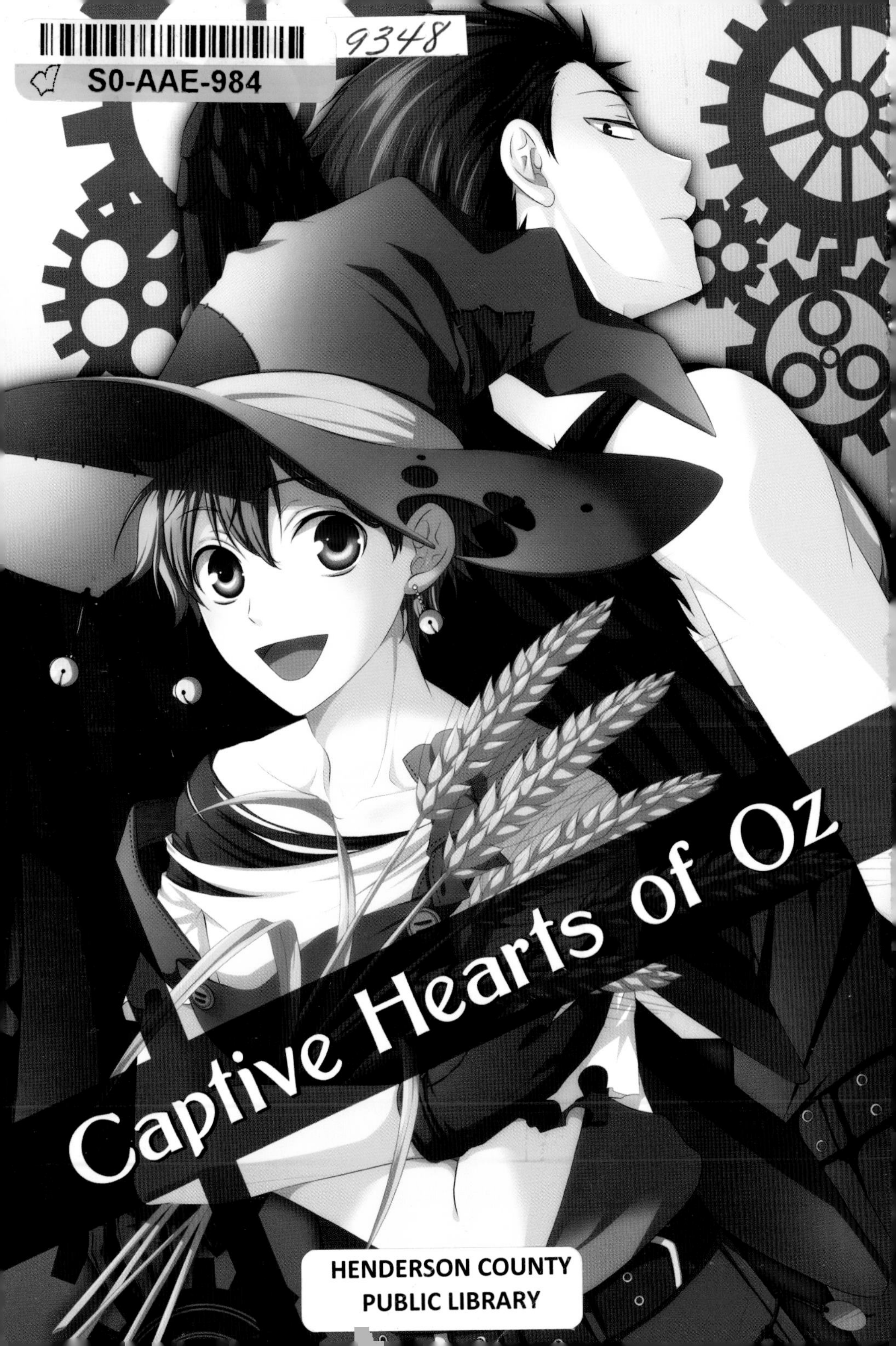
Captive Hearts of Oz

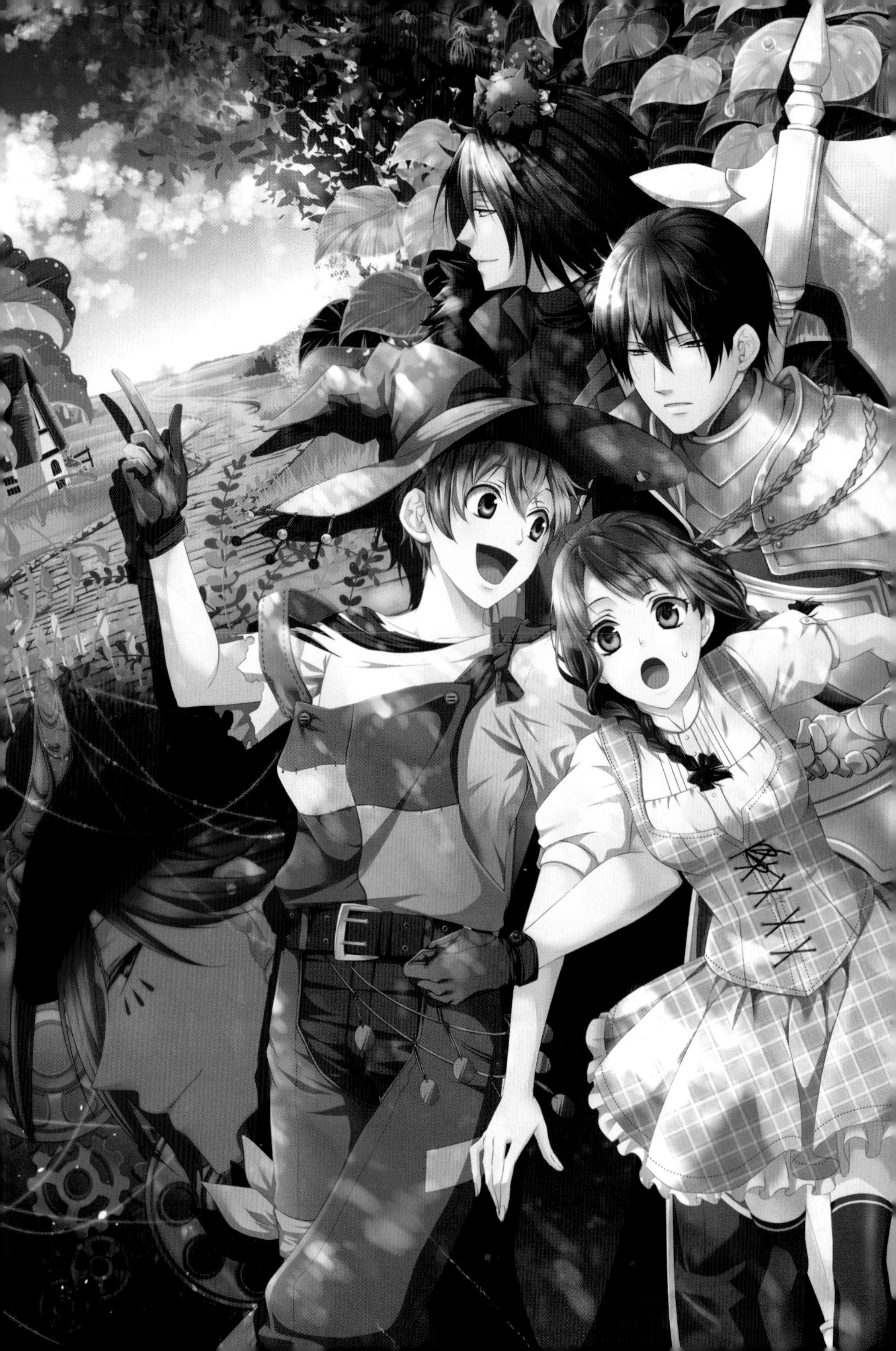

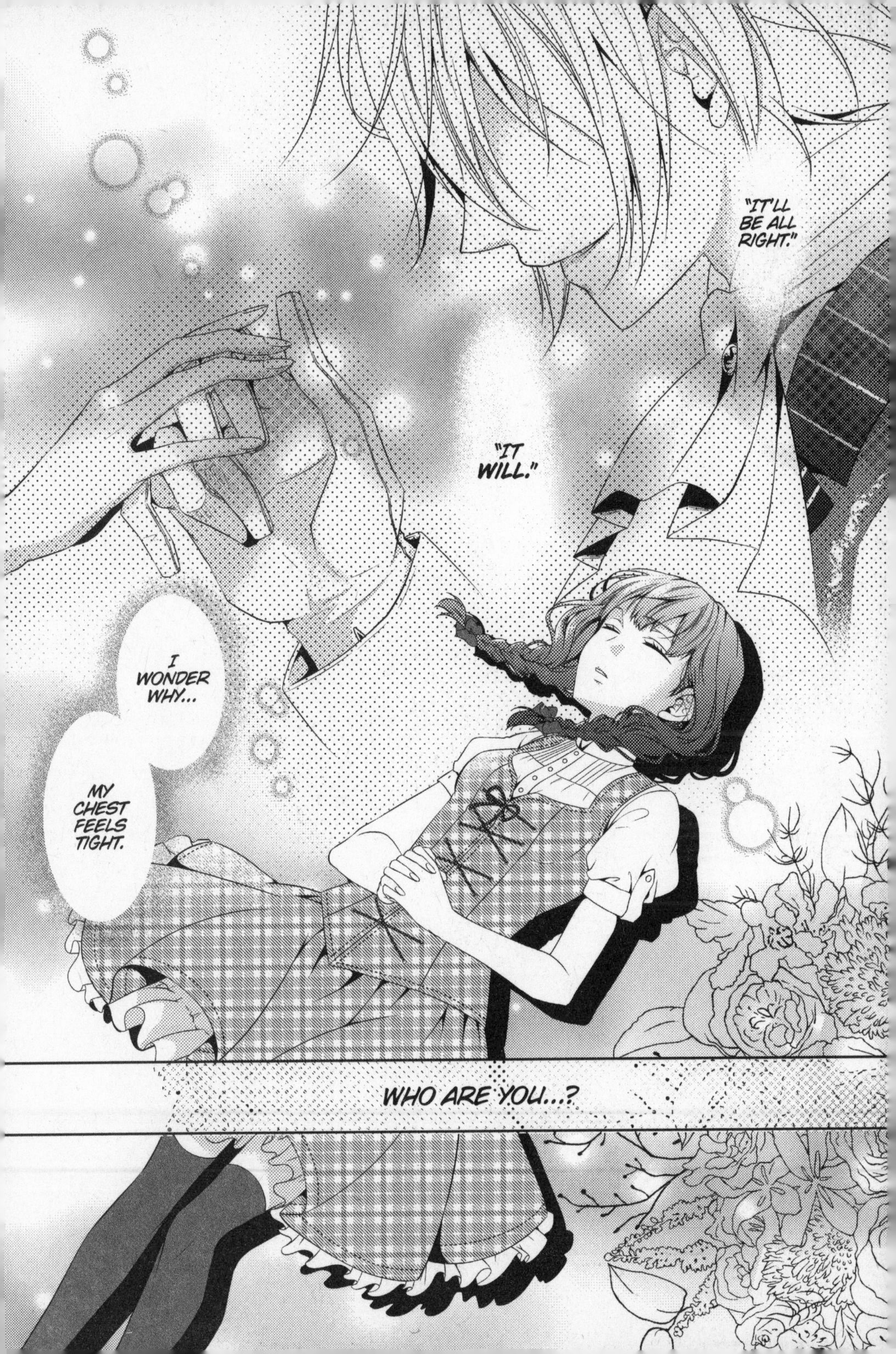
"IT'LL BE ALL RIGHT."
"IT WILL."
I WONDER WHY...
MY CHEST FEELS TIGHT.
WHO ARE YOU...?

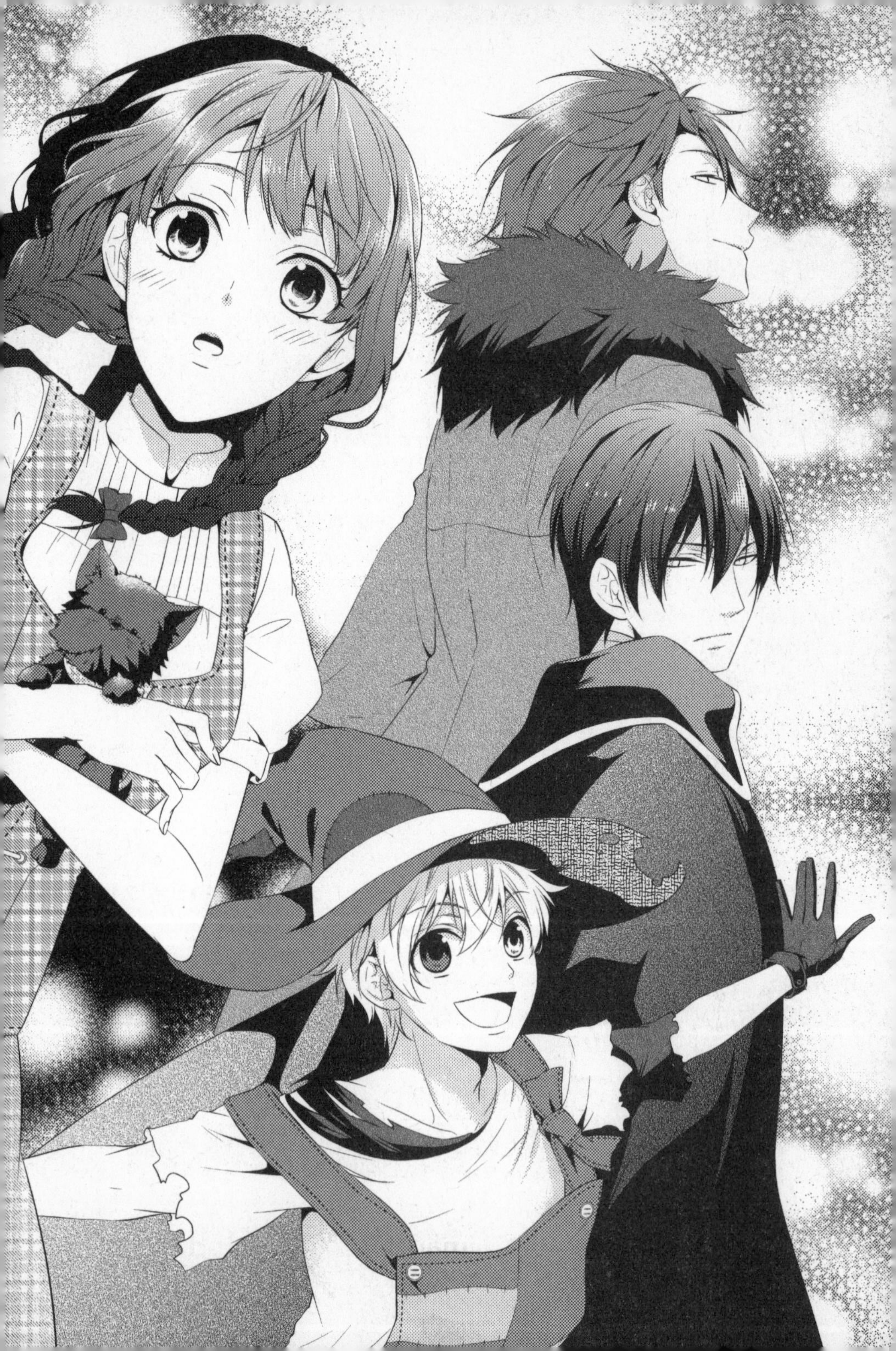

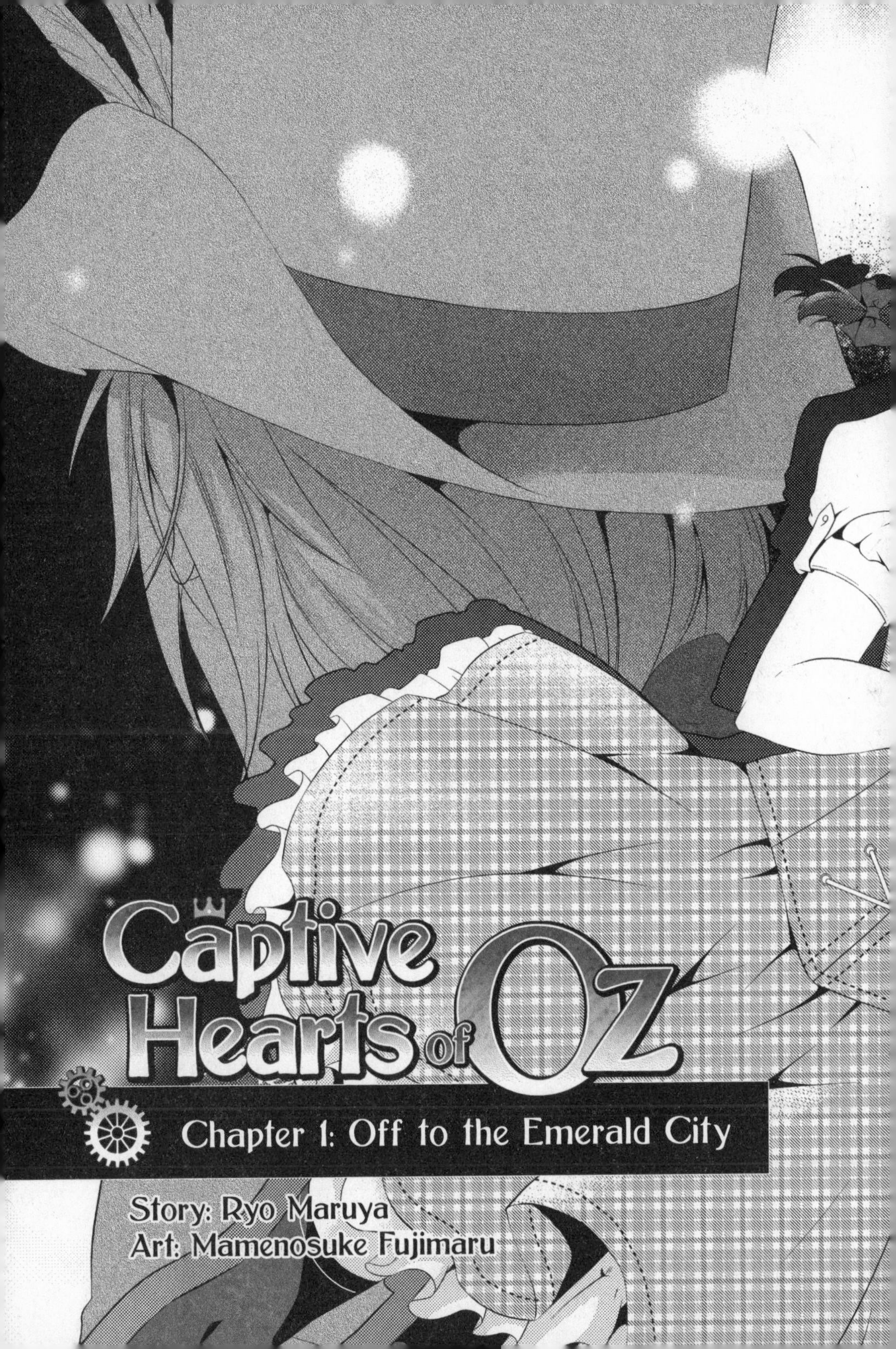
Captive Hearts of Oz
Chapter 1: Off to the Emerald City
Story: Ryo Maruya
Art: Mamenosuke Fujimaru

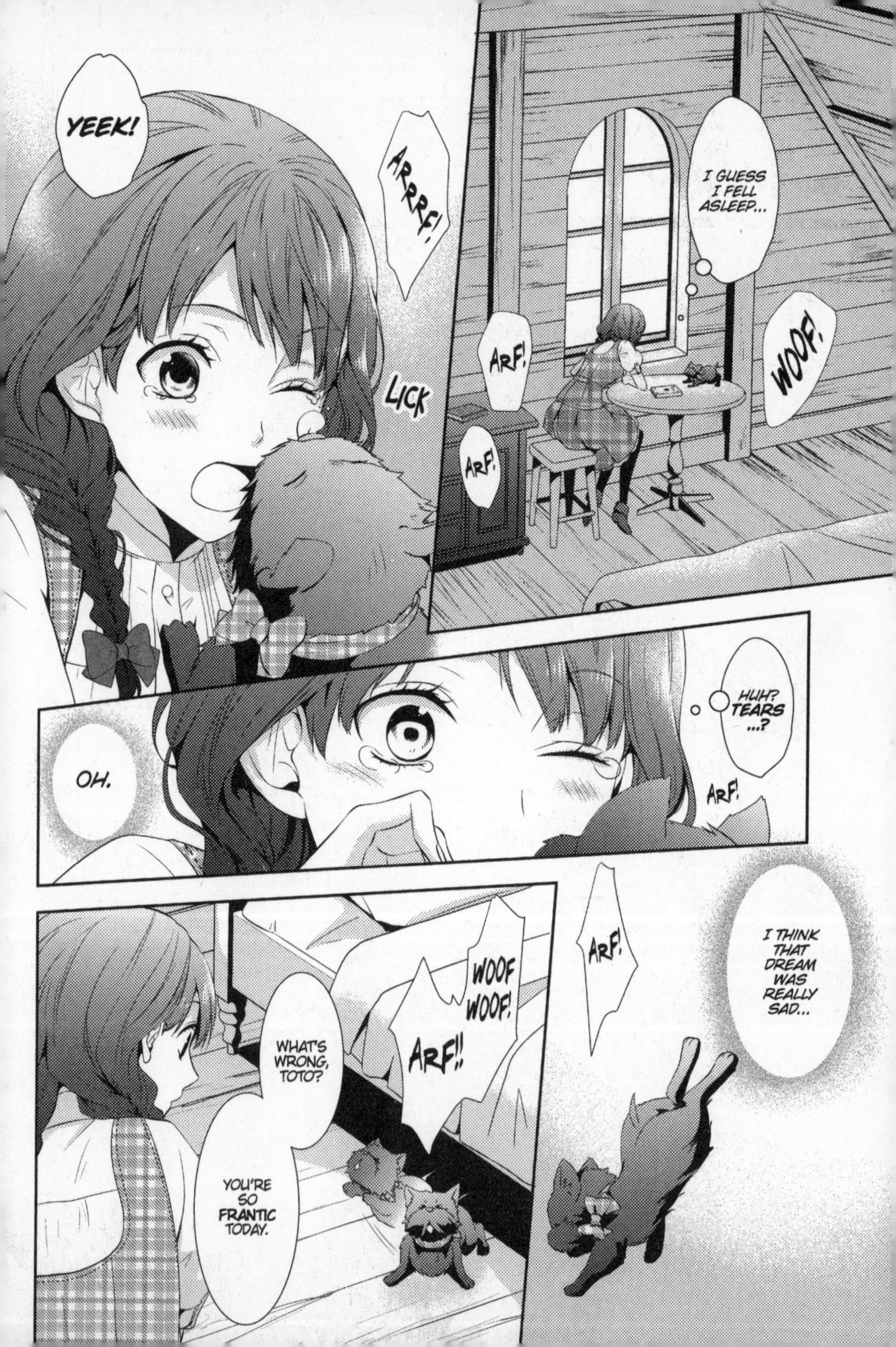
I GUESS I FELL ASLEEP...
WOOF!
ARF!
ARF!
YEEK!
ARRRF!
LICK
HUH? TEARS ...?
ARF!
OH.
I THINK THAT DREAM WAS REALLY SAD...
ARF!
WOOF WOOF!
ARF!!
WHAT'S WRONG, TOTO?
YOU'RE SO FRANTIC TODAY.

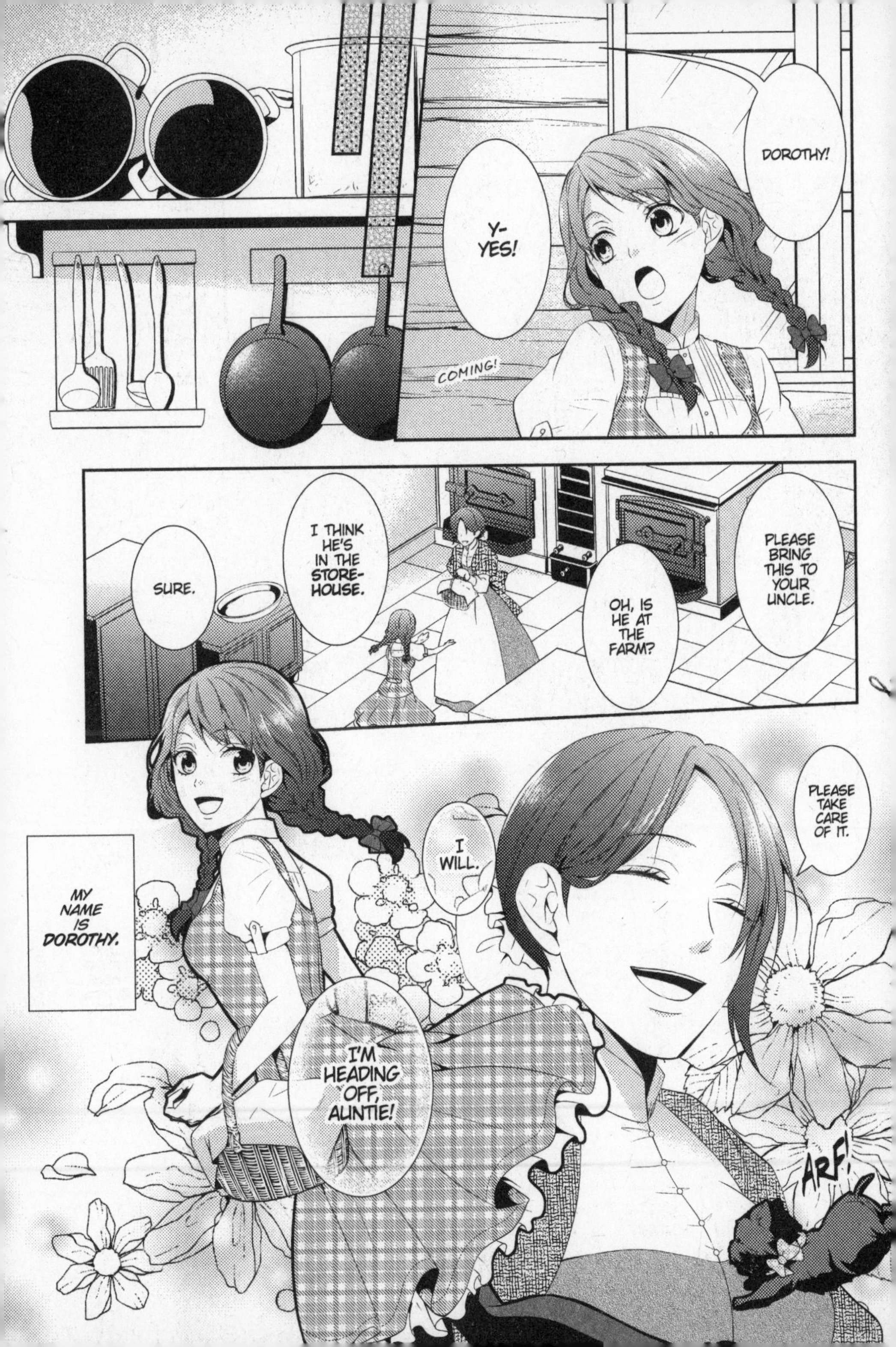
DOROTHY!
Y- YES!
COMING!
PLEASE BRING THIS TO YOUR UNCLE.
OH, IS HE AT THE FARM?
I THINK HE'S IN THE STORE-HOUSE.
SURE.
PLEASE TAKE CARE OF IT.
I WILL.
MY NAME IS DOROTHY.
I'M HEADING OFF, AUNTIE!
ARF!

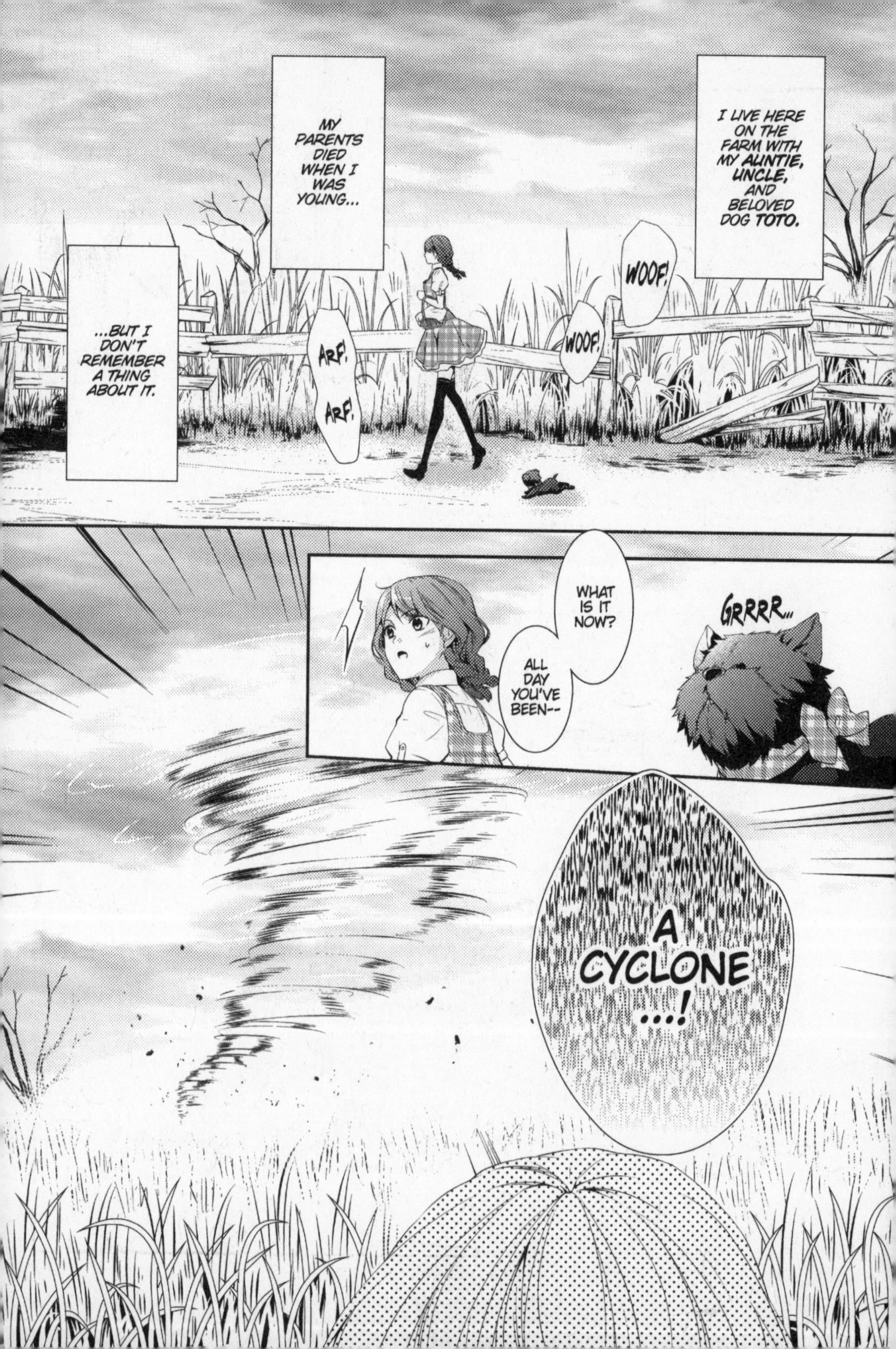
I LIVE HERE ON THE FARM WITH MY AUNTIE, UNCLE, AND BELOVED DOG TOTO.
MY PARENTS DIED WHEN I WAS YOUNG...
WOOF!
WOOF!
...BUT I DON'T REMEMBER A THING ABOUT IT.
ARF! ARF!
GRRRR...
WHAT IS IT NOW?
ALL DAY YOU'VE BEEN--
A CYCLONE...!

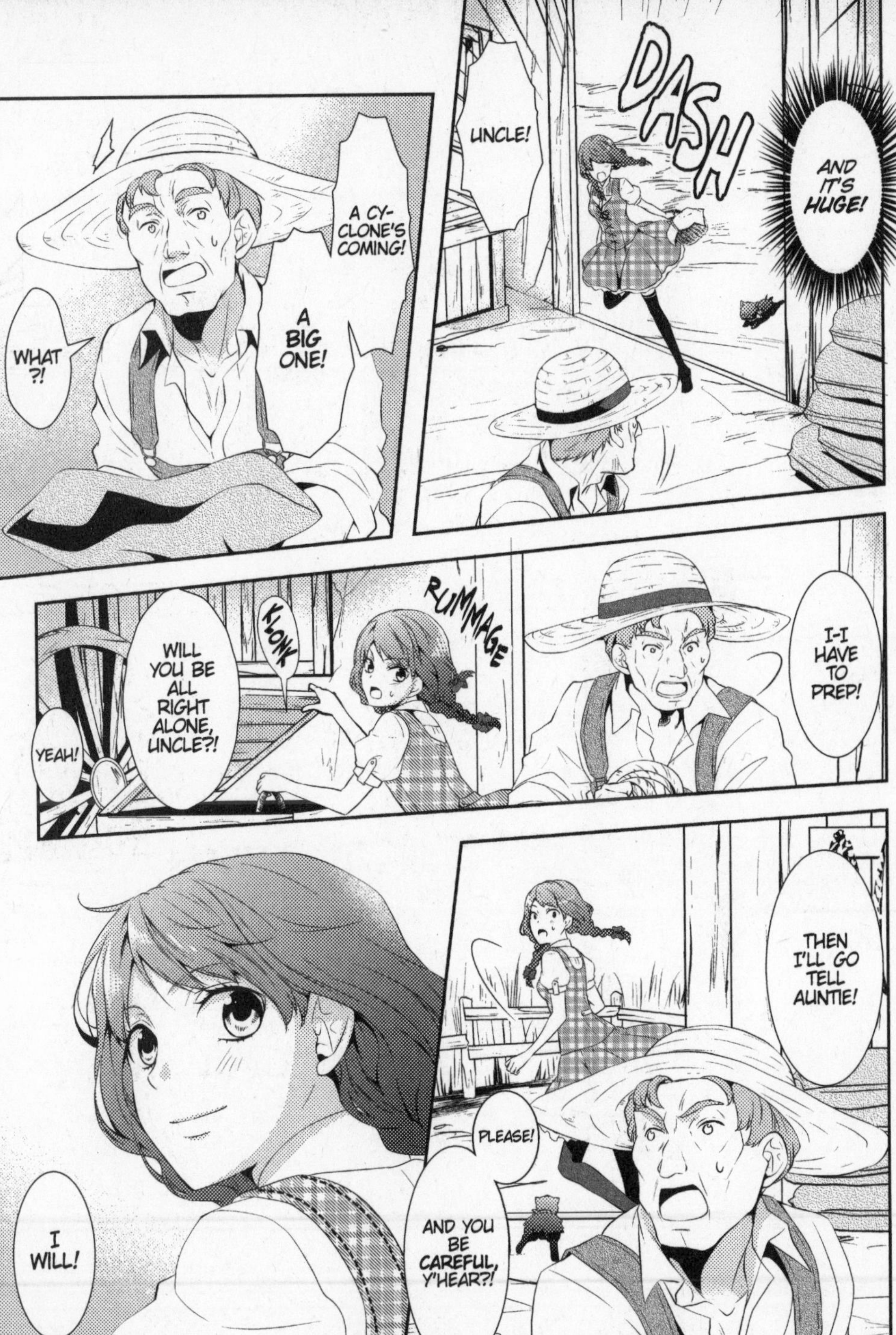
AND IT'S HUGE!
DASH
UNCLE!
A CY-CLONE'S COMING!
A BIG ONE!
WHAT?!
I-I HAVE TO PREP!
RUMMAGE
KLONK
WILL YOU BE ALL RIGHT ALONE, UNCLE?!
YEAH!
THEN I'LL GO TELL AUNTIE!
PLEASE!
AND YOU BE CAREFUL, Y'HEAR?!
I WILL!

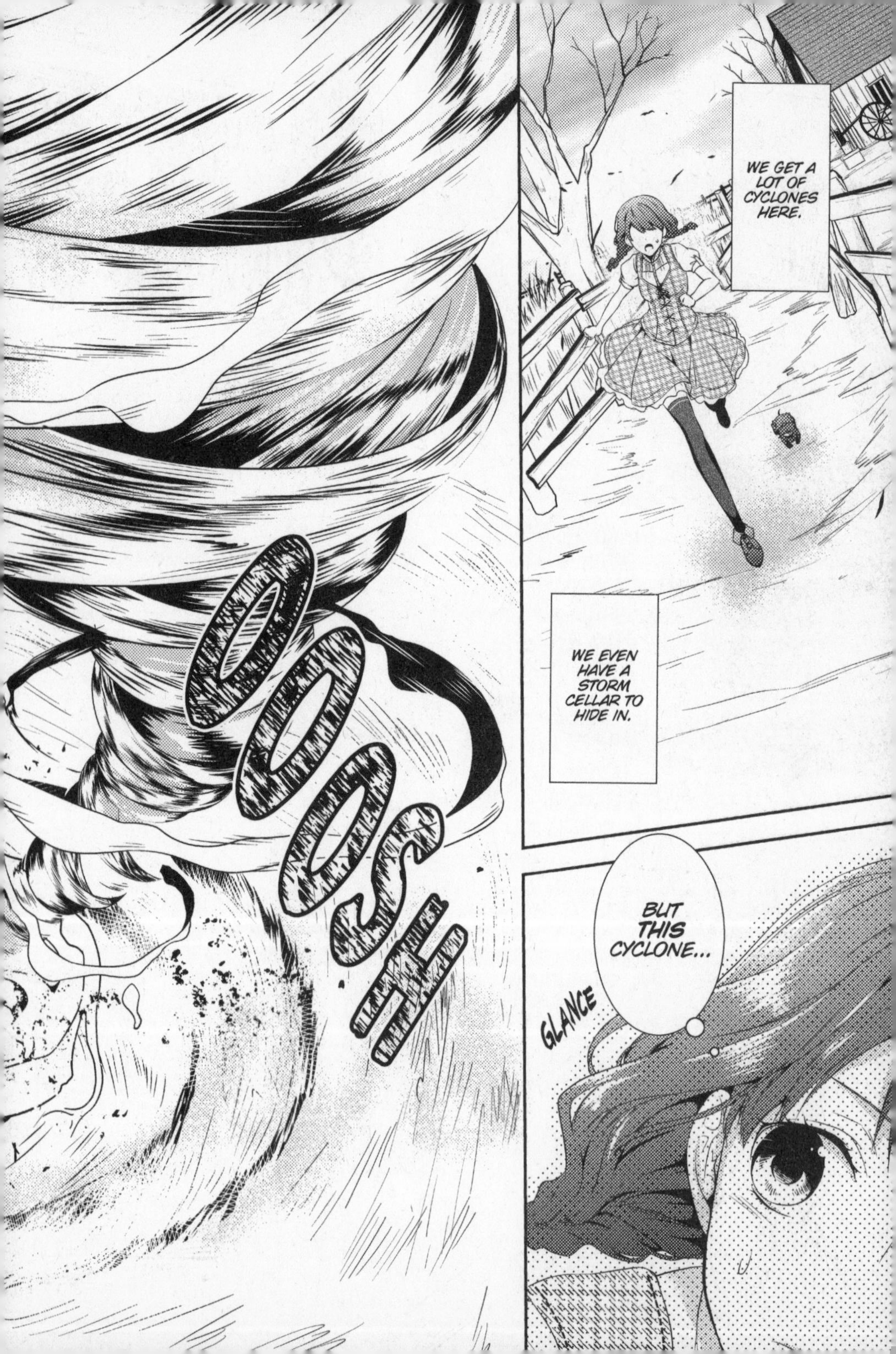
WE GET A LOT OF CYCLONES HERE.
WE EVEN HAVE A STORM CELLAR TO HIDE IN.
BUT THIS CYCLONE...
GLANCE
OOOSH

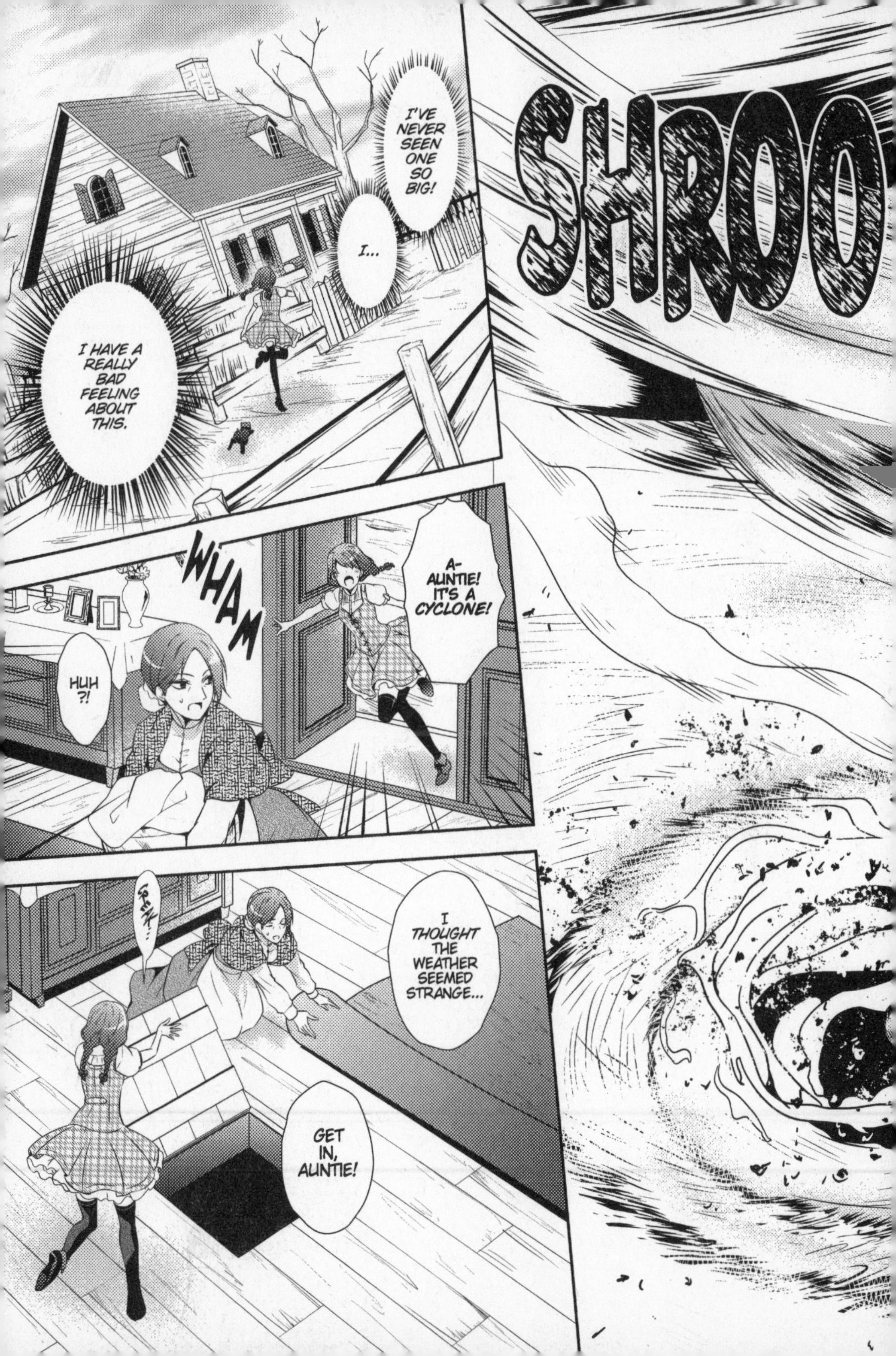
SHROO
I'VE NEVER SEEN ONE SO BIG!
I...
I HAVE A REALLY BAD FEELING ABOUT THIS.
WHAM
A-AUNTIE! IT'S A CYCLONE!
HUH?!
I THOUGHT THE WEATHER SEEMED STRANGE...
CREAK...
GET IN, AUNTIE!

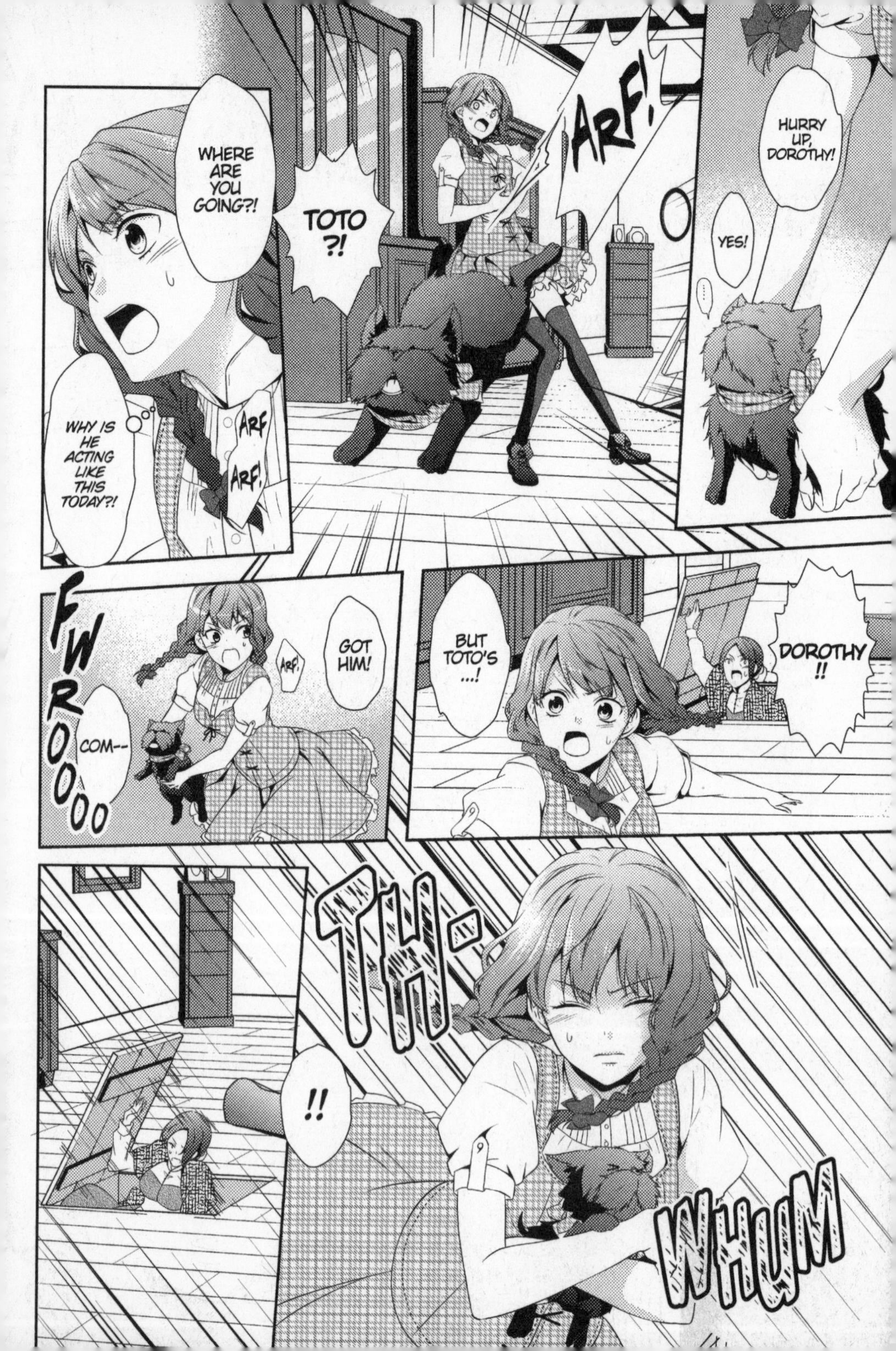
HURRY UP, DOROTHY!
YES!
...
ARF!
TOTO ?!
WHERE ARE YOU GOING?!
ARF
ARF!
WHY IS HE ACTING LIKE THIS TODAY?!
DOROTHY !!
BUT TOTO'S ...!
GOT HIM!
ARF!
COM--
FWROOOOO
TH-
WHUM
!!

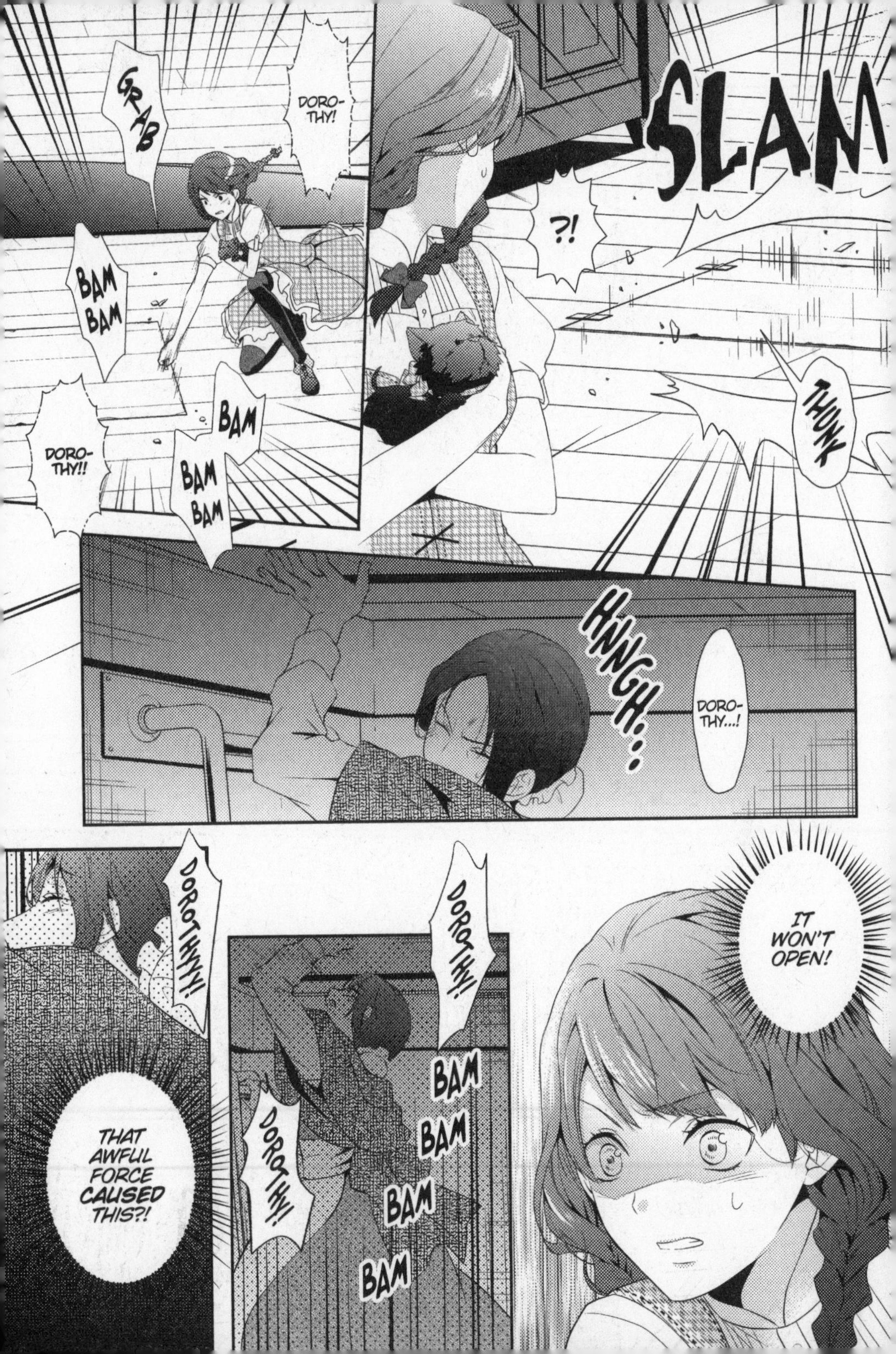
SLAM
?!
THUNK
DORO-THY!
GRAB
BAM BAM
BAM
BAM BAM
DORO-THY!!
HNNGH...
DORO-THY...!
IT WON'T OPEN!
DOROTHY!
BAM
BAM
BAM
BAM
DOROTHY!
DOROTHYYY!!
THAT AWFUL FORCE CAUSED THIS?!

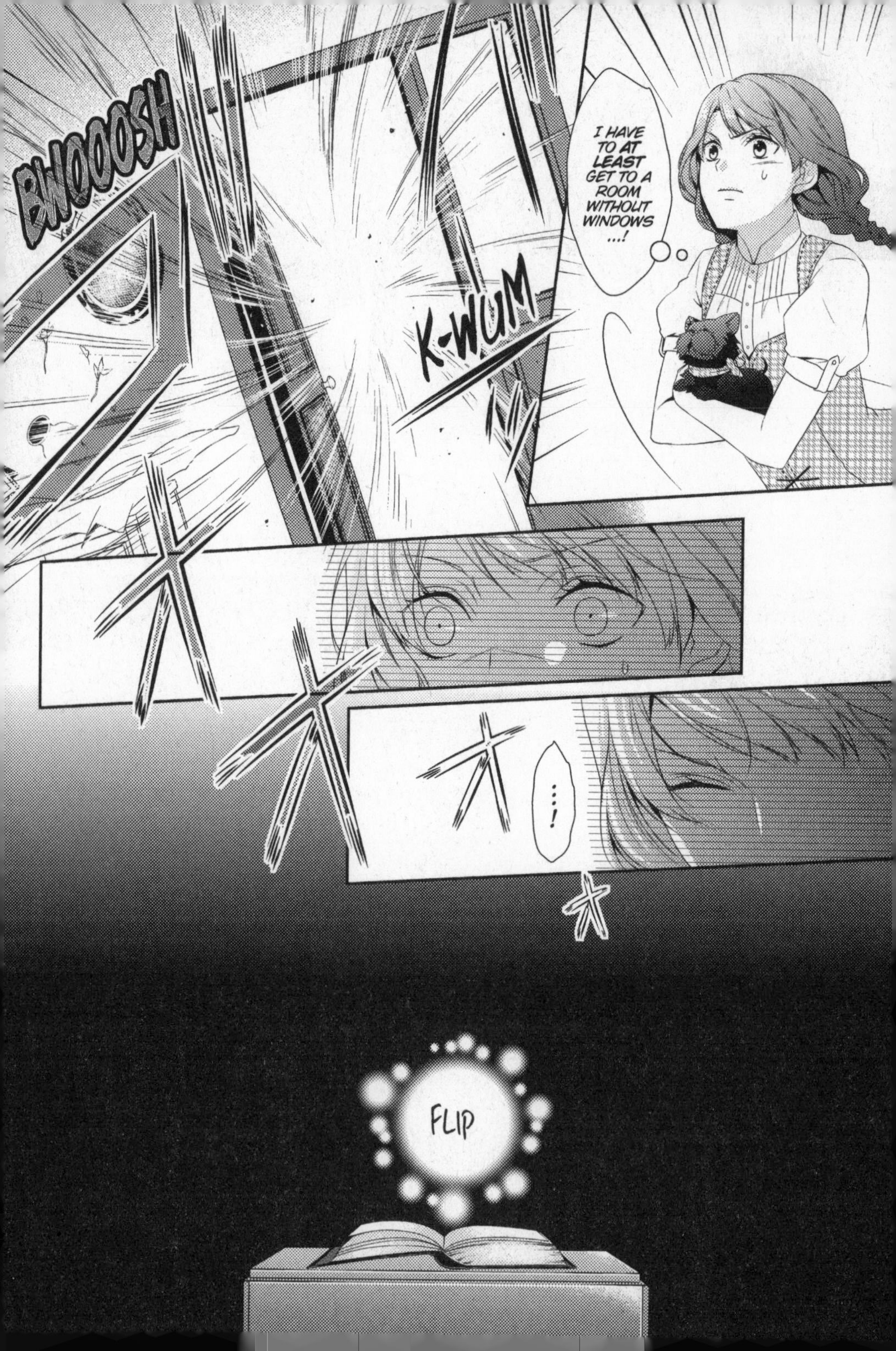
I HAVE TO AT LEAST GET TO A ROOM WITHOUT WINDOWS ...!
K-WUM
BWOOOSH
...!
FLIP

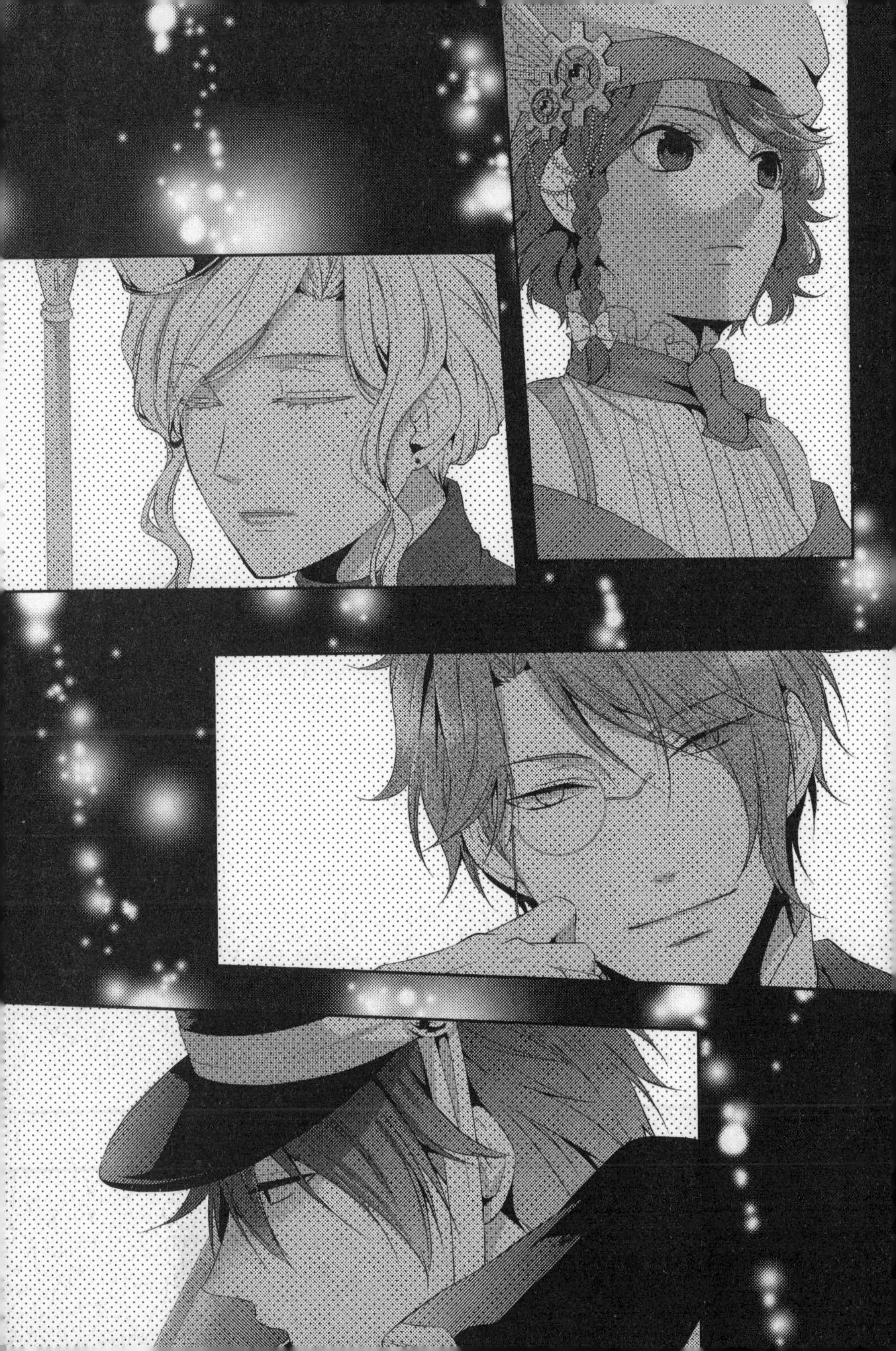

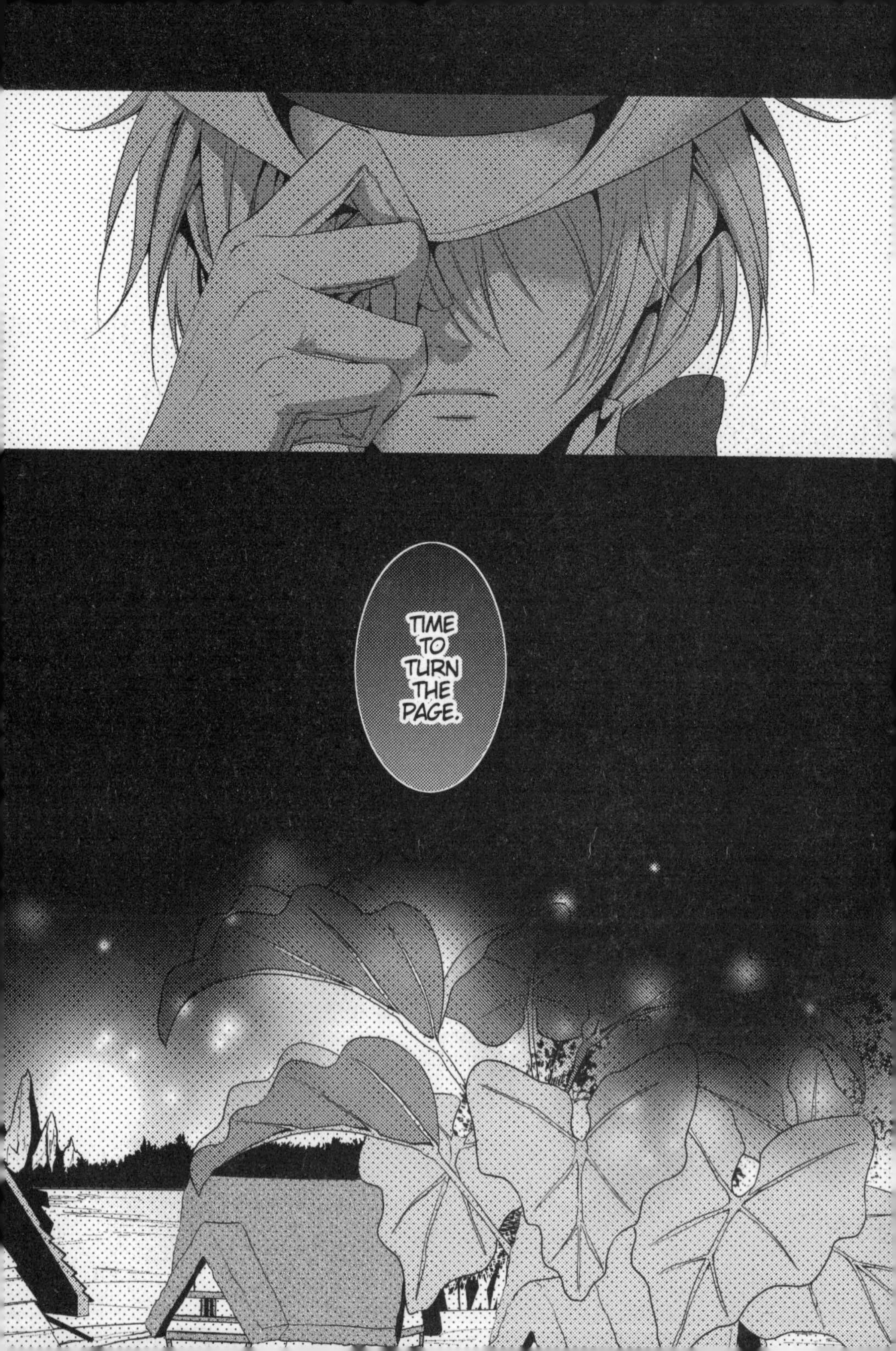
TIME TO TURN THE PAGE.

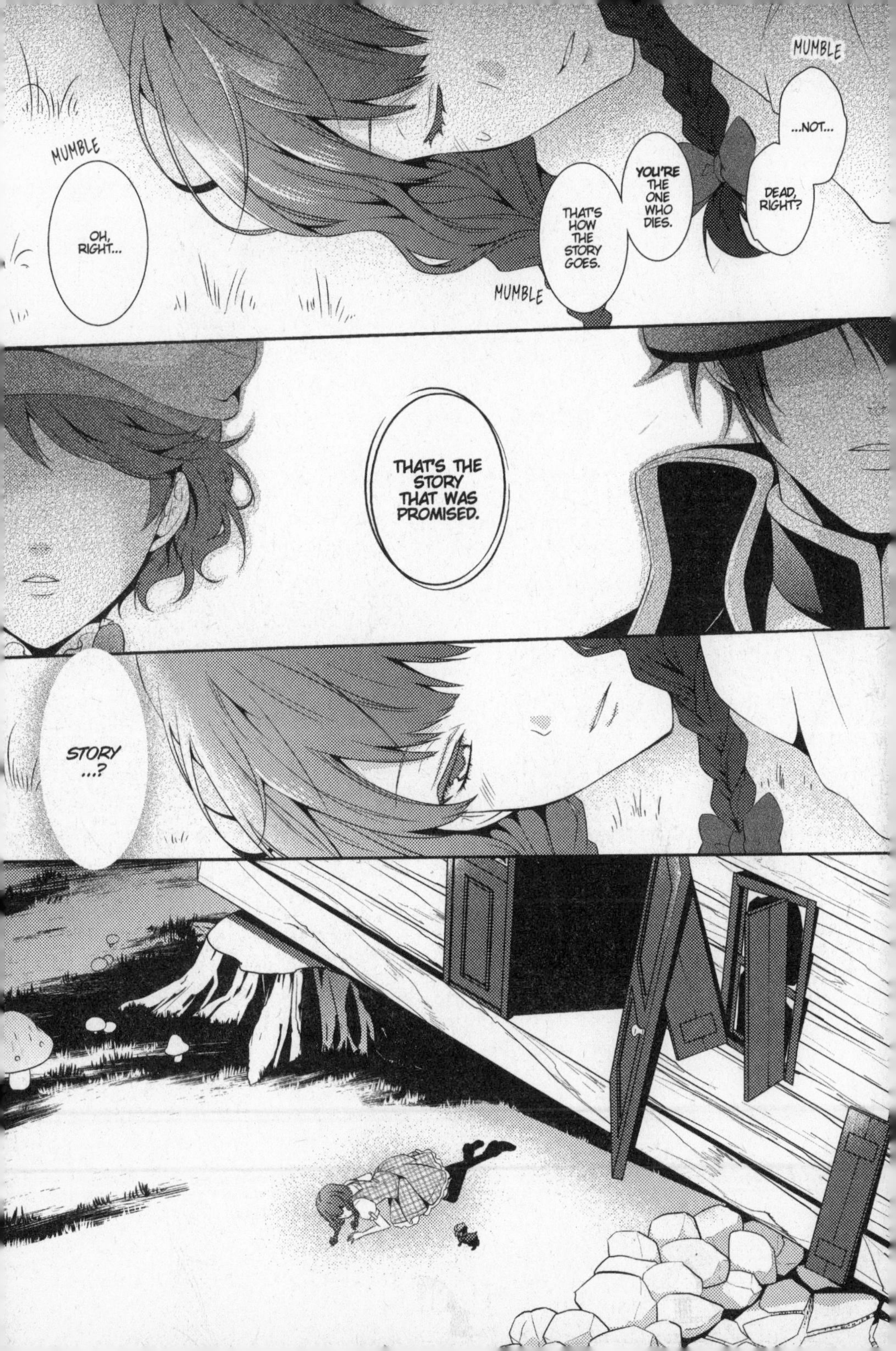
MUMBLE
...NOT...
DEAD, RIGHT?
YOU'RE THE ONE WHO DIES.
THAT'S HOW THE STORY GOES.
MUMBLE
MUMBLE
OH, RIGHT...
THAT'S THE STORY THAT WAS PROMISED.
STORY ...?

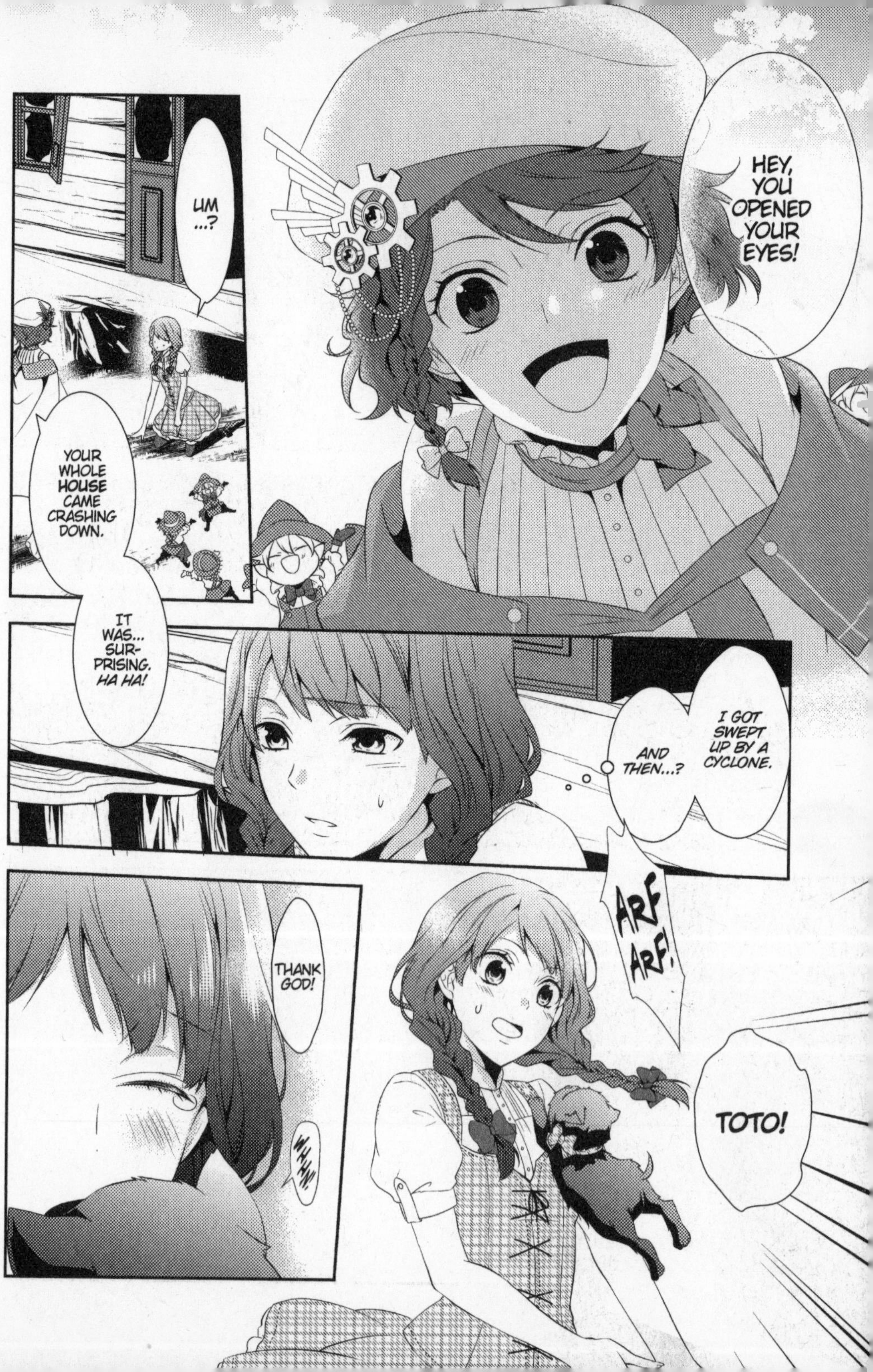
HEY, YOU OPENED YOUR EYES!
UM ...?
YOUR WHOLE HOUSE CAME CRASHING DOWN.
IT WAS... SUR-PRISING. HA HA!
I GOT SWEPT UP BY A CYCLONE.
AND THEN...?
ARF ARF!
TOTO!
THANK GOD!
WHIN!

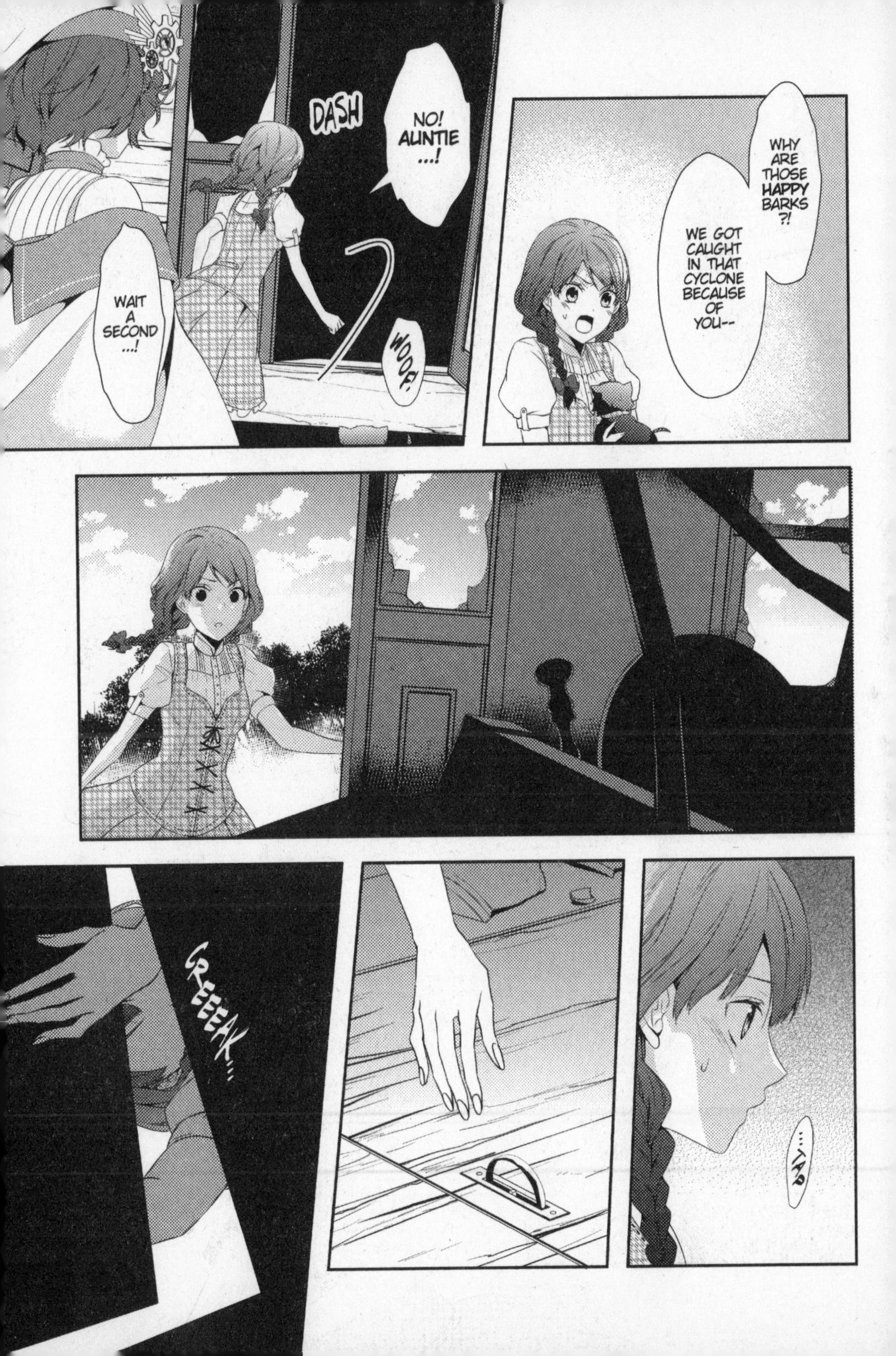
WHY ARE THOSE HAPPY BARKS ?!
WE GOT CAUGHT IN THAT CYCLONE BECAUSE OF YOU--
NO! AUNTIE ...!
DASH
WOOF!
WAIT A SECOND ...!
...?!
CREEEAK...

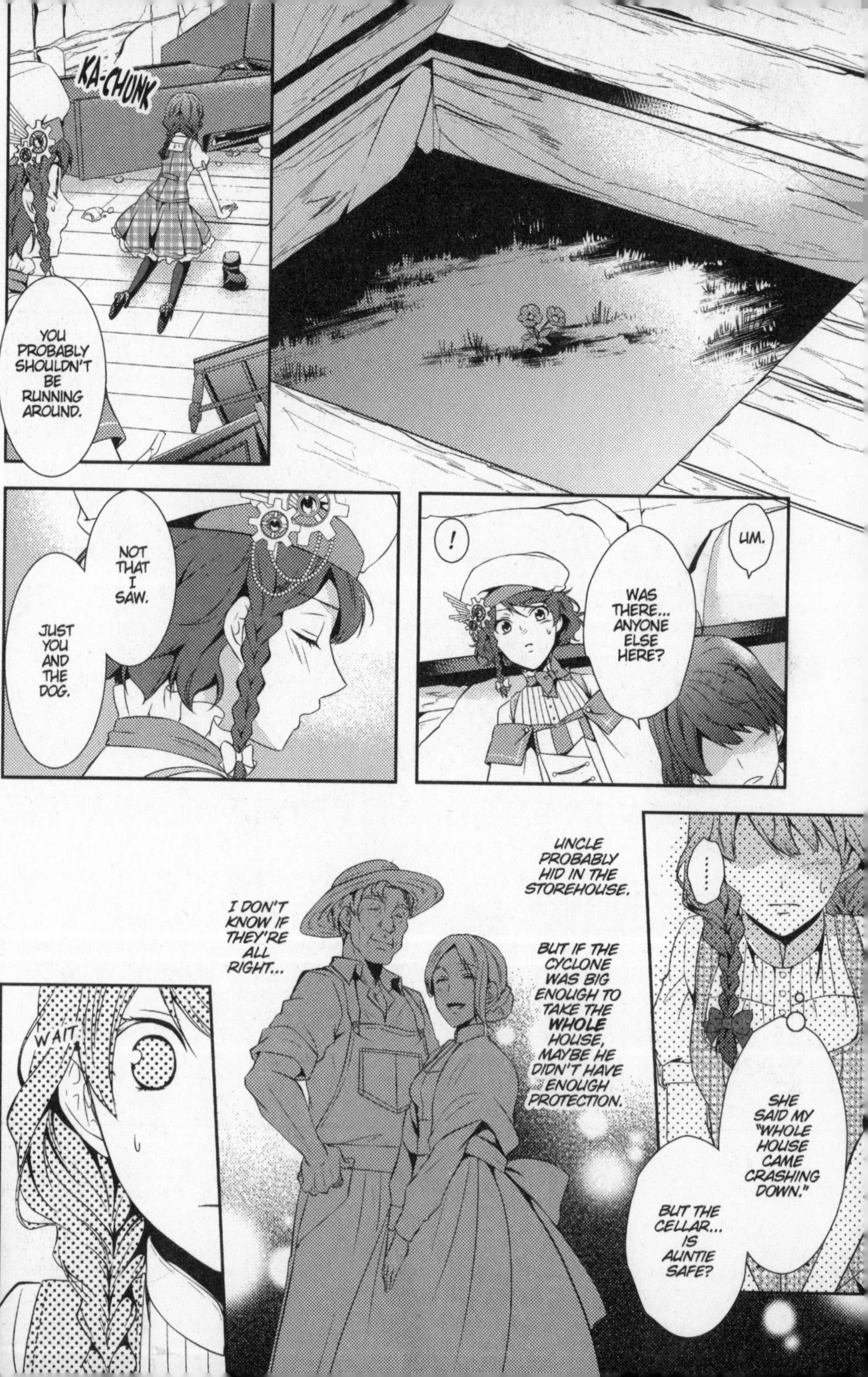

KA-CHUNK
YOU PROBABLY SHOULDN'T BE RUNNING AROUND.
UM.
WAS THERE... ANYONE ELSE HERE?
!
NOT THAT I SAW.
JUST YOU AND THE DOG.
......
SHE SAID MY "WHOLE HOUSE CAME CRASHING DOWN."
BUT THE CELLAR... IS AUNTIE SAFE?
UNCLE PROBABLY HID IN THE STOREHOUSE.
BUT IF THE CYCLONE WAS BIG ENOUGH TO TAKE THE **WHOLE** HOUSE, MAYBE HE DIDN'T HAVE ENOUGH PROTECTION.
I DON'T KNOW IF THEY'RE ALL RIGHT...
WAIT.

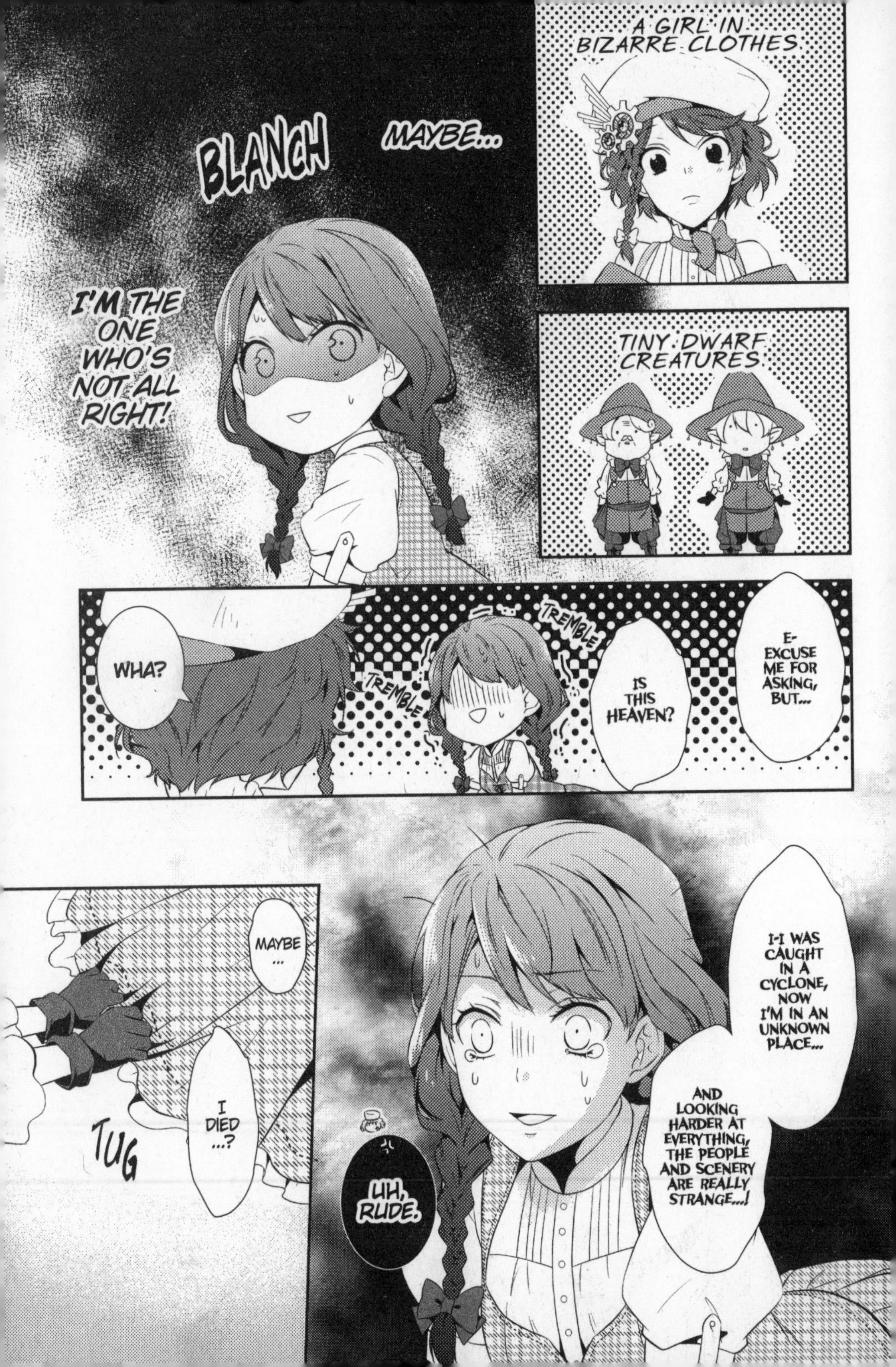
A GIRL IN BIZARRE CLOTHES
TINY DWARF CREATURES
MAYBE...
BLANCH
I'M THE ONE WHO'S NOT ALL RIGHT!
E-EXCUSE ME FOR ASKING, BUT...
IS THIS HEAVEN?
TREMBLE
TREMBLE
WHA?
I-I WAS CAUGHT IN A CYCLONE, NOW I'M IN AN UNKNOWN PLACE...
AND LOOKING HARDER AT EVERYTHING, THE PEOPLE AND SCENERY ARE REALLY STRANGE...!
UH, RUDE.
MAYBE ...
I DIED ...?
TUG

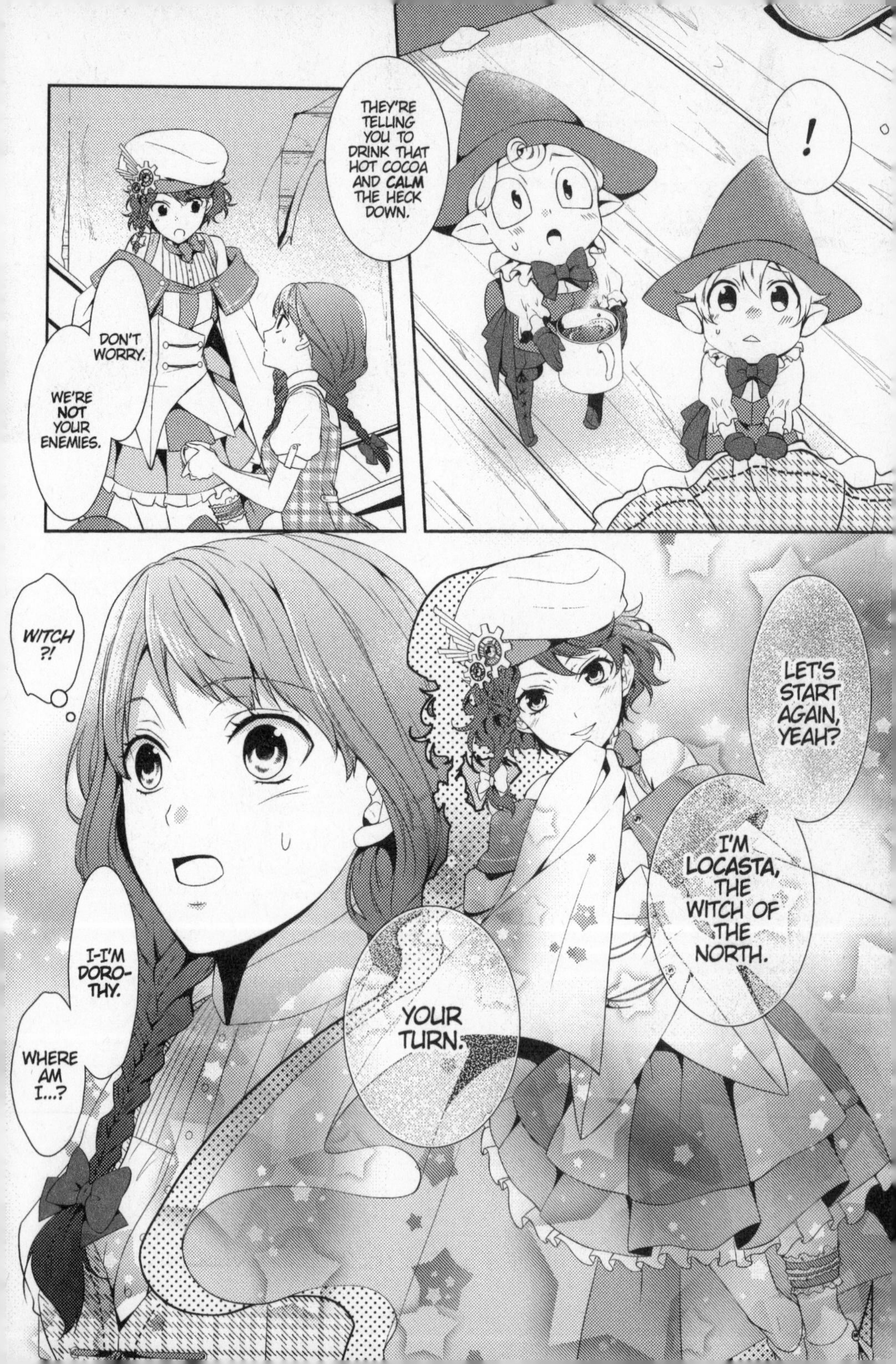
!
THEY'RE TELLING YOU TO DRINK THAT HOT COCOA AND CALM THE HECK DOWN.
DON'T WORRY.
WE'RE NOT YOUR ENEMIES.
LET'S START AGAIN, YEAH?
I'M LOCASTA, THE WITCH OF THE NORTH.
WITCH?!
YOUR TURN.
I-I'M DORO-THY.
WHERE AM I...?

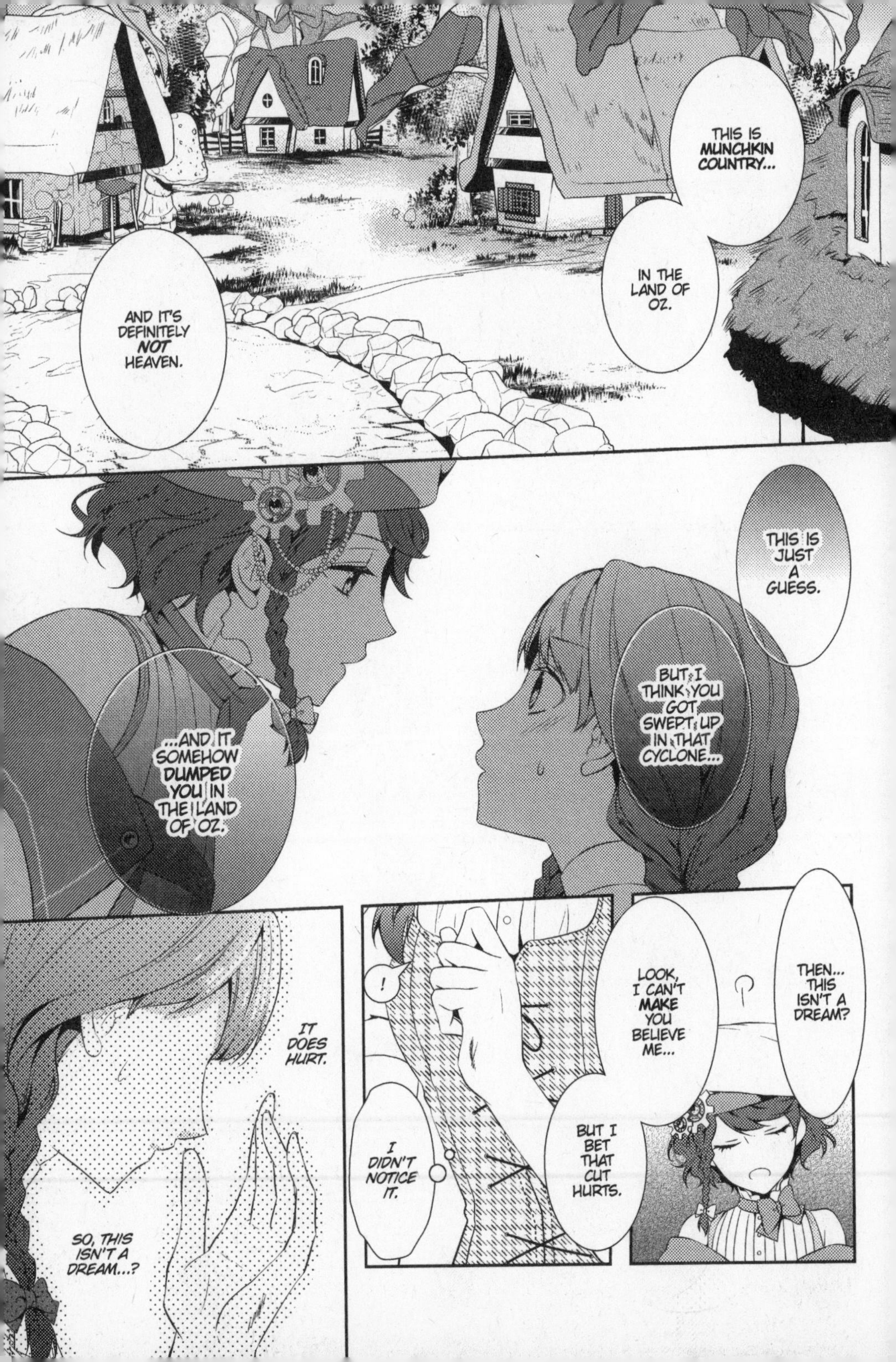
THIS IS MUNCHKIN COUNTRY...
IN THE LAND OF OZ.
AND IT'S DEFINITELY NOT HEAVEN.
THIS IS JUST A GUESS.
BUT I THINK YOU GOT SWEPT UP IN THAT CYCLONE...
...AND IT SOMEHOW DUMPED YOU IN THE LAND OF OZ.
THEN... THIS ISN'T A DREAM?
?
LOOK, I CAN'T MAKE YOU BELIEVE ME...
BUT I BET THAT CUT HURTS.
!
I DIDN'T NOTICE IT.
IT DOES HURT.
SO, THIS ISN'T A DREAM...?

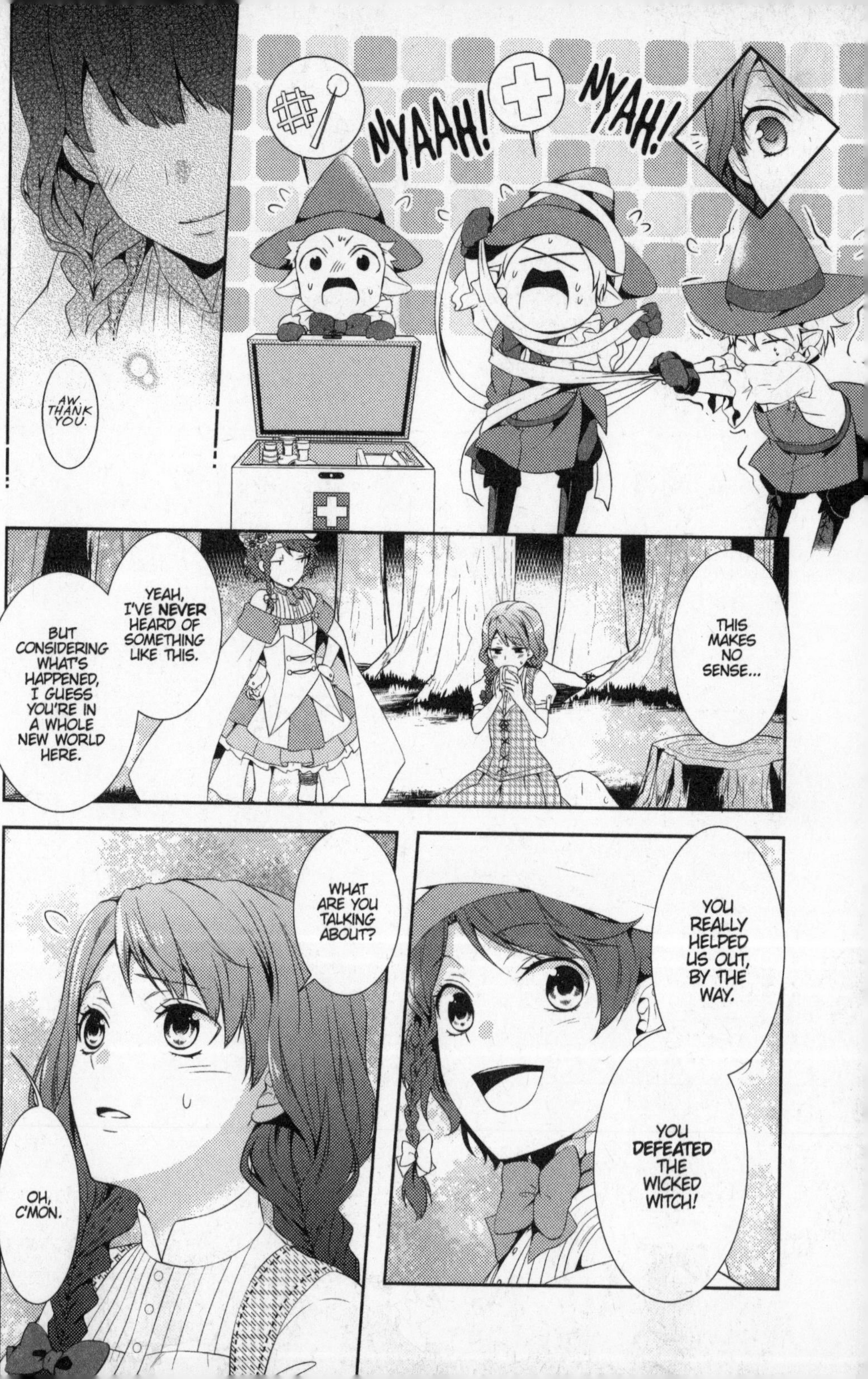
NYAH!
NYAAH!
AW. THANK YOU.
THIS MAKES NO SENSE...
YEAH, I'VE **NEVER** HEARD OF SOMETHING LIKE THIS.
BUT CONSIDERING WHAT'S HAPPENED, I GUESS YOU'RE IN A WHOLE NEW WORLD HERE.
YOU REALLY HELPED US OUT, BY THE WAY.
YOU DEFEATED THE WICKED WITCH!
WHAT ARE YOU TALKING ABOUT?
OH, C'MON.

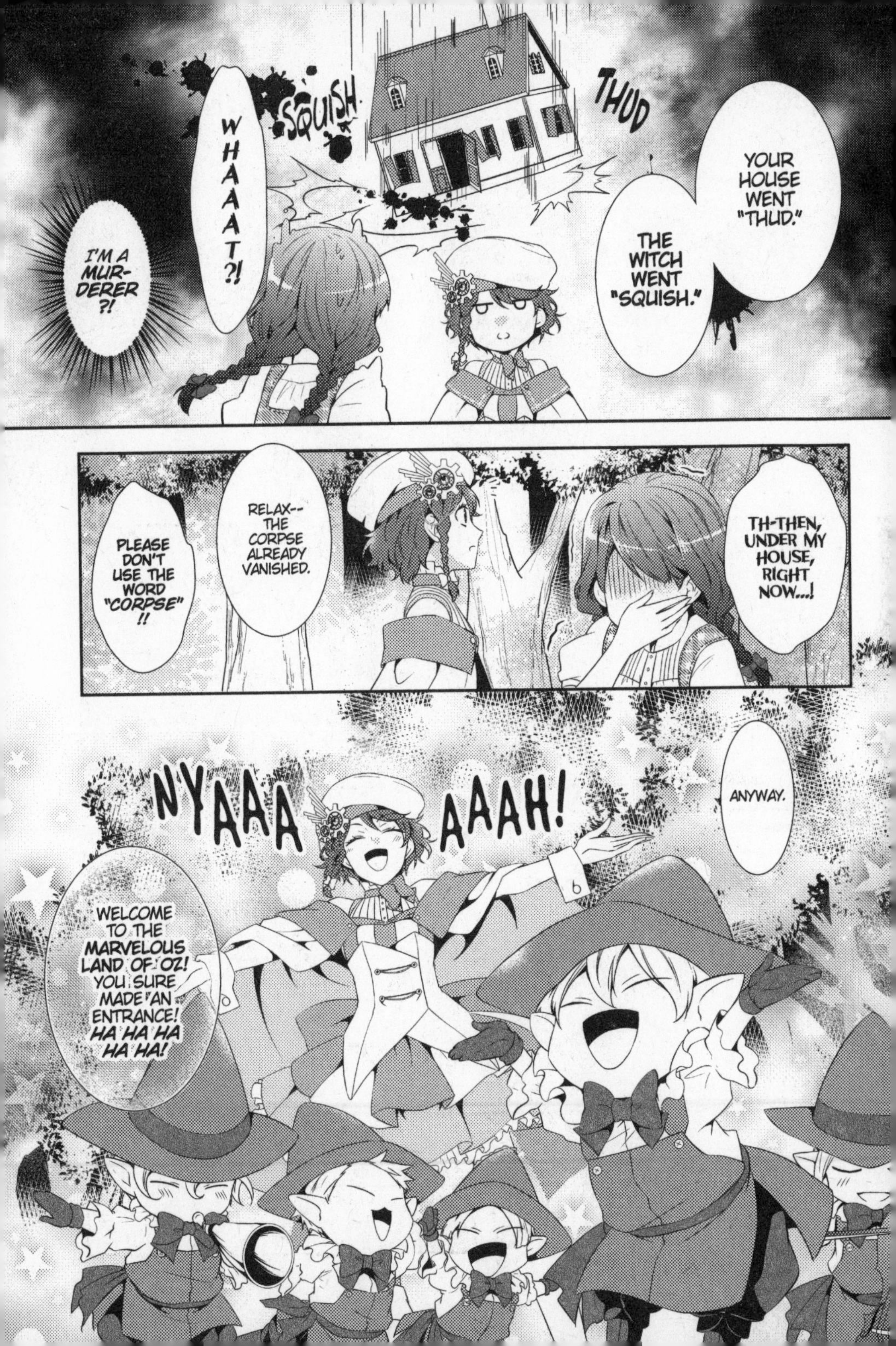
YOUR HOUSE WENT "THUD."
THUD
THE WITCH WENT "SQUISH."
SQUISH
WHAAAAT?!
I'M A MURDERER?!
TH-THEN, UNDER MY HOUSE, RIGHT NOW...!
RELAX-- THE CORPSE ALREADY VANISHED.
PLEASE DON'T USE THE WORD "CORPSE"!!
ANYWAY.
NYAAAAAAH!
WELCOME TO THE MARVELOUS LAND OF OZ! YOU SURE MADE AN ENTRANCE! HA HA HA HA HA!

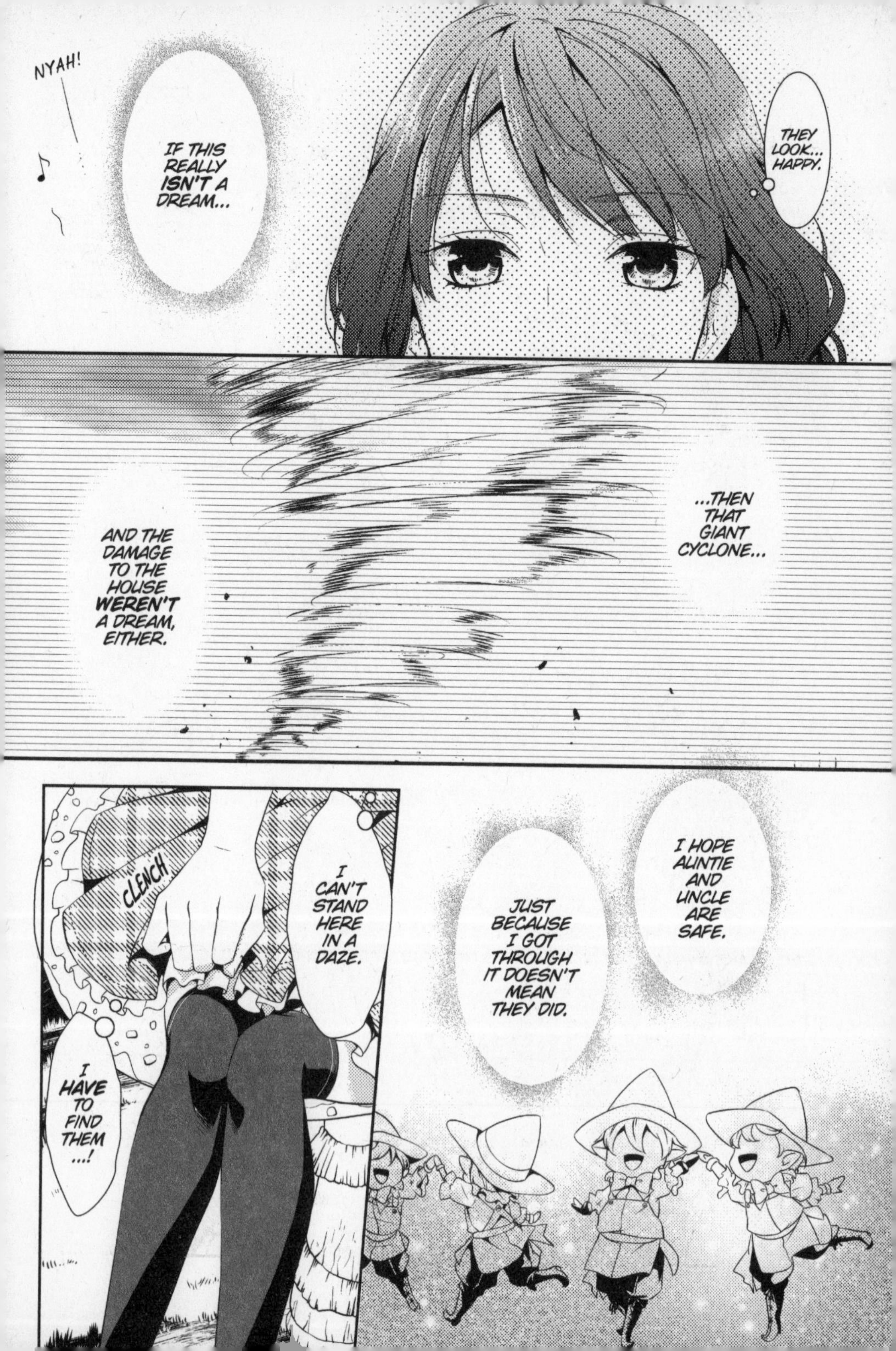
THEY LOOK... HAPPY.
NYAH!
IF THIS REALLY ISN'T A DREAM...
...THEN THAT GIANT CYCLONE...
AND THE DAMAGE TO THE HOUSE WEREN'T A DREAM, EITHER.
I HOPE AUNTIE AND UNCLE ARE SAFE.
JUST BECAUSE I GOT THROUGH IT DOESN'T MEAN THEY DID.
I CAN'T STAND HERE IN A DAZE.
CLENCH
I HAVE TO FIND THEM...!

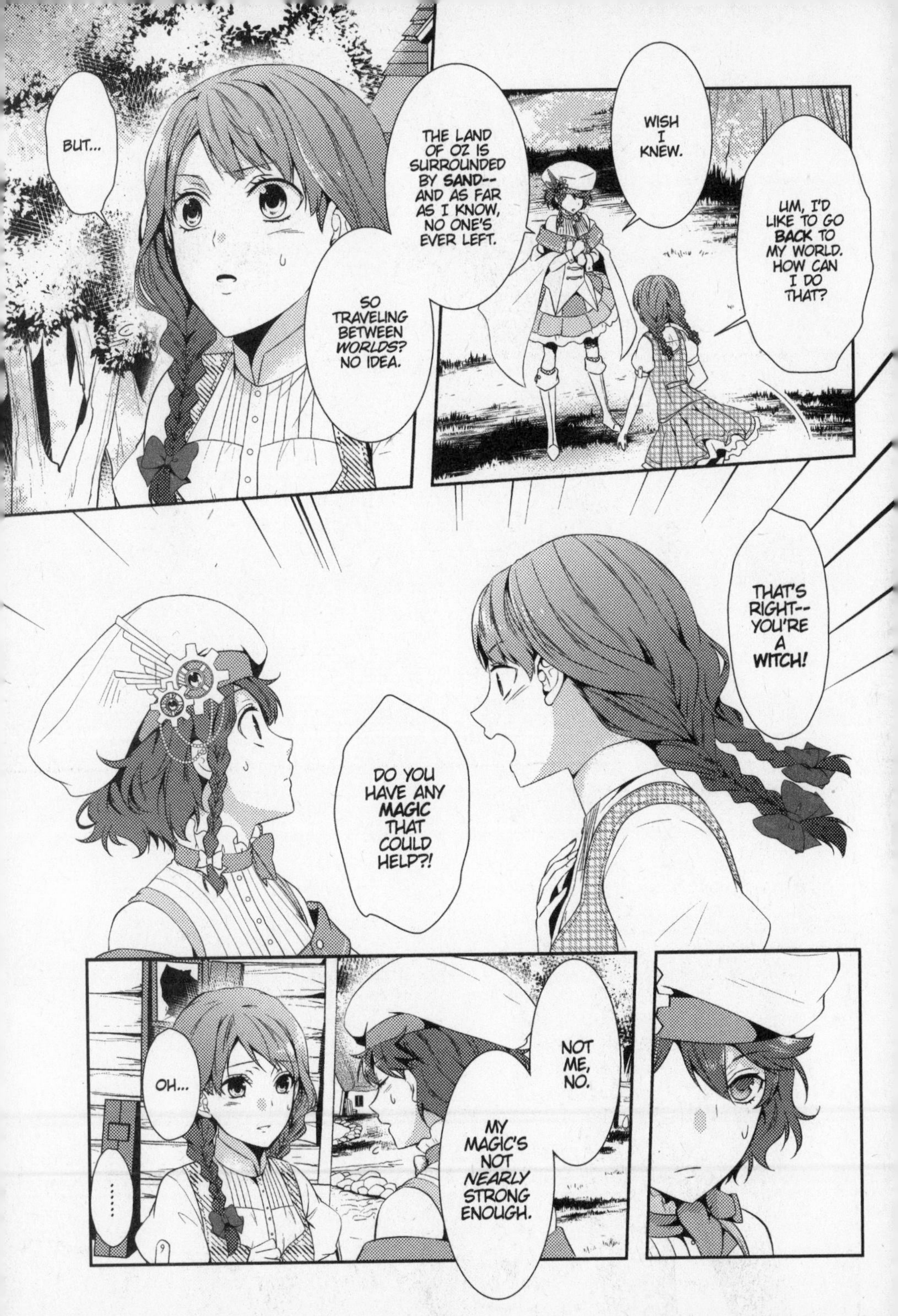
UM, I'D LIKE TO GO BACK TO MY WORLD. HOW CAN I DO THAT?
WISH I KNEW.
THE LAND OF OZ IS SURROUNDED BY SAND-- AND AS FAR AS I KNOW, NO ONE'S EVER LEFT.
SO TRAVELING BETWEEN WORLDS? NO IDEA.
BUT...
THAT'S RIGHT-- YOU'RE A WITCH!
DO YOU HAVE ANY MAGIC THAT COULD HELP?!
NOT ME, NO.
MY MAGIC'S NOT NEARLY STRONG ENOUGH.
OH...
......

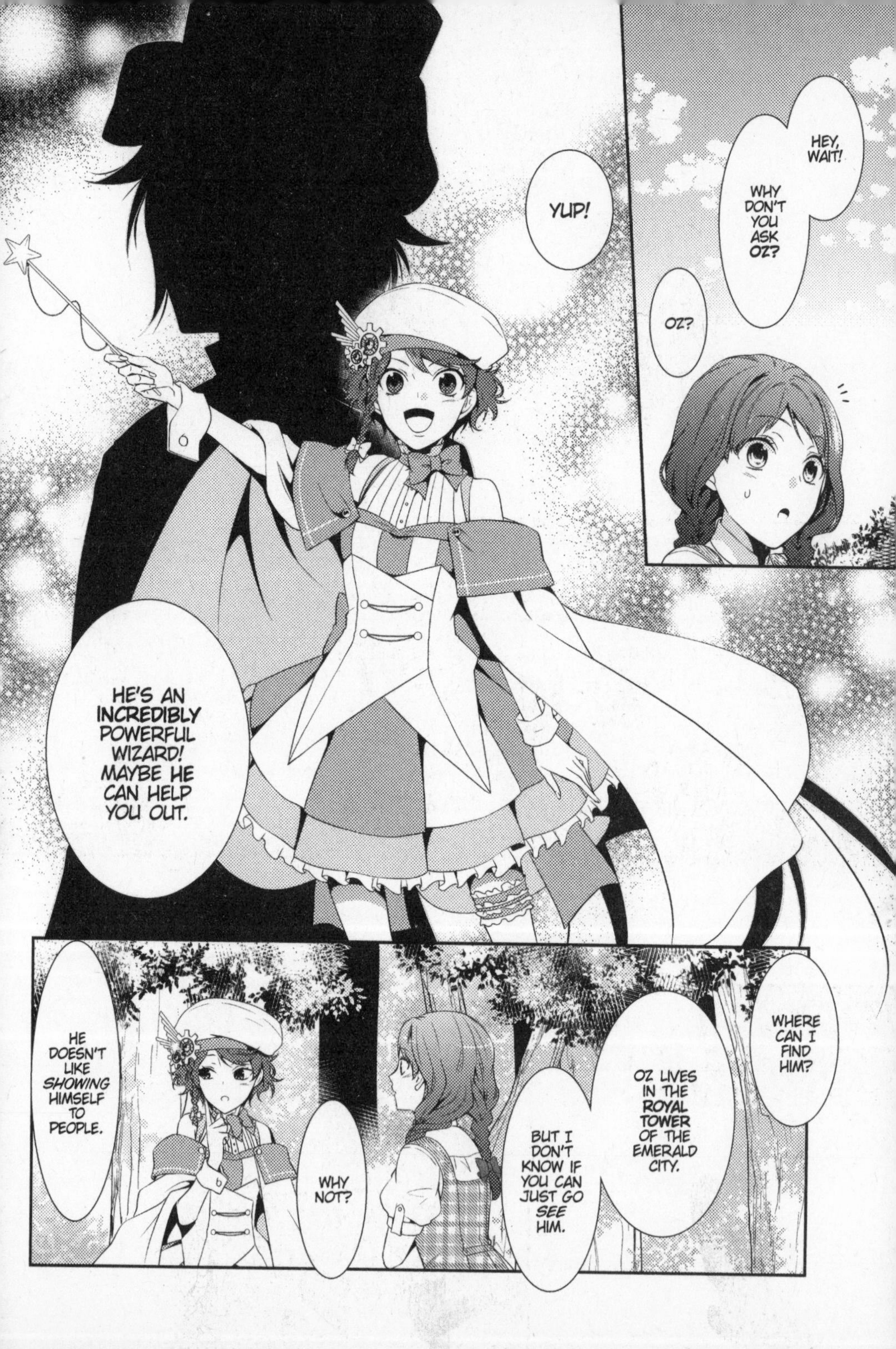
HEY, WAIT!
WHY DON'T YOU ASK OZ?
OZ?
YUP!
HE'S AN INCREDIBLY POWERFUL WIZARD! MAYBE HE CAN HELP YOU OUT.
WHERE CAN I FIND HIM?
OZ LIVES IN THE ROYAL TOWER OF THE EMERALD CITY.
BUT I DON'T KNOW IF YOU CAN JUST GO SEE HIM.
WHY NOT?
HE DOESN'T LIKE SHOWING HIMSELF TO PEOPLE.

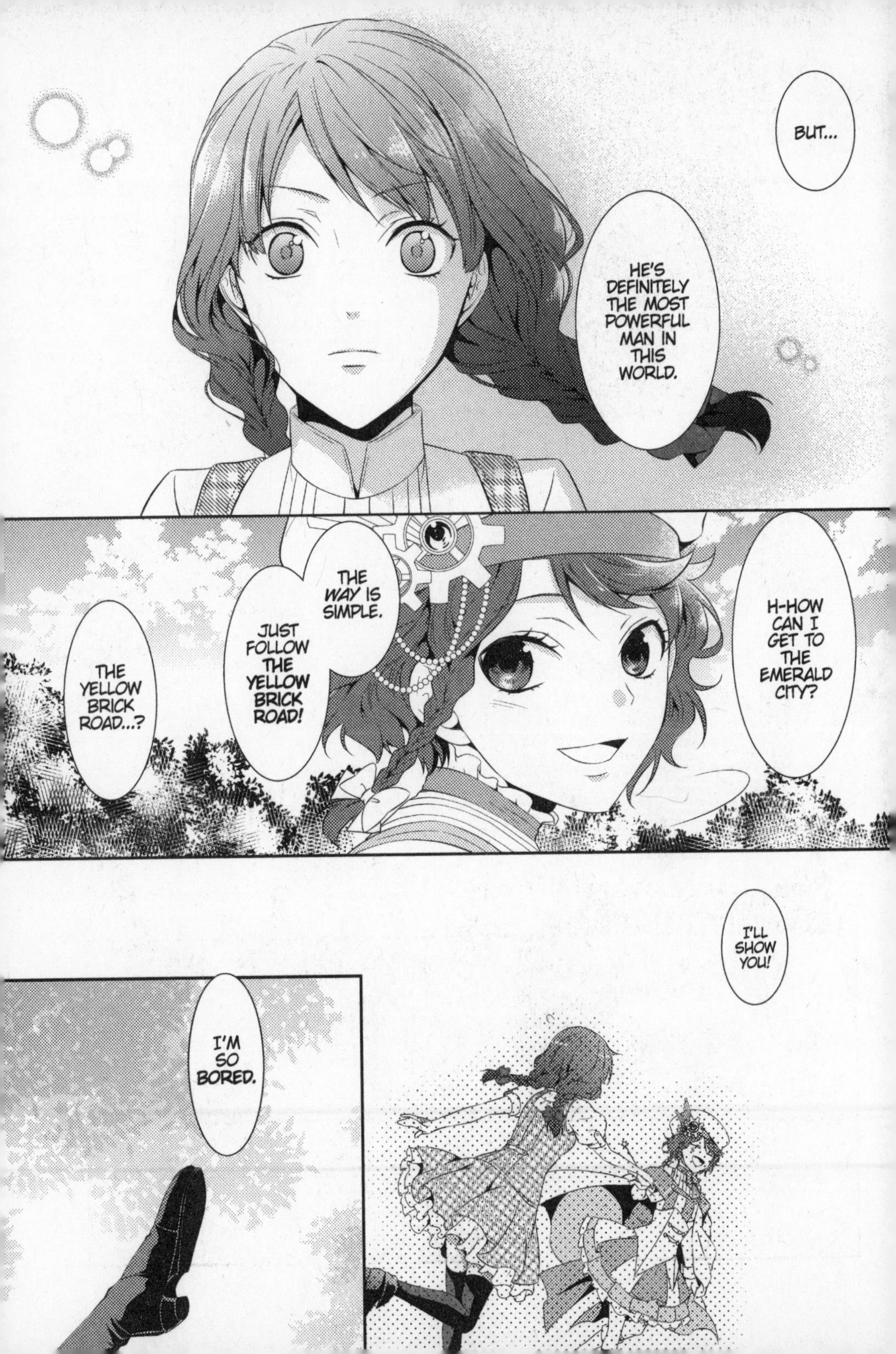
BUT...
HE'S DEFINITELY THE MOST POWERFUL MAN IN THIS WORLD.
H-HOW CAN I GET TO THE EMERALD CITY?
THE *WAY* IS SIMPLE.
JUST FOLLOW THE YELLOW BRICK ROAD!
THE YELLOW BRICK ROAD...?
I'LL SHOW YOU!
I'M SO BORED.

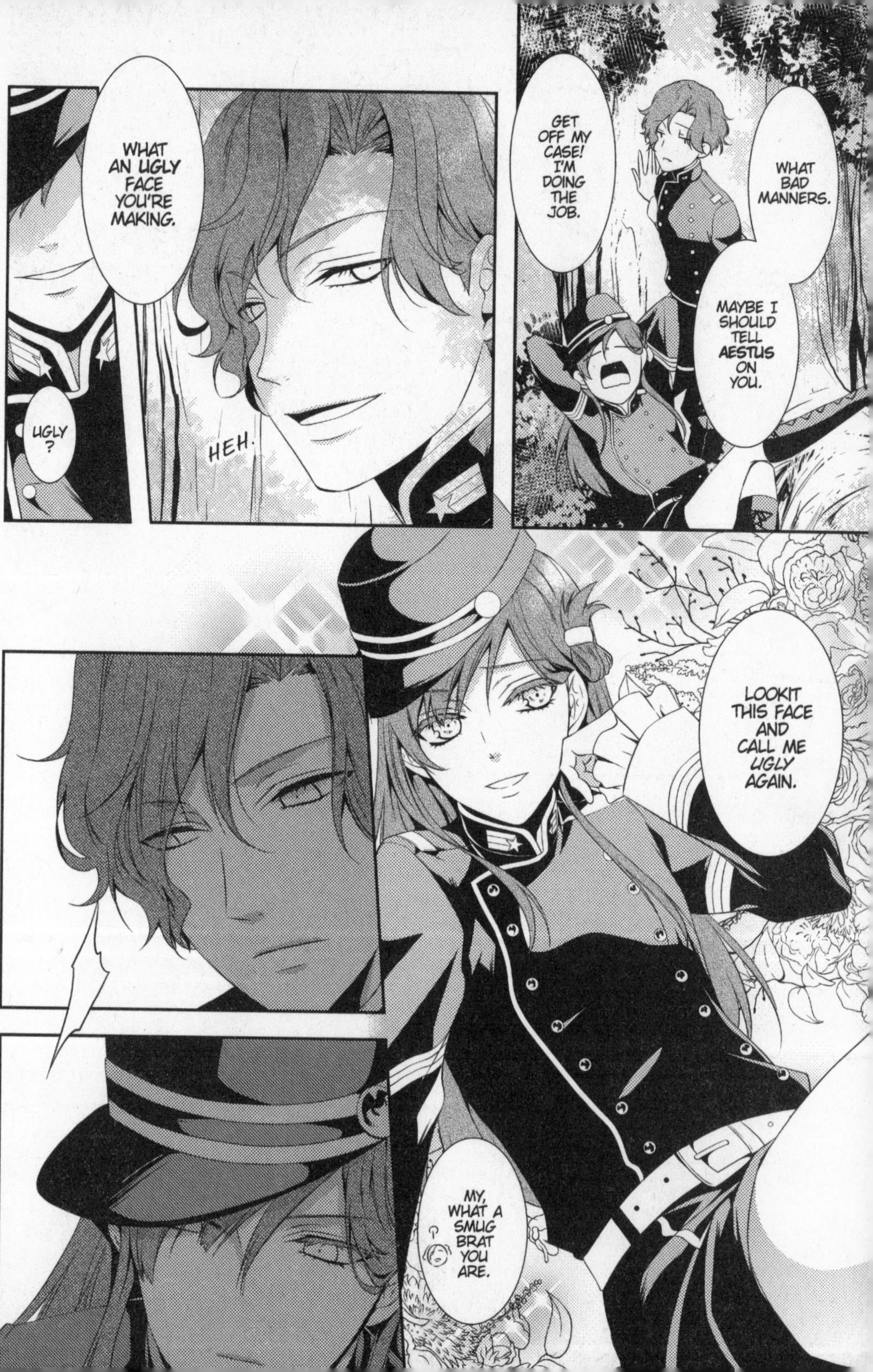
WHAT BAD MANNERS.
MAYBE I SHOULD TELL AESTUS ON YOU.
GET OFF MY CASE! I'M DOING THE JOB.
WHAT AN UGLY FACE YOU'RE MAKING.
HEH.
UGLY?
LOOKIT THIS FACE AND CALL ME UGLY AGAIN.
MY, WHAT A SMUG BRAT YOU ARE.

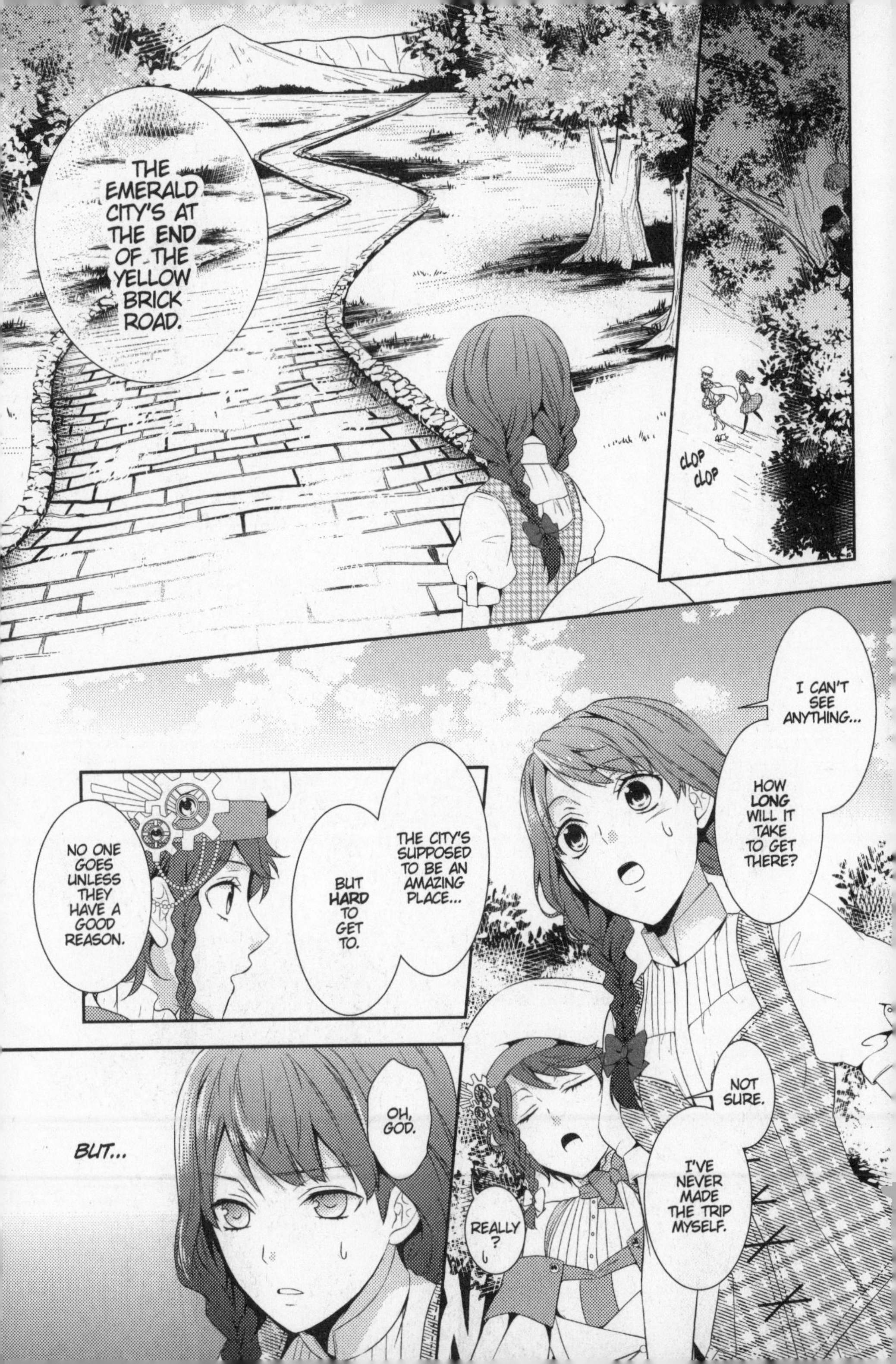
CLOP CLOP
THE EMERALD CITY'S AT THE END OF THE YELLOW BRICK ROAD.
I CAN'T SEE ANYTHING...
HOW LONG WILL IT TAKE TO GET THERE?
THE CITY'S SUPPOSED TO BE AN AMAZING PLACE...
BUT HARD TO GET TO.
NO ONE GOES UNLESS THEY HAVE A GOOD REASON.
NOT SURE.
I'VE NEVER MADE THE TRIP MYSELF.
REALLY?
OH, GOD.
BUT...

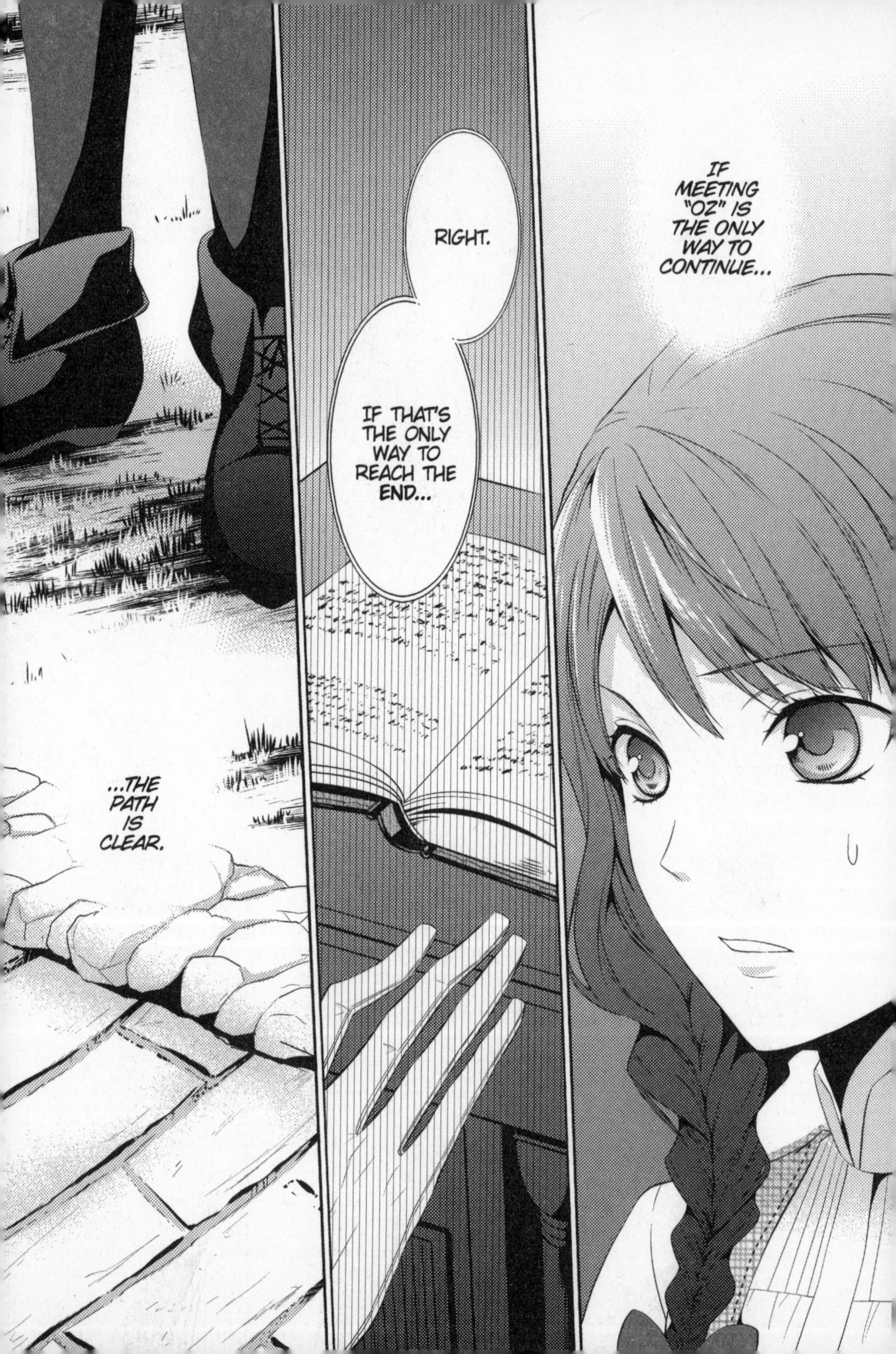
IF MEETING "OZ" IS THE ONLY WAY TO CONTINUE...
RIGHT.
IF THAT'S THE ONLY WAY TO REACH THE END...
...THE PATH IS CLEAR.

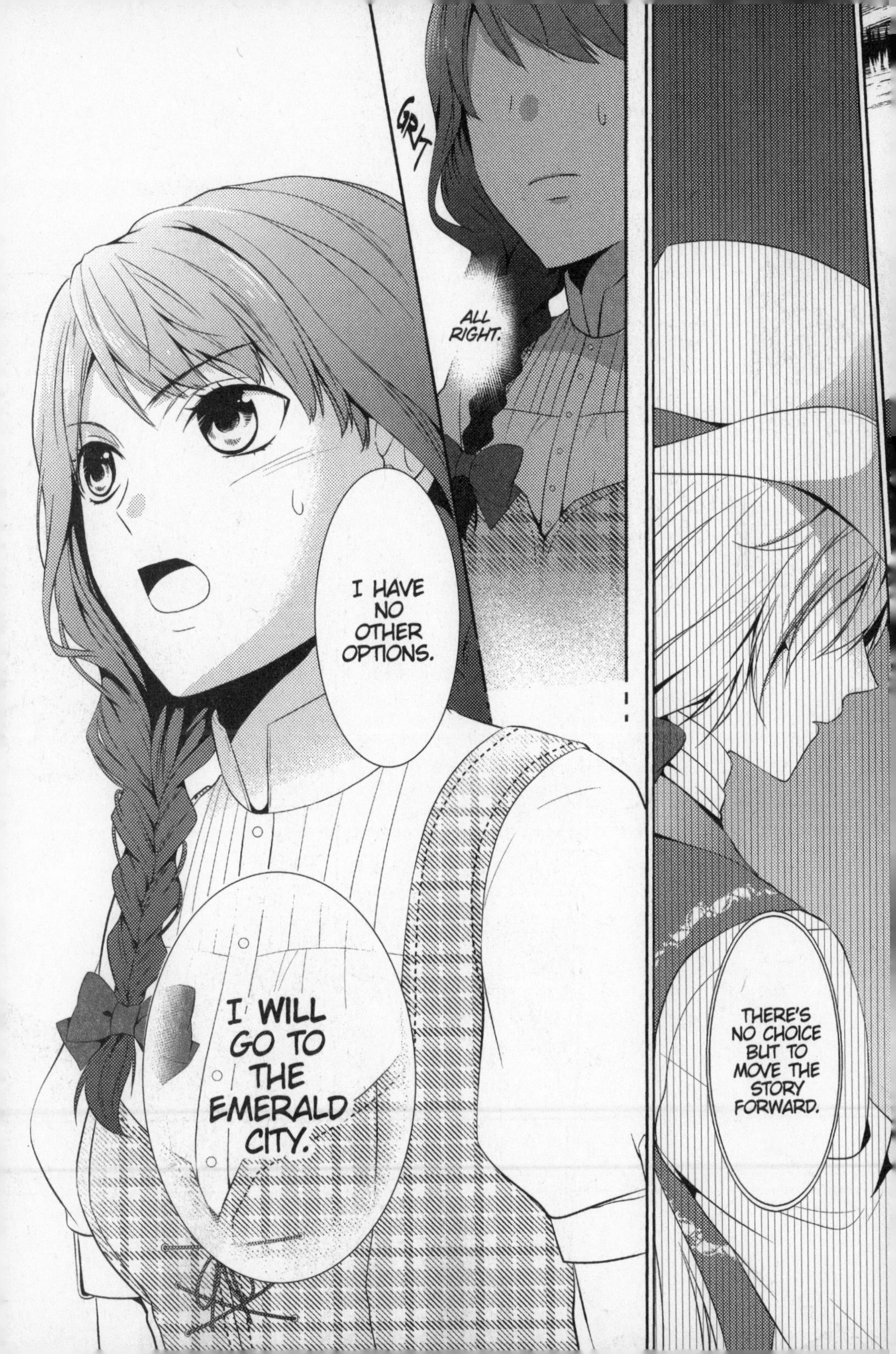
THERE'S NO CHOICE BUT TO MOVE THE STORY FORWARD.
GRIT
ALL RIGHT.
I HAVE NO OTHER OPTIONS.
I WILL GO TO THE EMERALD CITY.

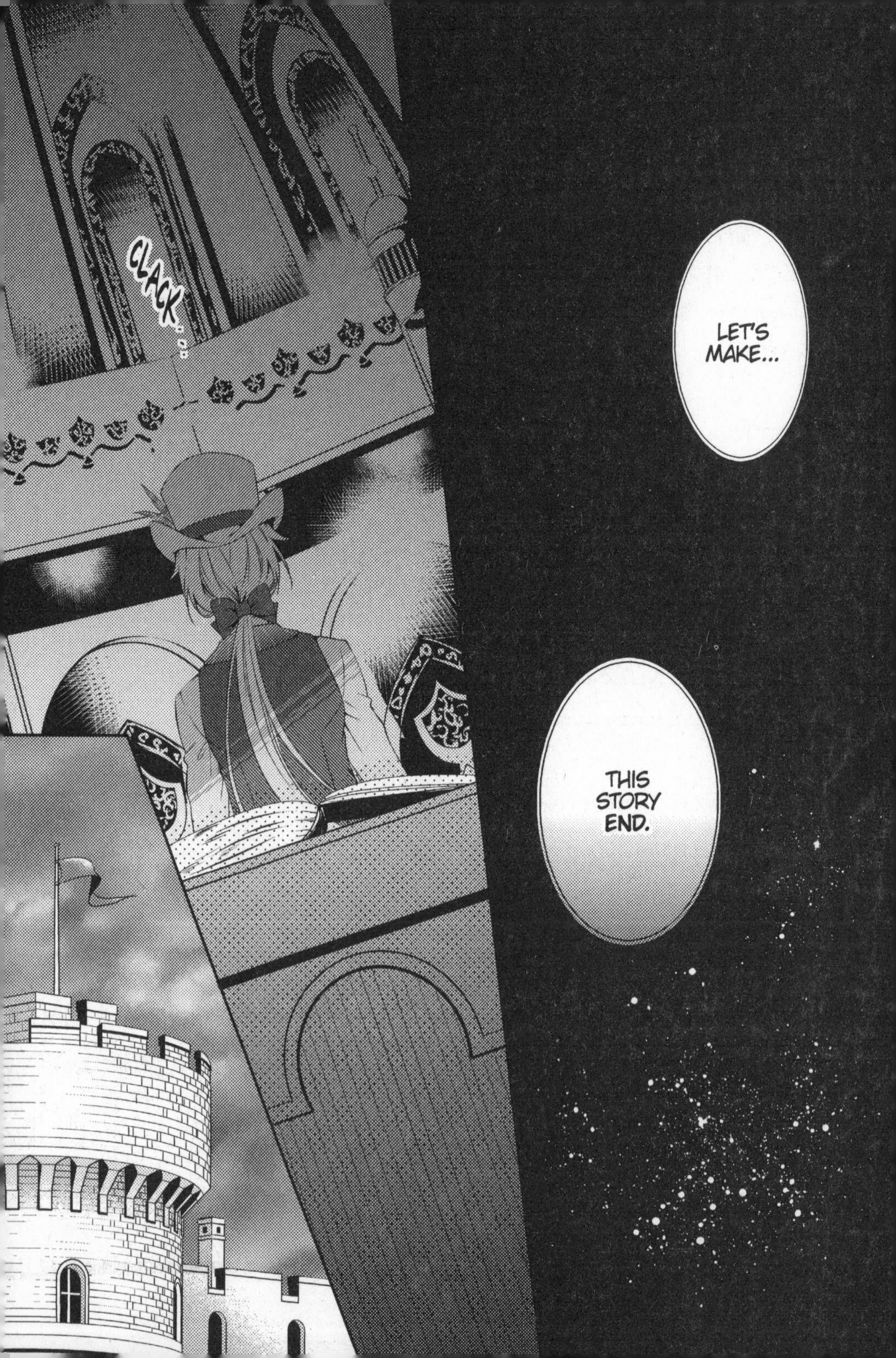
LET'S MAKE...
THIS STORY END.
CLACK

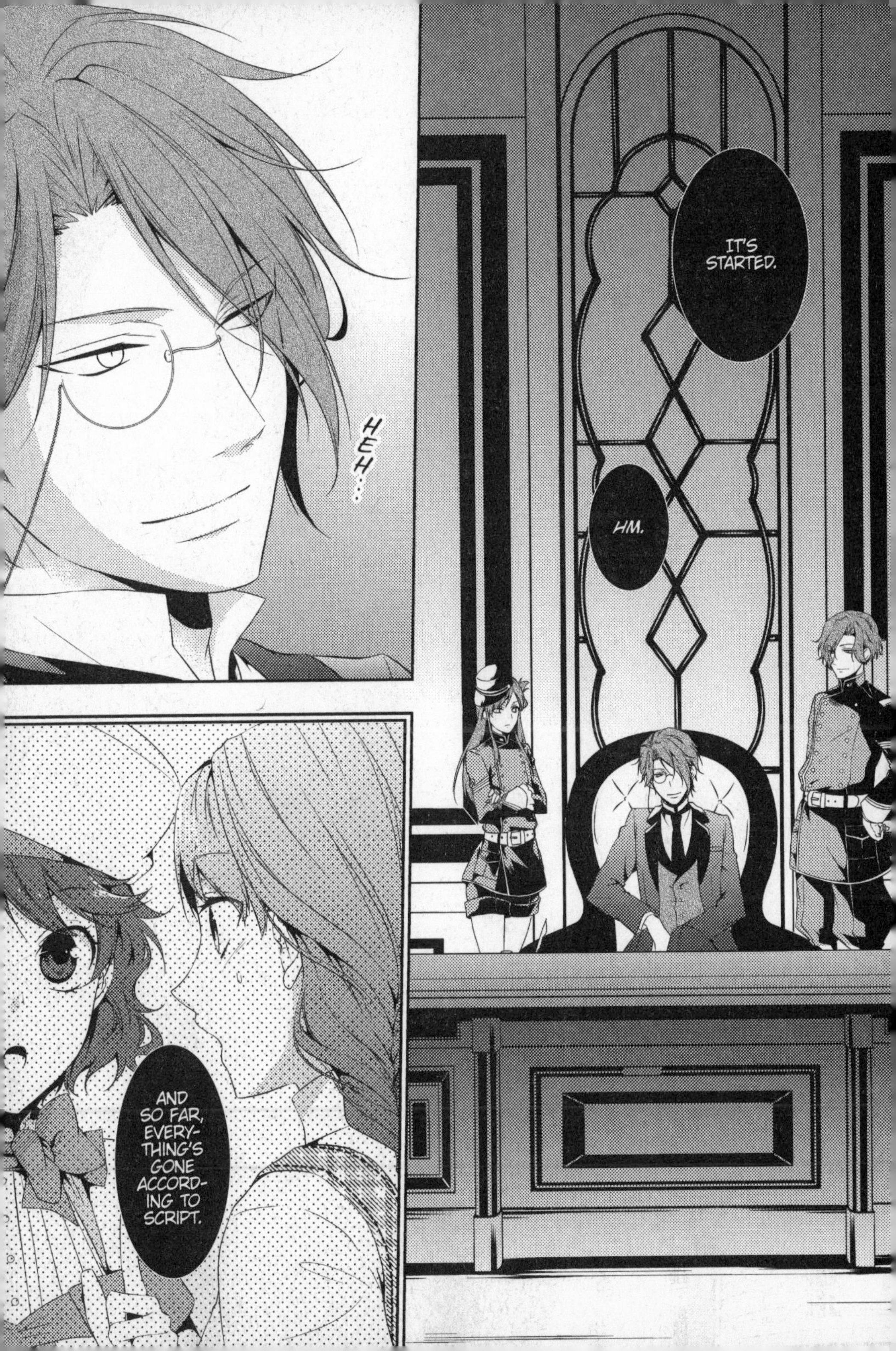
IT'S STARTED.
HM.
HEH...
AND SO FAR, EVERYTHING'S GONE ACCORDING TO SCRIPT.

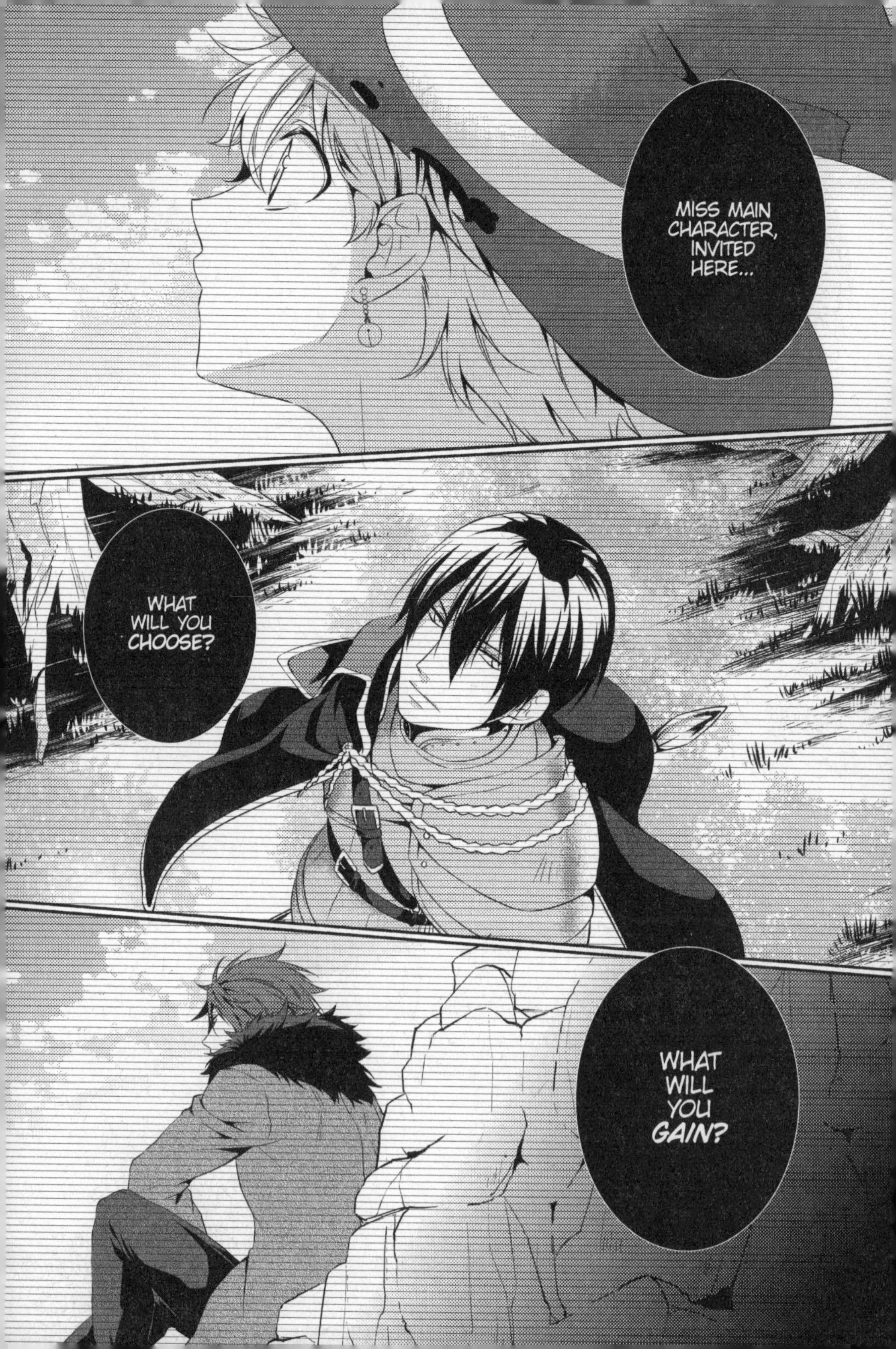
MISS MAIN CHARACTER, INVITED HERE...
WHAT WILL YOU CHOOSE?
WHAT WILL YOU GAIN?

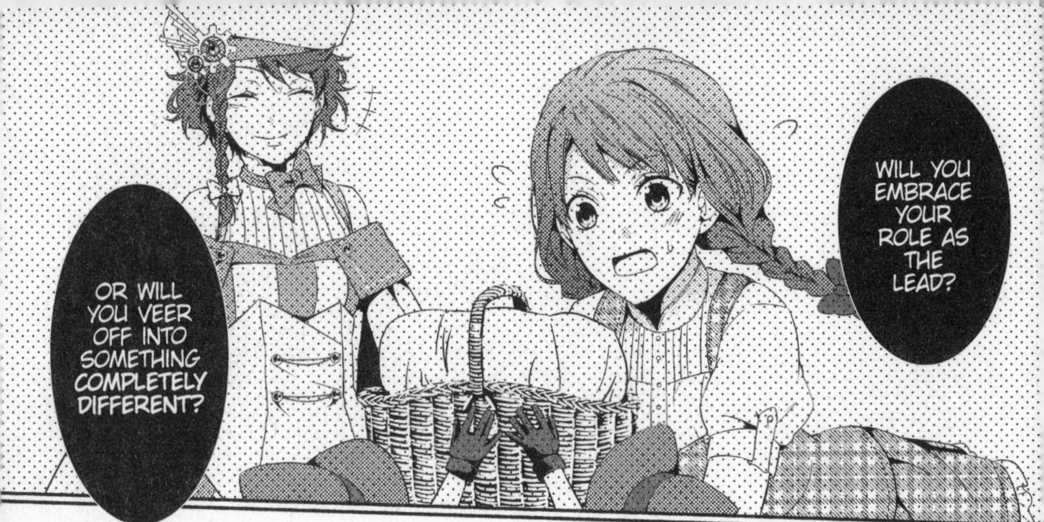
WILL YOU EMBRACE YOUR ROLE AS THE LEAD?
OR WILL YOU VEER OFF INTO SOMETHING COMPLETELY DIFFERENT?
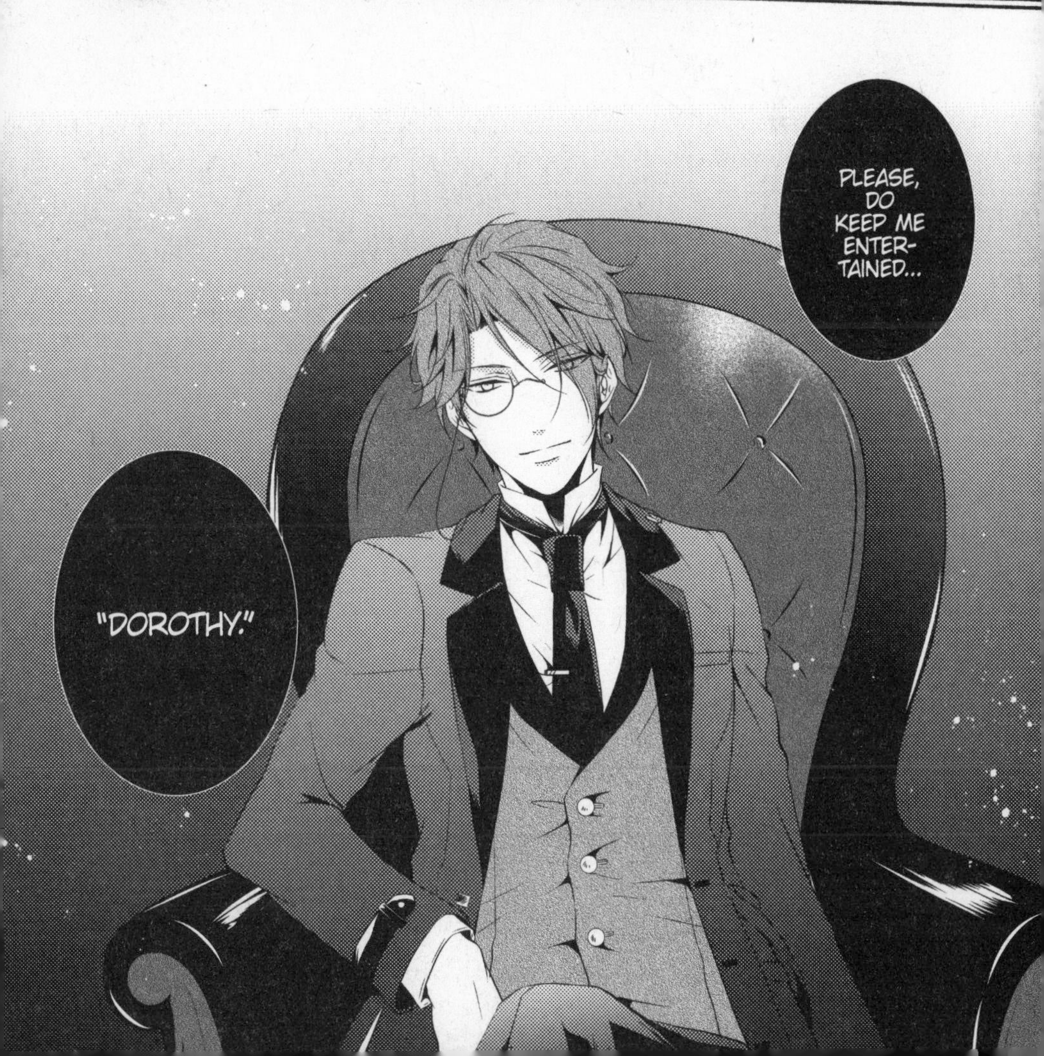
PLEASE, DO KEEP ME ENTER-TAINED...
"DOROTHY."

Captive Hearts of Oz

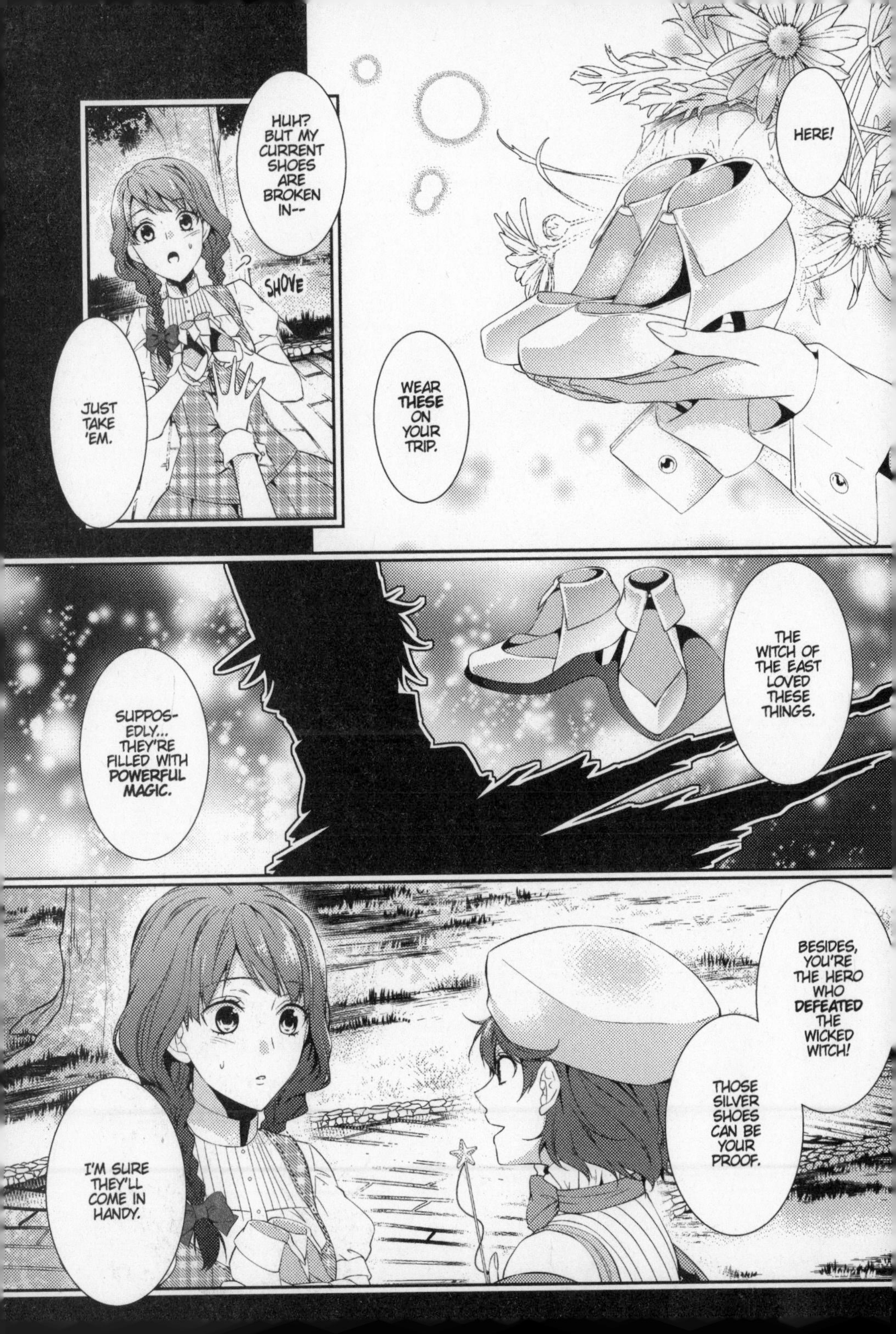
HERE!
WEAR THESE ON YOUR TRIP.
HUH? BUT MY CURRENT SHOES ARE BROKEN IN--
SHOVE
JUST TAKE 'EM.
THE WITCH OF THE EAST LOVED THESE THINGS.
SUPPOS-EDLY... THEY'RE FILLED WITH POWERFUL MAGIC.
BESIDES, YOU'RE THE HERO WHO DEFEATED THE WICKED WITCH!
THOSE SILVER SHOES CAN BE YOUR PROOF.
I'M SURE THEY'LL COME IN HANDY.

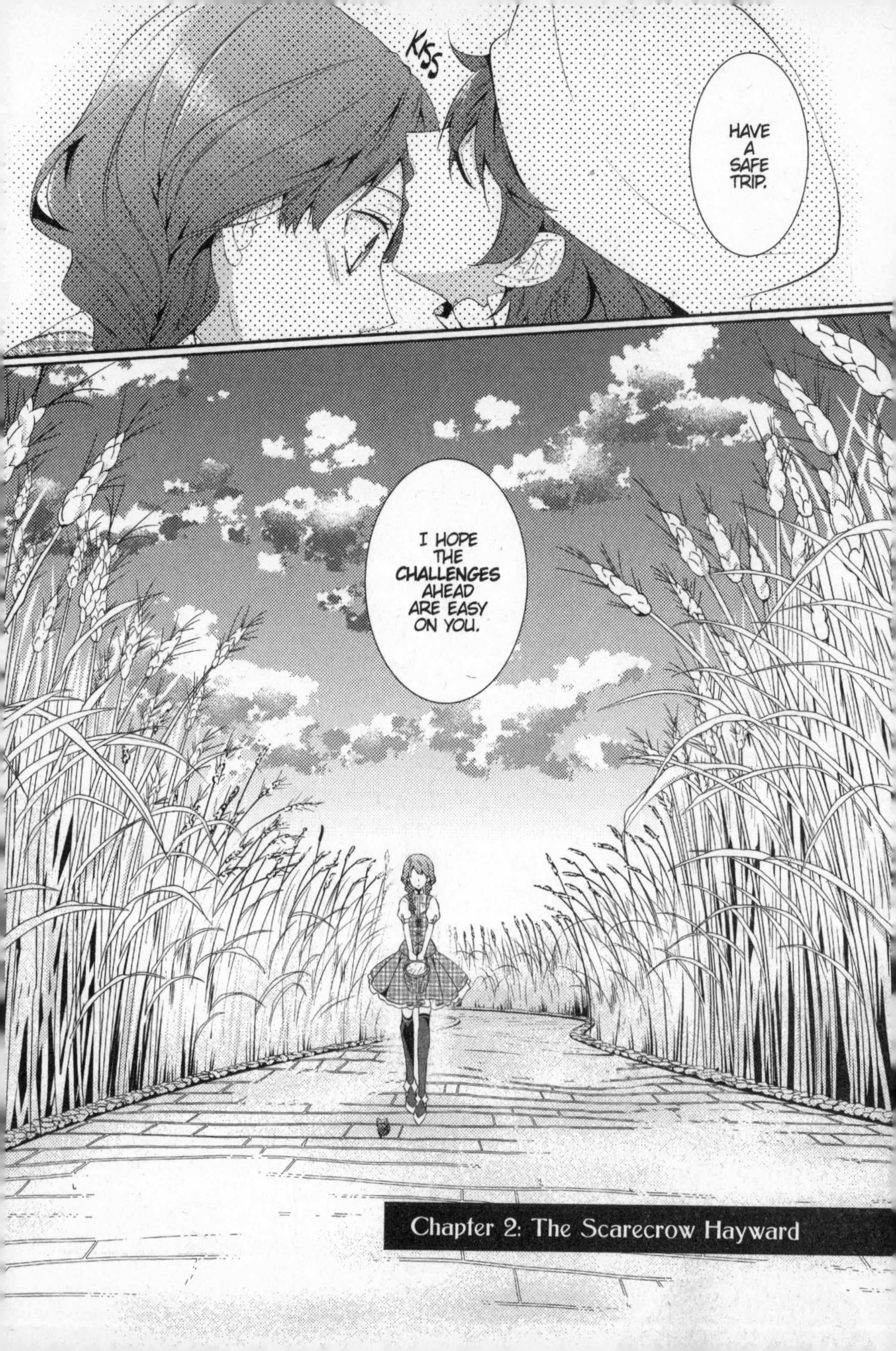
KISS
HAVE A SAFE TRIP.
I HOPE THE CHALLENGES AHEAD ARE EASY ON YOU.
Chapter 2: The Scarecrow Hayward

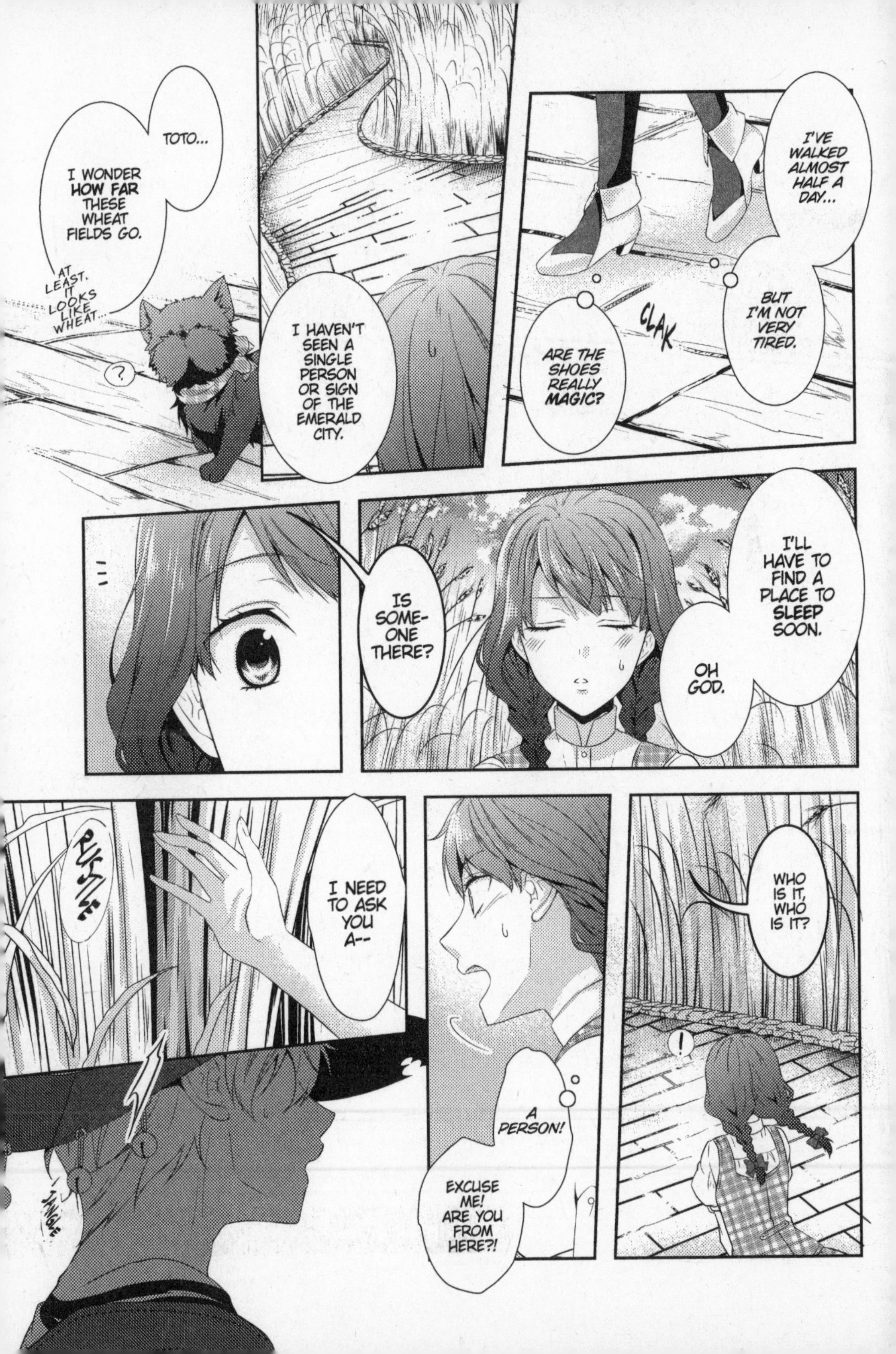

I'VE WALKED ALMOST HALF A DAY...
BUT I'M NOT VERY TIRED.
CLAK
ARE THE SHOES REALLY MAGIC?
I HAVEN'T SEEN A SINGLE PERSON OR SIGN OF THE EMERALD CITY.
TOTO...
I WONDER HOW FAR THESE WHEAT FIELDS GO.
AT LEAST, IT LOOKS LIKE WHEAT...
?
I'LL HAVE TO FIND A PLACE TO SLEEP SOON.
OH GOD.
IS SOME-ONE THERE?
WHO IS IT, WHO IS IT?
!
A PERSON!
EXCUSE ME! ARE YOU FROM HERE?!
I NEED TO ASK YOU A--
RUSTLE
JANGLE

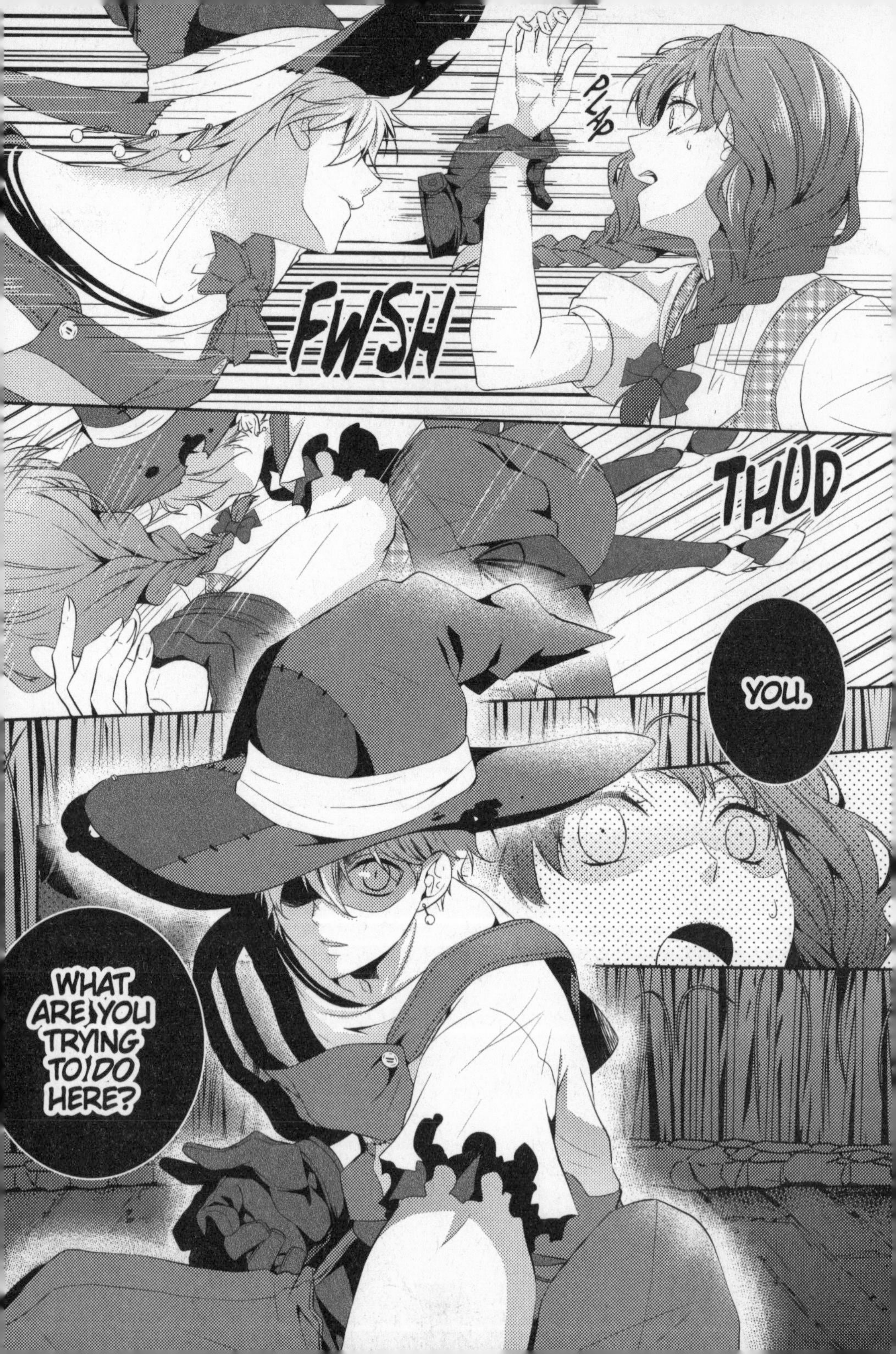
PLAP
FWSH
THUD
YOU.
WHAT ARE YOU TRYING TO DO HERE?

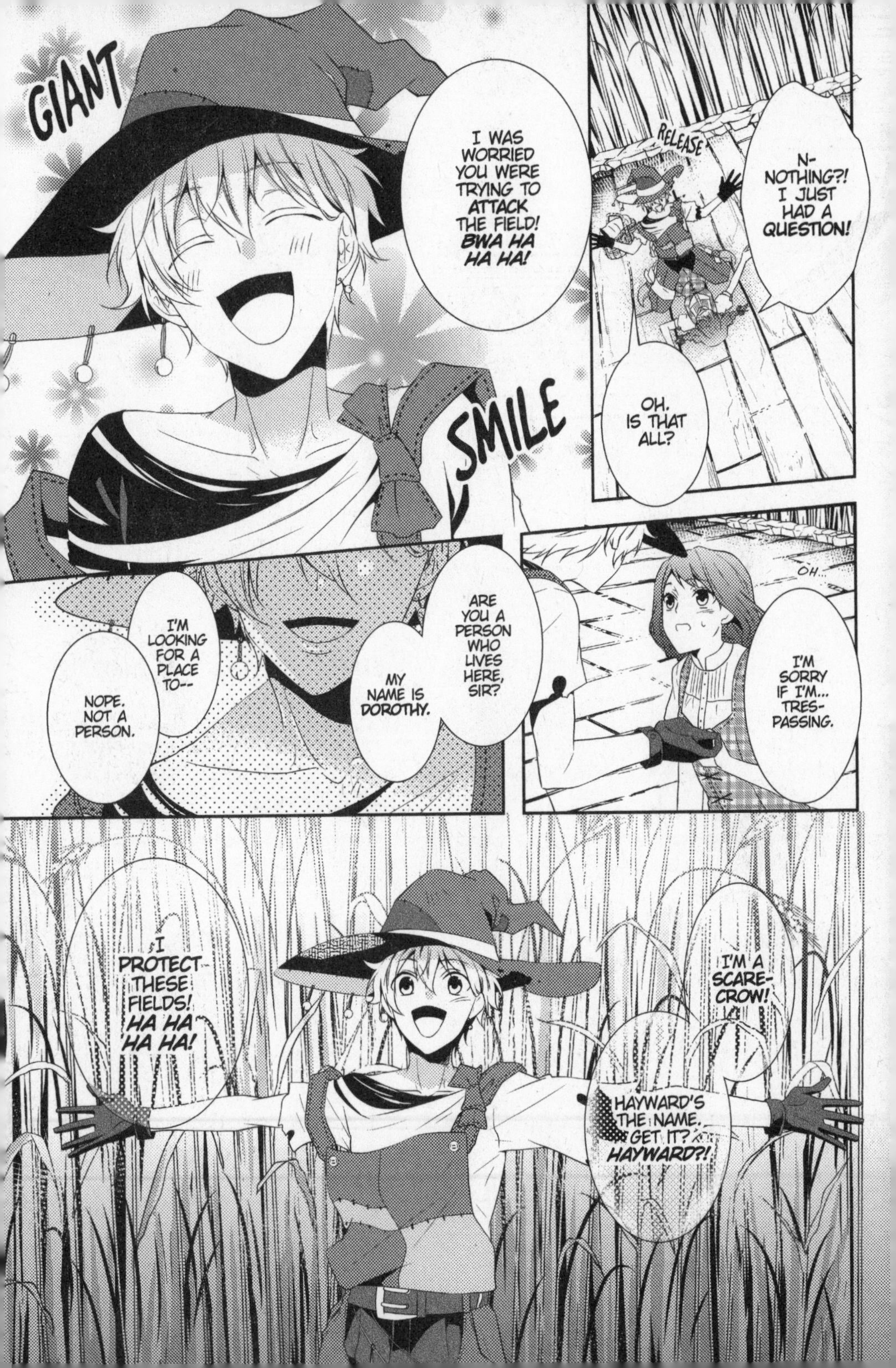
RELEASE
N-NOTHING?! I JUST HAD A QUESTION!
OH. IS THAT ALL?
GIANT
I WAS WORRIED YOU WERE TRYING TO ATTACK THE FIELD! BWA HA HA HA!
SMILE
OH...
I'M SORRY IF I'M... TRES-PASSING.
ARE YOU A PERSON WHO LIVES HERE, SIR?
MY NAME IS DOROTHY.
I'M LOOKING FOR A PLACE TO--
NOPE. NOT A PERSON.
I'M A SCARE-CROW!
HAYWARD'S THE NAME. GET IT? HAYWARD?!
I PROTECT THESE FIELDS! HA HA HA HA!

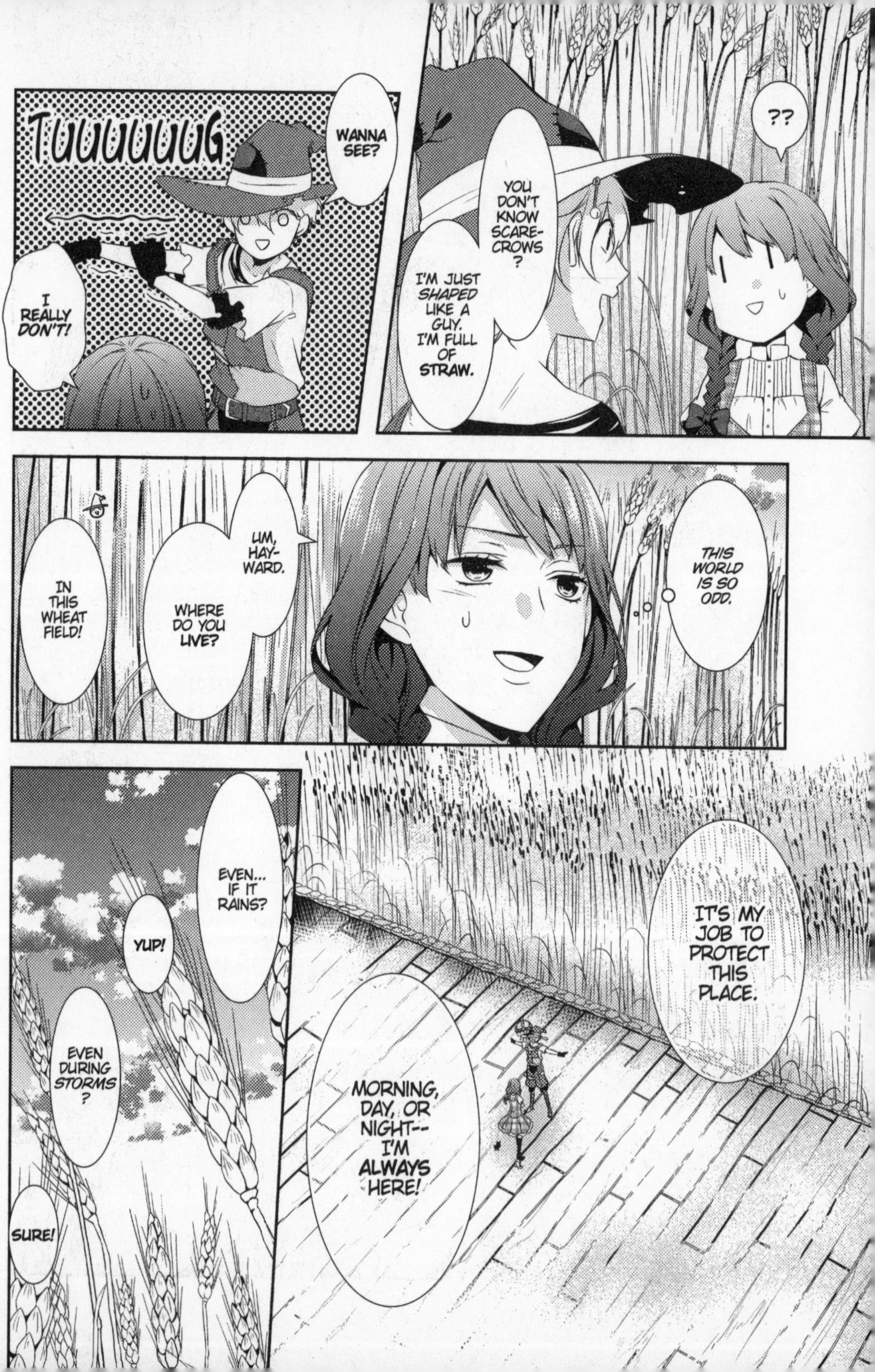
??
YOU DON'T KNOW SCARE-CROWS?
I'M JUST SHAPED LIKE A GUY. I'M FULL OF STRAW.
WANNA SEE?
TUUUUUUUG
I REALLY DON'T!
THIS WORLD IS SO ODD.
UM, HAYWARD.
WHERE DO YOU LIVE?
IN THIS WHEAT FIELD!
IT'S MY JOB TO PROTECT THIS PLACE.
MORNING, DAY, OR NIGHT-- I'M ALWAYS HERE!
EVEN... IF IT RAINS?
YUP!
EVEN DURING STORMS?
SURE!

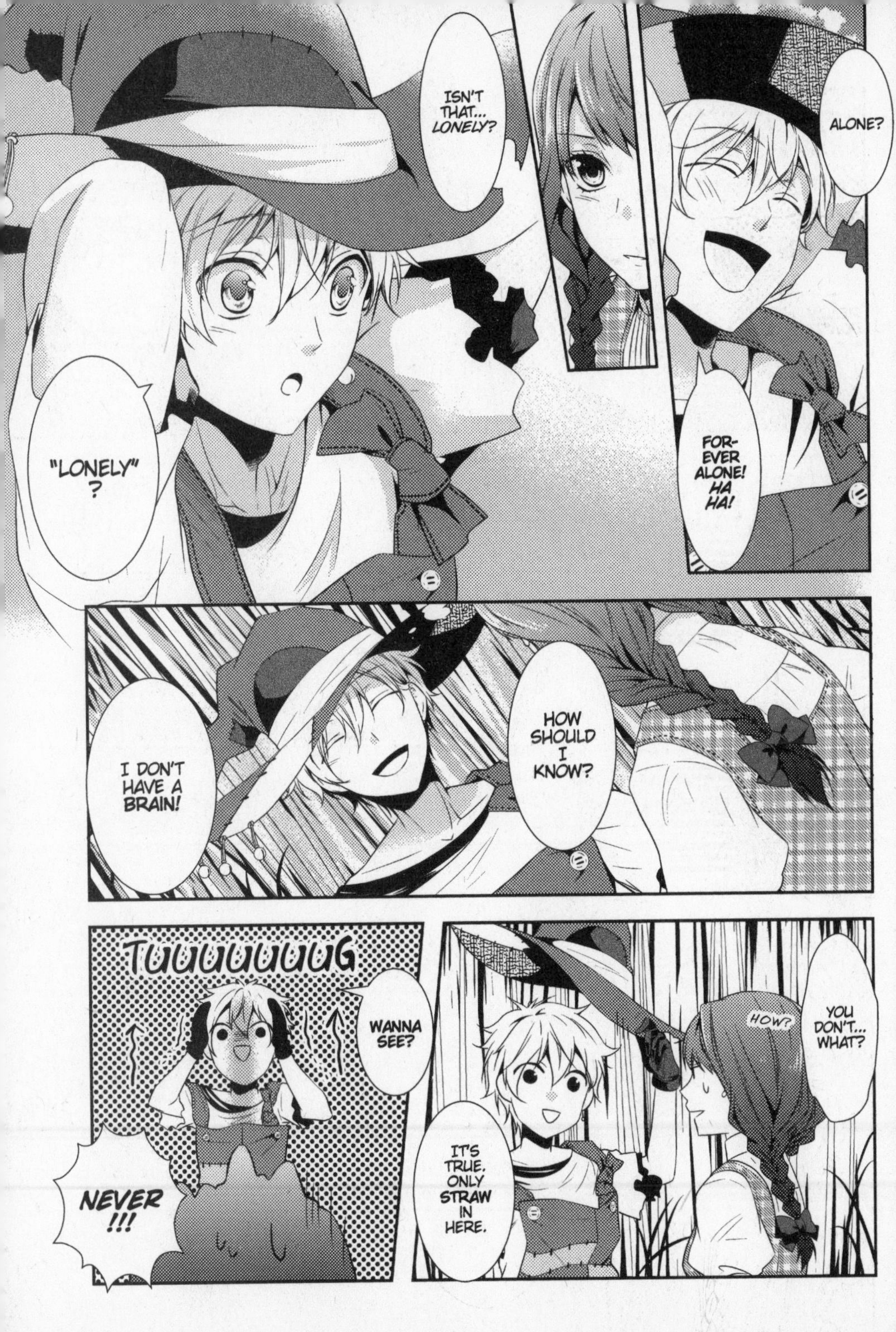

ALONE?
FOR-EVER ALONE! HA HA!
ISN'T THAT... LONELY?
"LONELY" ?
HOW SHOULD I KNOW?
I DON'T HAVE A BRAIN!
YOU DON'T... WHAT?
HOW?
IT'S TRUE. ONLY STRAW IN HERE.
TUUUUUUUG
WANNA SEE?
NEVER !!!

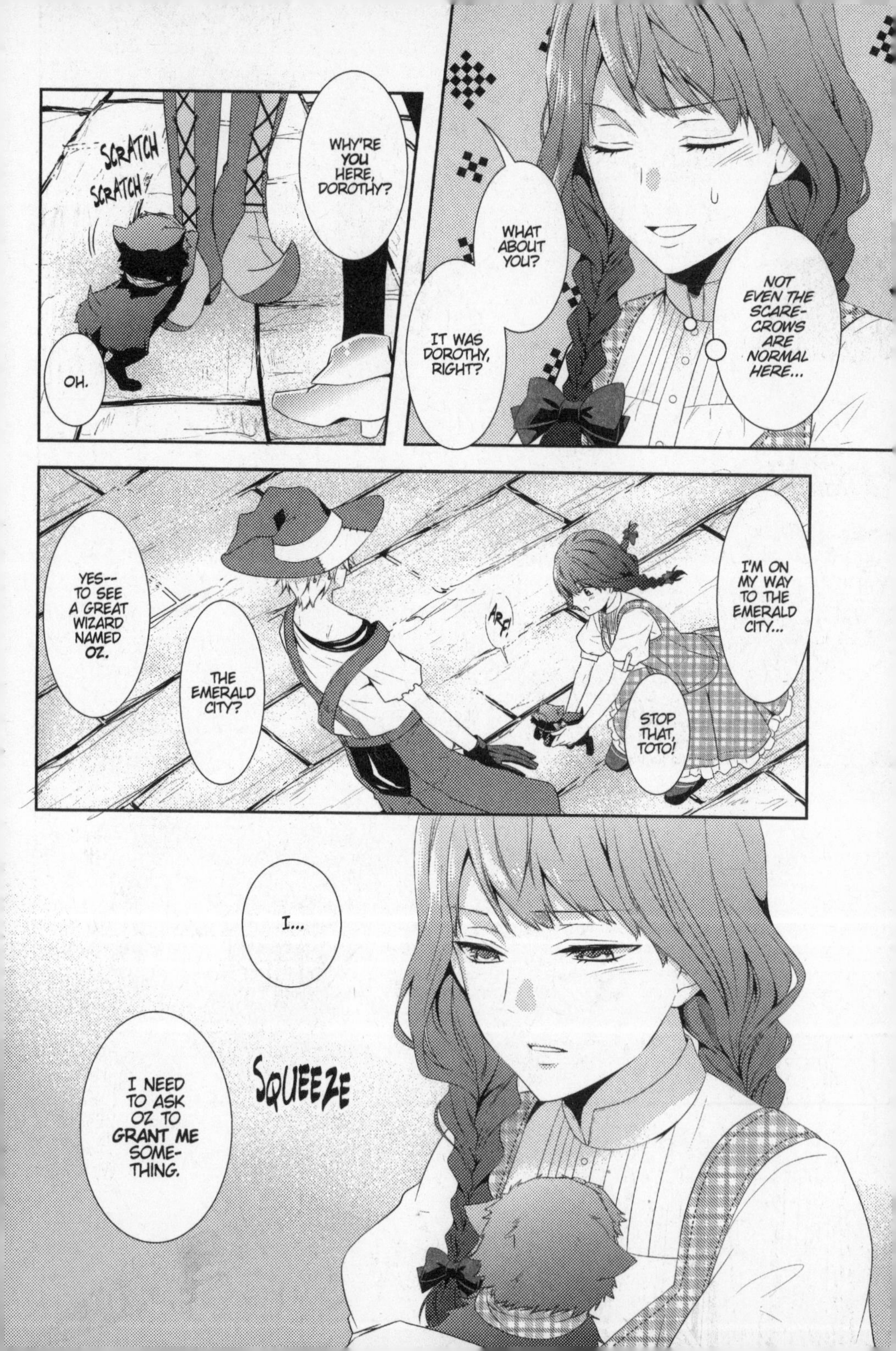
NOT EVEN THE SCARE-CROWS ARE NORMAL HERE...
WHAT ABOUT YOU?
IT WAS DOROTHY, RIGHT?
WHY'RE YOU HERE, DOROTHY?
SCRATCH SCRATCH
OH.
I'M ON MY WAY TO THE EMERALD CITY...
STOP THAT, TOTO!
ARF!
THE EMERALD CITY?
YES-- TO SEE A GREAT WIZARD NAMED OZ.
I...
SQUEEZE
I NEED TO ASK OZ TO GRANT ME SOME-THING.

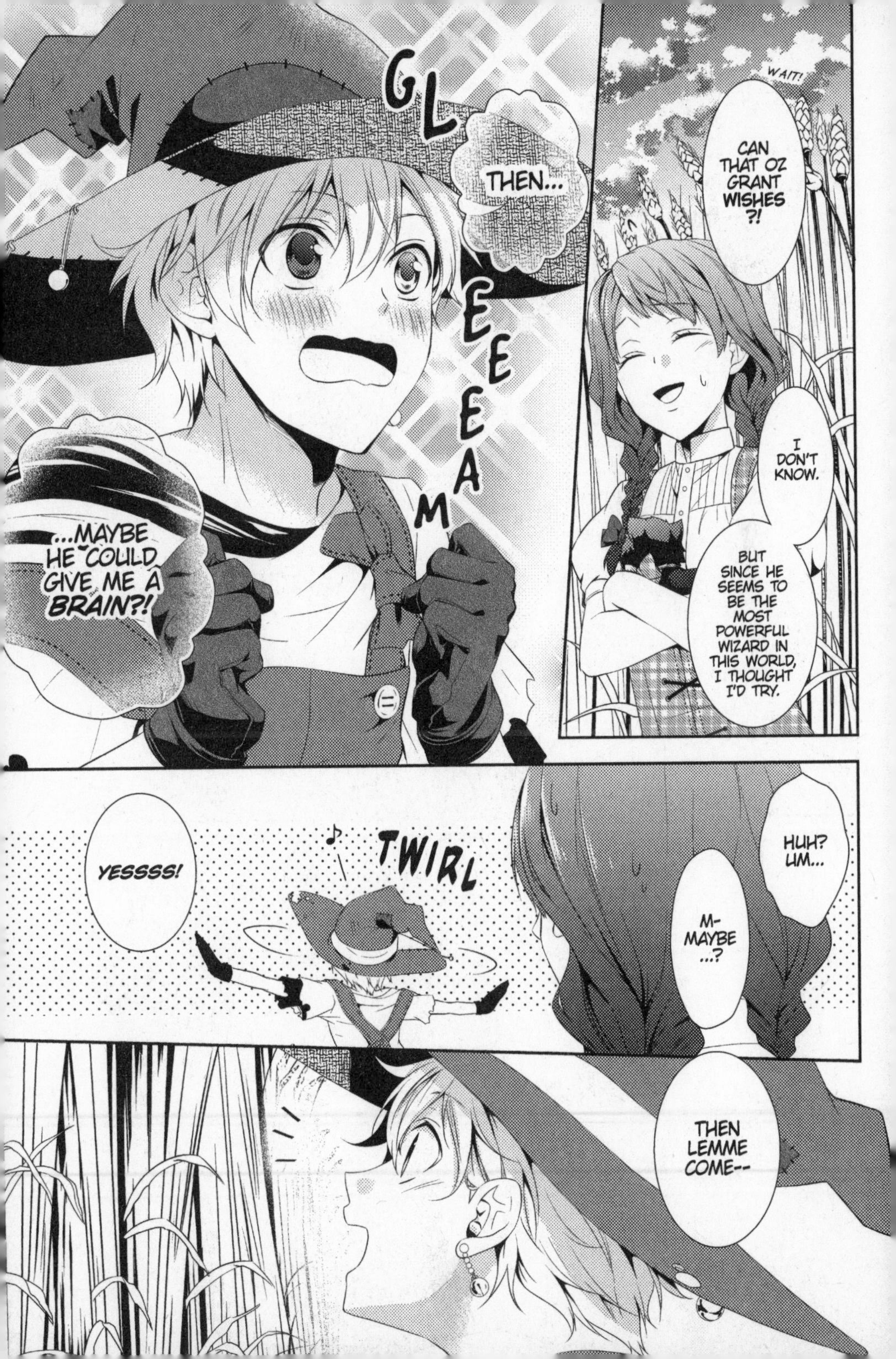

WAIT!
CAN THAT OZ GRANT WISHES?!
I DON'T KNOW.
BUT SINCE HE SEEMS TO BE THE MOST POWERFUL WIZARD IN THIS WORLD, I THOUGHT I'D TRY.
GLEEEEAM
THEN...
...MAYBE HE COULD GIVE ME A BRAIN?!
HUH? UM...
M-MAYBE...?
YESSSS!
TWIRL
THEN LEMME COME--

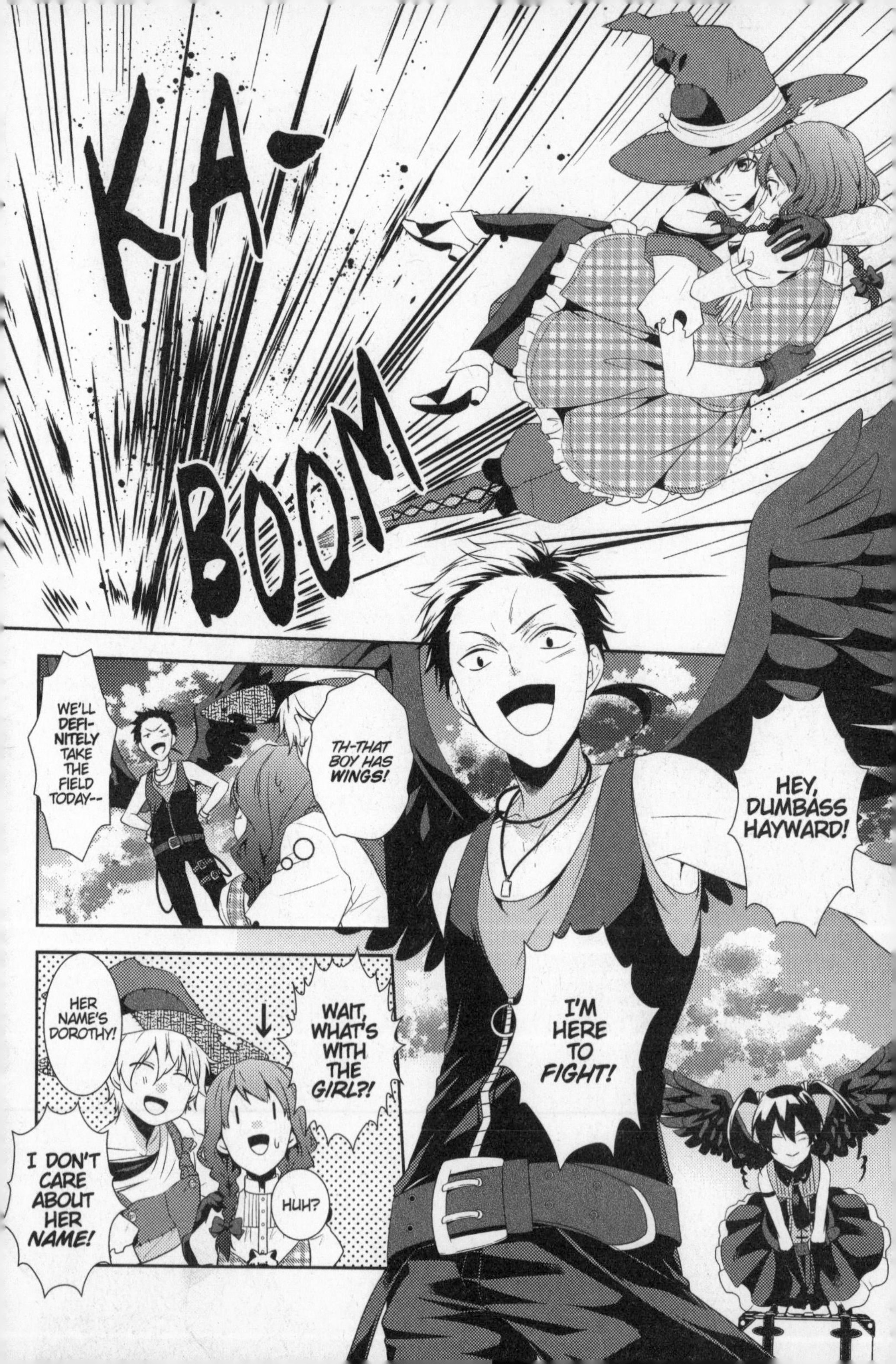
KA-BOOM
HEY, DUMBASS HAYWARD!
I'M HERE TO FIGHT!
TH-THAT BOY HAS WINGS!
WE'LL DEFINITELY TAKE THE FIELD TODAY--
WAIT, WHAT'S WITH THE GIRL?!
HER NAME'S DOROTHY!
HUH?
I DON'T CARE ABOUT HER NAME!

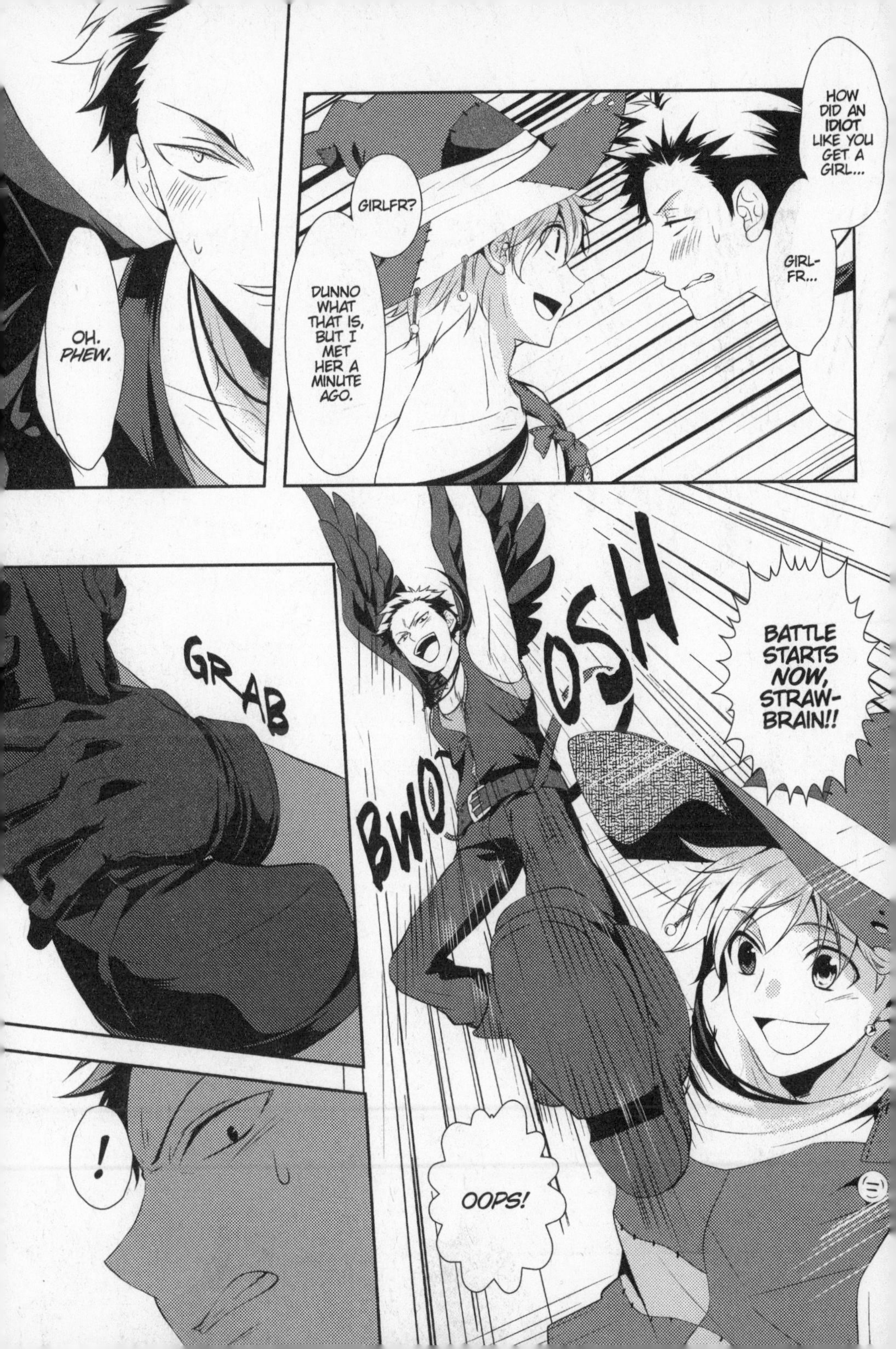
HOW DID AN IDIOT LIKE YOU GET A GIRL...
GIRL-FR...
GIRLFR?
DUNNO WHAT THAT IS, BUT I MET HER A MINUTE AGO.
OH. PHEW.
BATTLE STARTS NOW, STRAW-BRAIN!!
BWO
OSH
OOPS!
GRAB
!

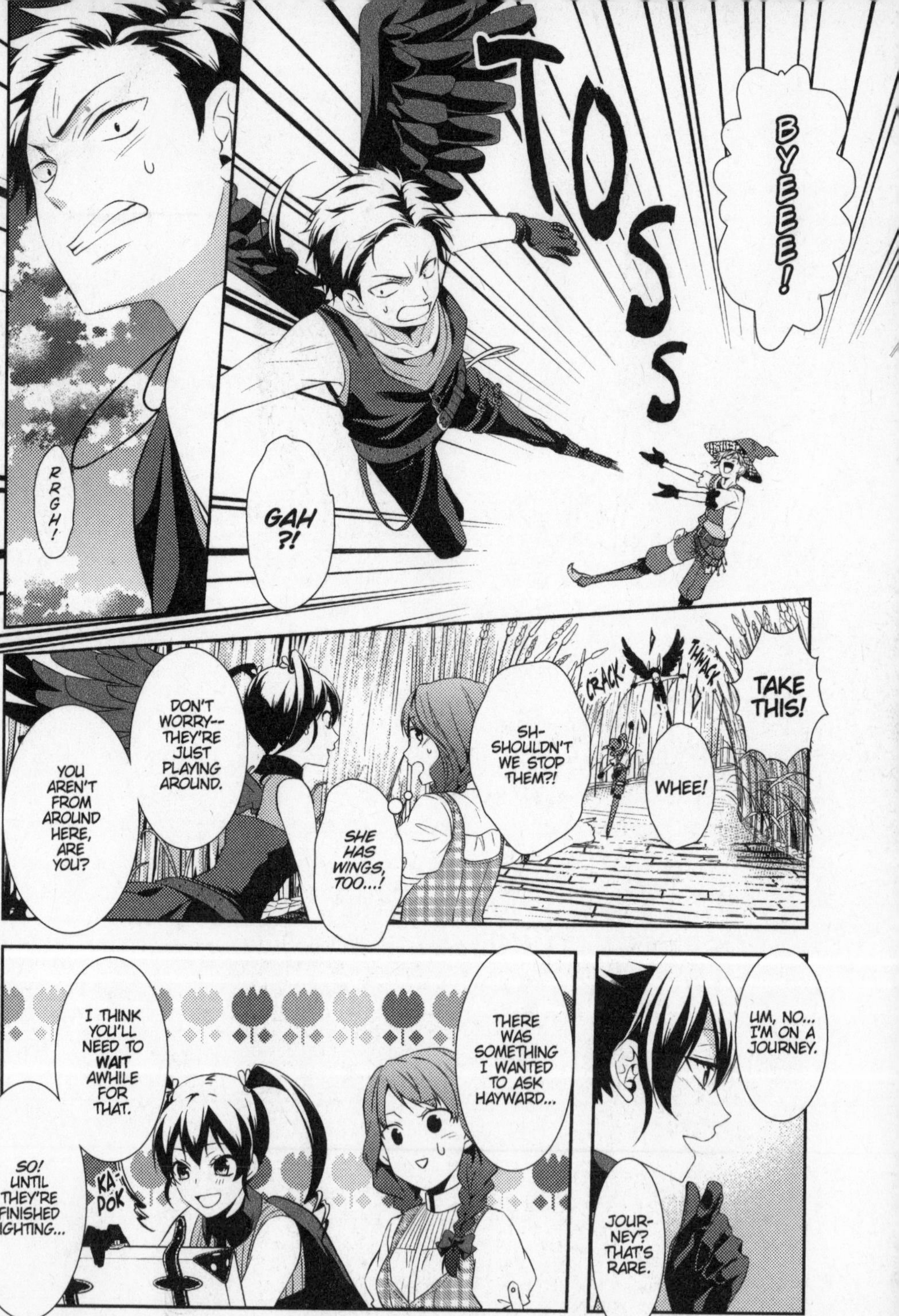
BYEEE!
TOSS
GAH?!
RRGH!
TAKE THIS!
THWACK
CRACK-
WHEE!
SH-SHOULDN'T WE STOP THEM?!
SHE HAS WINGS, TOO...!
DON'T WORRY--THEY'RE JUST PLAYING AROUND.
YOU AREN'T FROM AROUND HERE, ARE YOU?
UM, NO... I'M ON A JOURNEY.
JOURNEY? THAT'S RARE.
THERE WAS SOMETHING I WANTED TO ASK HAYWARD...
I THINK YOU'LL NEED TO WAIT AWHILE FOR THAT.
KA-DOK
SO! UNTIL THEY'RE FINISHED FIGHTING...

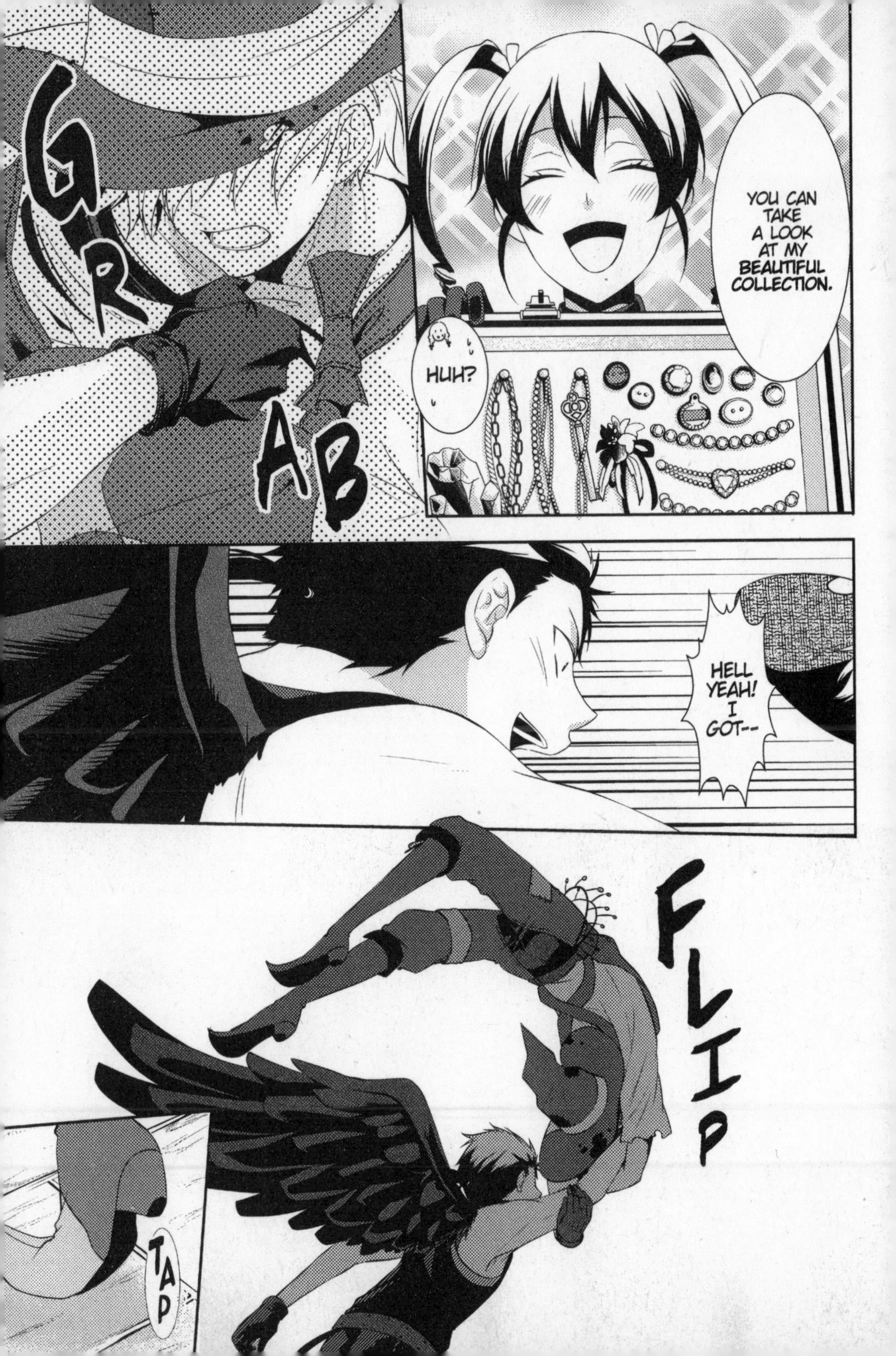
YOU CAN TAKE A LOOK AT MY BEAUTIFUL COLLECTION.
HUH?
GRAB
HELL YEAH! I GOT--
FLIP
TAP

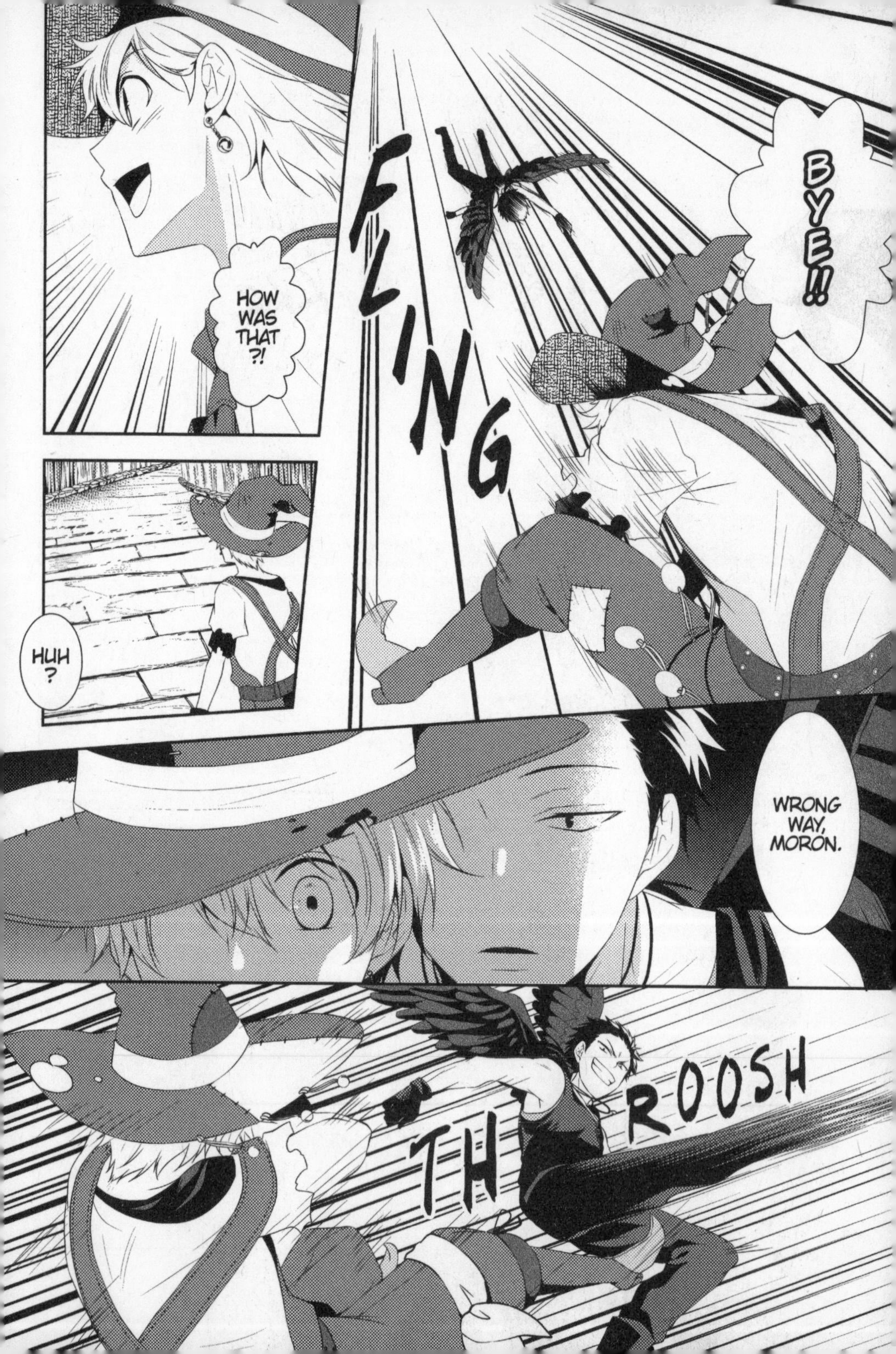
BYE!!
FLING
HOW WAS THAT?!
HUH?
WRONG WAY, MORON.
THROOSH

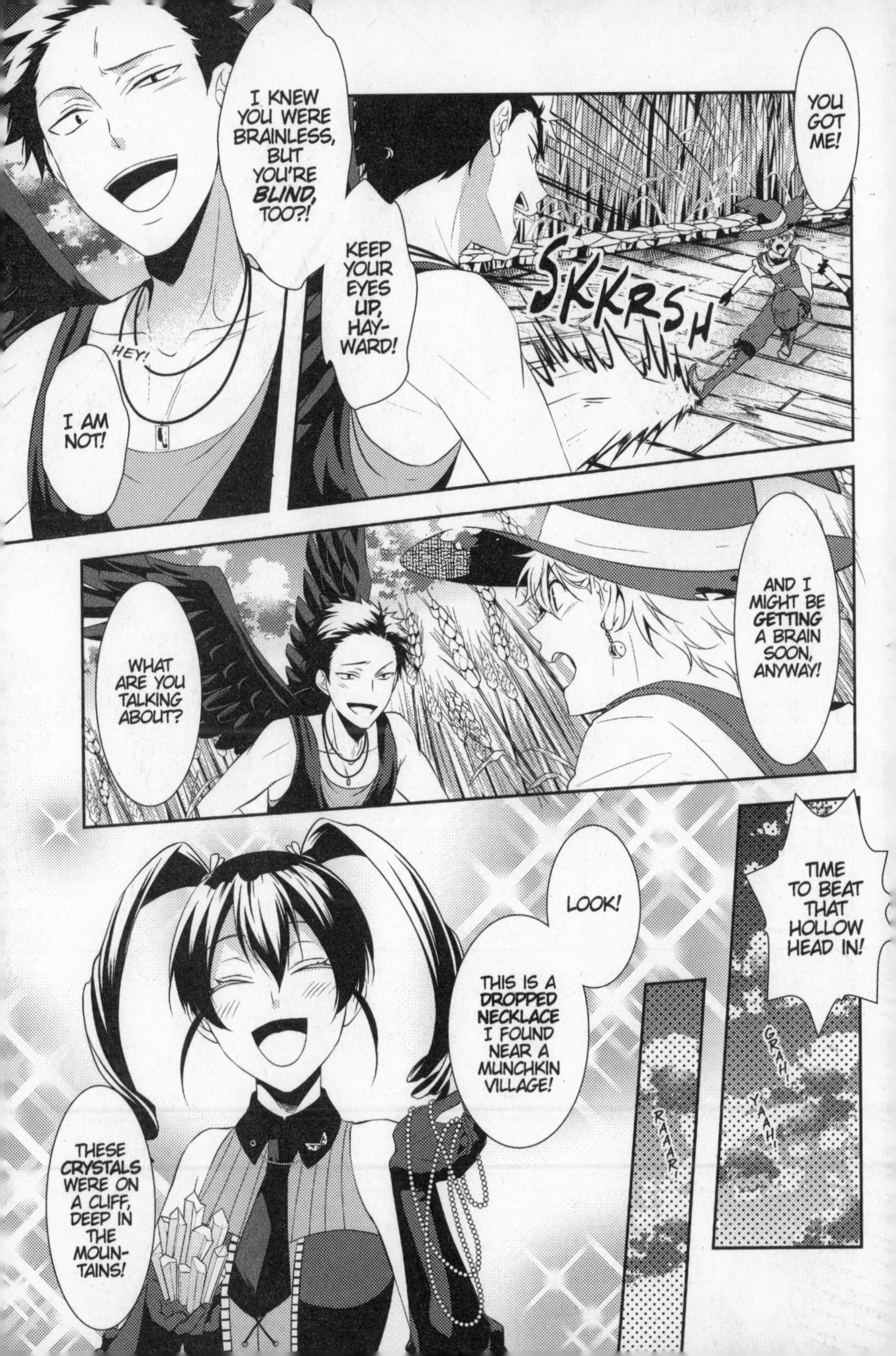
YOU GOT ME!
SKKRSH
I KNEW YOU WERE BRAINLESS, BUT YOU'RE BLIND, TOO?!
KEEP YOUR EYES UP, HAY-WARD!
HEY!
I AM NOT!
AND I MIGHT BE GETTING A BRAIN SOON, ANYWAY!
WHAT ARE YOU TALKING ABOUT?
TIME TO BEAT THAT HOLLOW HEAD IN!
GRAH!
YAAH!
RAAAR!
LOOK!
THIS IS A DROPPED NECKLACE I FOUND NEAR A MUNCHKIN VILLAGE!
THESE CRYSTALS WERE ON A CLIFF, DEEP IN THE MOUN-TAINS!

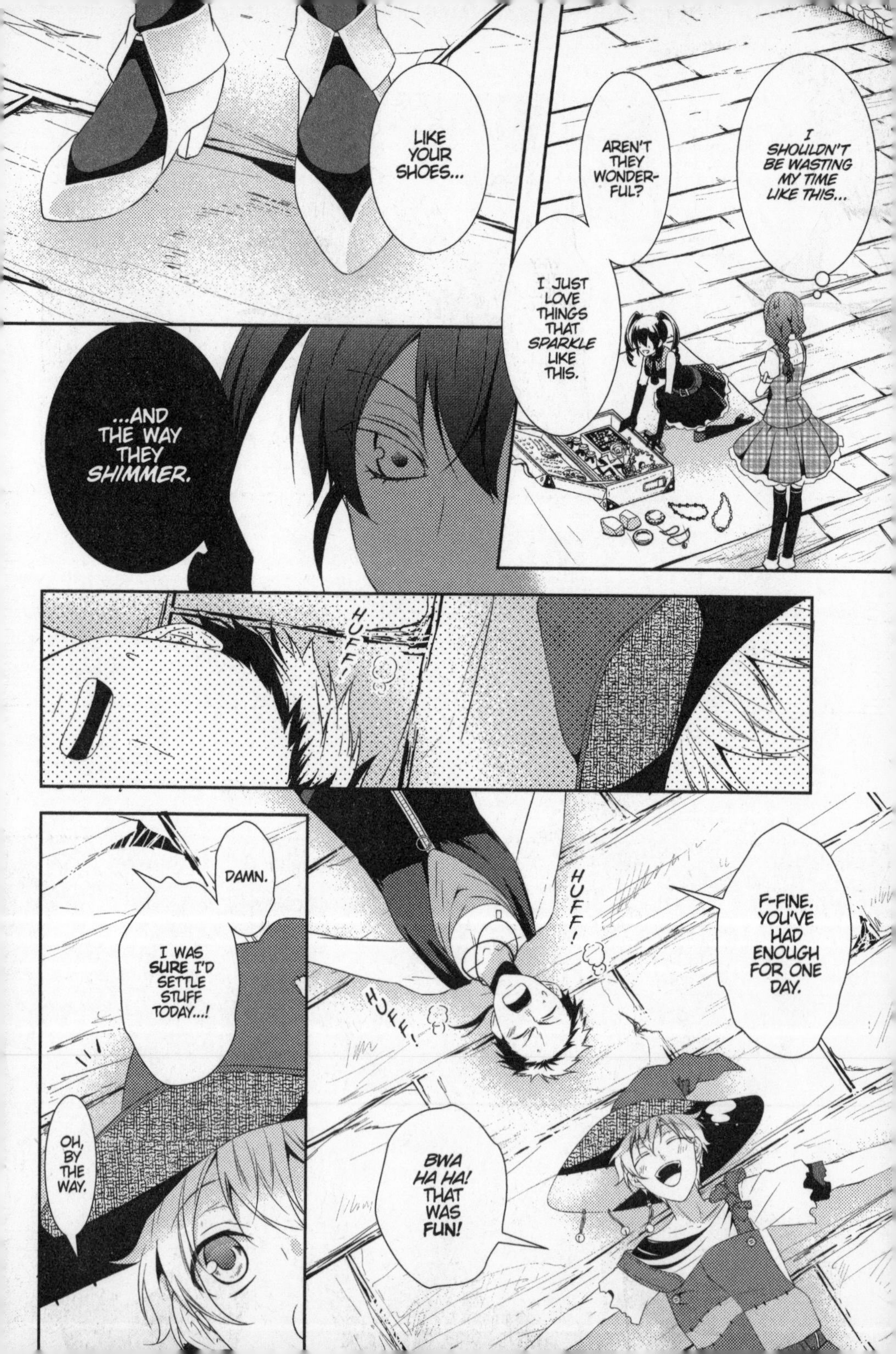
I SHOULDN'T BE WASTING MY TIME LIKE THIS...
AREN'T THEY WONDERFUL?
I JUST LOVE THINGS THAT *SPARKLE* LIKE THIS.
LIKE YOUR SHOES...
...AND THE WAY THEY *SHIMMER.*
HUFF!
F-FINE. YOU'VE HAD ENOUGH FOR ONE DAY.
HUFF!
HUFF!
BWA HA HA! THAT WAS FUN!
DAMN.
I WAS SURE I'D SETTLE STUFF TODAY...!
OH, BY THE WAY.

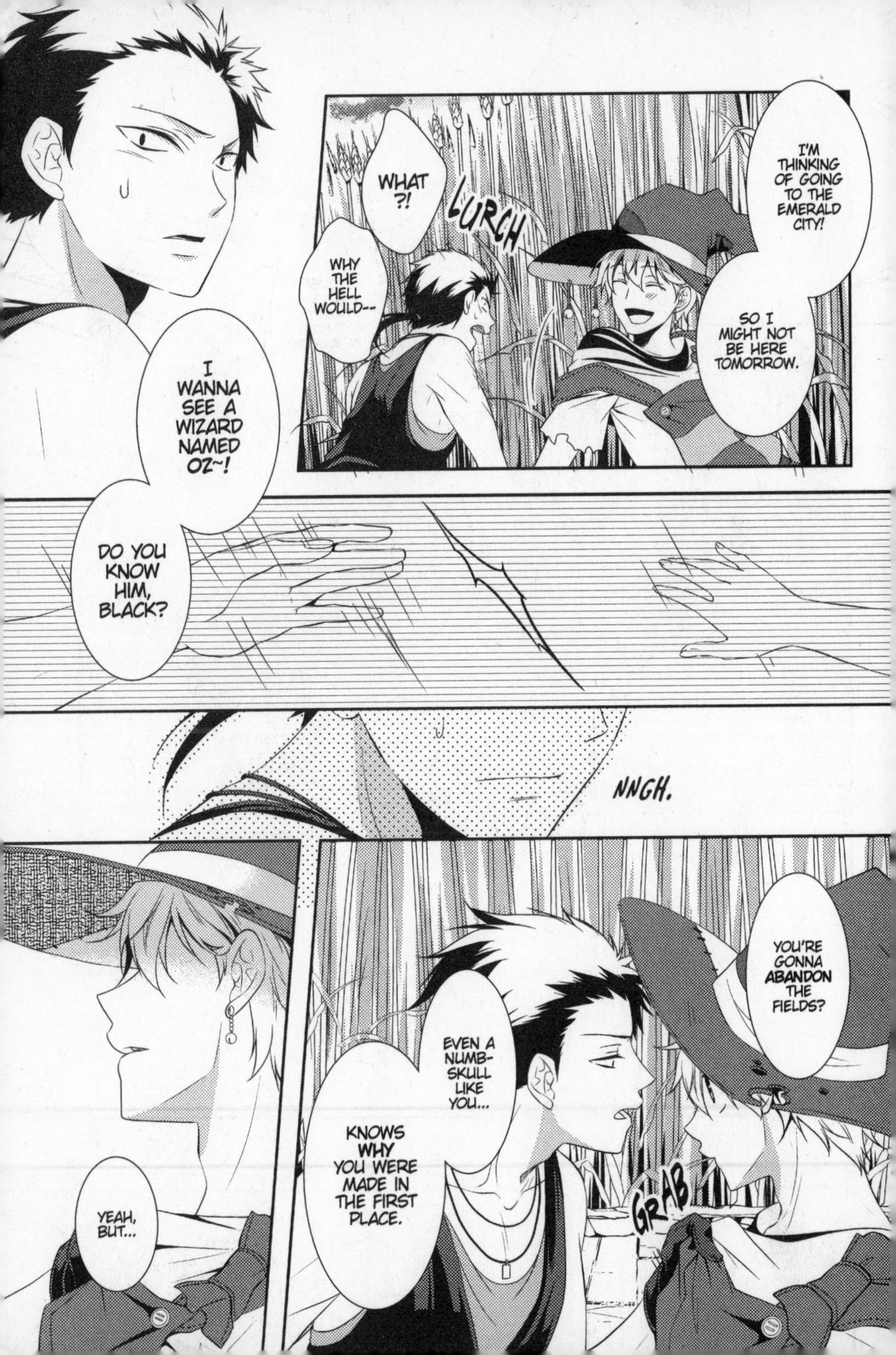
I'M THINKING OF GOING TO THE EMERALD CITY!
SO I MIGHT NOT BE HERE TOMORROW.
LURCH
WHAT ?!
WHY THE HELL WOULD--
I WANNA SEE A WIZARD NAMED OZ~!
DO YOU KNOW HIM, BLACK?
NNGH.
YOU'RE GONNA ABANDON THE FIELDS?
EVEN A NUMB-SKULL LIKE YOU...
KNOWS WHY YOU WERE MADE IN THE FIRST PLACE.
GRAB
YEAH, BUT...

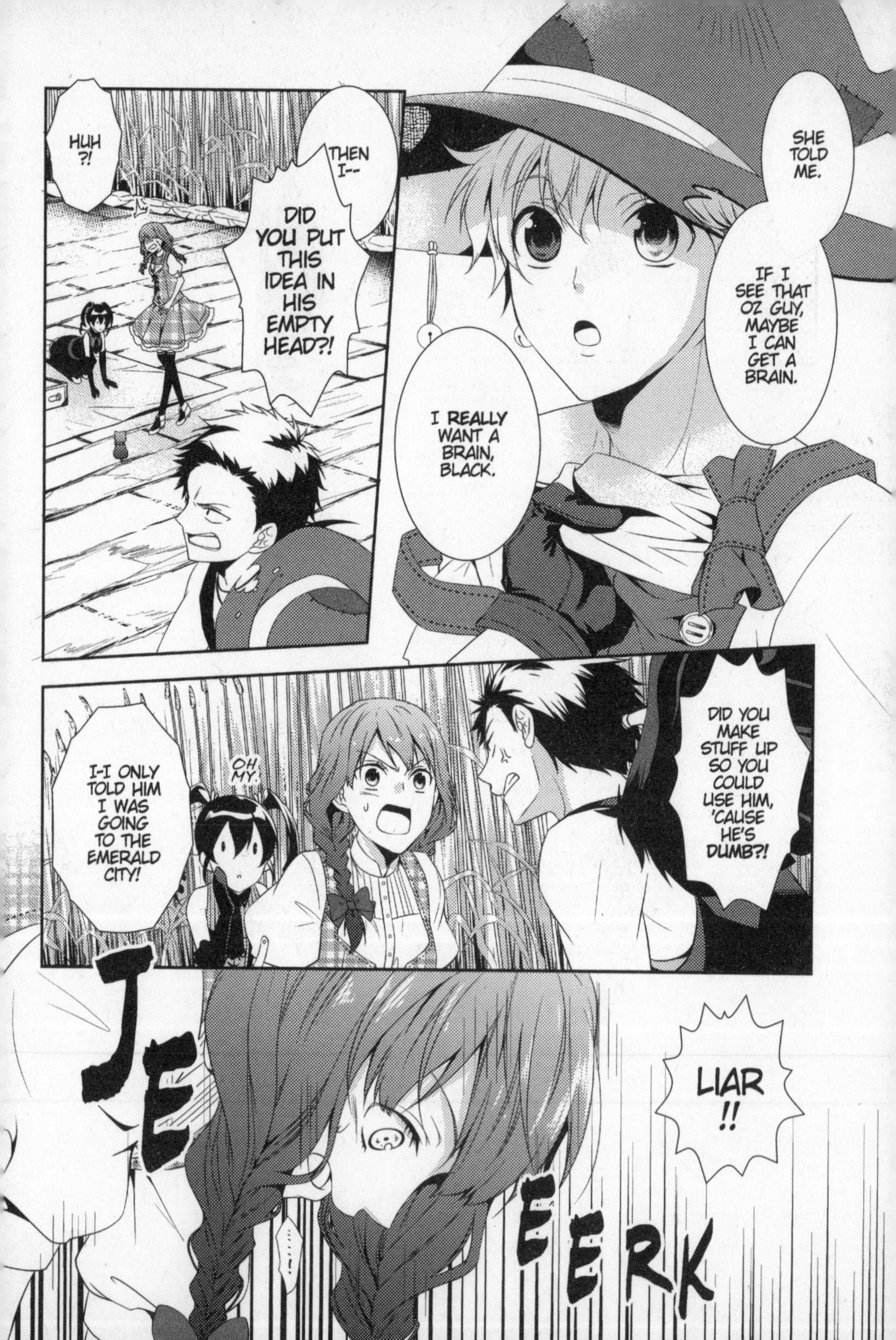

SHE TOLD ME.
IF I SEE THAT OZ GUY, MAYBE I CAN GET A BRAIN.
I REALLY WANT A BRAIN, BLACK.
THEN I--
DID YOU PUT THIS IDEA IN HIS EMPTY HEAD?!
HUH ?!
DID YOU MAKE STUFF UP SO YOU COULD USE HIM, 'CAUSE HE'S DUMB?!
OH MY.
I-I ONLY TOLD HIM I WAS GOING TO THE EMERALD CITY!
LIAR !!
JEEERK

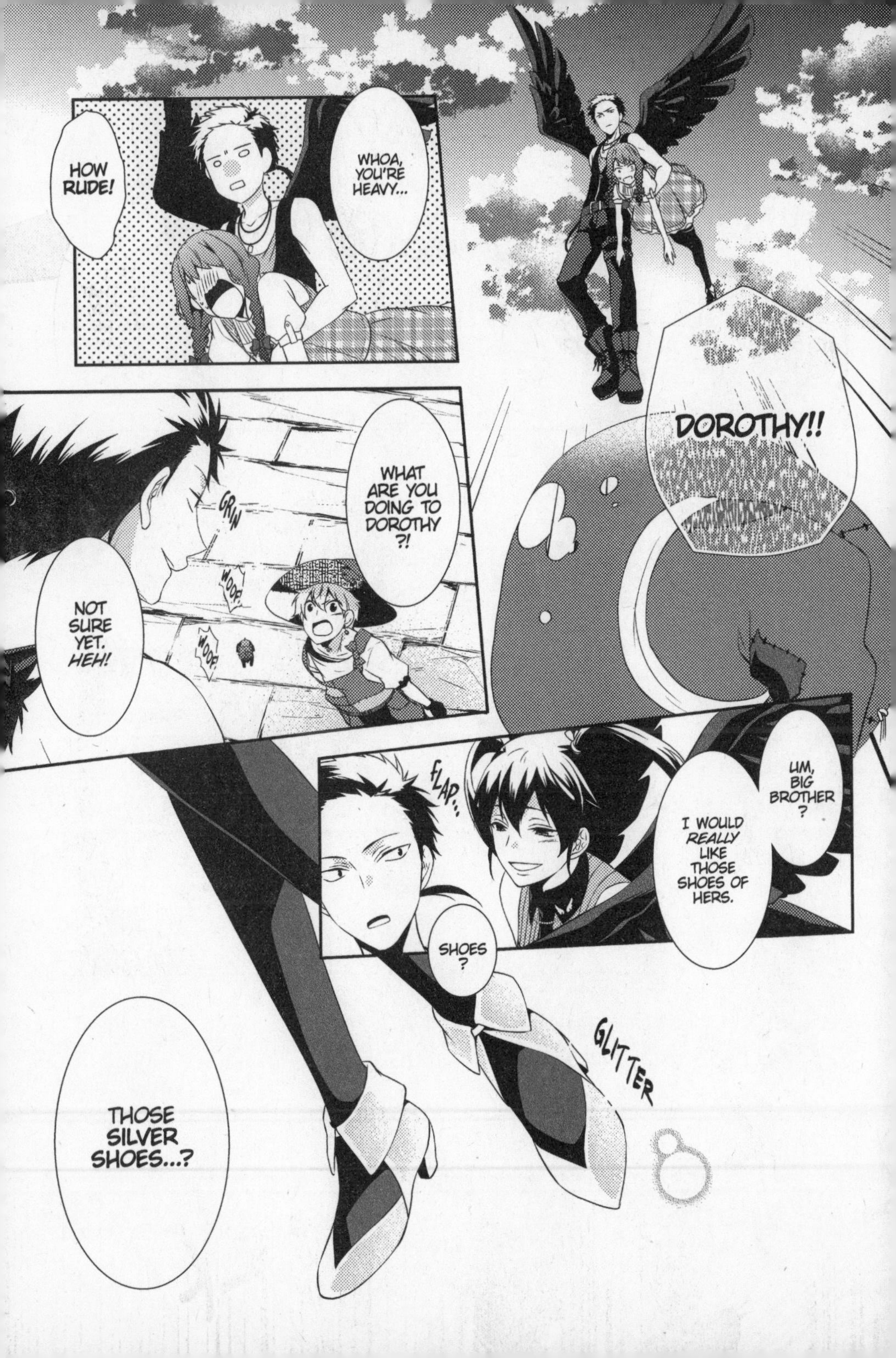
WHOA, YOU'RE HEAVY...
HOW RUDE!
DOROTHY!!
WHAT ARE YOU DOING TO DOROTHY?!
GRIN
WOOF
WOOF
NOT SURE YET. HEH!
UM, BIG BROTHER?
I WOULD REALLY LIKE THOSE SHOES OF HERS.
FLAP...
SHOES?
GLITTER
THOSE SILVER SHOES...?

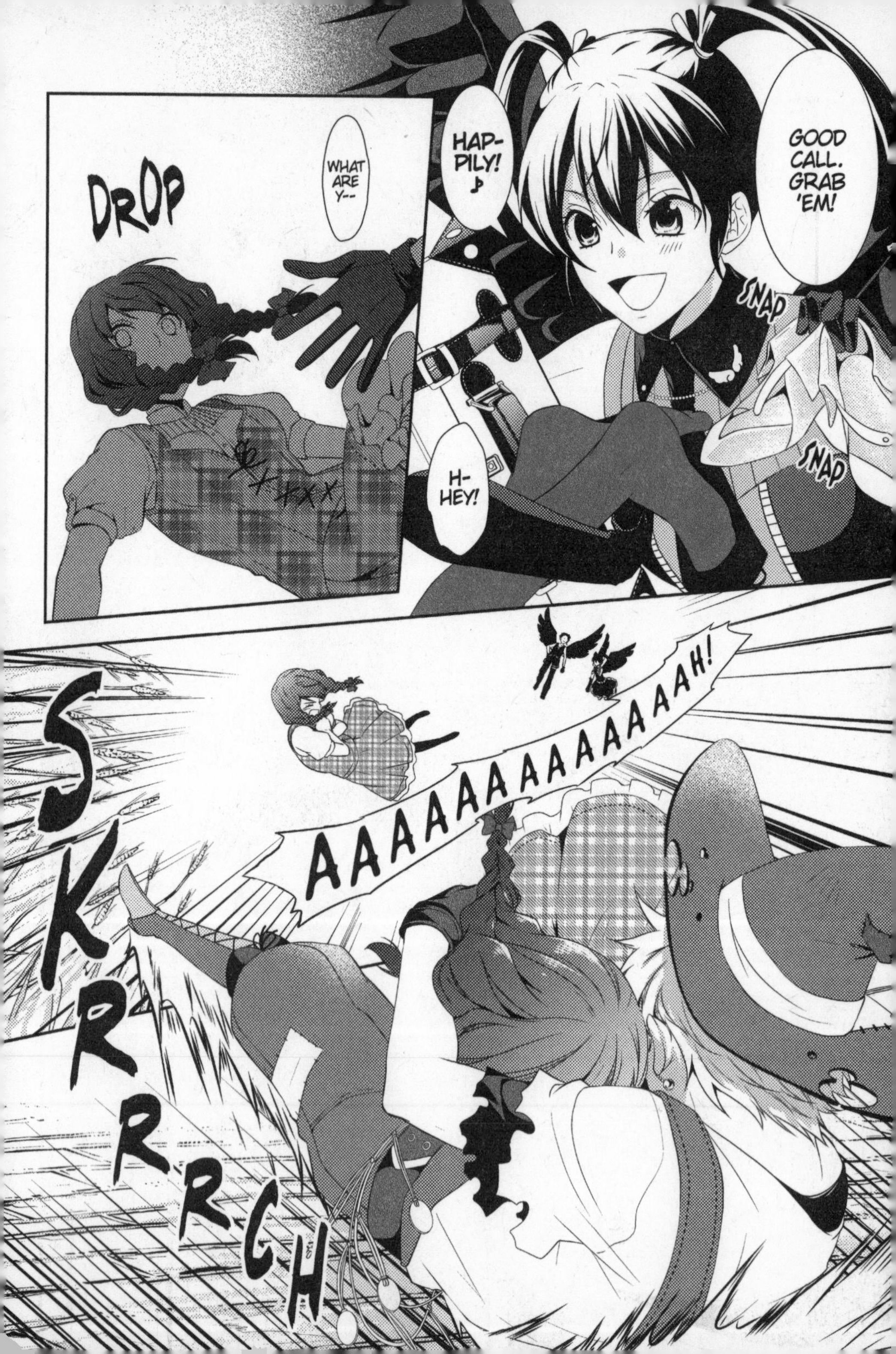
GOOD CALL. GRAB 'EM!
HAP-PILY! ♪
SNAP
SNAP
H-HEY!
WHAT ARE Y--
DROP
AAAAAAAAAAAAAAAAAAAAH!
SKRRRCH

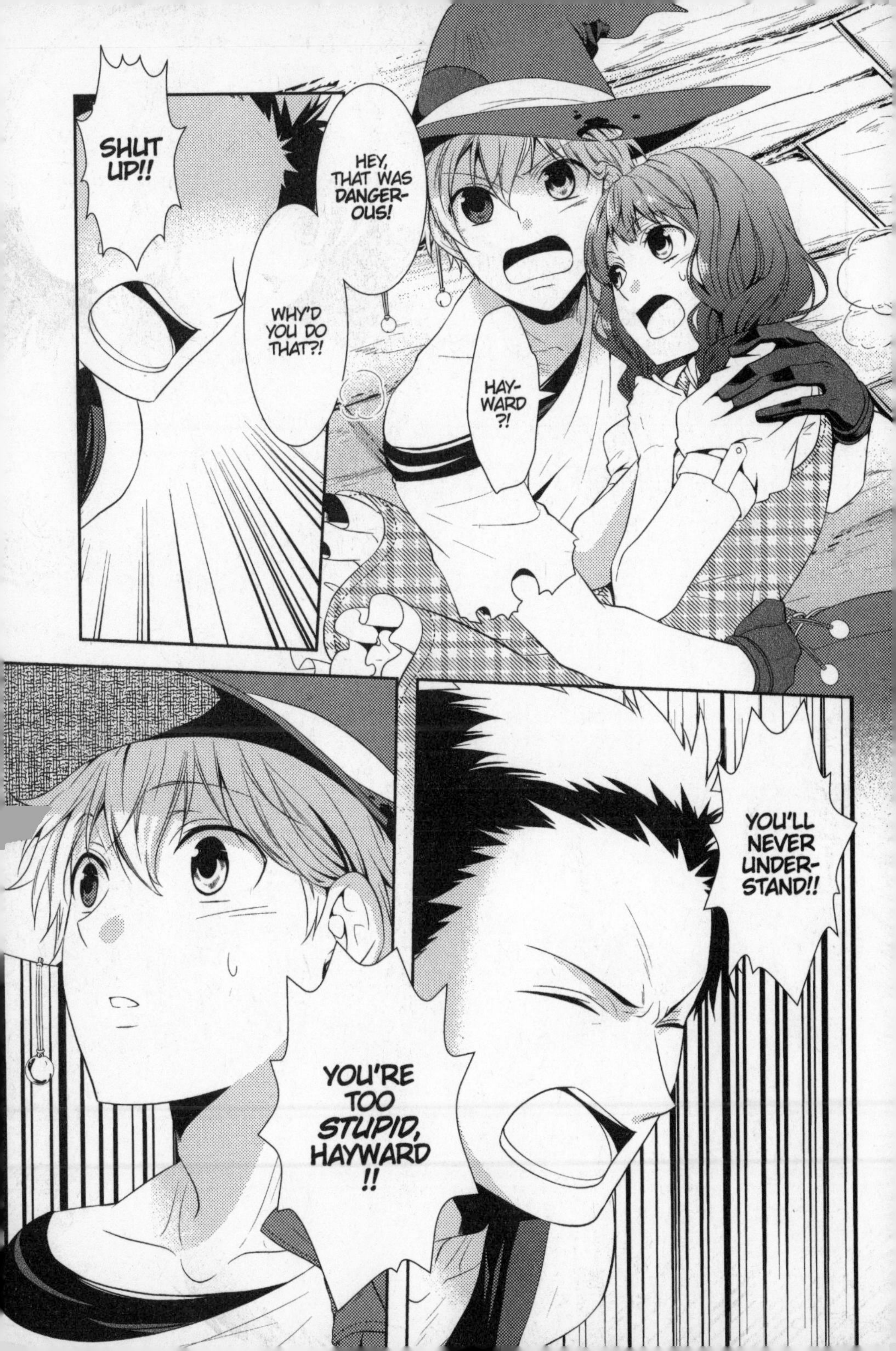
HEY, THAT WAS DANGER-OUS!
WHY'D YOU DO THAT?!
HAY-WARD?!
SHUT UP!!
YOU'LL NEVER UNDER-STAND!!
YOU'RE TOO STUPID, HAYWARD!!

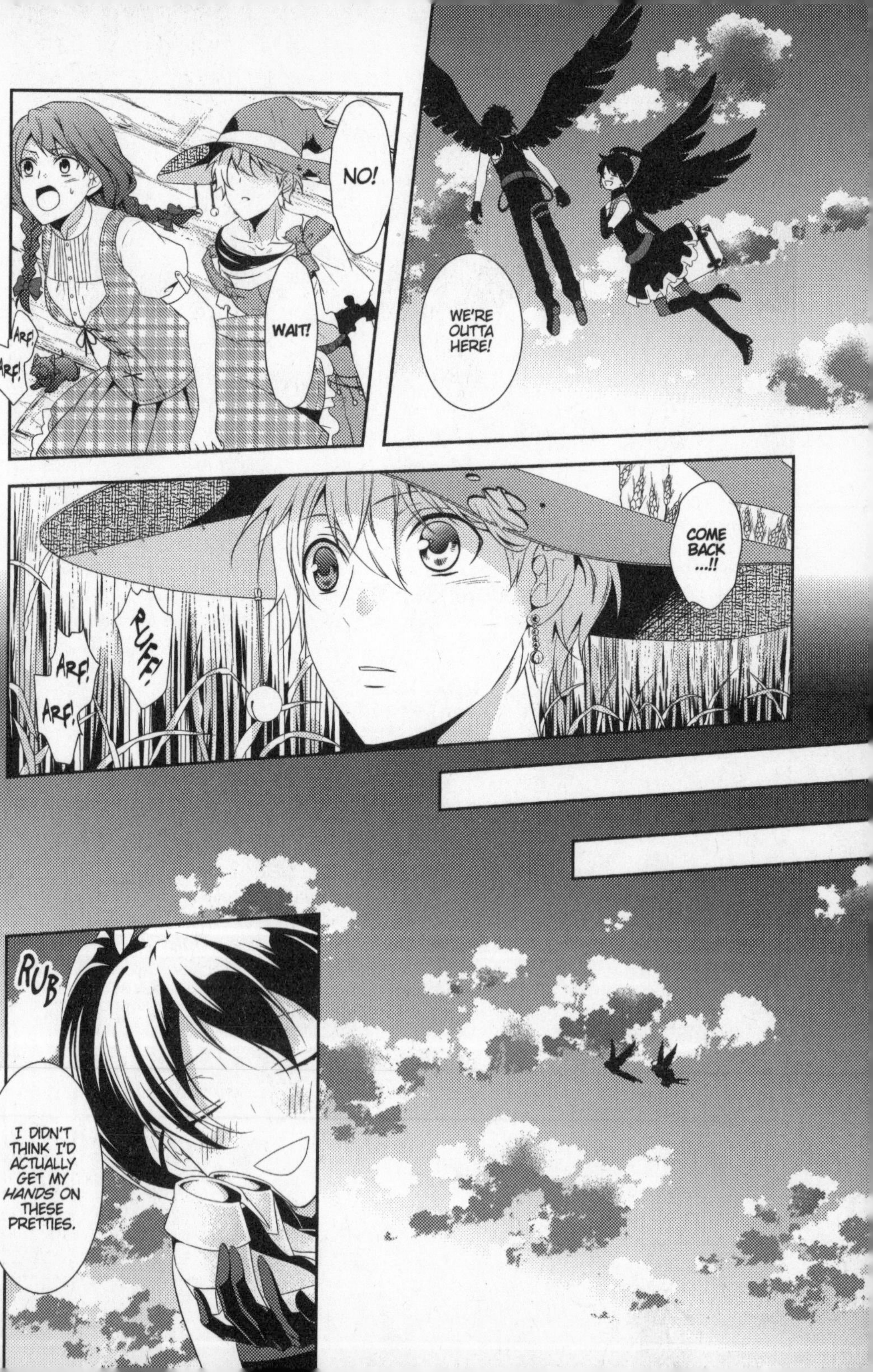
WE'RE OUTTA HERE!
NO!
WAIT!
ARF!
ARF!
COME BACK ...!!
RUFF!
ARF!
ARF!
RUB
I DIDN'T THINK I'D ACTUALLY GET MY *HANDS* ON THESE PRETTIES.

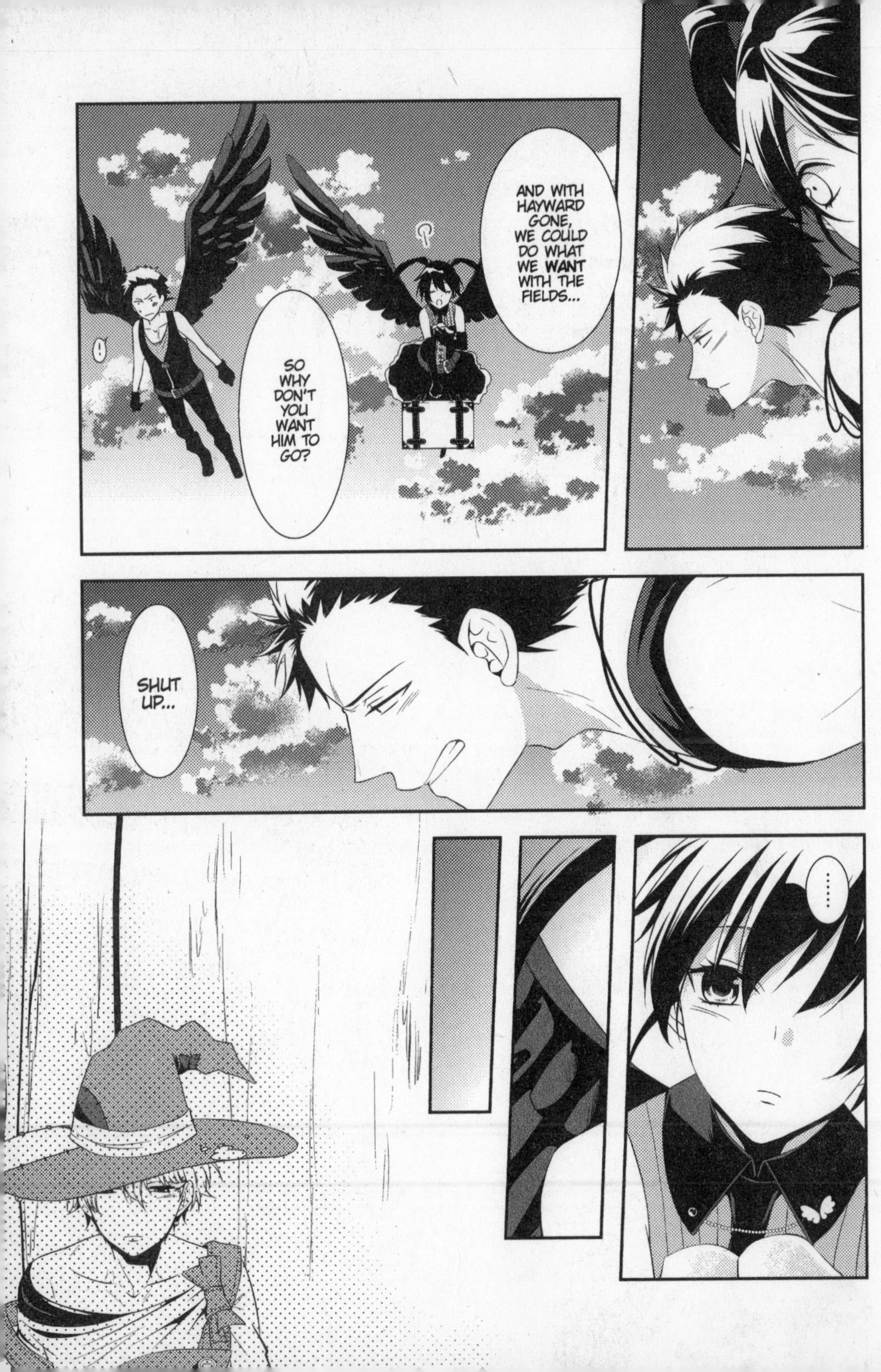
AND WITH HAYWARD GONE, WE COULD DO WHAT WE WANT WITH THE FIELDS...
SO WHY DON'T YOU WANT HIM TO GO?
SHUT UP...
......

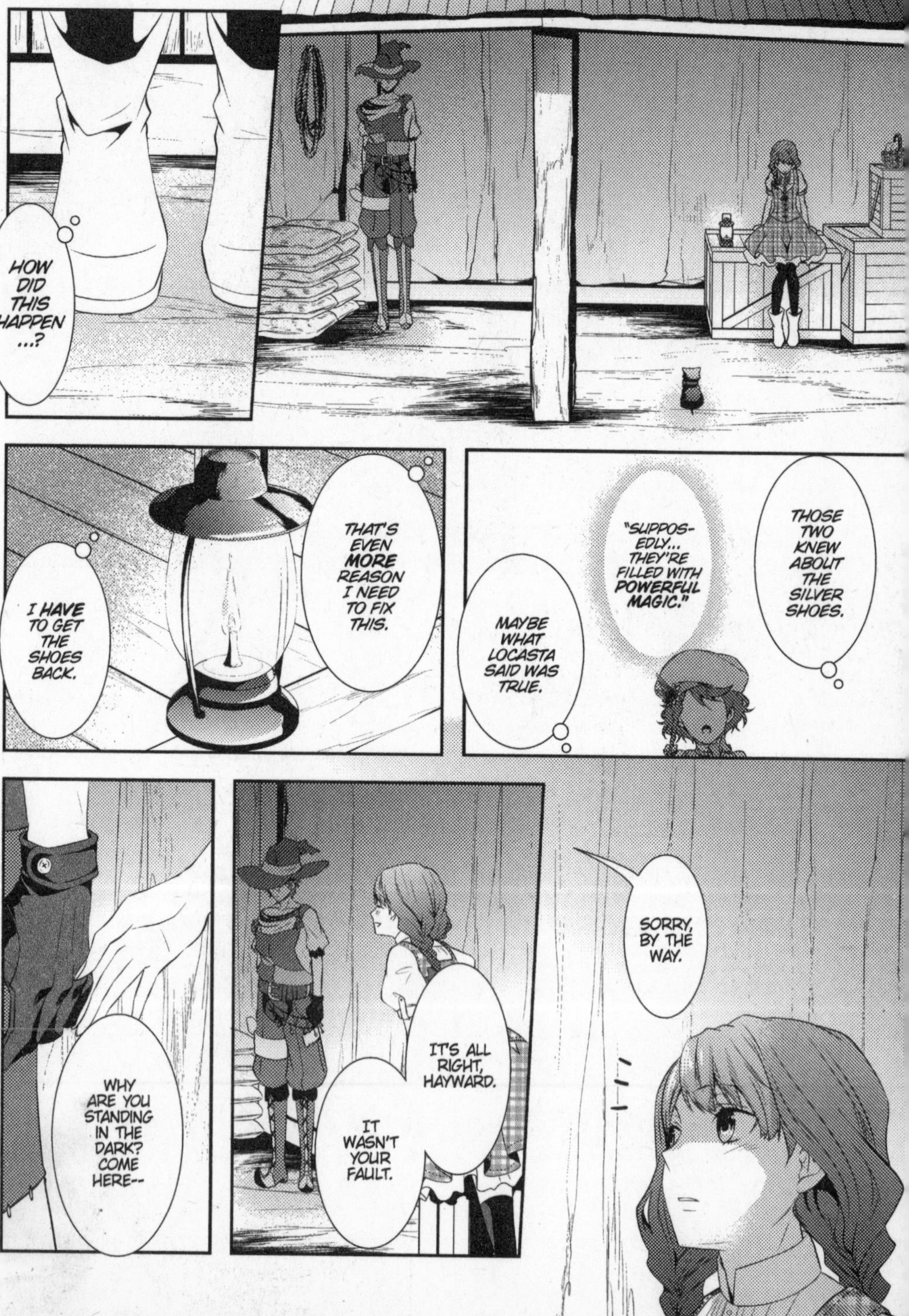
HOW DID THIS HAPPEN ...?
THOSE TWO KNEW ABOUT THE SILVER SHOES.
"SUPPOS-EDLY... THEY'RE FILLED WITH POWERFUL MAGIC."
MAYBE WHAT LOCASTA SAID WAS TRUE.
THAT'S EVEN MORE REASON I NEED TO FIX THIS.
I HAVE TO GET THE SHOES BACK.
SORRY, BY THE WAY.
IT'S ALL RIGHT, HAYWARD.
IT WASN'T YOUR FAULT.
WHY ARE YOU STANDING IN THE DARK? COME HERE--

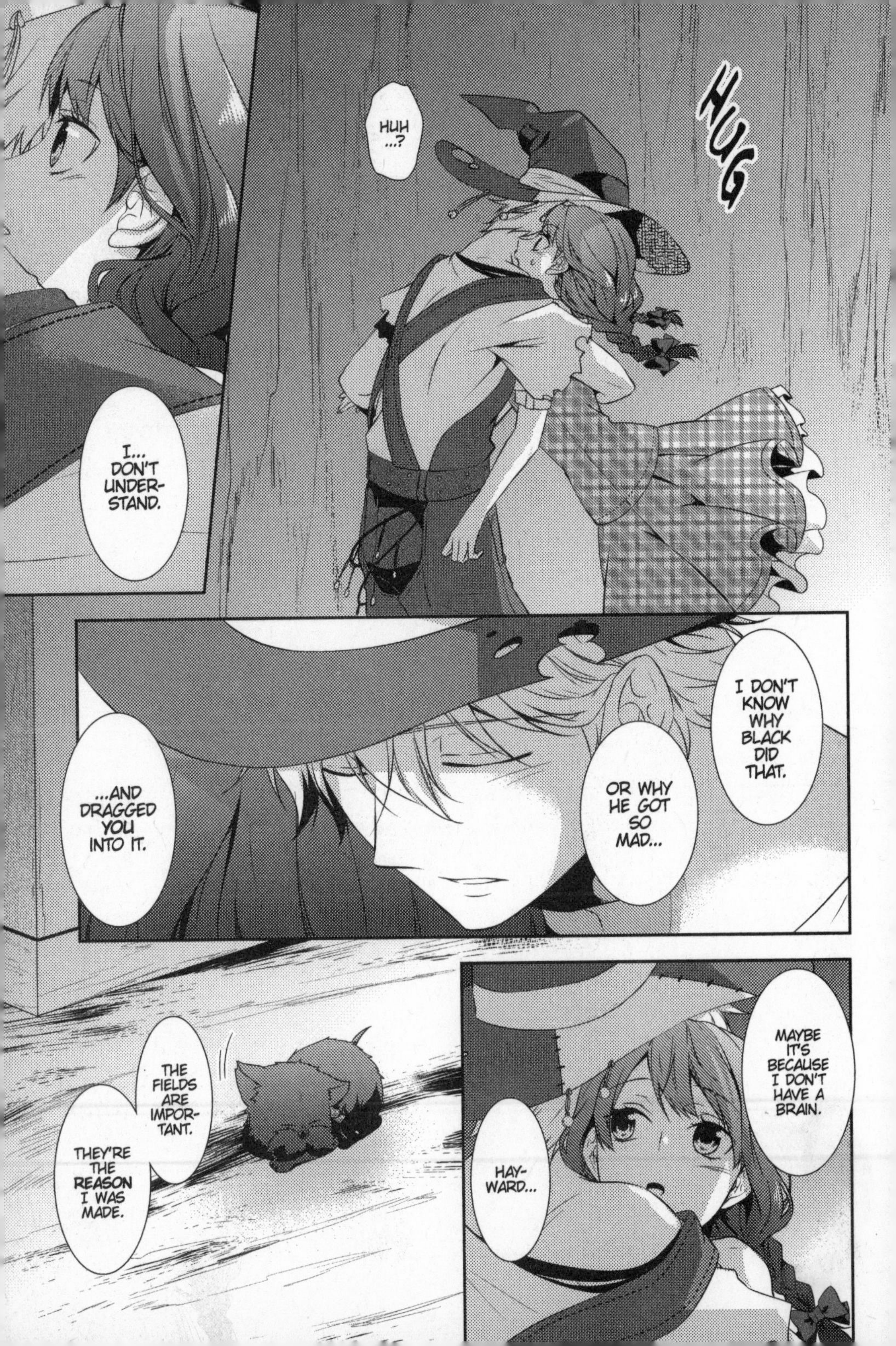
HUG
HUH ...?
I... DON'T UNDERSTAND.
I DON'T KNOW WHY BLACK DID THAT.
OR WHY HE GOT SO MAD...
...AND DRAGGED YOU INTO IT.
MAYBE IT'S BECAUSE I DON'T HAVE A BRAIN.
HAYWARD...
THE FIELDS ARE IMPORTANT.
THEY'RE THE REASON I WAS MADE.

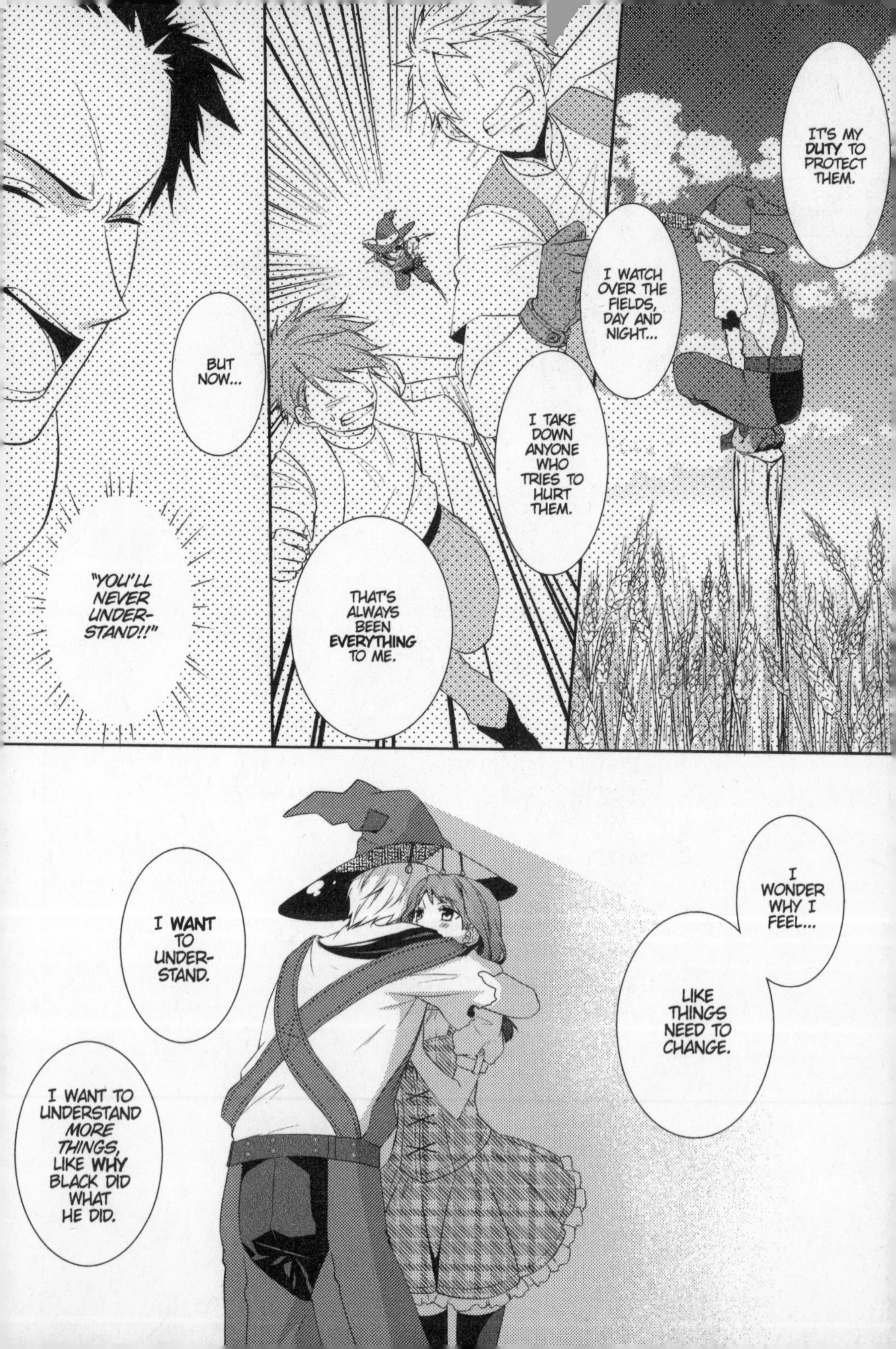
IT'S MY DUTY TO PROTECT THEM.
I WATCH OVER THE FIELDS, DAY AND NIGHT...
I TAKE DOWN ANYONE WHO TRIES TO HURT THEM.
THAT'S ALWAYS BEEN EVERYTHING TO ME.
BUT NOW...
"YOU'LL NEVER UNDER-STAND!!"
I WONDER WHY I FEEL...
LIKE THINGS NEED TO CHANGE.
I WANT TO UNDER-STAND.
I WANT TO UNDERSTAND *MORE* THINGS, LIKE WHY BLACK DID WHAT HE DID.

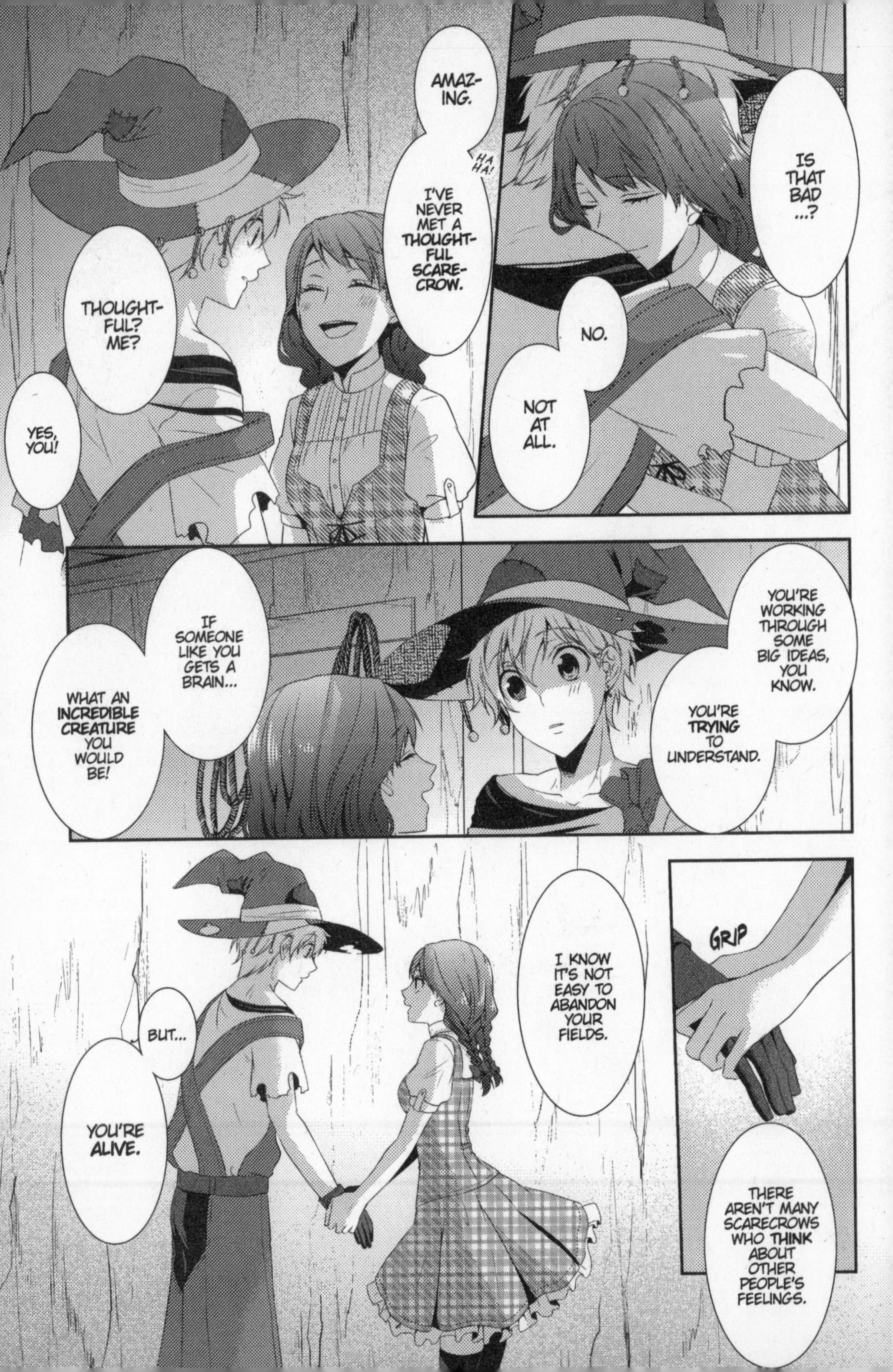
IS THAT BAD ...?
NO.
NOT AT ALL.
AMAZ-ING.
HA HA!
I'VE NEVER MET A THOUGHT-FUL SCARE-CROW.
THOUGHT-FUL? ME?
YES, YOU!
YOU'RE WORKING THROUGH SOME BIG IDEAS, YOU KNOW.
YOU'RE **TRYING** TO UNDERSTAND.
IF SOMEONE LIKE YOU GETS A BRAIN...
WHAT AN **INCREDIBLE CREATURE** YOU WOULD BE!
GRIP
THERE AREN'T MANY SCARECROWS WHO **THINK** ABOUT OTHER PEOPLE'S FEELINGS.
I KNOW IT'S NOT EASY TO ABANDON YOUR FIELDS.
BUT...
YOU'RE **ALIVE.**

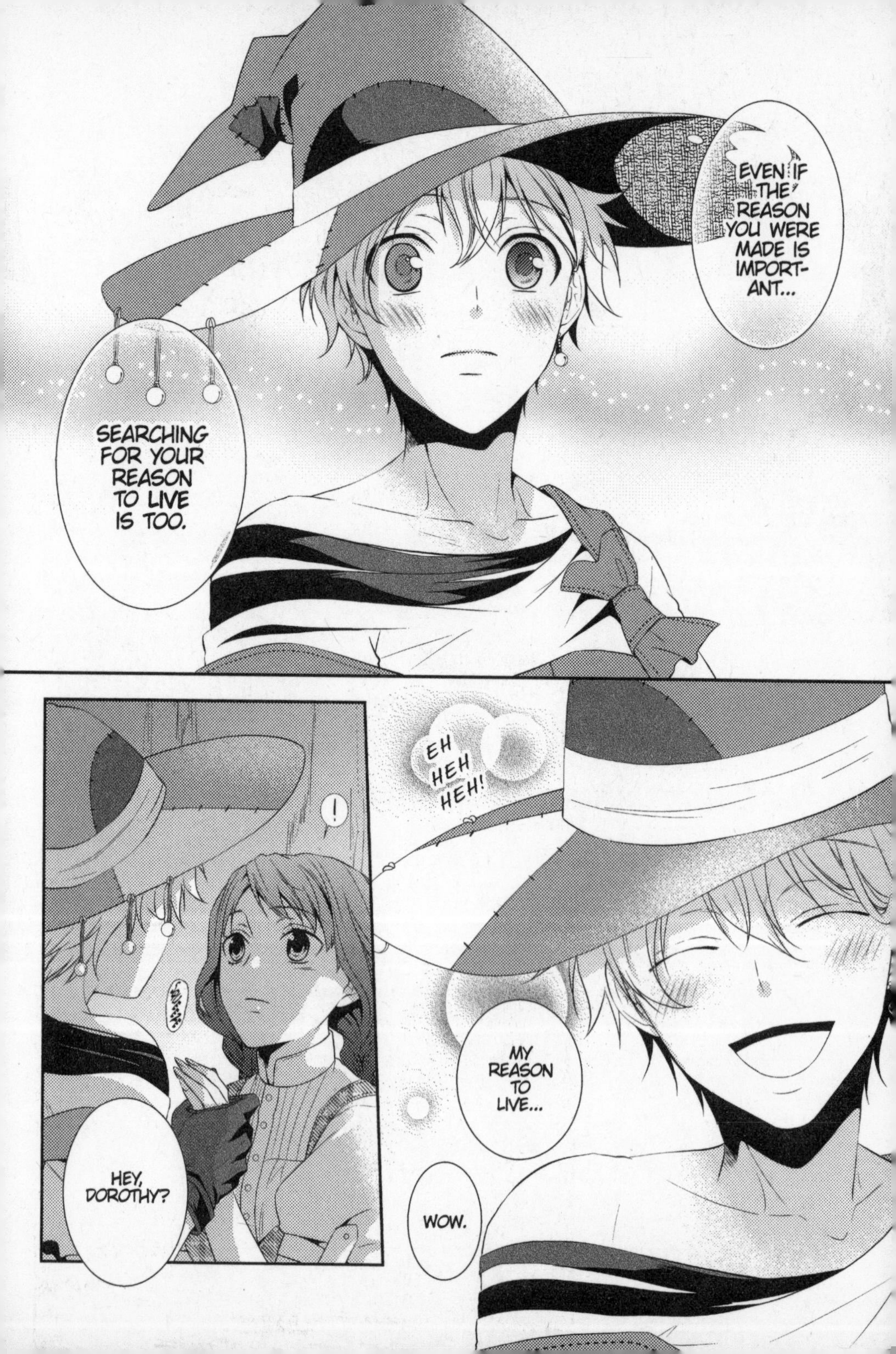
EVEN IF THE REASON YOU WERE MADE IS IMPORT-ANT...
SEARCHING FOR YOUR REASON TO LIVE IS TOO.
EH HEH HEH!
MY REASON TO LIVE...
WOW.
!
HEY, DOROTHY?

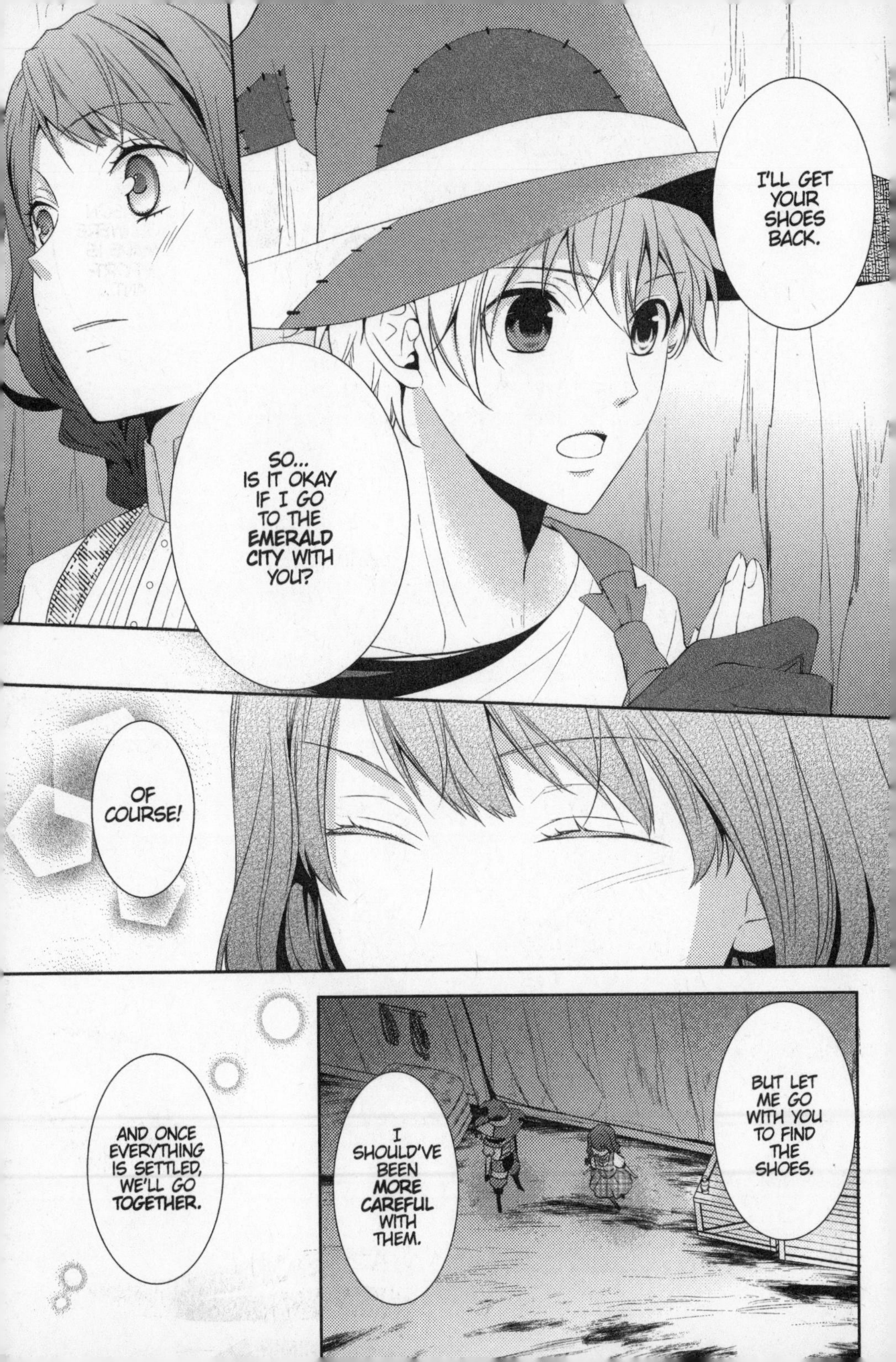
I'LL GET YOUR SHOES BACK.
SO... IS IT OKAY IF I GO TO THE EMERALD CITY WITH YOU?
OF COURSE!
BUT LET ME GO WITH YOU TO FIND THE SHOES.
I SHOULD'VE BEEN MORE CAREFUL WITH THEM.
AND ONCE EVERYTHING IS SETTLED, WE'LL GO TOGETHER.

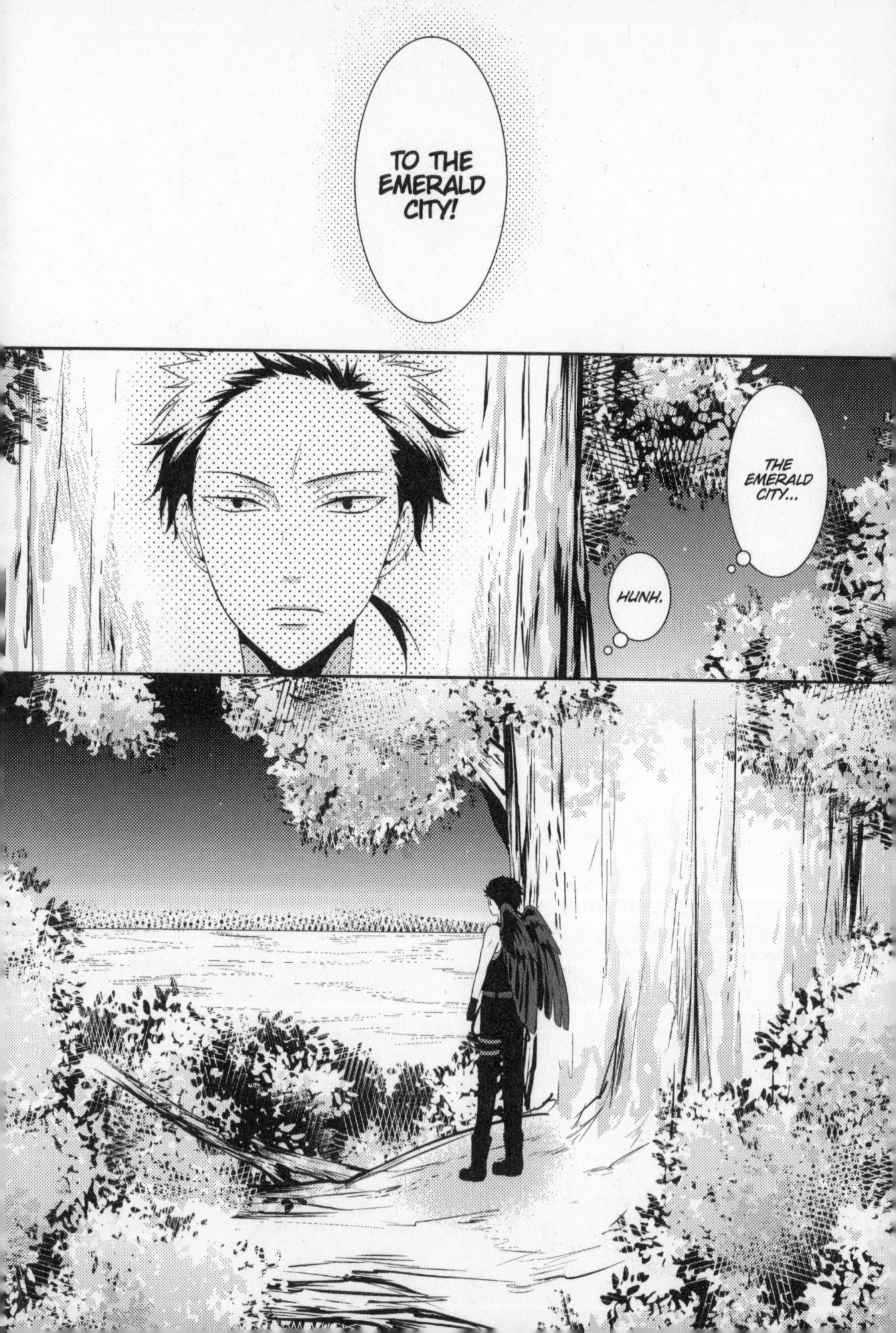
TO THE EMERALD CITY!
THE EMERALD CITY...
HUNH.

Captive
Hearts
of Oz

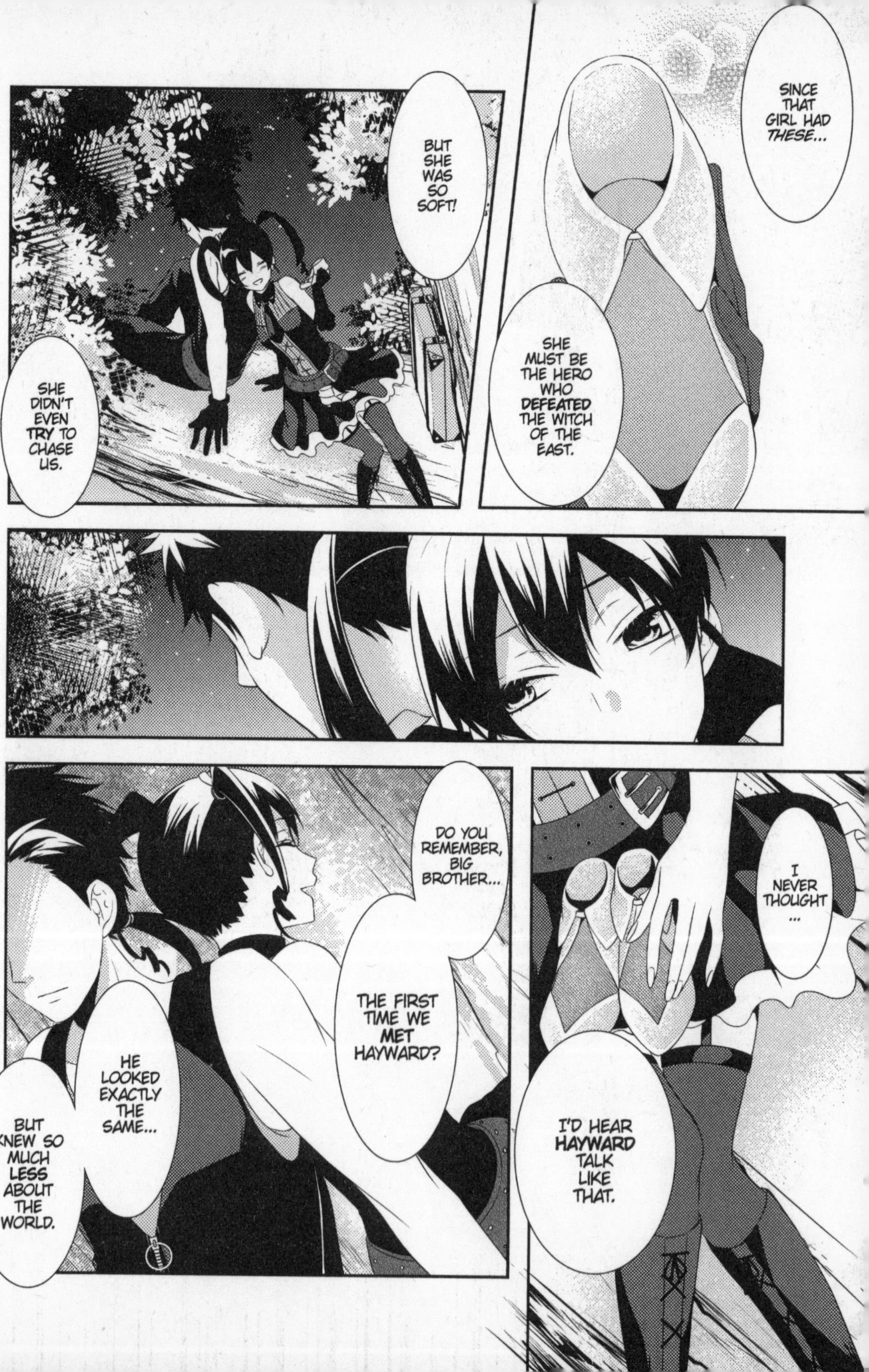
SINCE THAT GIRL HAD THESE...
SHE MUST BE THE HERO WHO DEFEATED THE WITCH OF THE EAST.
BUT SHE WAS SO SOFT!
SHE DIDN'T EVEN TRY TO CHASE US.
I NEVER THOUGHT...
I'D HEAR HAYWARD TALK LIKE THAT.
DO YOU REMEMBER, BIG BROTHER...
THE FIRST TIME WE MET HAYWARD?
HE LOOKED EXACTLY THE SAME...
BUT KNEW SO MUCH LESS ABOUT THE WORLD.

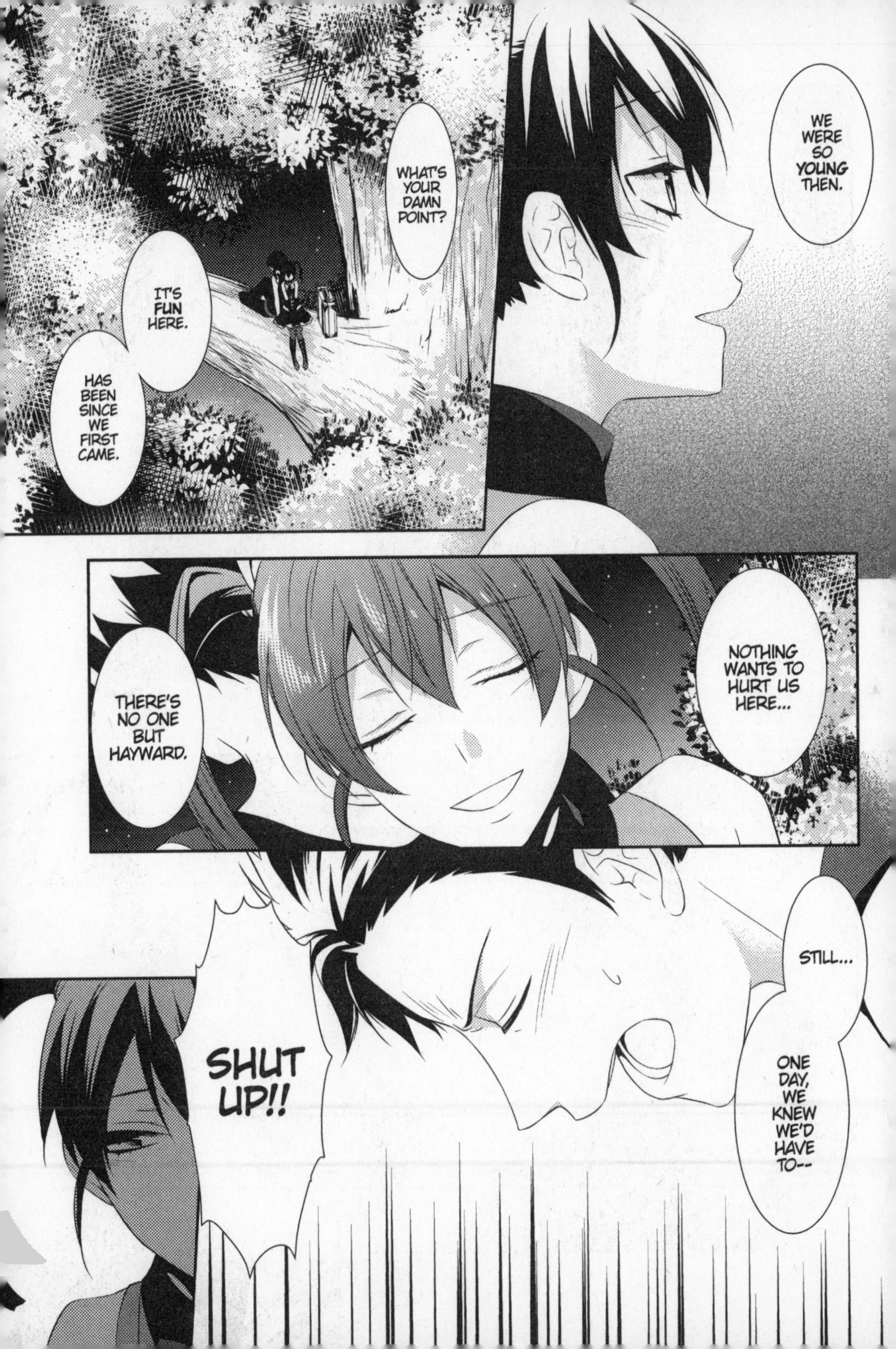
WE WERE SO YOUNG THEN.
WHAT'S YOUR DAMN POINT?
IT'S FUN HERE.
HAS BEEN SINCE WE FIRST CAME.
NOTHING WANTS TO HURT US HERE...
THERE'S NO ONE BUT HAYWARD.
STILL...
ONE DAY, WE KNEW WE'D HAVE TO--
SHUT UP!!

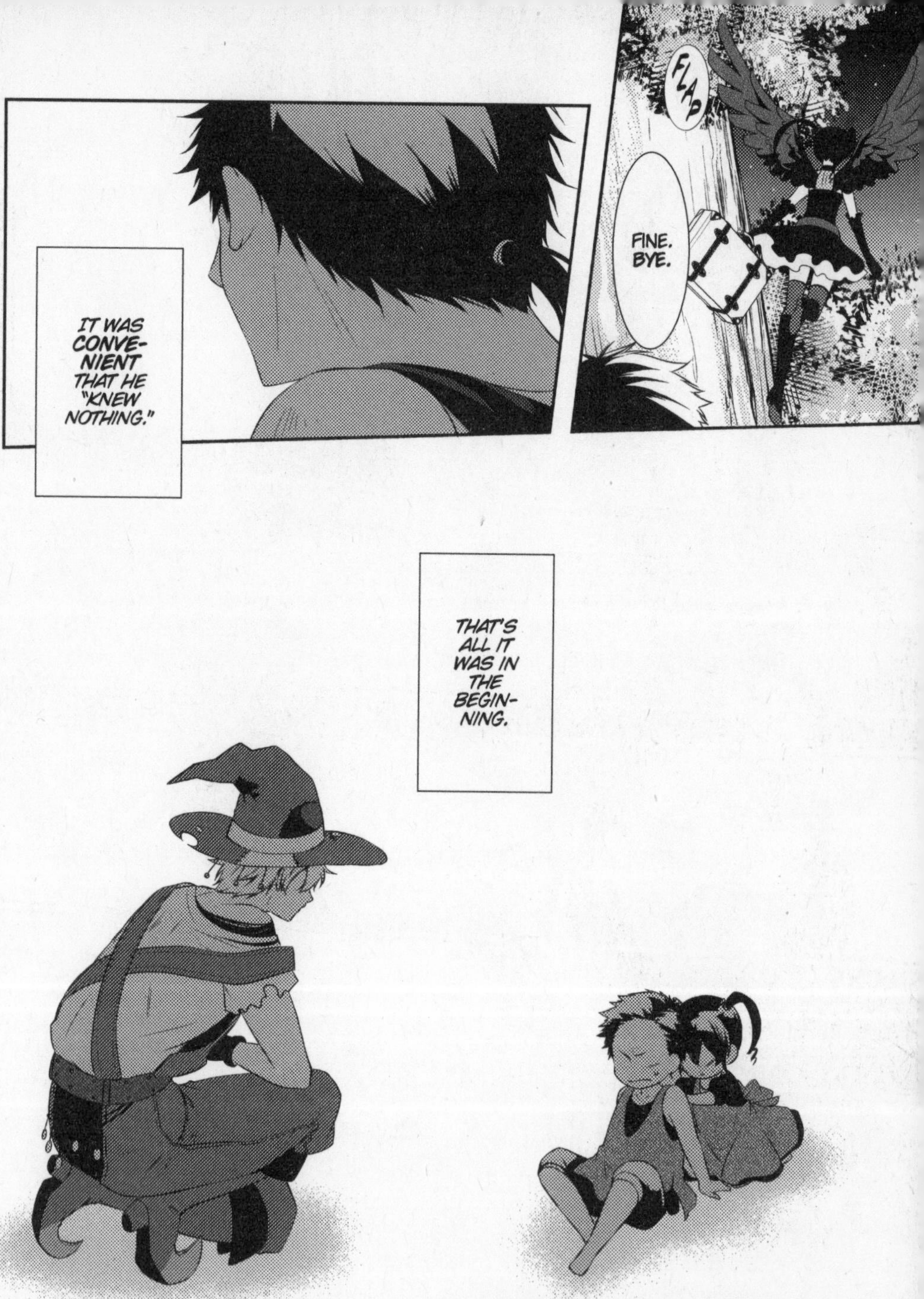
FLAP
FINE. BYE.
IT WAS CONVENIENT THAT HE "KNEW NOTHING."
THAT'S ALL IT WAS IN THE BEGINNING.

Chapter 3: Resolve

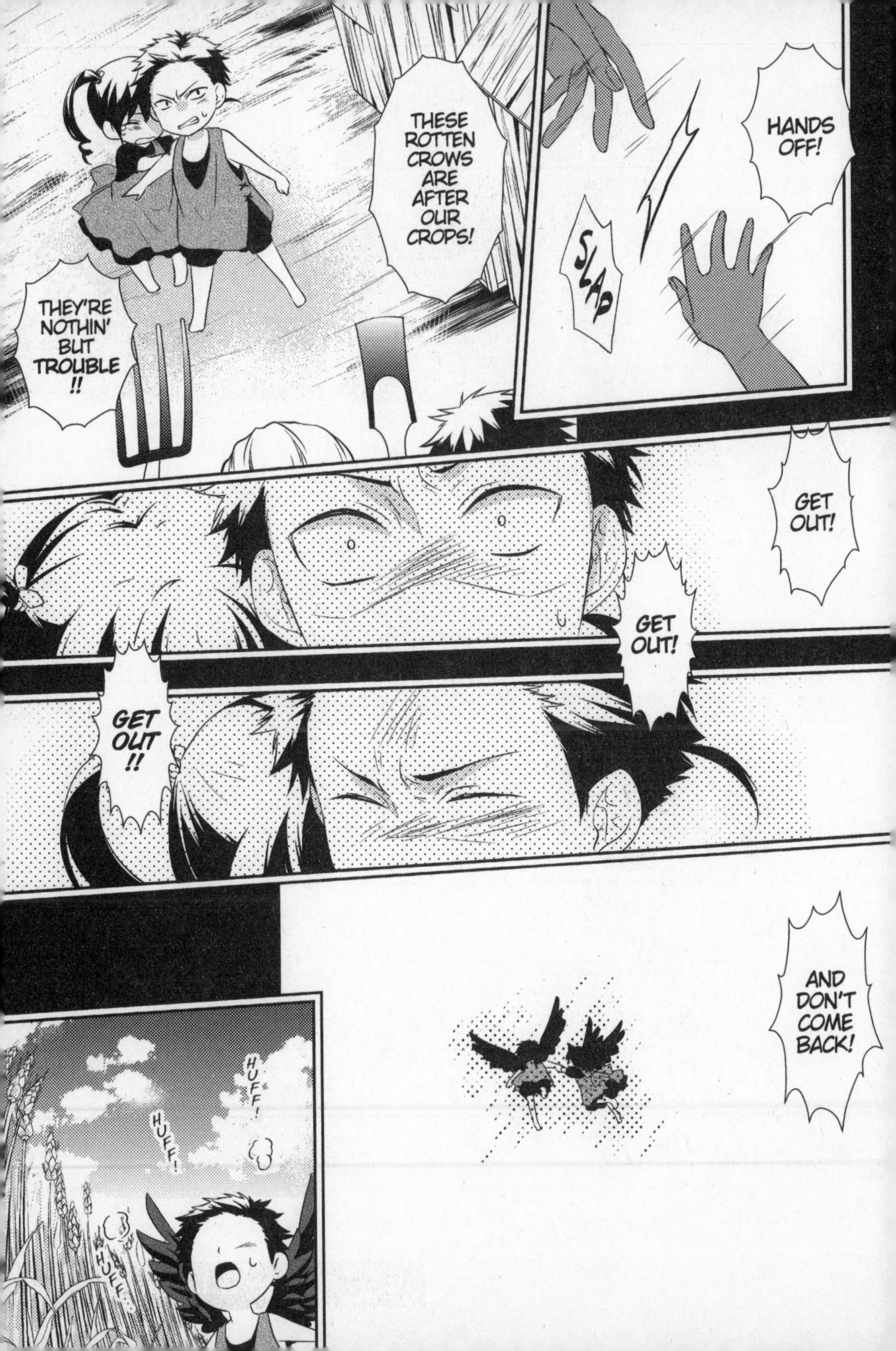
HANDS OFF!
SLAP
THESE ROTTEN CROWS ARE AFTER OUR CROPS!
THEY'RE NOTHIN' BUT TROUBLE!!
GET OUT!
GET OUT!
GET OUT!!
AND DON'T COME BACK!
HUFF!
HUFF!
HUFF

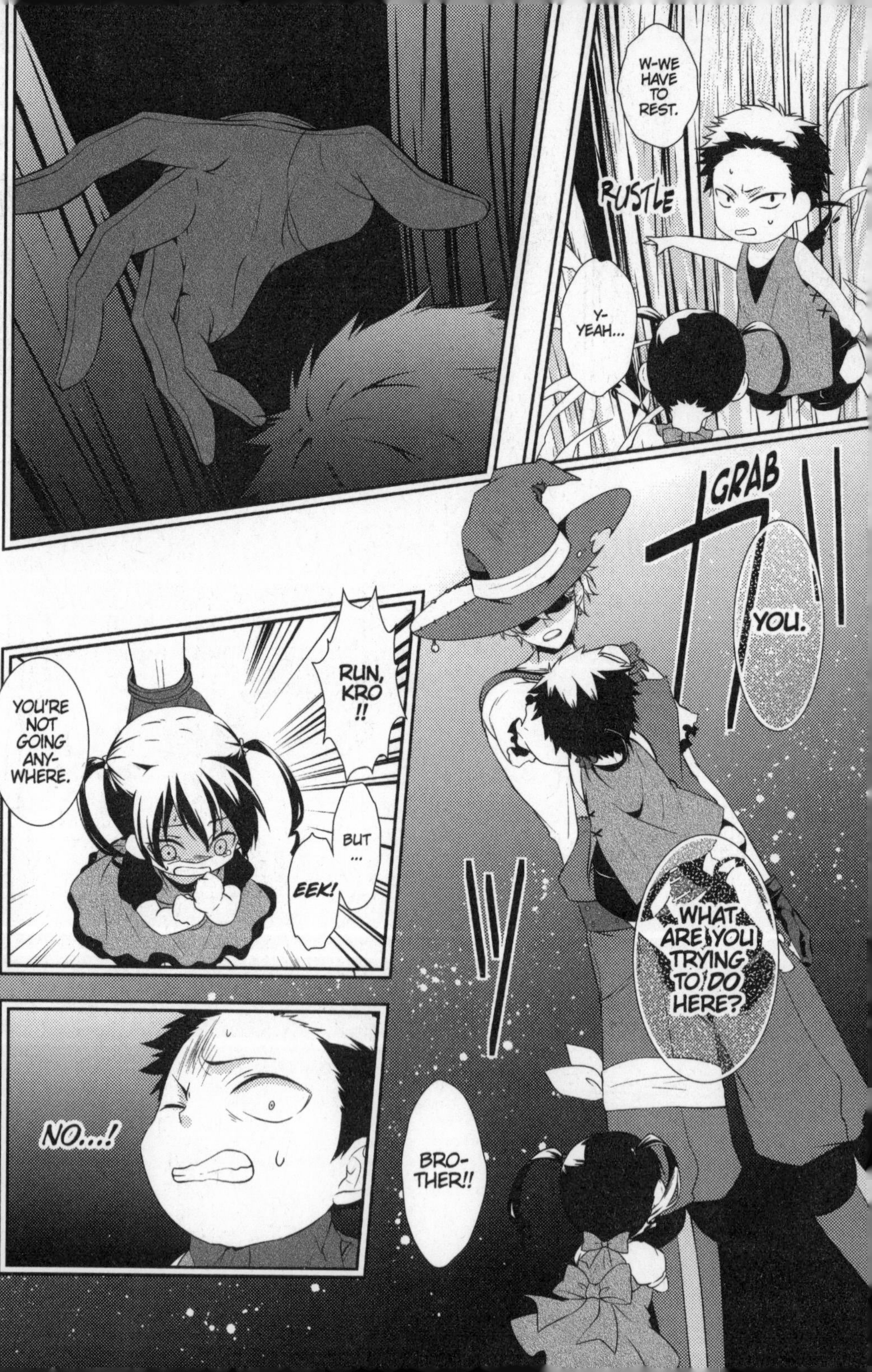

W-WE HAVE TO REST.
RUSTLE
Y-YEAH...
GRAB
YOU.
WHAT ARE YOU TRYING TO DO HERE?
BRO-THER!!
RUN, KRO!!
YOU'RE NOT GOING ANY-WHERE.
BUT...
EEK!
NO...!

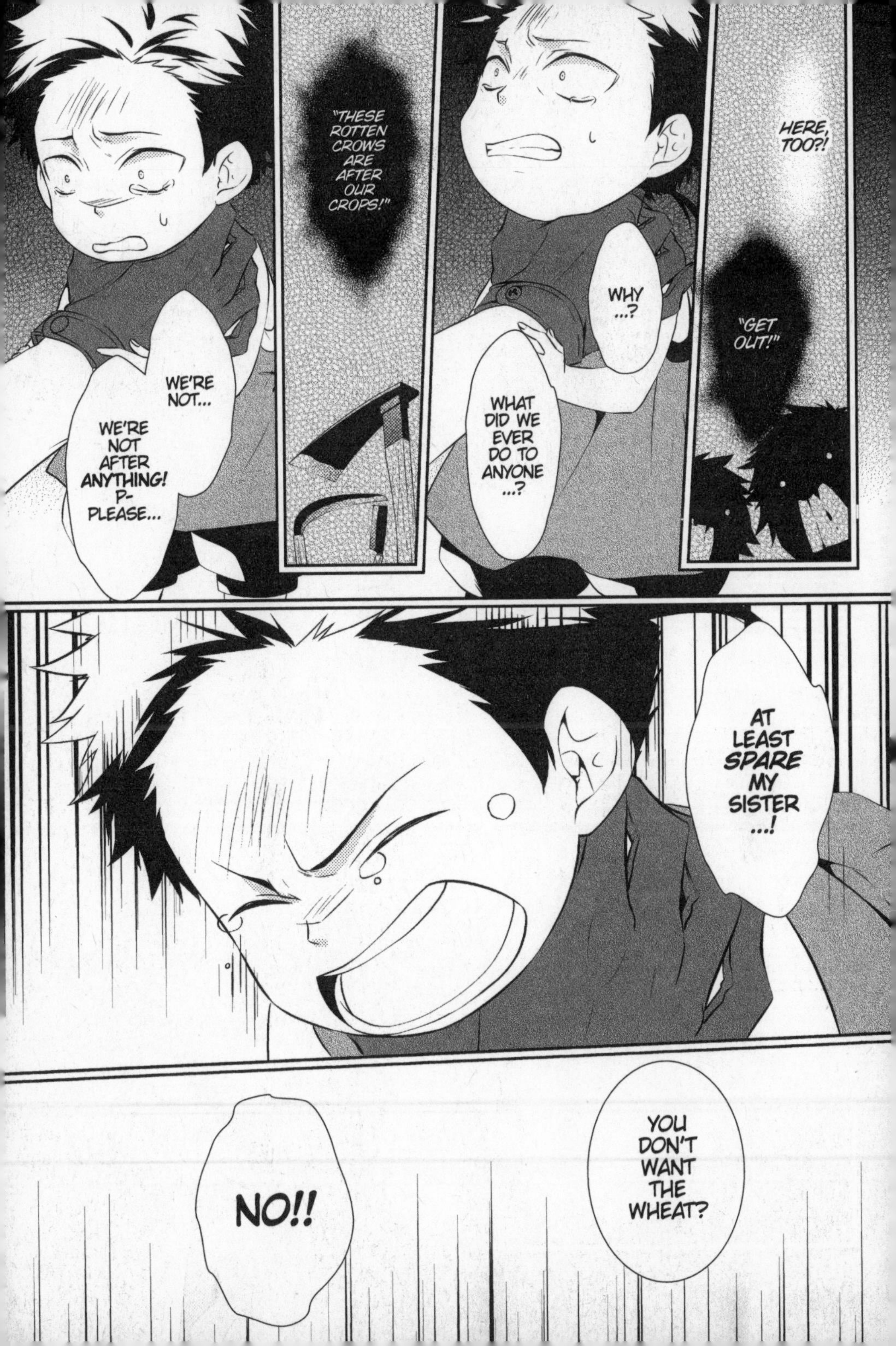
HERE, TOO?!
"GET OUT!"
WHY ...?
WHAT DID WE EVER DO TO ANYONE ...?
"THESE ROTTEN CROWS ARE AFTER OUR CROPS!"
WE'RE NOT...
WE'RE NOT AFTER ANYTHING! P-PLEASE...
AT LEAST SPARE MY SISTER ...!
YOU DON'T WANT THE WHEAT?
NO!!

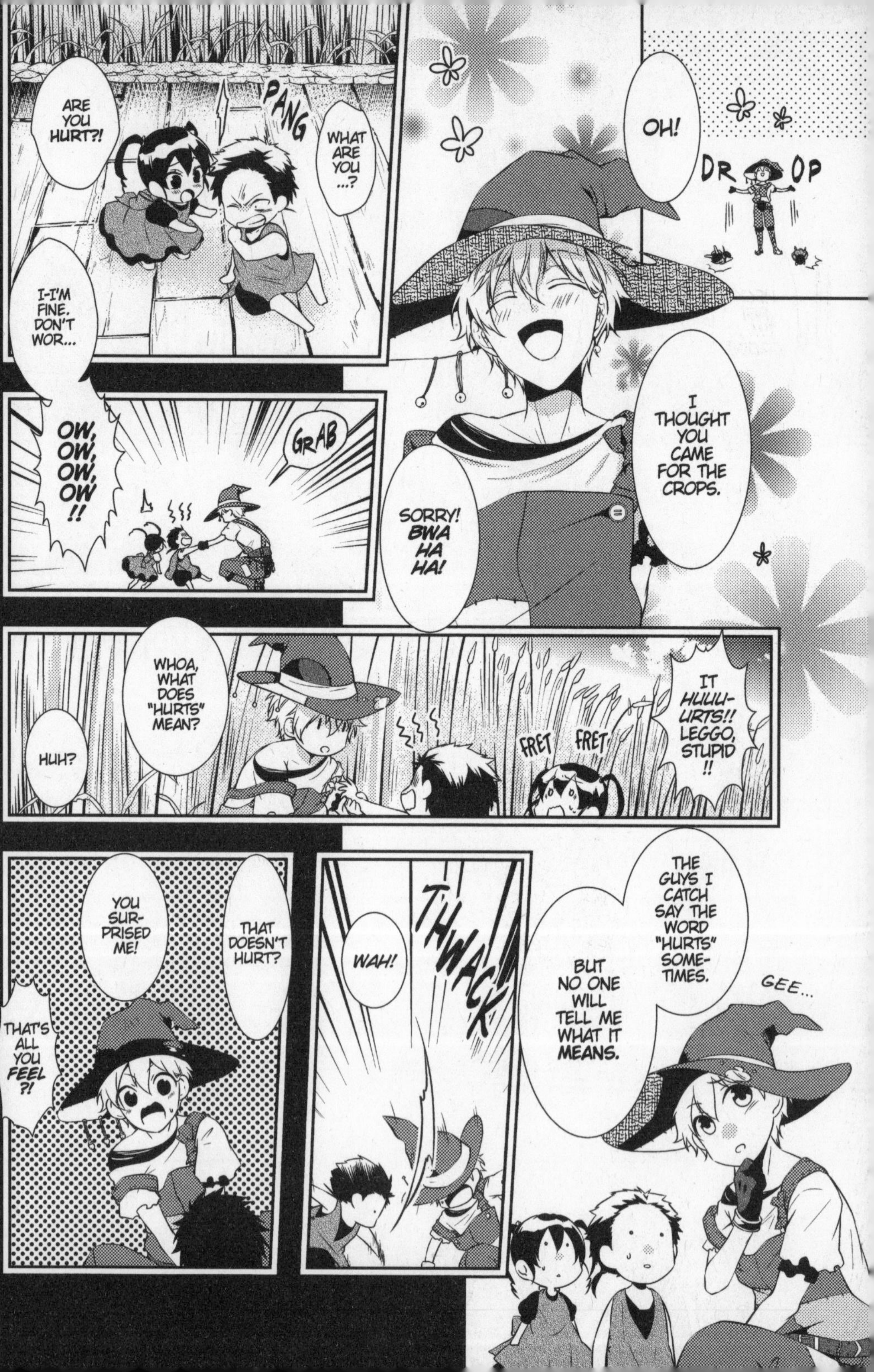

DR OP
OH!
I THOUGHT YOU CAME FOR THE CROPS.
SORRY! BWA HA HA!
PANG
WHAT ARE YOU ...?
ARE YOU HURT?!
I-I'M FINE. DON'T WOR...
GRAB
OW, OW, OW, OW!!
IT HUUUURTS!! LEGGO, STUPID!!
FRET FRET
WHOA, WHAT DOES "HURTS" MEAN?
HUH?
GEE...
THE GUYS I CATCH SAY THE WORD "HURTS" SOMETIMES.
BUT NO ONE WILL TELL ME WHAT IT MEANS.
THWACK
WAH!
THAT DOESN'T HURT?
YOU SURPRISED ME!
THAT'S ALL YOU FEEL?!

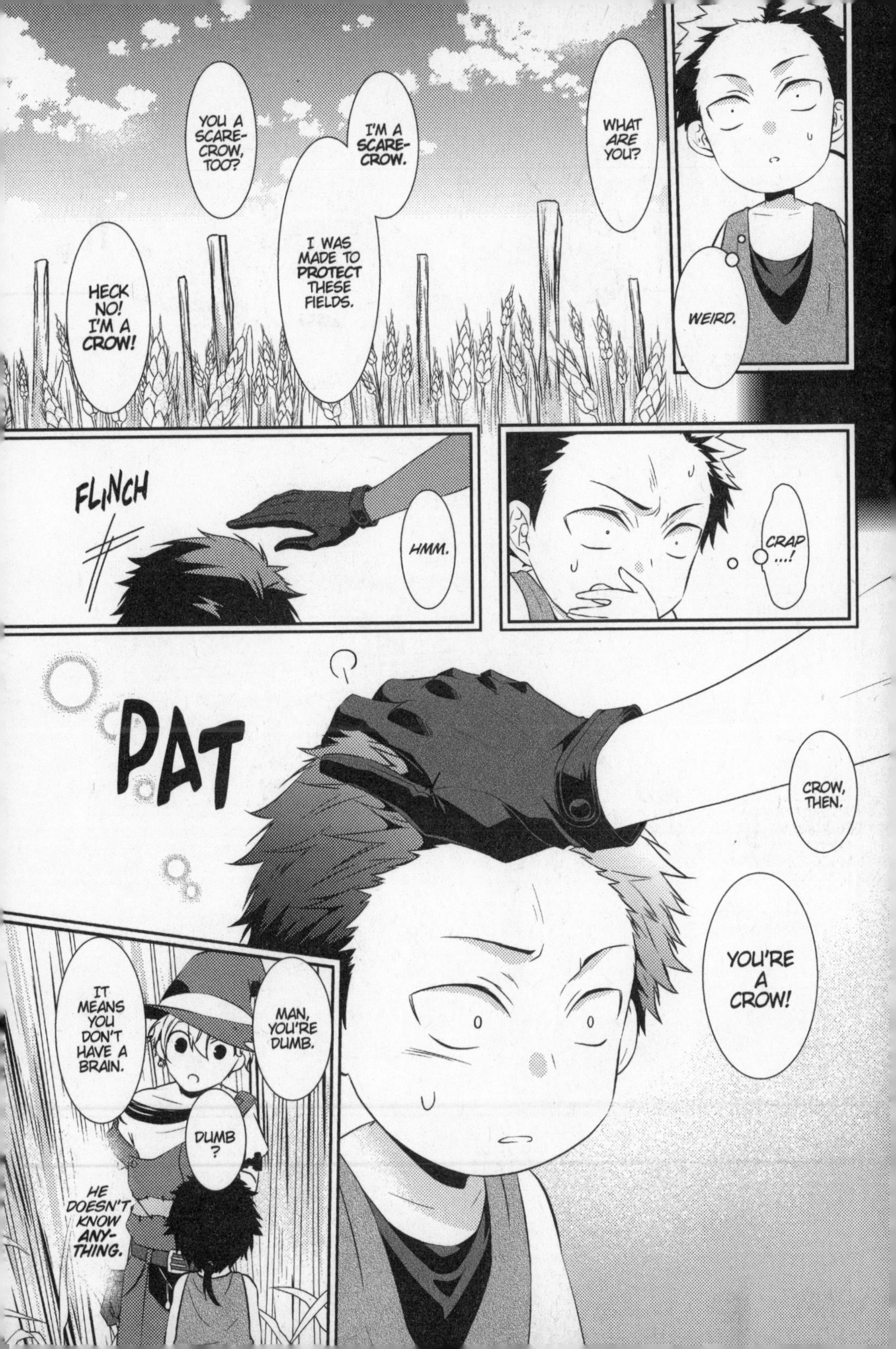
WHAT ARE YOU?
WEIRD.
I'M A SCARECROW.
YOU A SCARECROW, TOO?
I WAS MADE TO PROTECT THESE FIELDS.
HECK NO! I'M A CROW!
CRAP ...!
HMM.
FLINCH
CROW, THEN.
YOU'RE A CROW!
PAT
MAN, YOU'RE DUMB.
IT MEANS YOU DON'T HAVE A BRAIN.
DUMB?
HE DOESN'T KNOW ANYTHING.

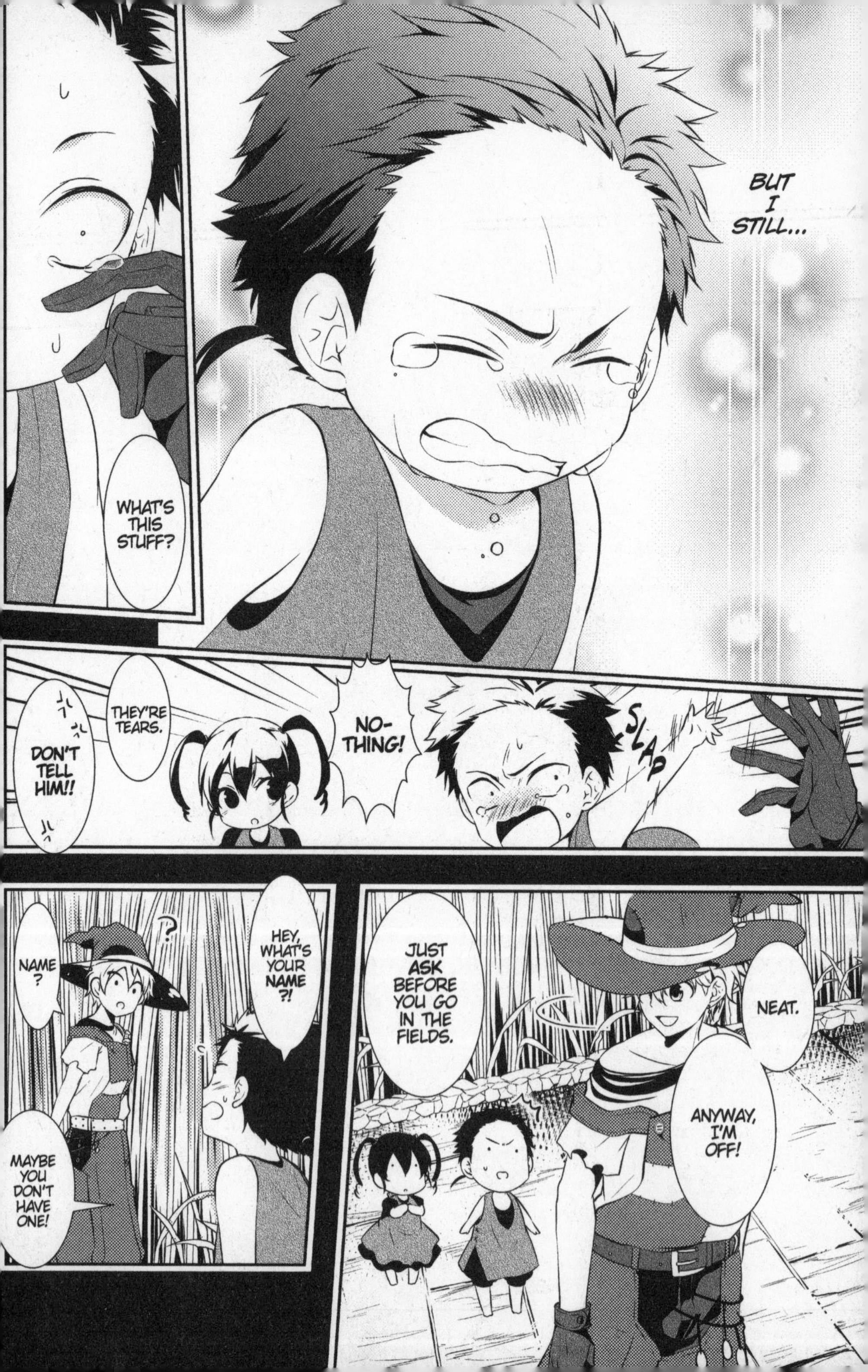
BUT I STILL...
WHAT'S THIS STUFF?
NO-THING!
SLAP
THEY'RE TEARS.
DON'T TELL HIM!!
NEAT.
JUST ASK BEFORE YOU GO IN THE FIELDS.
ANYWAY, I'M OFF!
HEY, WHAT'S YOUR NAME?!
NAME?
MAYBE YOU DON'T HAVE ONE!

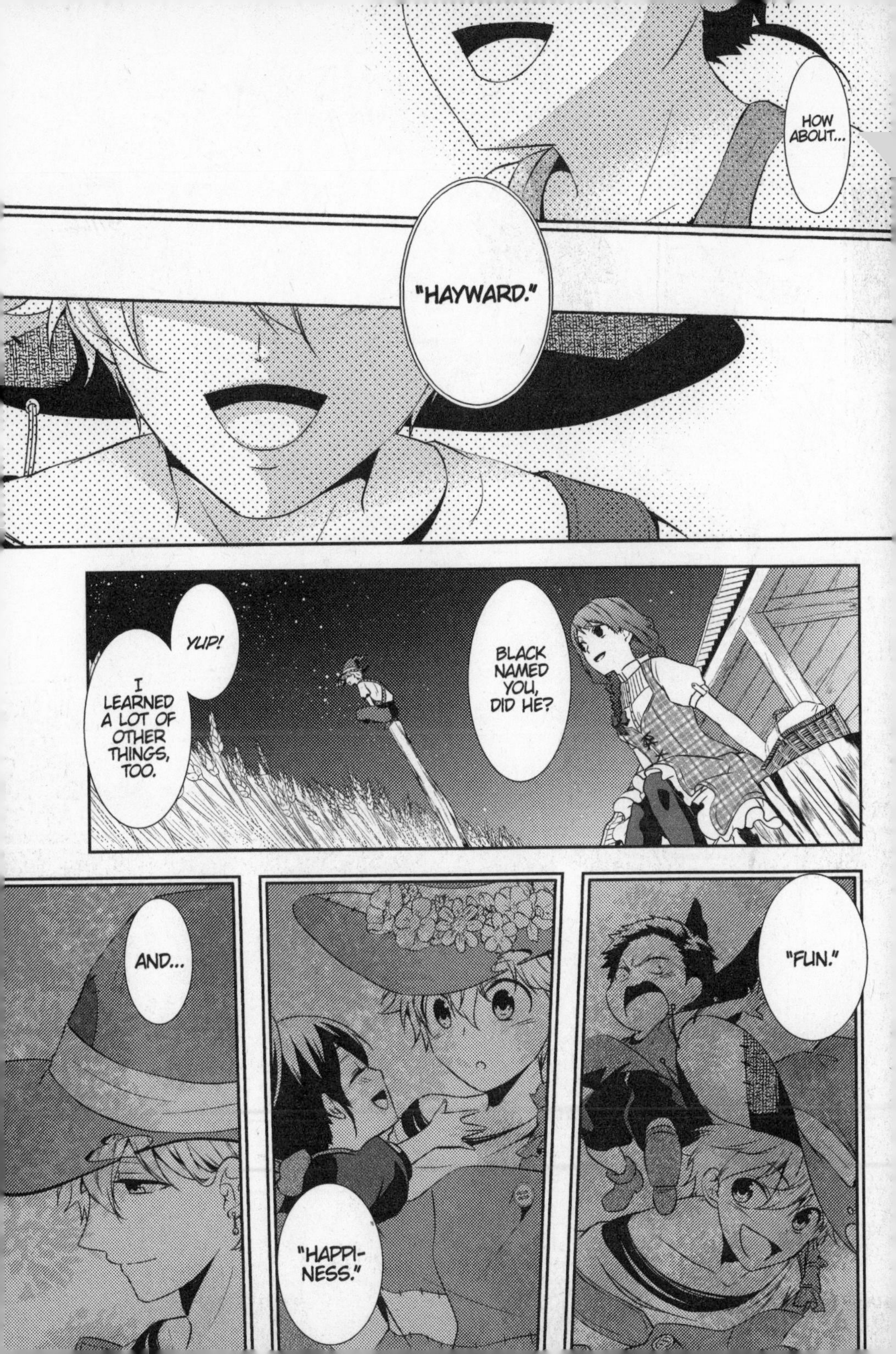
HOW ABOUT...
"HAYWARD."
BLACK NAMED YOU, DID HE?
YUP!
I LEARNED A LOT OF OTHER THINGS, TOO.
"FUN."
"HAPPI-NESS."
AND...

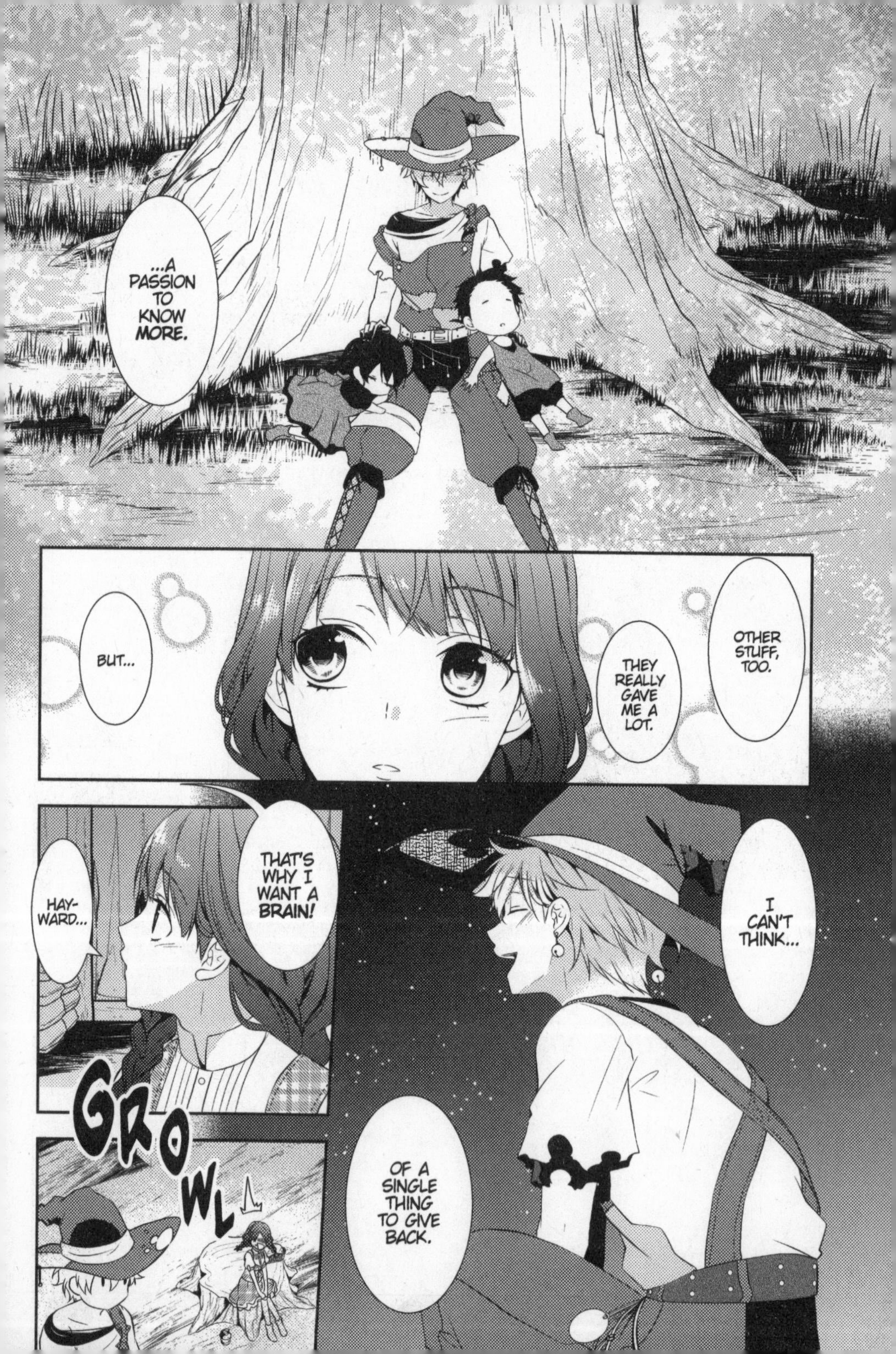
...A PASSION TO KNOW MORE.
OTHER STUFF, TOO.
THEY REALLY GAVE ME A LOT.
BUT...
I CAN'T THINK...
OF A SINGLE THING TO GIVE BACK.
THAT'S WHY I WANT A BRAIN!
HAY-WARD...
GROWL

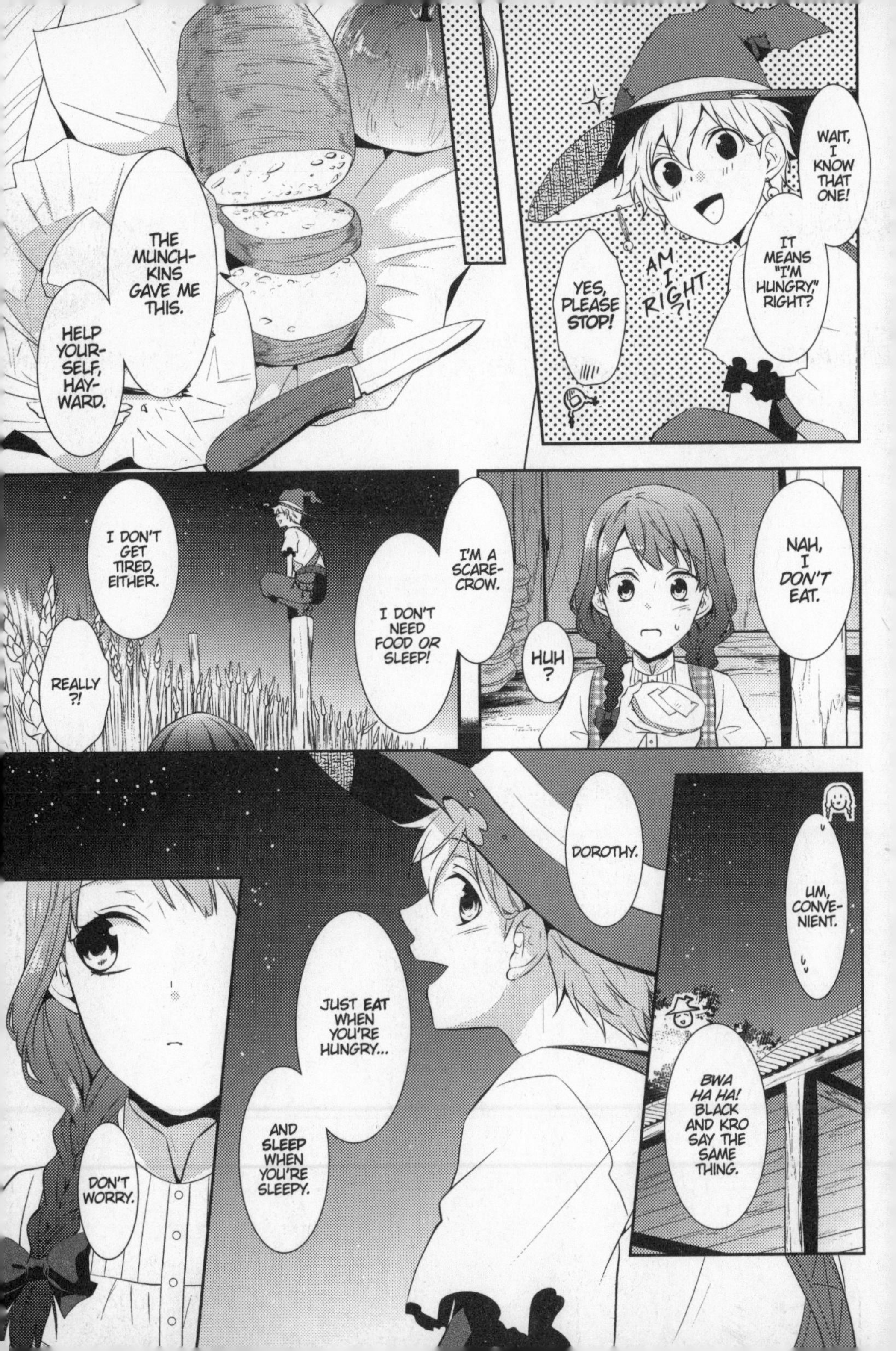
WAIT, I KNOW THAT ONE!
IT MEANS "I'M HUNGRY," RIGHT?
AM I RIGHT?!
YES, PLEASE STOP!
THE MUNCHKINS GAVE ME THIS.
HELP YOURSELF, HAYWARD.
NAH, I DON'T EAT.
HUH?
I'M A SCARECROW.
I DON'T NEED FOOD OR SLEEP!
I DON'T GET TIRED, EITHER.
REALLY?!
UM, CONVENIENT.
BWA HA HA! BLACK AND KRO SAY THE SAME THING.
DOROTHY.
JUST EAT WHEN YOU'RE HUNGRY...
AND SLEEP WHEN YOU'RE SLEEPY.
DON'T WORRY.

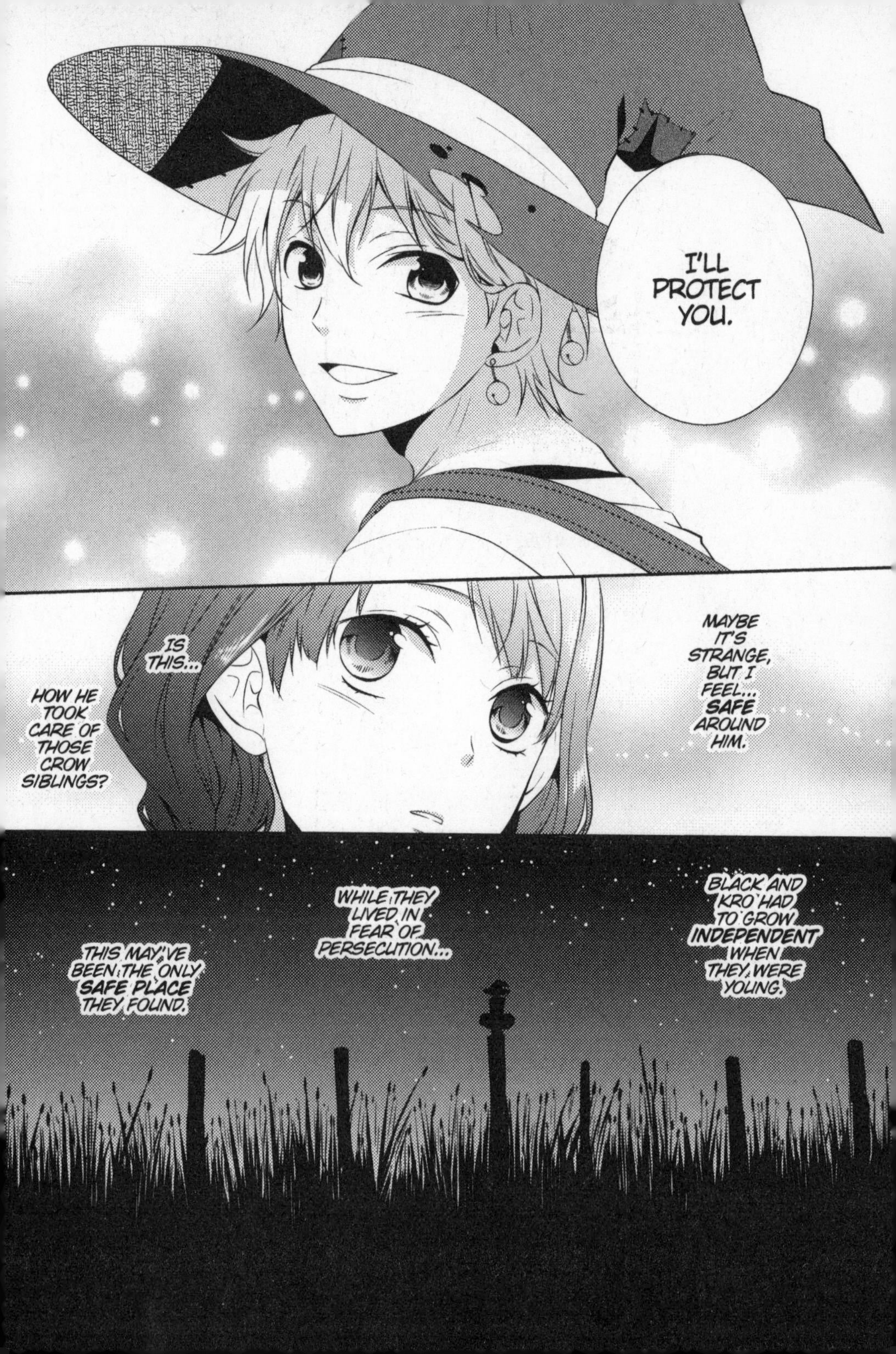
I'LL PROTECT YOU.
MAYBE IT'S STRANGE, BUT I FEEL... SAFE AROUND HIM.
IS THIS...
HOW HE TOOK CARE OF THOSE CROW SIBLINGS?
BLACK AND KRO HAD TO GROW INDEPENDENT WHEN THEY WERE YOUNG.
WHILE THEY LIVED IN FEAR OF PERSECUTION...
THIS MAY'VE BEEN THE ONLY SAFE PLACE THEY FOUND.

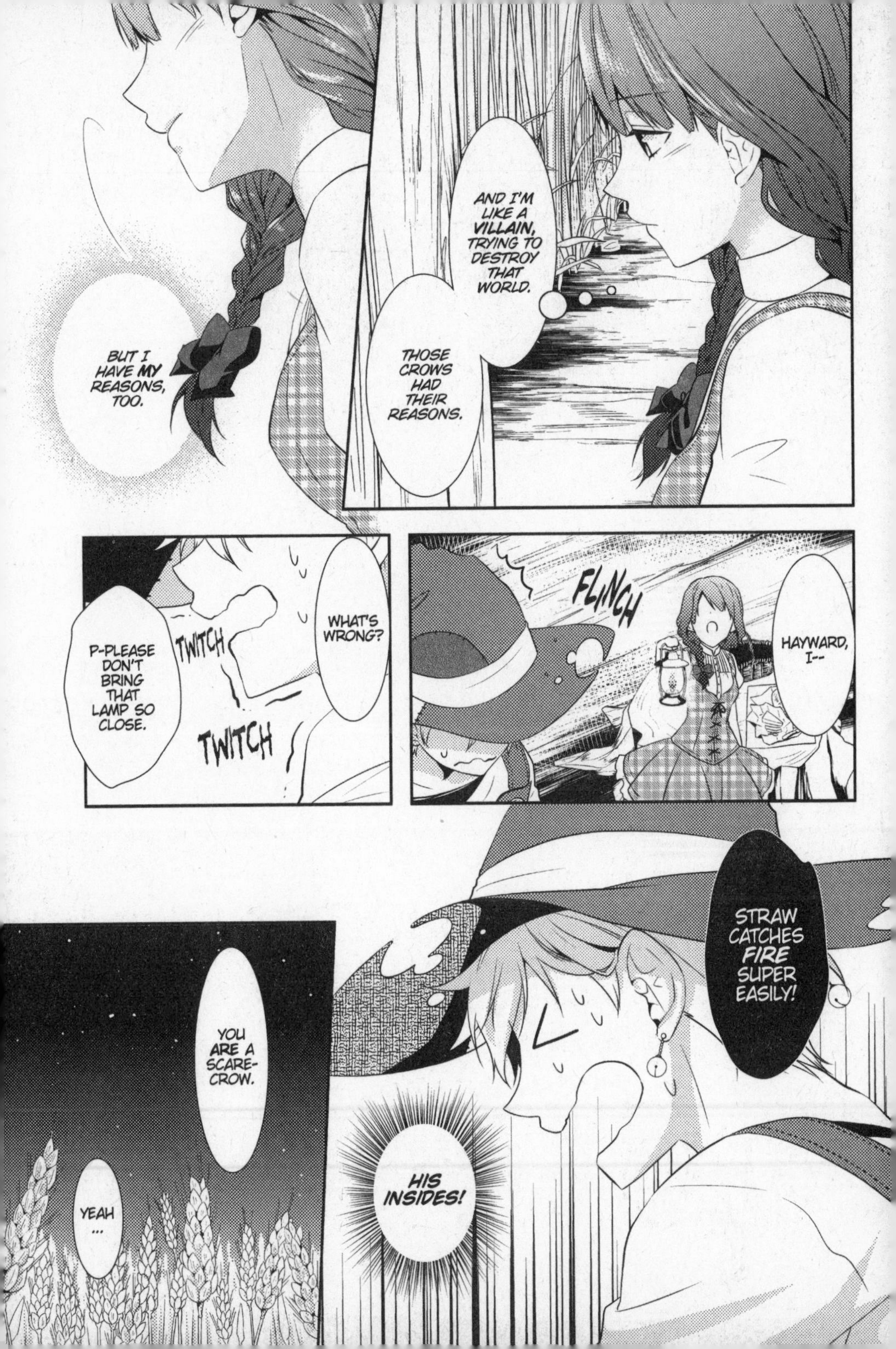
AND I'M LIKE A VILLAIN, TRYING TO DESTROY THAT WORLD.
THOSE CROWS HAD THEIR REASONS.
BUT I HAVE MY REASONS, TOO.
HAYWARD, I--
FLINCH
WHAT'S WRONG?
TWITCH
P-PLEASE DON'T BRING THAT LAMP SO CLOSE.
TWITCH
STRAW CATCHES FIRE SUPER EASILY!
HIS INSIDES!
YOU ARE A SCARE-CROW.
YEAH ...

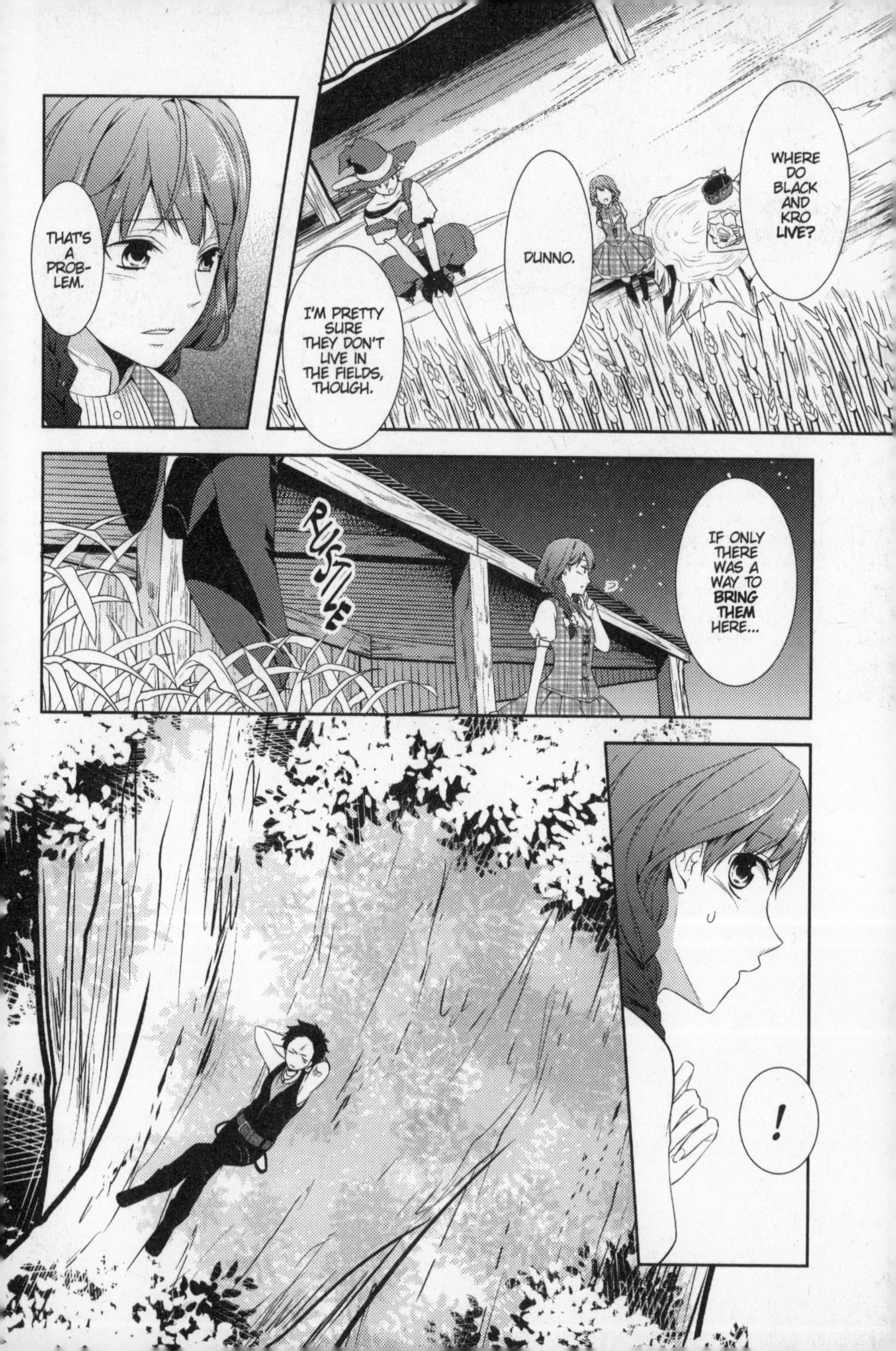
WHERE DO BLACK AND KRO LIVE?
DUNNO.
I'M PRETTY SURE THEY DON'T LIVE IN THE FIELDS, THOUGH.
THAT'S A PROB-LEM.
IF ONLY THERE WAS A WAY TO BRING THEM HERE...
RUSTLE
!

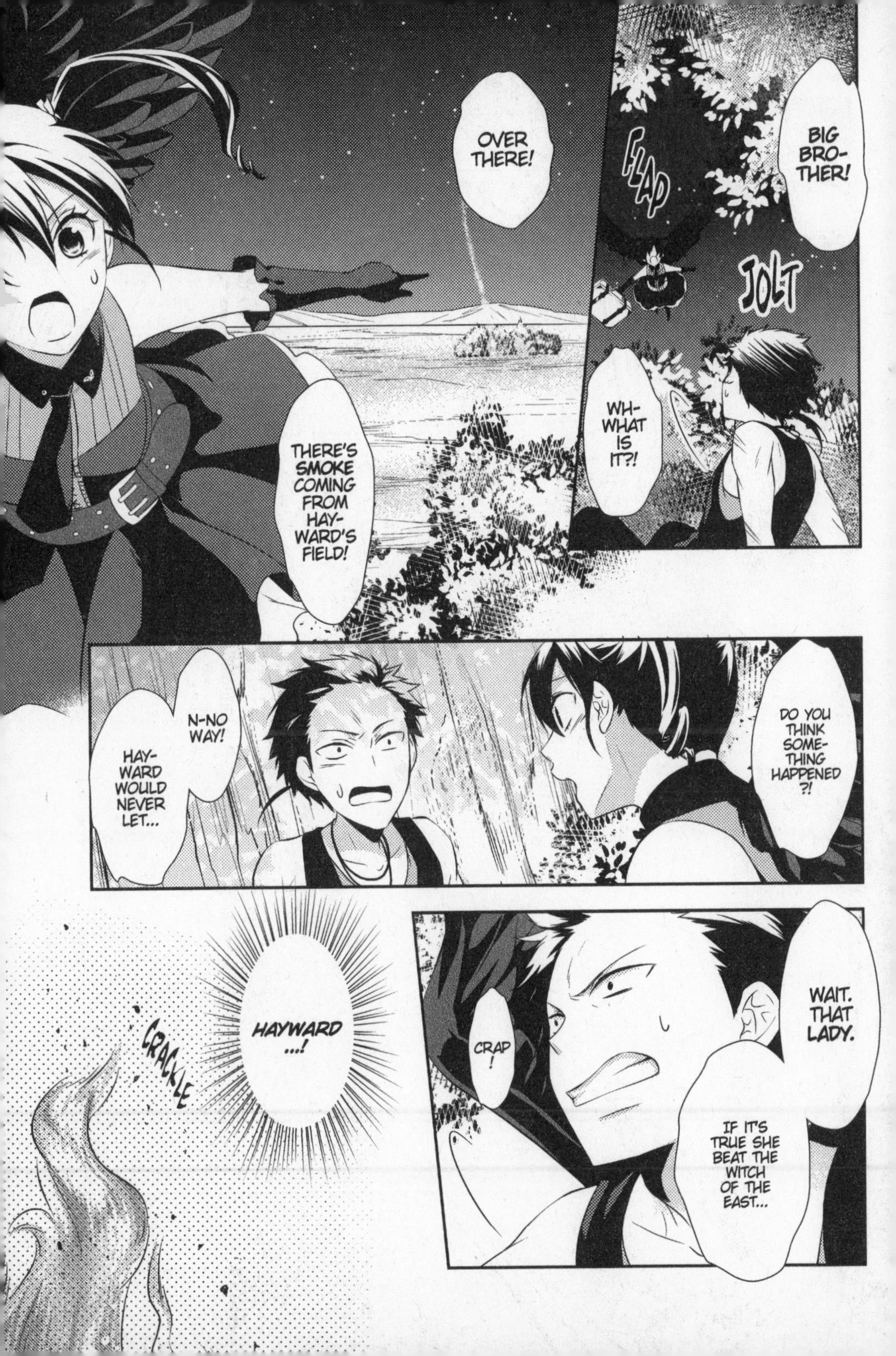
BIG BROTHER!
FLAP
JOLT
WH-WHAT IS IT?!
OVER THERE!
THERE'S SMOKE COMING FROM HAYWARD'S FIELD!
DO YOU THINK SOMETHING HAPPENED?!
N-NO WAY!
HAYWARD WOULD NEVER LET...
WAIT. THAT LADY.
CRAP!
IF IT'S TRUE SHE BEAT THE WITCH OF THE EAST...
HAYWARD...!
CRACKLE

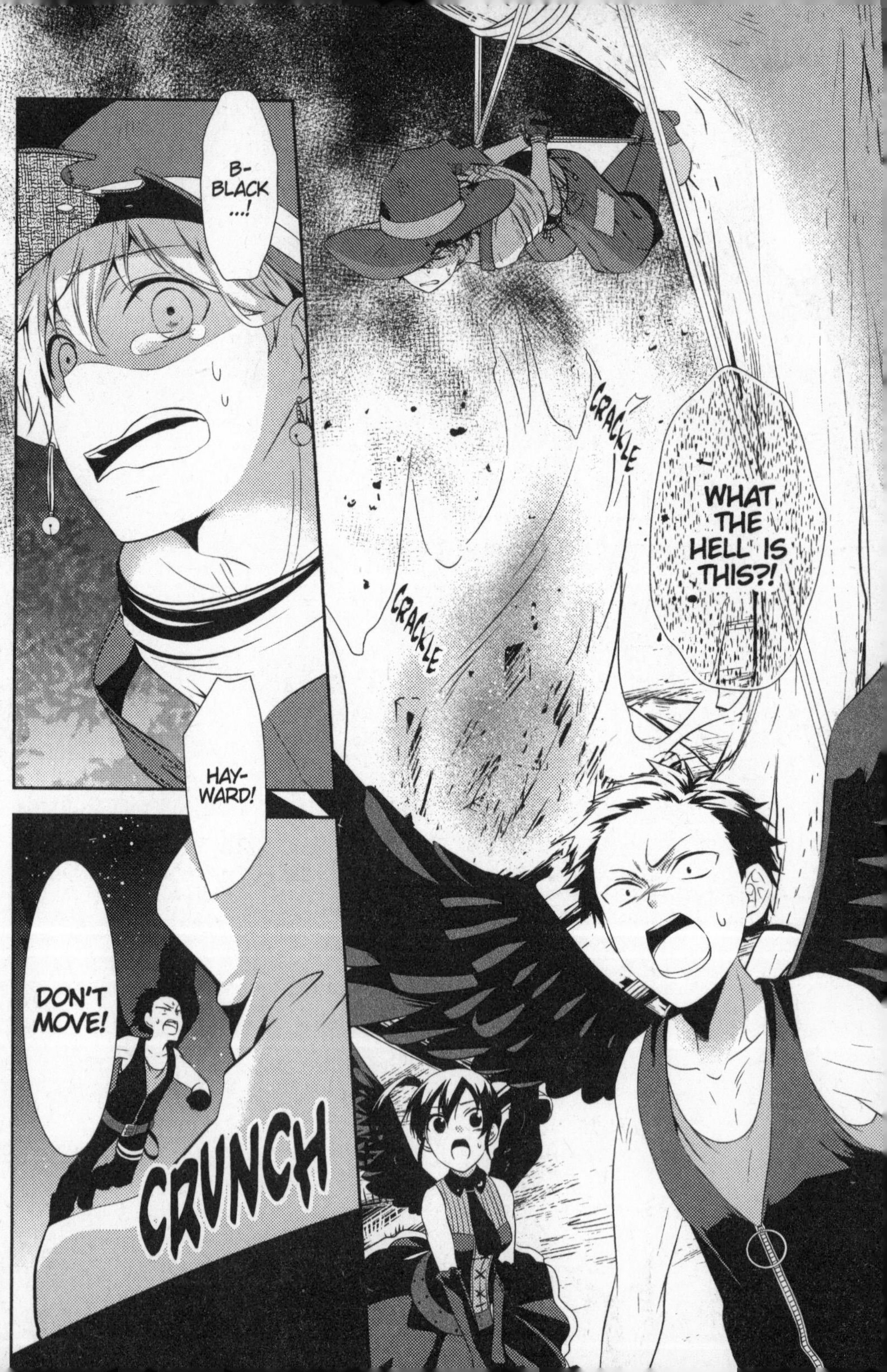
CRACKLE
CRACKLE
WHAT THE HELL IS THIS?!
HAY-WARD!
B-BLACK ...!
DON'T MOVE!
CRUNCH

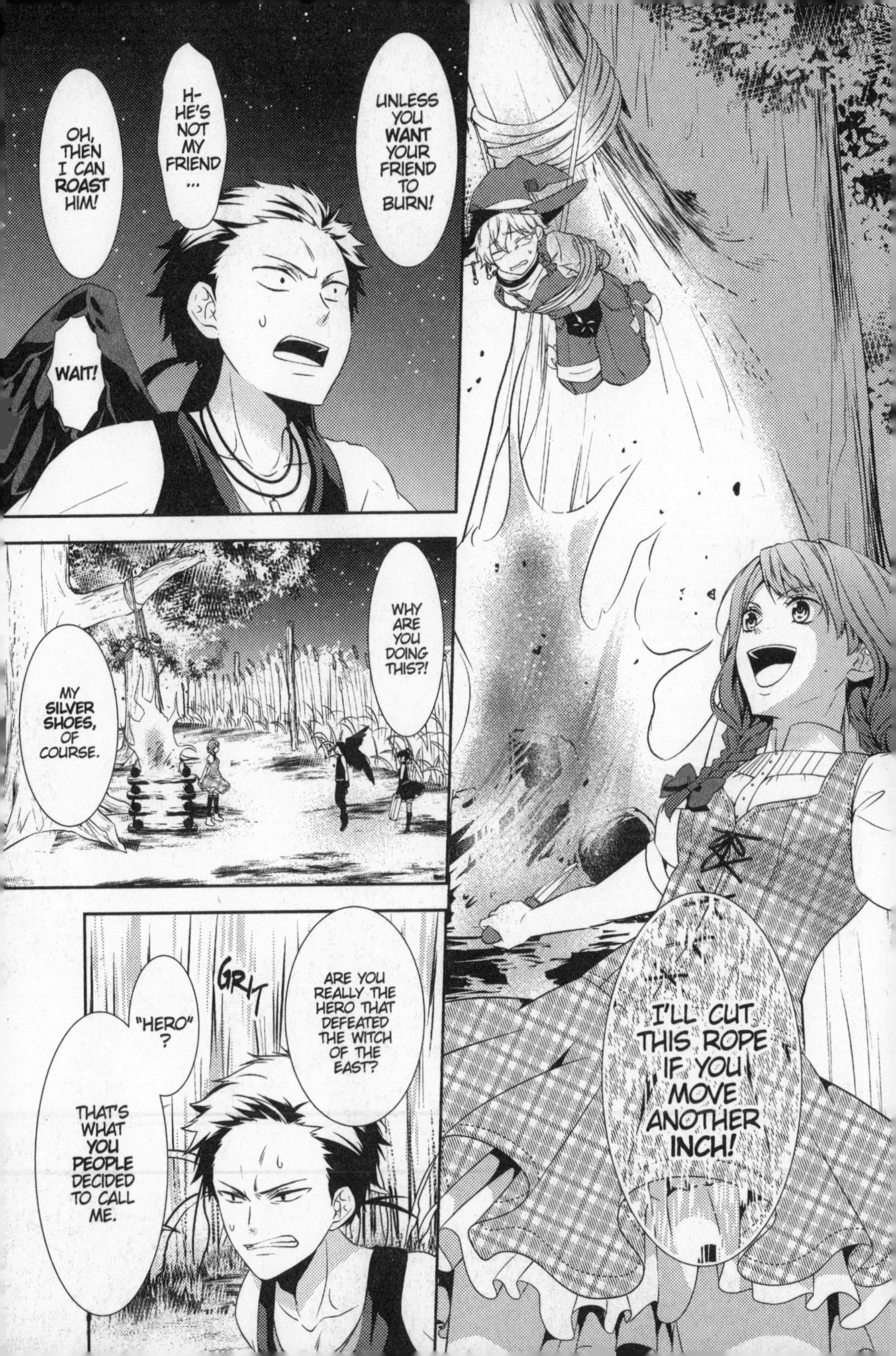

I'LL CUT THIS ROPE IF YOU MOVE ANOTHER INCH!
UNLESS YOU WANT YOUR FRIEND TO BURN!
H-HE'S NOT MY FRIEND...
OH, THEN I CAN ROAST HIM!
WAIT!
WHY ARE YOU DOING THIS?!
MY SILVER SHOES, OF COURSE.
GRIT
ARE YOU REALLY THE HERO THAT DEFEATED THE WITCH OF THE EAST?
"HERO"?
THAT'S WHAT YOU PEOPLE DECIDED TO CALL ME.

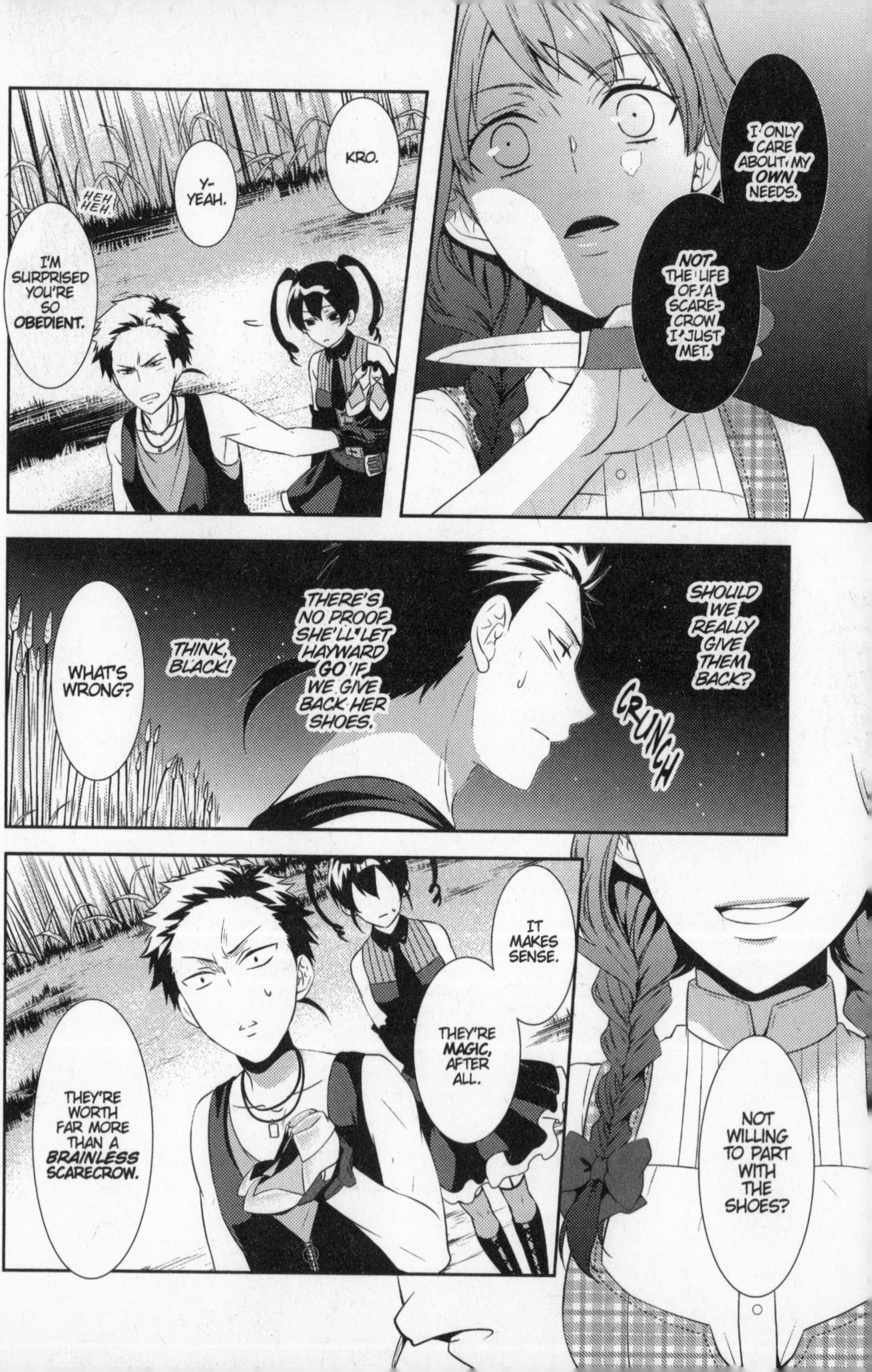
I ONLY CARE ABOUT MY OWN NEEDS.
NOT THE LIFE OF A SCARECROW I JUST MET.
KRO.
Y-YEAH.
HEH HEH
I'M SURPRISED YOU'RE SO OBEDIENT.
SHOULD WE REALLY GIVE THEM BACK?
CRUNCH
THERE'S NO PROOF SHE'LL LET HAYWARD GO IF WE GIVE BACK HER SHOES.
THINK, BLACK!
WHAT'S WRONG?
NOT WILLING TO PART WITH THE SHOES?
IT MAKES SENSE.
THEY'RE MAGIC, AFTER ALL.
THEY'RE WORTH FAR MORE THAN A BRAINLESS SCARECROW.

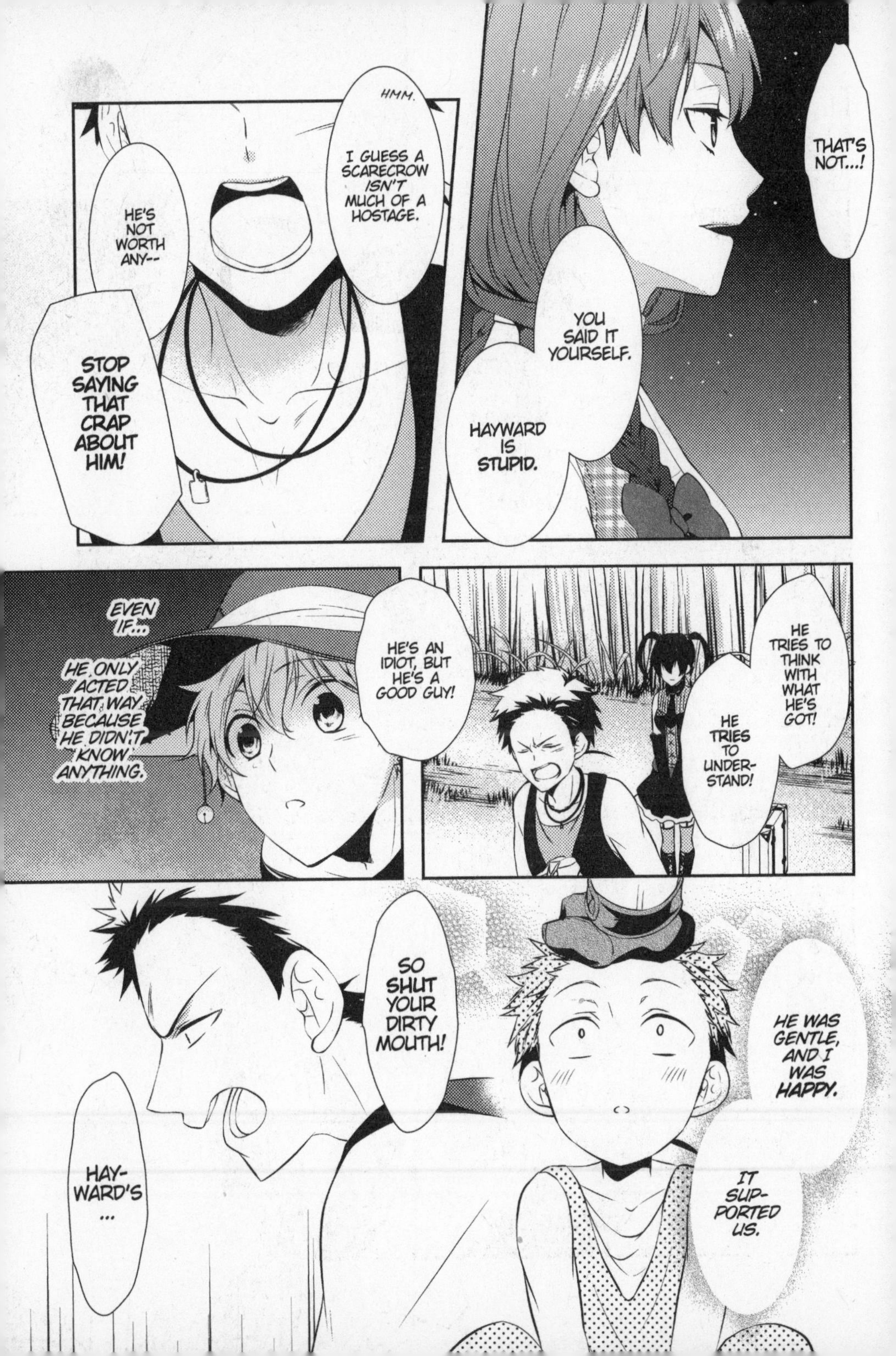
THAT'S NOT...!
YOU SAID IT YOURSELF.
HAYWARD IS STUPID.
HMM.
I GUESS A SCARECROW ISN'T MUCH OF A HOSTAGE.
HE'S NOT WORTH ANY--
STOP SAYING THAT CRAP ABOUT HIM!
HE TRIES TO THINK WITH WHAT HE'S GOT!
HE TRIES TO UNDER-STAND!
HE'S AN IDIOT, BUT HE'S A GOOD GUY!
EVEN IF...
HE ONLY ACTED THAT WAY BECAUSE HE DIDN'T KNOW ANYTHING.
HE WAS GENTLE, AND I WAS HAPPY.
IT SUP-PORTED US.
SO SHUT YOUR DIRTY MOUTH!
HAY-WARD'S...

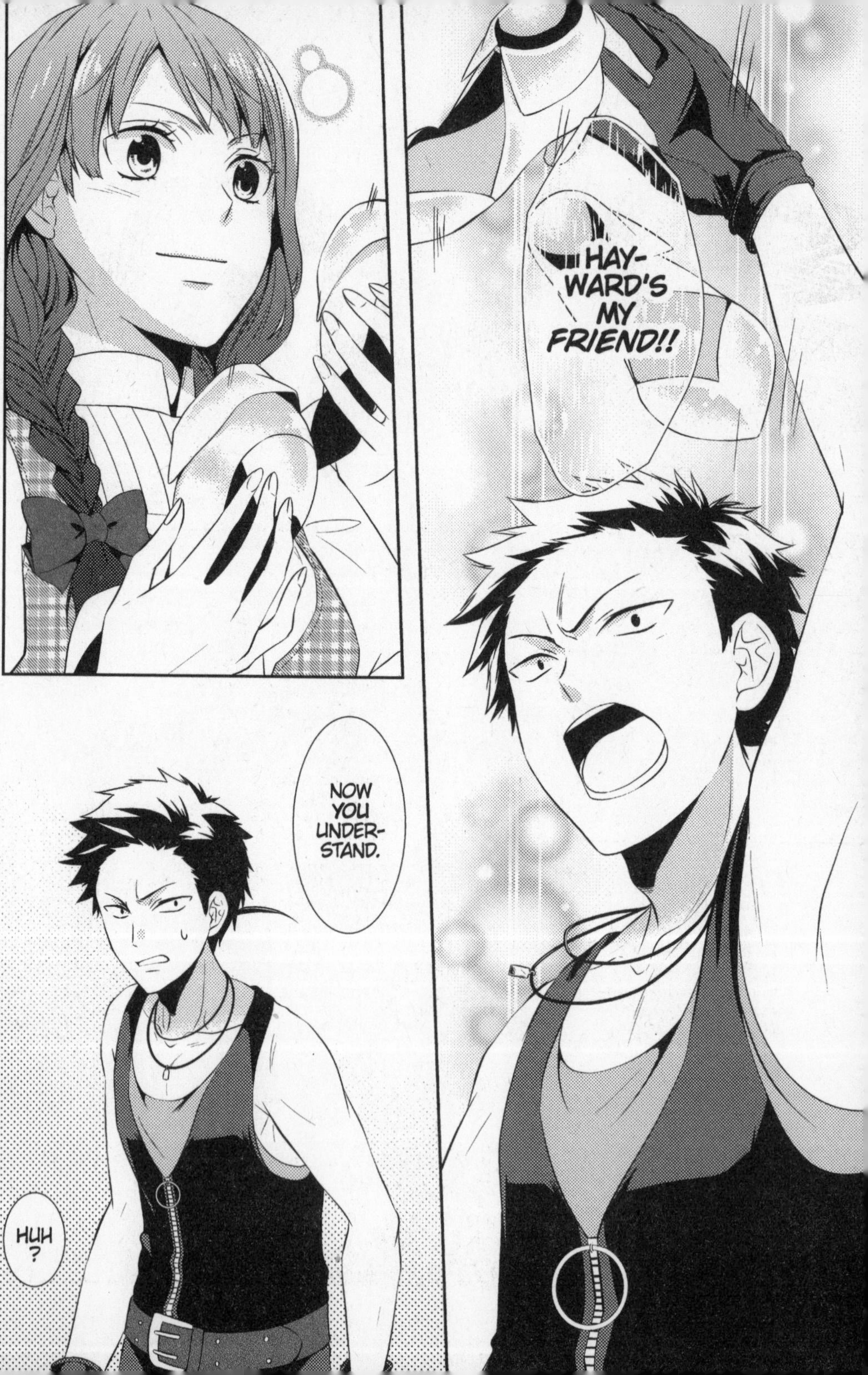
HAY-
WARD'S
MY
FRIEND!!
NOW
YOU
UNDER-
STAND.
HUH
?

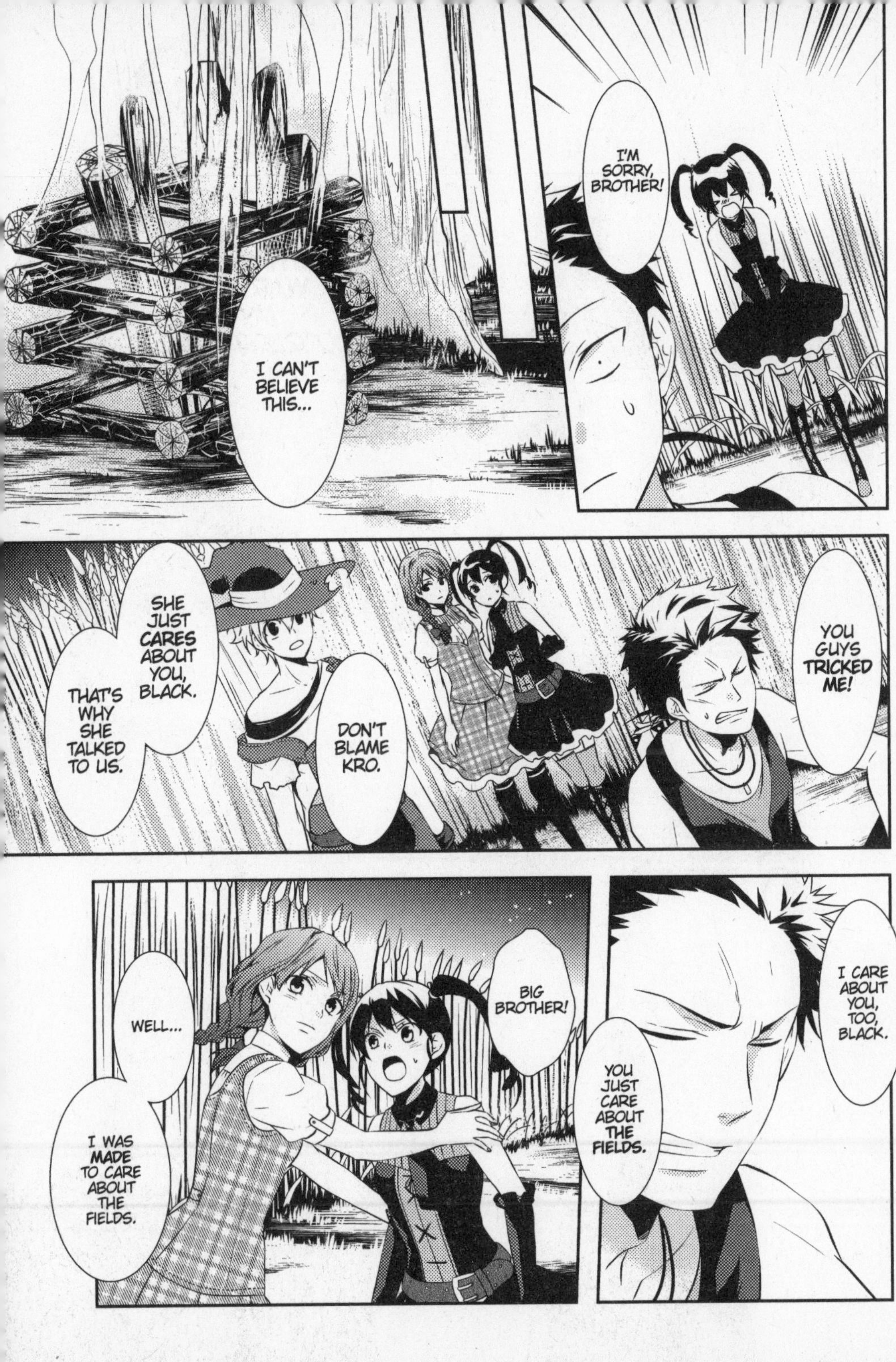
I'M SORRY, BROTHER!
I CAN'T BELIEVE THIS...
YOU GUYS TRICKED ME!
DON'T BLAME KRO.
SHE JUST CARES ABOUT YOU, BLACK.
THAT'S WHY SHE TALKED TO US.
I CARE ABOUT YOU, TOO, BLACK.
YOU JUST CARE ABOUT THE FIELDS.
BIG BROTHER!
WELL...
I WAS MADE TO CARE ABOUT THE FIELDS.

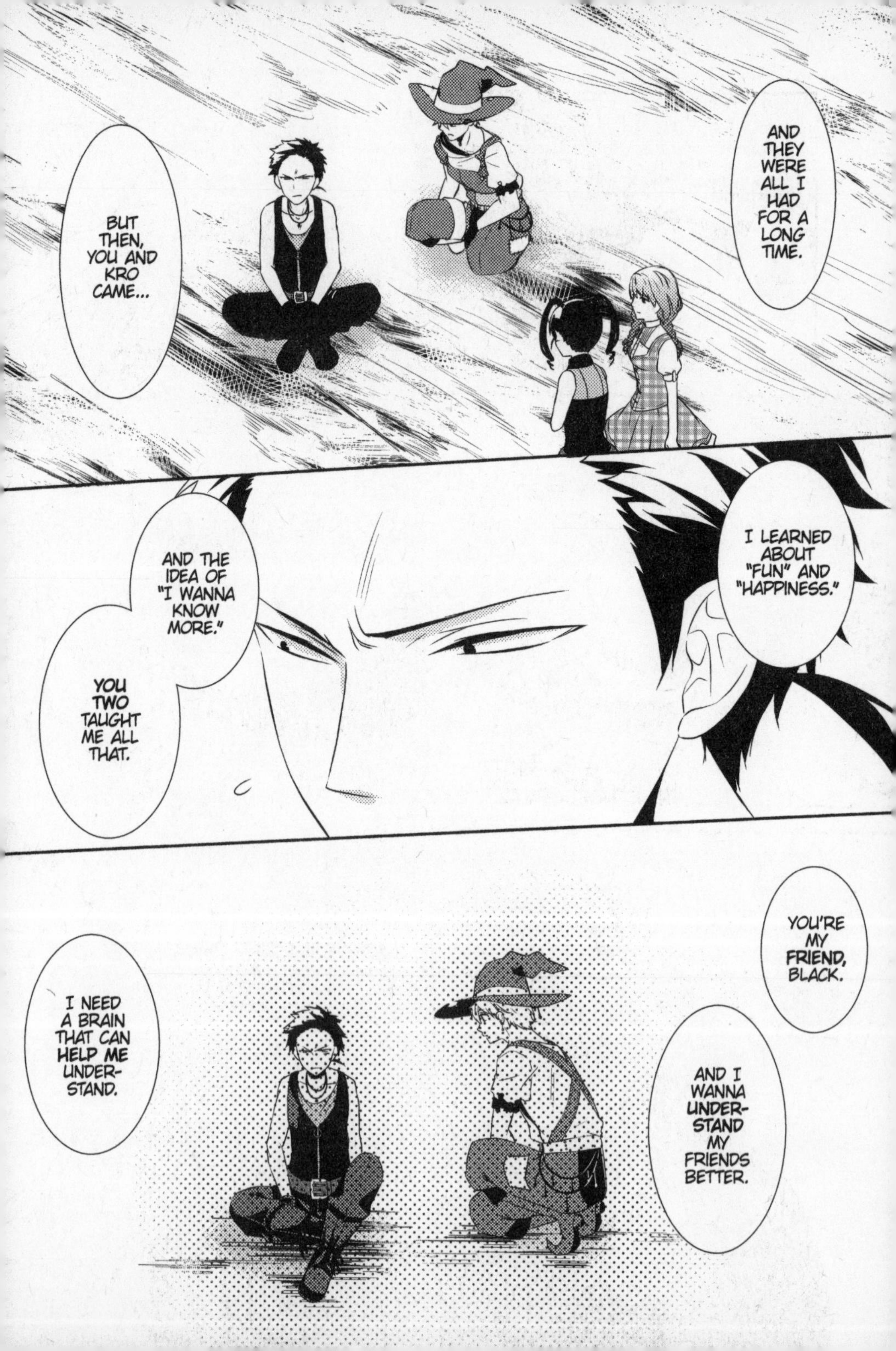
AND THEY WERE ALL I HAD FOR A LONG TIME.
BUT THEN, YOU AND KRO CAME...
I LEARNED ABOUT "FUN" AND "HAPPINESS."
AND THE IDEA OF "I WANNA KNOW MORE."
YOU TWO TAUGHT ME ALL THAT.
YOU'RE MY FRIEND, BLACK.
AND I WANNA UNDER-STAND MY FRIENDS BETTER.
I NEED A BRAIN THAT CAN HELP ME UNDER-STAND.

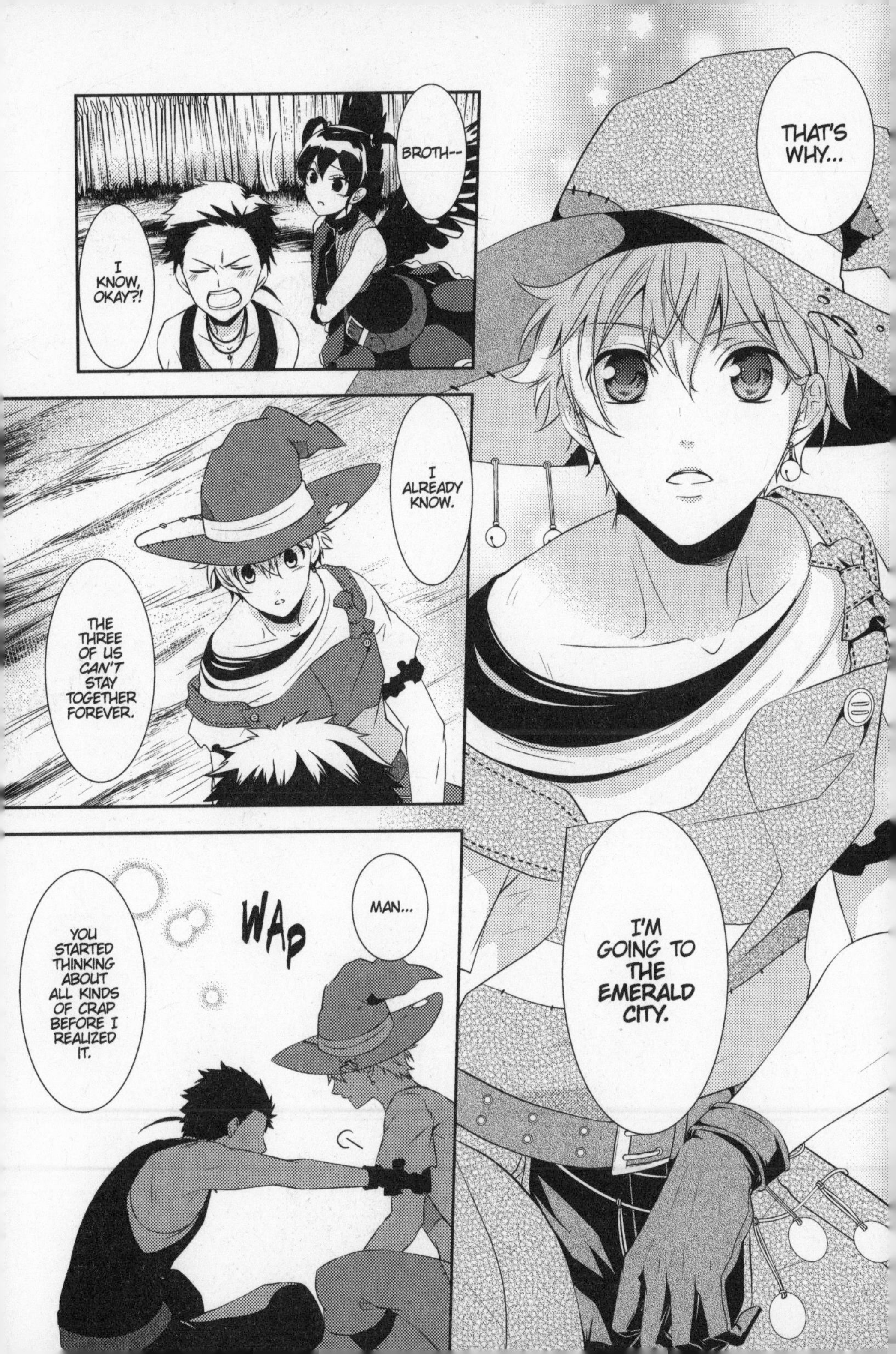
THAT'S WHY...
I'M GOING TO THE EMERALD CITY.
BROTH--
I KNOW, OKAY?!
I ALREADY KNOW.
THE THREE OF US CAN'T STAY TOGETHER FOREVER.
MAN...
WAP
YOU STARTED THINKING ABOUT ALL KINDS OF CRAP BEFORE I REALIZED IT.

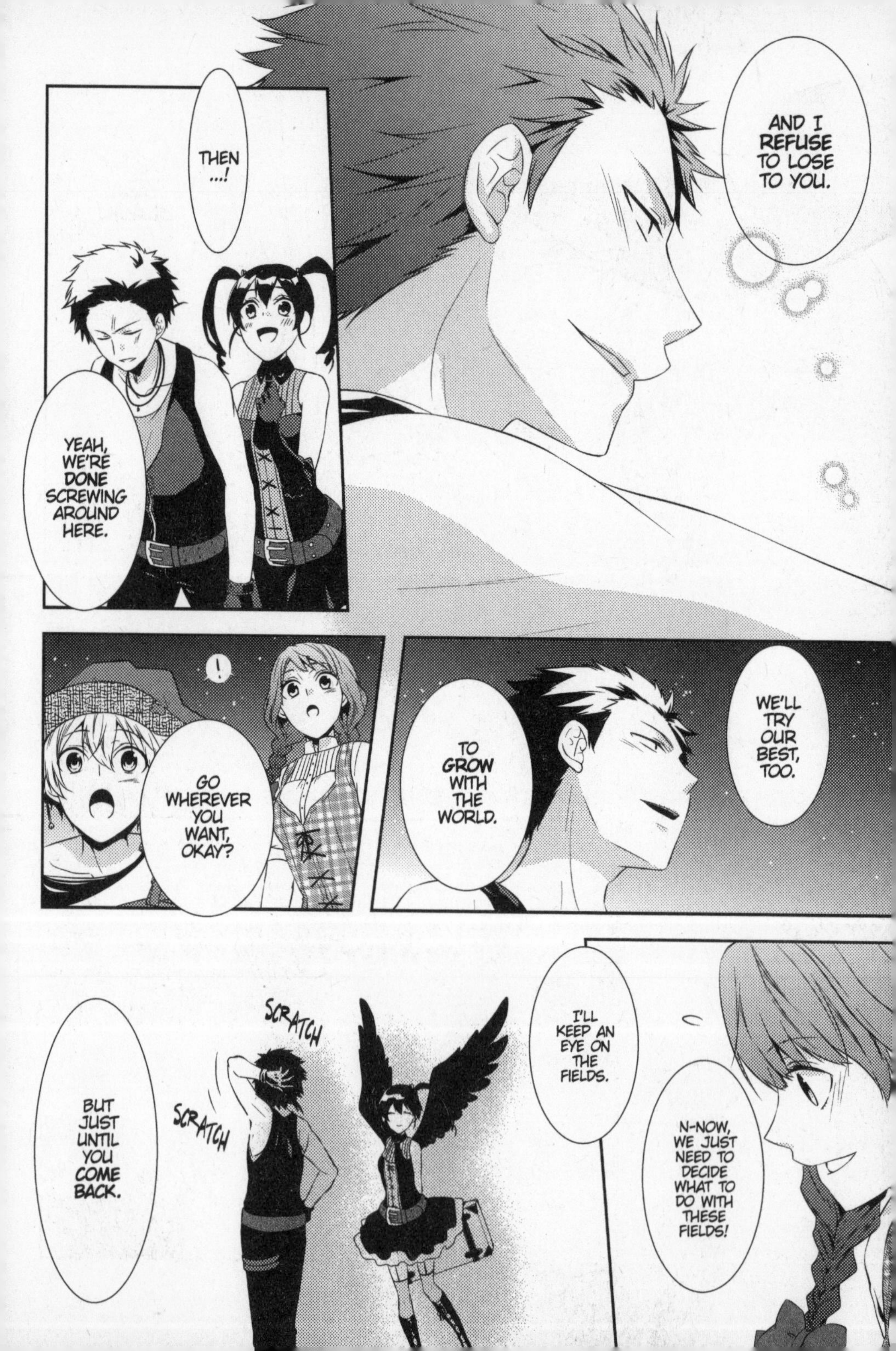
AND I REFUSE TO LOSE TO YOU.
THEN ...!
YEAH, WE'RE DONE SCREWING AROUND HERE.
WE'LL TRY OUR BEST, TOO.
TO GROW WITH THE WORLD.
!
GO WHEREVER YOU WANT, OKAY?
N-NOW, WE JUST NEED TO DECIDE WHAT TO DO WITH THESE FIELDS!
I'LL KEEP AN EYE ON THE FIELDS.
SCRATCH
SCRATCH
BUT JUST UNTIL YOU COME BACK.

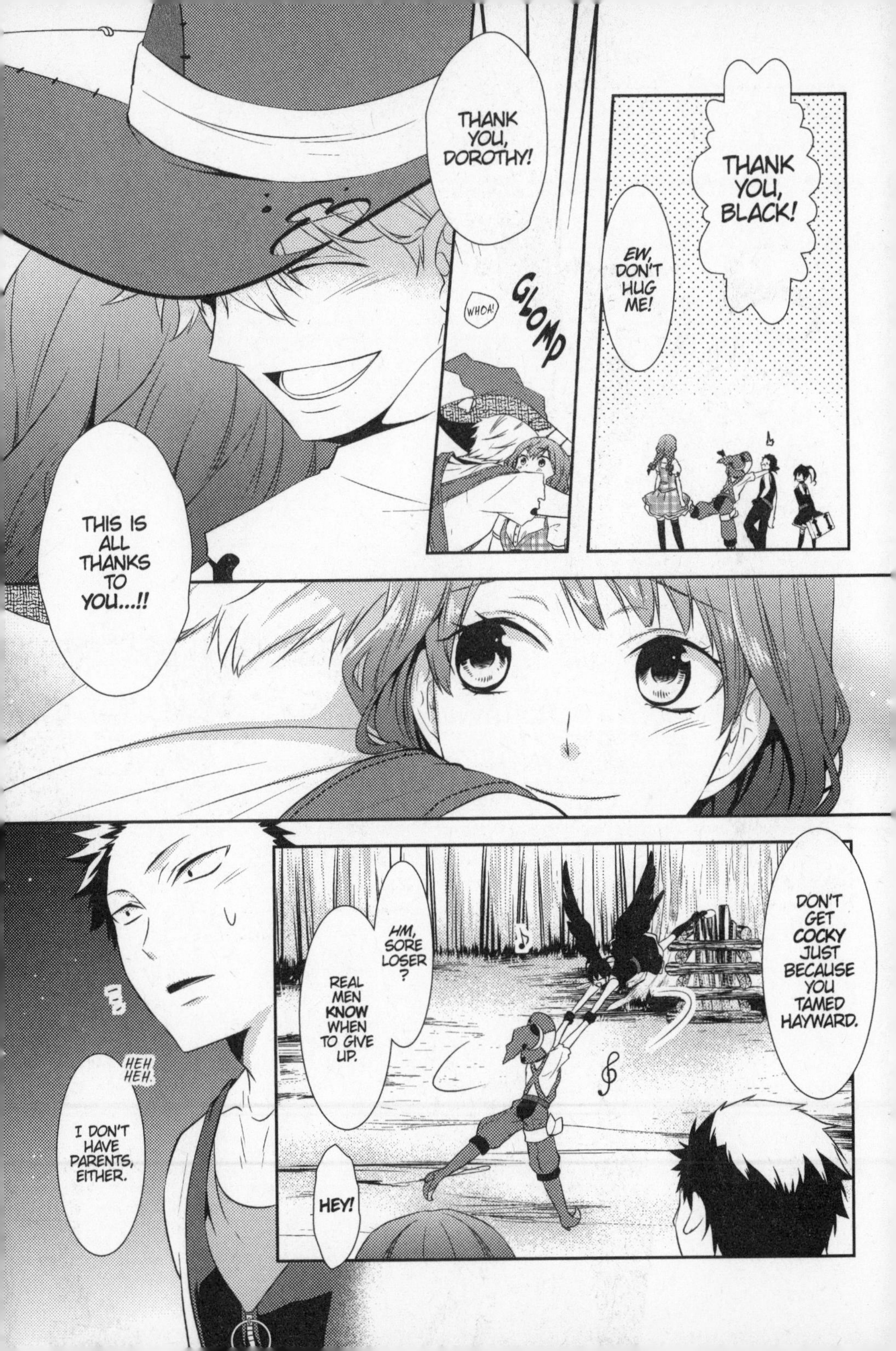
THANK YOU, BLACK!
EW, DON'T HUG ME!
THANK YOU, DOROTHY!
GLOMP
WHOA!
THIS IS ALL THANKS TO YOU...!!
DON'T GET COCKY JUST BECAUSE YOU TAMED HAYWARD.
HM, SORE LOSER?
REAL MEN KNOW WHEN TO GIVE UP.
HEY!
HEH HEH.
I DON'T HAVE PARENTS, EITHER.

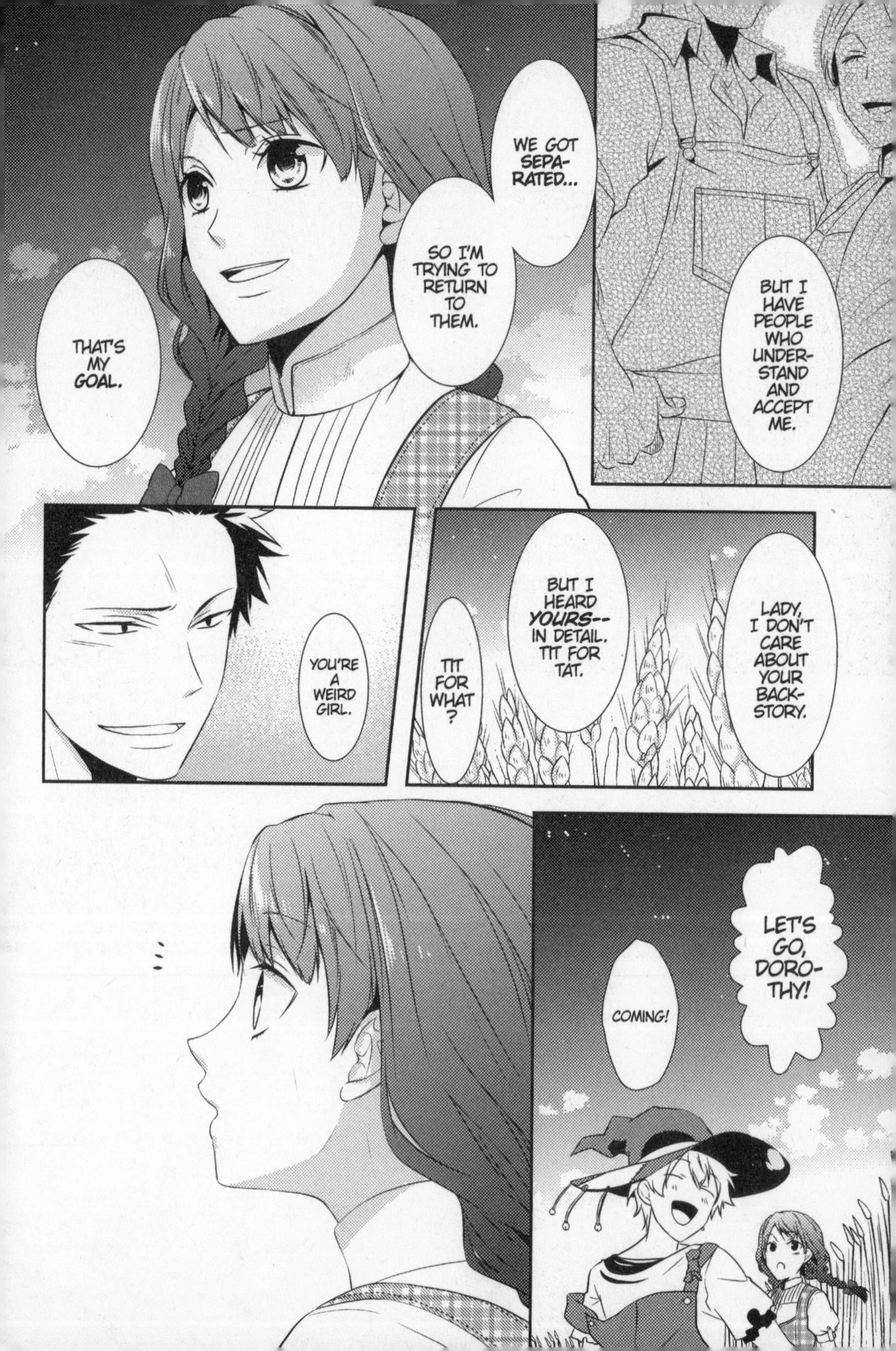
BUT I HAVE PEOPLE WHO UNDERSTAND AND ACCEPT ME.
WE GOT SEPARATED...
SO I'M TRYING TO RETURN TO THEM.
THAT'S MY GOAL.
LADY, I DON'T CARE ABOUT YOUR BACKSTORY.
BUT I HEARD *YOURS*-- IN DETAIL. TIT FOR TAT.
TIT FOR WHAT?
YOU'RE A WEIRD GIRL.
LET'S GO, DOROTHY!
COMING!

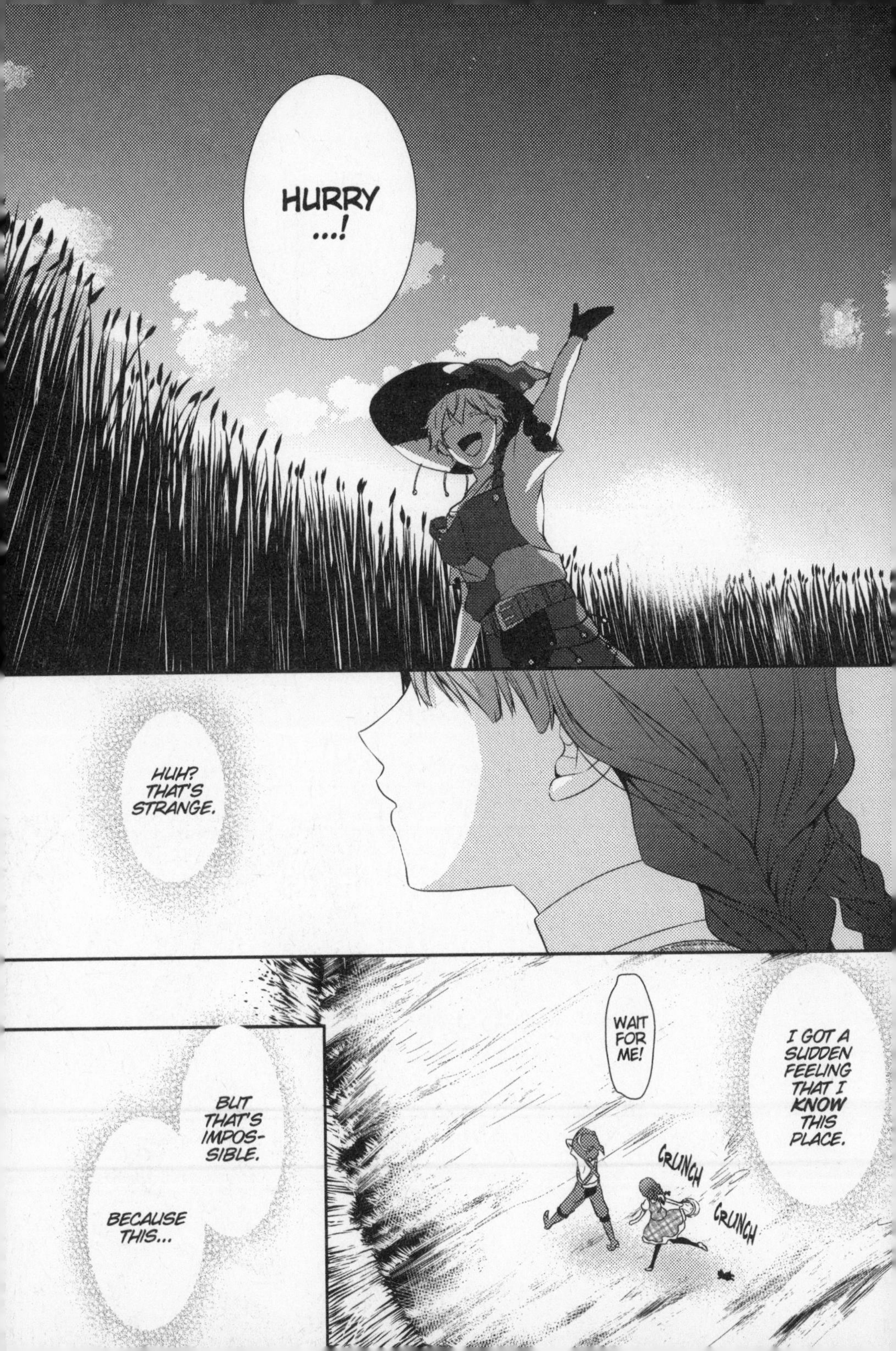
HURRY ...!
HUH? THAT'S STRANGE.
I GOT A SUDDEN FEELING THAT I KNOW THIS PLACE.
WAIT FOR ME!
CRUNCH
CRUNCH
BUT THAT'S IMPOS-SIBLE.
BECAUSE THIS...

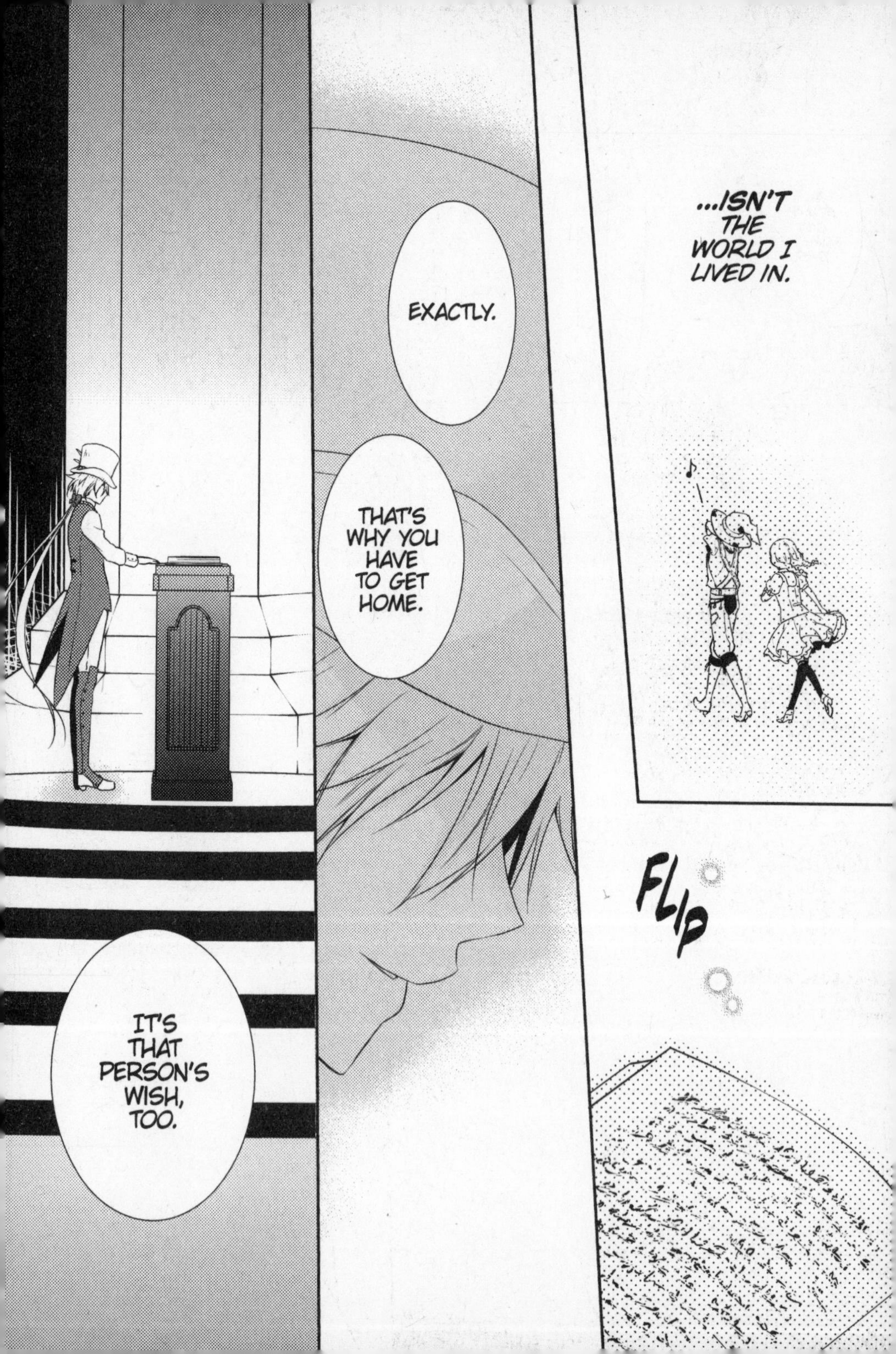
...ISN'T THE WORLD I LIVED IN.
FLIP
EXACTLY.
THAT'S WHY YOU HAVE TO GET HOME.
IT'S THAT PERSON'S WISH, TOO.

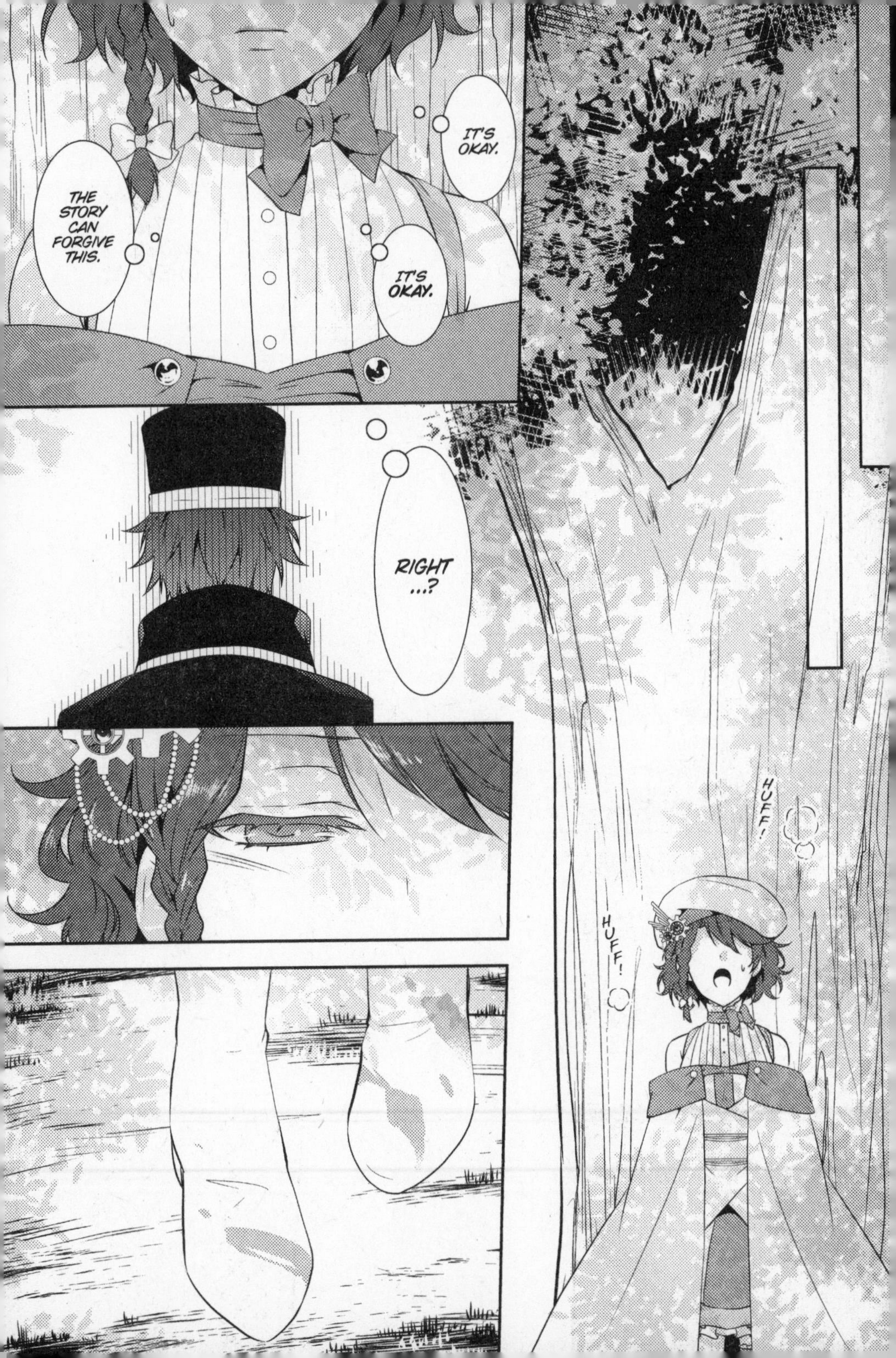
HUFF!
HUFF!
IT'S OKAY.
IT'S OKAY.
THE STORY CAN FORGIVE THIS.
RIGHT ...?

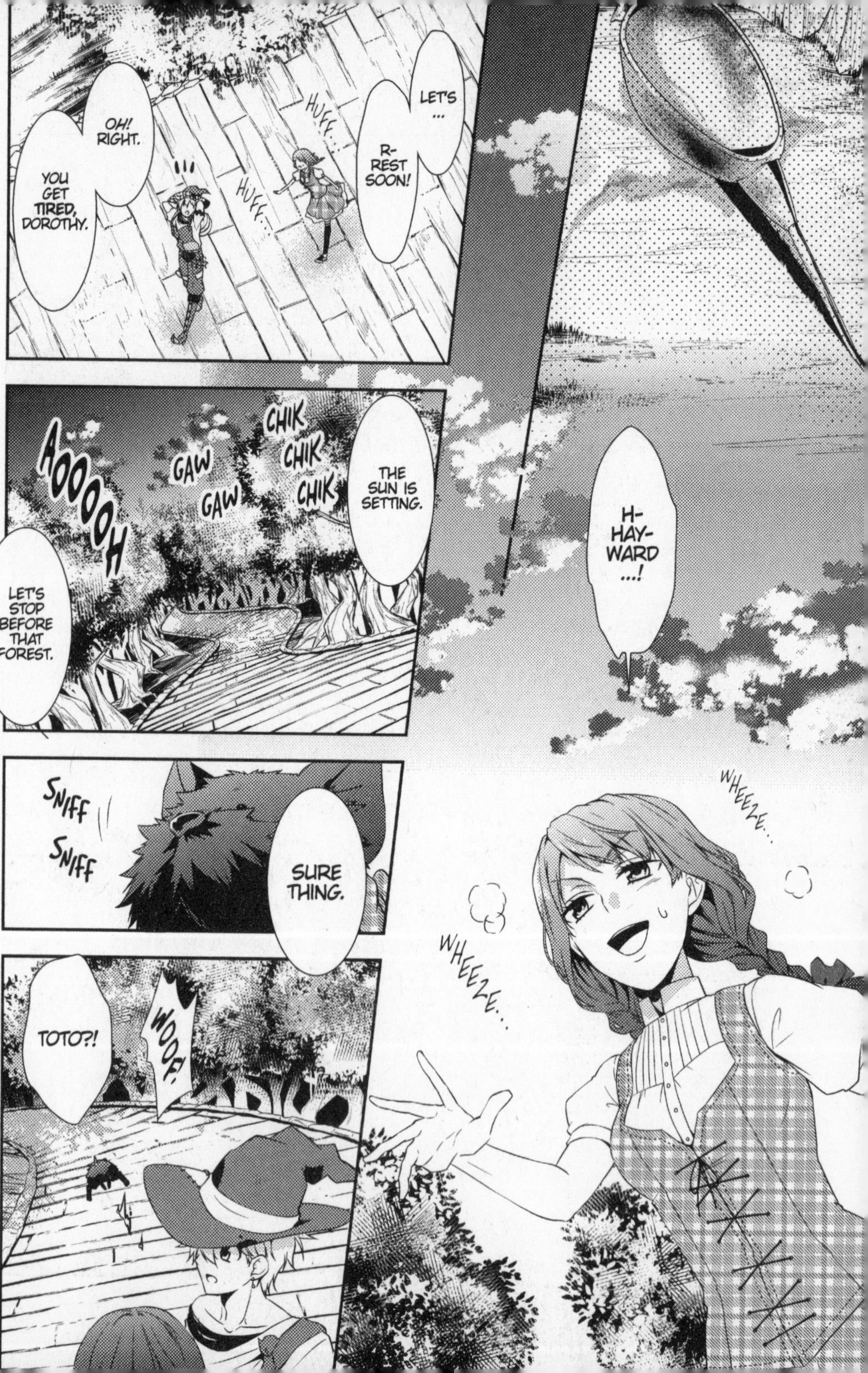
H-HAYWARD...!
WHEEZE...
WHEEZE...
LET'S... R-REST SOON!
HUFF... HUFF...
OH! RIGHT. YOU GET TIRED, DOROTHY.
THE SUN IS SETTING.
CHIK CHIK CHIK
GAW GAW
AOOOOOH
LET'S STOP BEFORE THAT FOREST.
SURE THING.
SNIFF SNIFF
WOOF!
TOTO?!

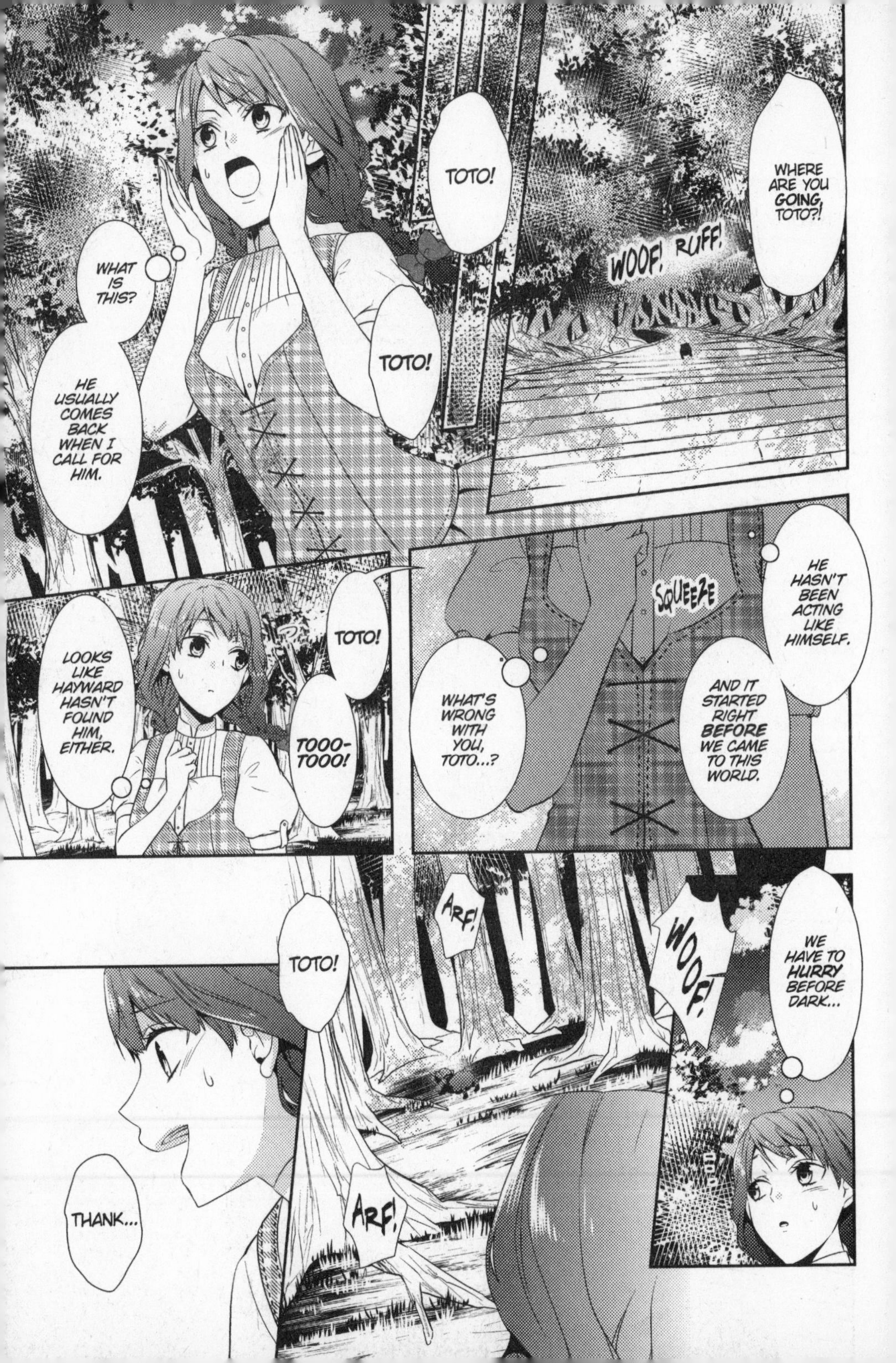
WHERE ARE YOU GOING, TOTO?!
WOOF! RUFF!
TOTO!
TOTO!
WHAT IS THIS?
HE USUALLY COMES BACK WHEN I CALL FOR HIM.
HE HASN'T BEEN ACTING LIKE HIMSELF.
AND IT STARTED RIGHT BEFORE WE CAME TO THIS WORLD.
SQUEEZE
WHAT'S WRONG WITH YOU, TOTO...?
TOTO!
TOOO-TOOO!
LOOKS LIKE HAYWARD HASN'T FOUND HIM, EITHER.
WE HAVE TO HURRY BEFORE DARK...
WOOF!
ARF!
TOTO!
ARF!
THANK...

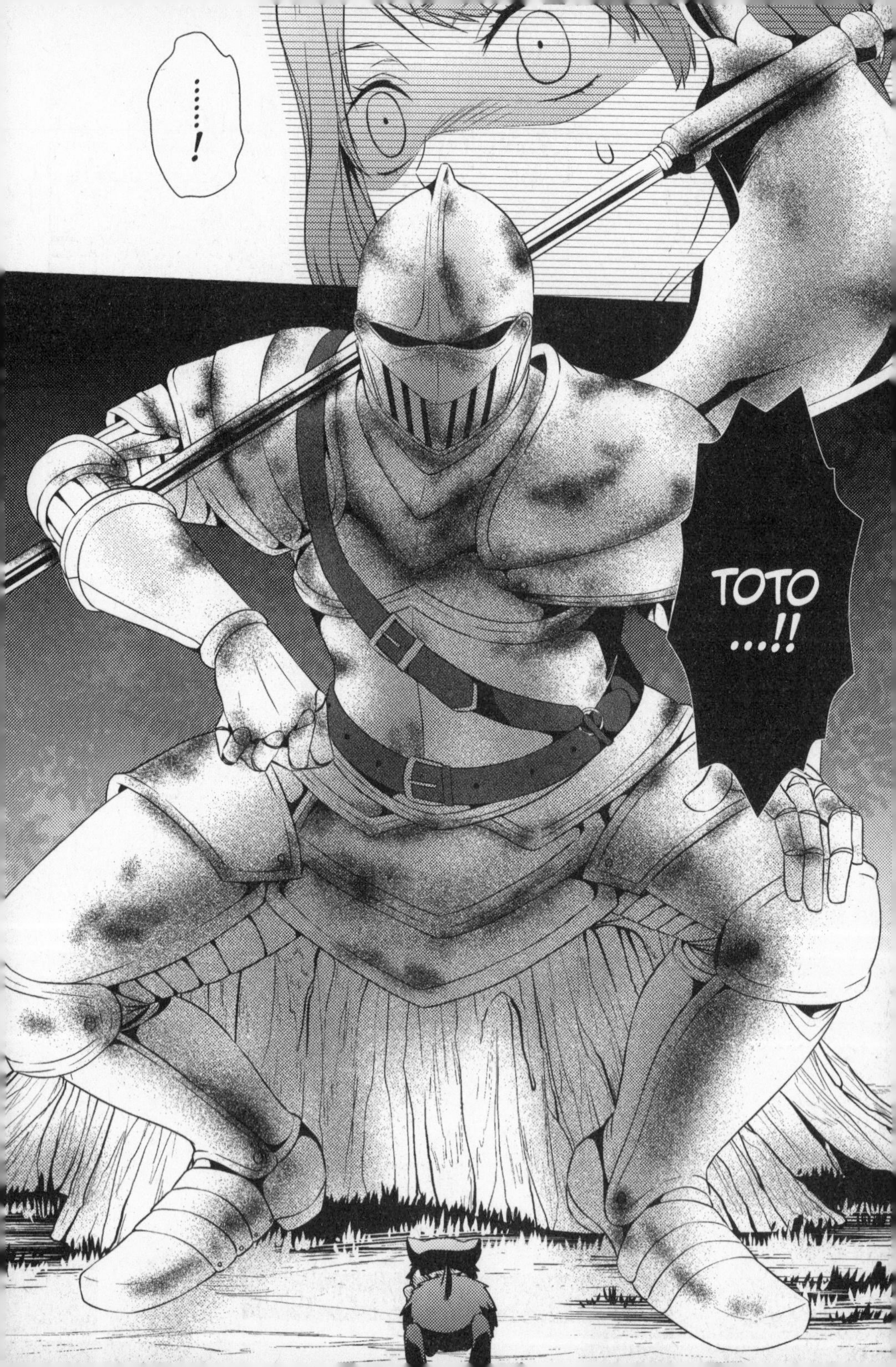

.....!
TOTO ...!!

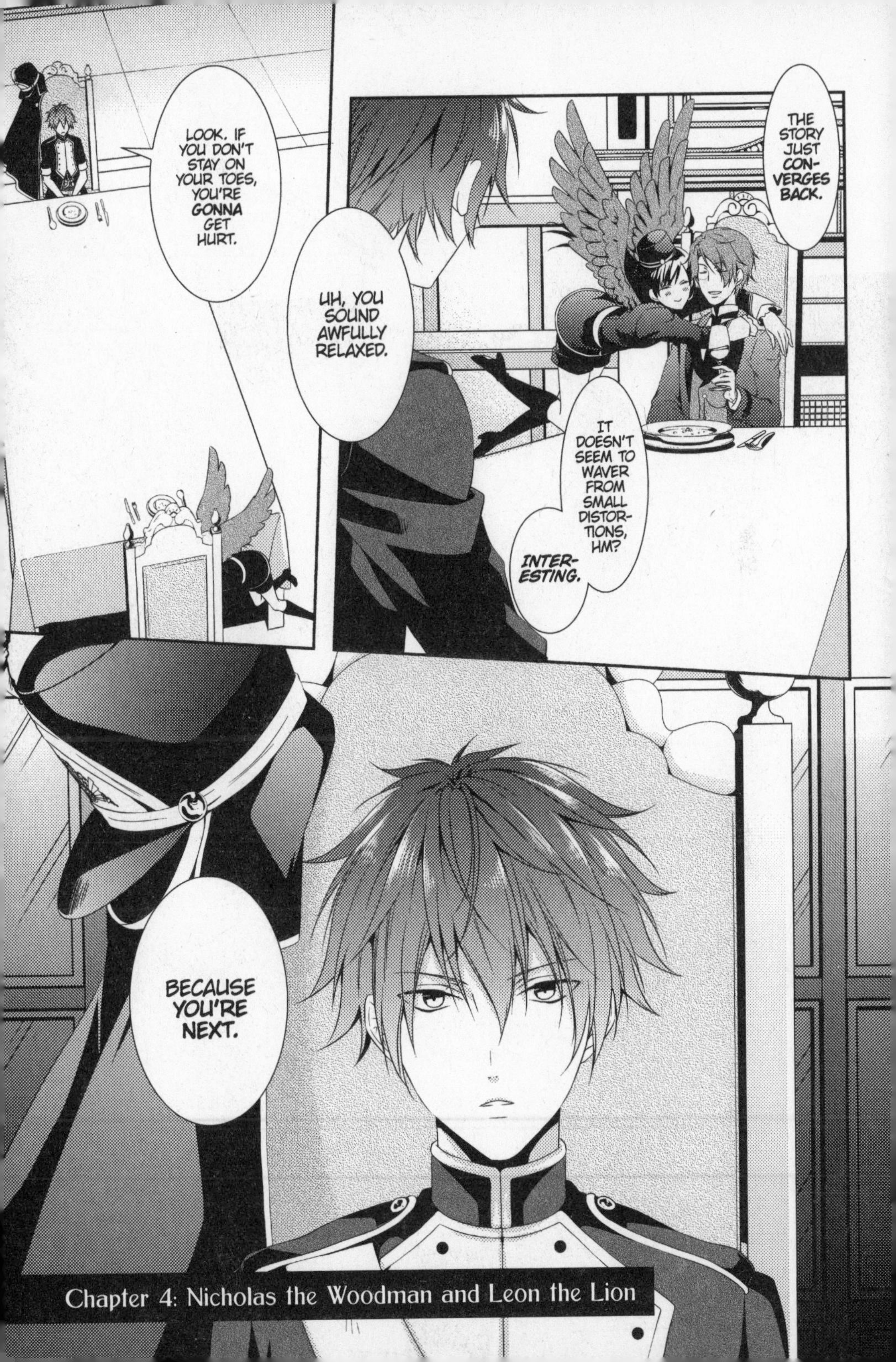
THE STORY JUST CON-VERGES BACK.
IT DOESN'T SEEM TO WAVER FROM SMALL DISTOR-TIONS, HM?
INTER-ESTING.
UH, YOU SOUND AWFULLY RELAXED.
LOOK. IF YOU DON'T STAY ON YOUR TOES, YOU'RE GONNA GET HURT.
BECAUSE YOU'RE NEXT.

Chapter 4: Nicholas the Woodman and Leon the Lion

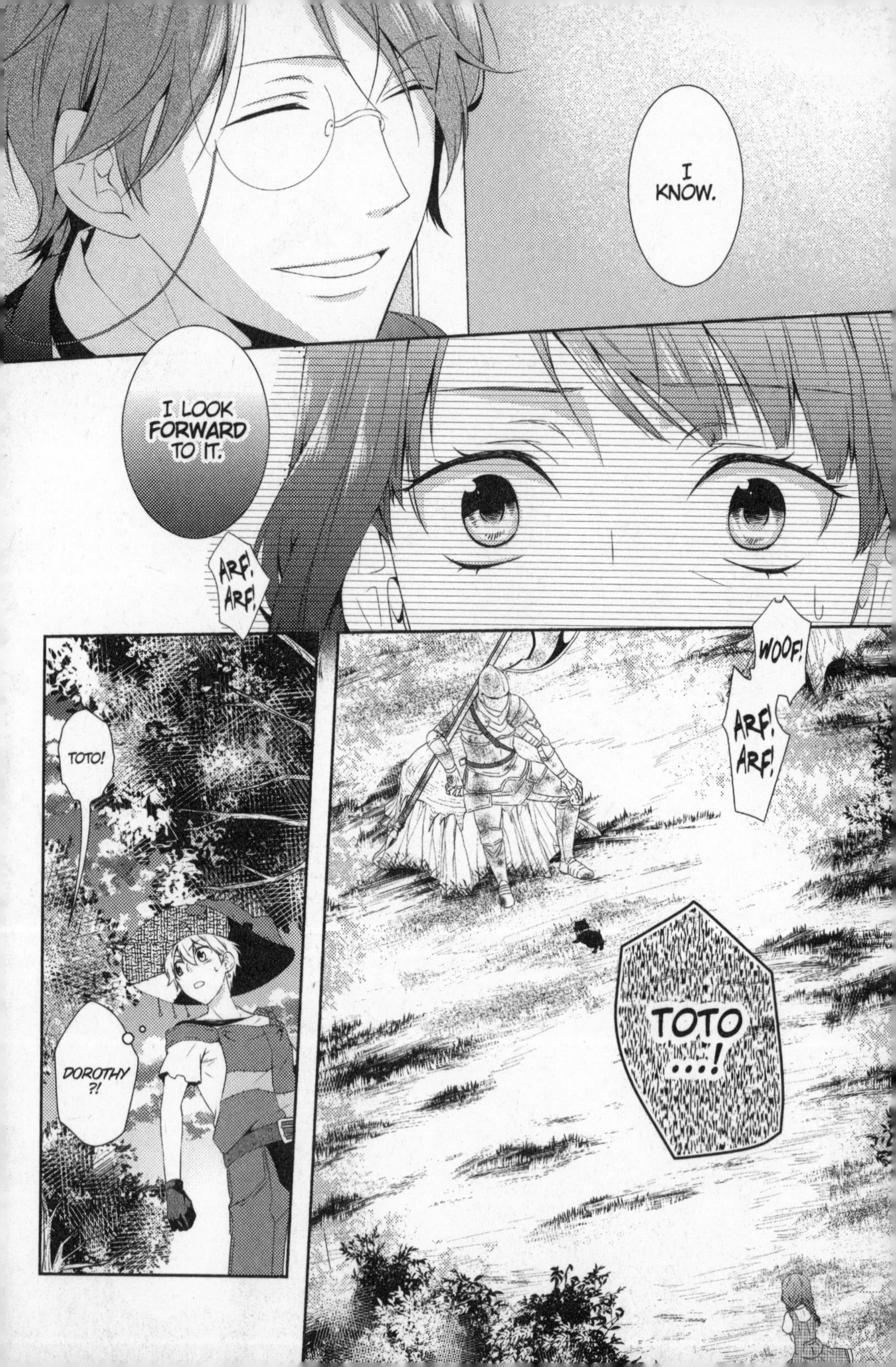
I KNOW.
I LOOK FORWARD TO IT.
ARF! ARF!
WOOF!
ARF! ARF!
TOTO ...!
TOTO!
DOROTHY ?!

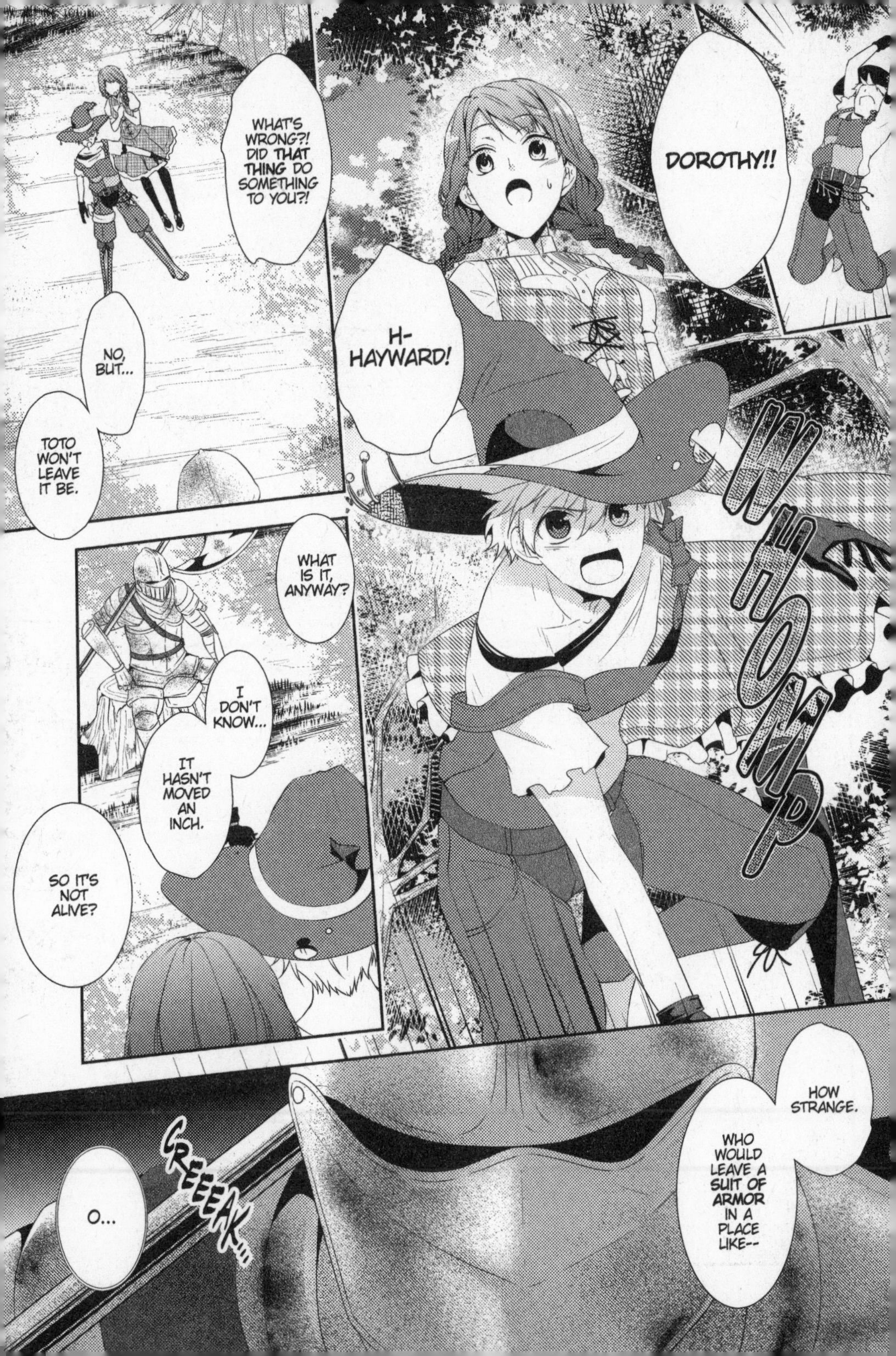
DOROTHY!!
H-HAYWARD!
WHOMP
WHAT'S WRONG?! DID THAT THING DO SOMETHING TO YOU?!
NO, BUT...
TOTO WON'T LEAVE IT BE.
WHAT IS IT, ANYWAY?
I DON'T KNOW...
IT HASN'T MOVED AN INCH.
SO IT'S NOT ALIVE?
HOW STRANGE.
WHO WOULD LEAVE A SUIT OF ARMOR IN A PLACE LIKE--
CREEEAK...
O...

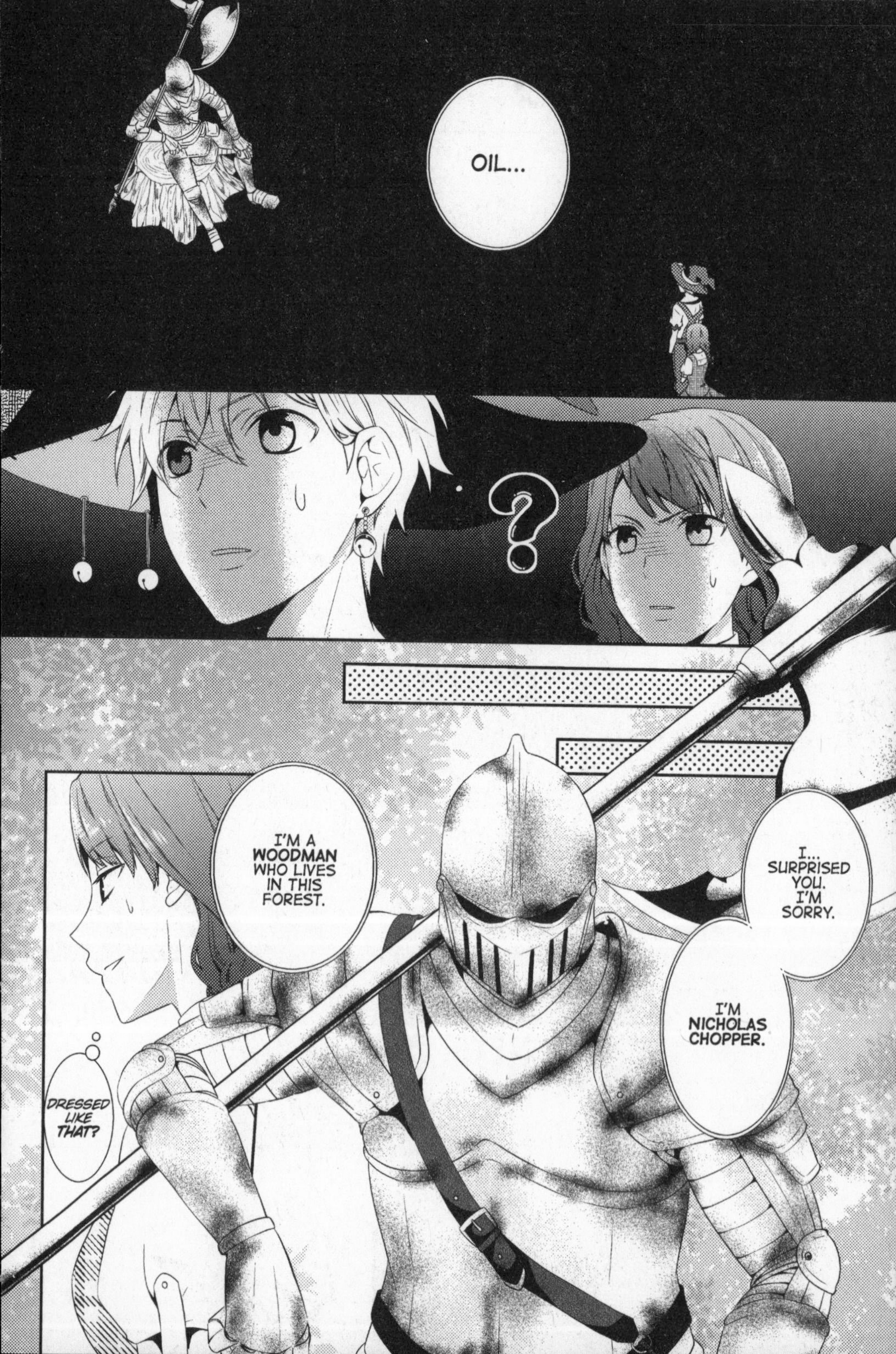
OIL...
?
I... SURPRISED YOU. I'M SORRY.
I'M NICHOLAS CHOPPER.
I'M A WOODMAN WHO LIVES IN THIS FOREST.
DRESSED LIKE THAT?

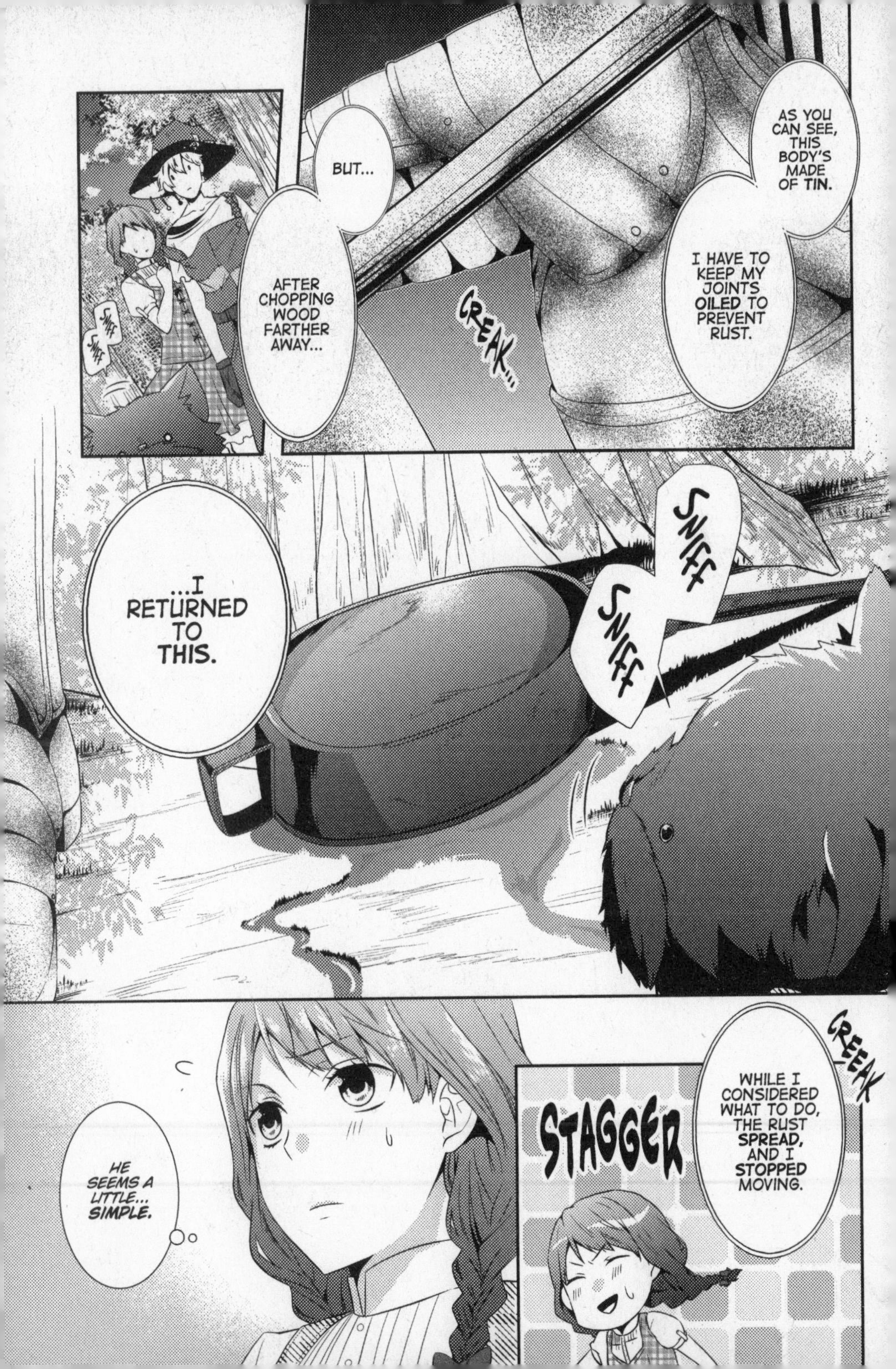
AS YOU CAN SEE, THIS BODY'S MADE OF TIN.
I HAVE TO KEEP MY JOINTS OILED TO PREVENT RUST.
CREAK...
BUT...
AFTER CHOPPING WOOD FARTHER AWAY...
SNIFF SNIFF
SNIFF SNIFF
...I RETURNED TO THIS.
CREEAK
WHILE I CONSIDERED WHAT TO DO, THE RUST SPREAD, AND I STOPPED MOVING.
STAGGER
HE SEEMS A LITTLE... SIMPLE.

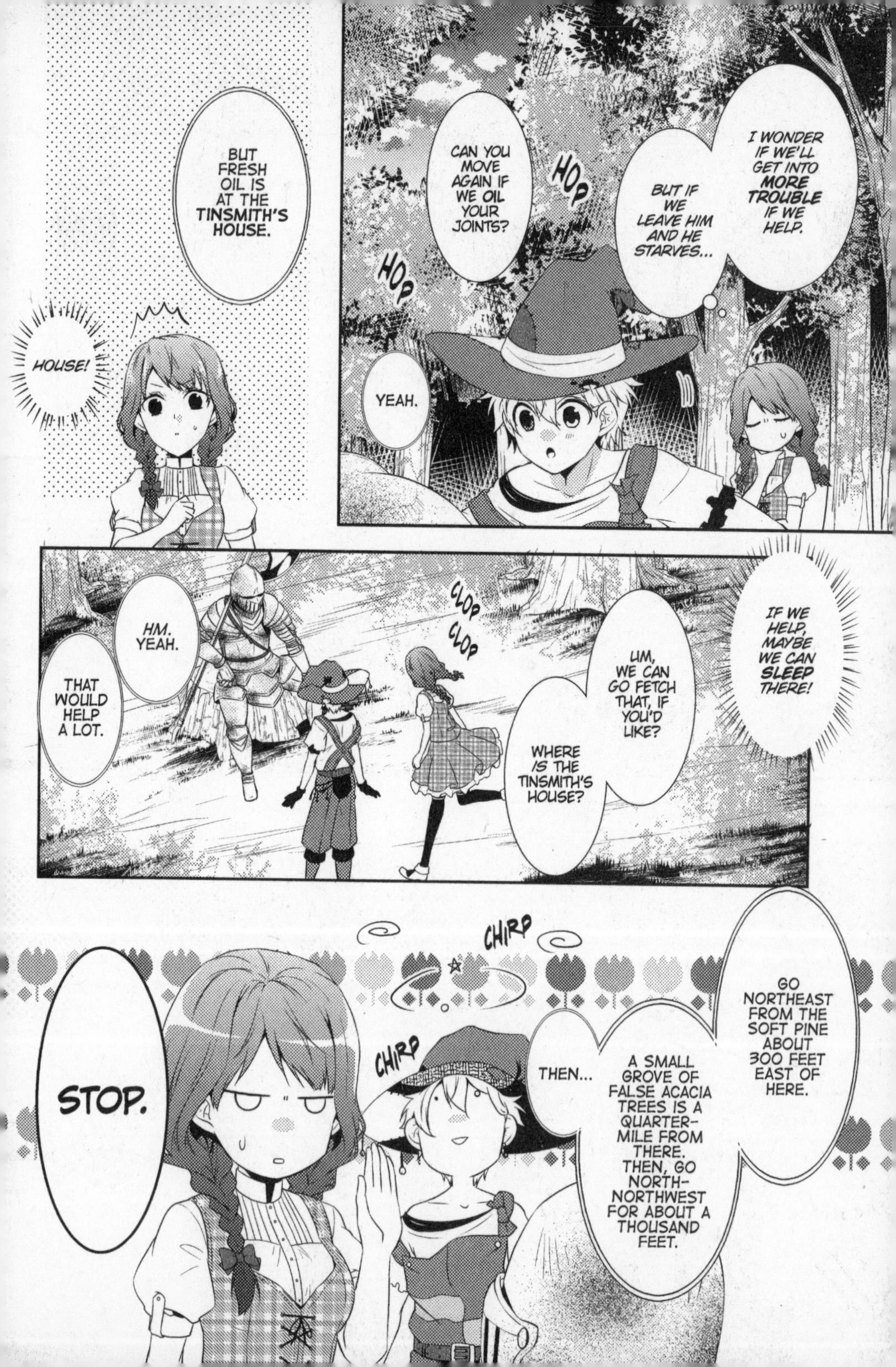
I WONDER IF WE'LL GET INTO MORE TROUBLE IF WE HELP.
BUT IF WE LEAVE HIM AND HE STARVES...
HOP
CAN YOU MOVE AGAIN IF WE OIL YOUR JOINTS?
HOP
YEAH.
BUT FRESH OIL IS AT THE TINSMITH'S HOUSE.
HOUSE!
IF WE HELP, MAYBE WE CAN SLEEP THERE!
UM, WE CAN GO FETCH THAT, IF YOU'D LIKE?
WHERE IS THE TINSMITH'S HOUSE?
CLOP
CLOP
HM. YEAH.
THAT WOULD HELP A LOT.
GO NORTHEAST FROM THE SOFT PINE ABOUT 300 FEET EAST OF HERE.
A SMALL GROVE OF FALSE ACACIA TREES IS A QUARTER-MILE FROM THERE. THEN, GO NORTH-NORTHWEST FOR ABOUT A THOUSAND FEET.
THEN...
CHIRP
CHIRP
STOP.

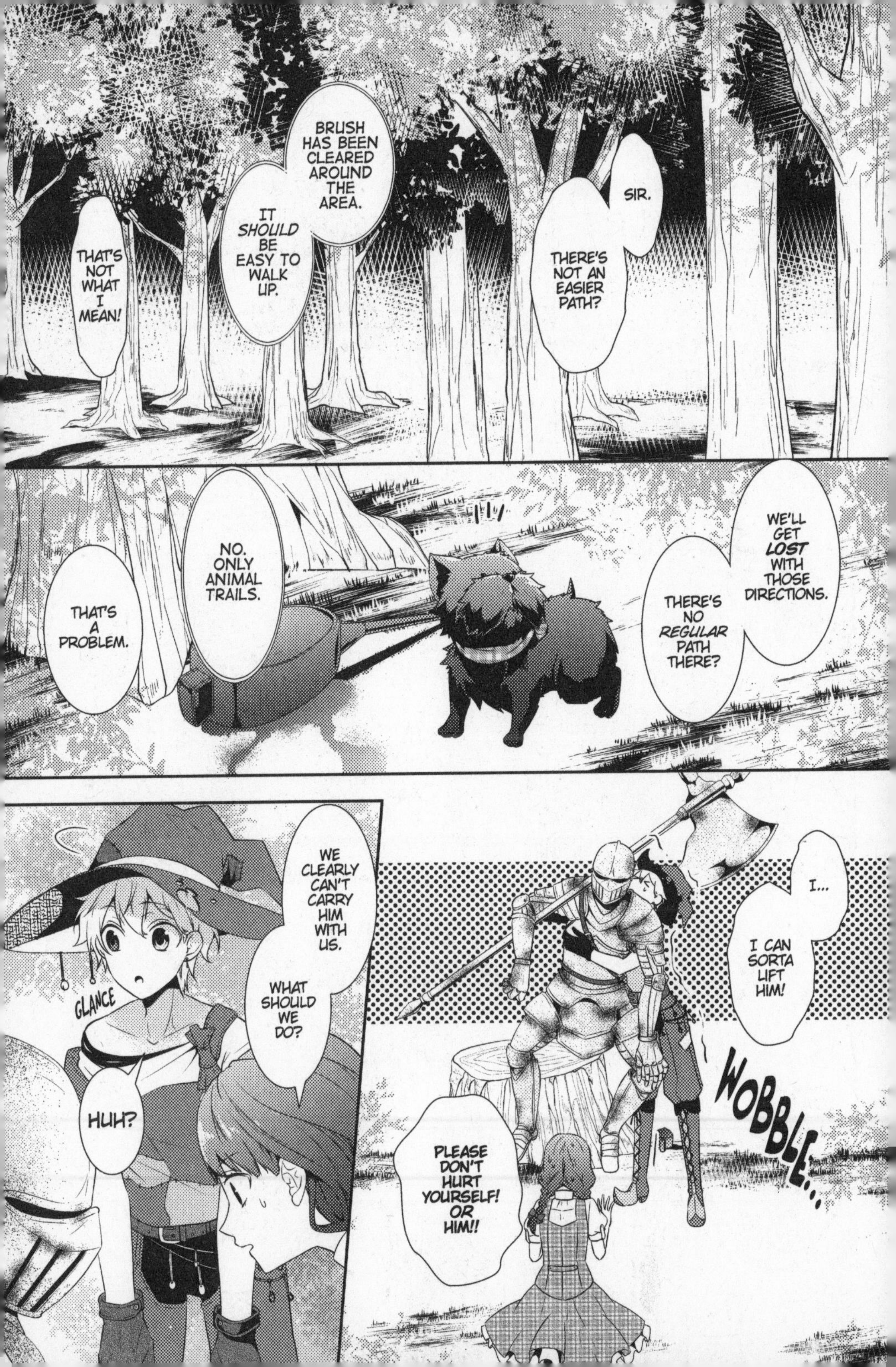
SIR.
THERE'S NOT AN EASIER PATH?
BRUSH HAS BEEN CLEARED AROUND THE AREA.
IT *SHOULD* BE EASY TO WALK UP.
THAT'S NOT WHAT I MEAN!
WE'LL GET ***LOST*** WITH THOSE DIRECTIONS.
THERE'S NO *REGULAR* PATH THERE?
NO. ONLY ANIMAL TRAILS.
THAT'S A PROBLEM.
I...
I CAN SORTA LIFT HIM!
WOBBLE...
PLEASE DON'T HURT YOURSELF! OR HIM!!
WE CLEARLY CAN'T CARRY HIM WITH US.
WHAT SHOULD WE DO?
GLANCE
HUH?

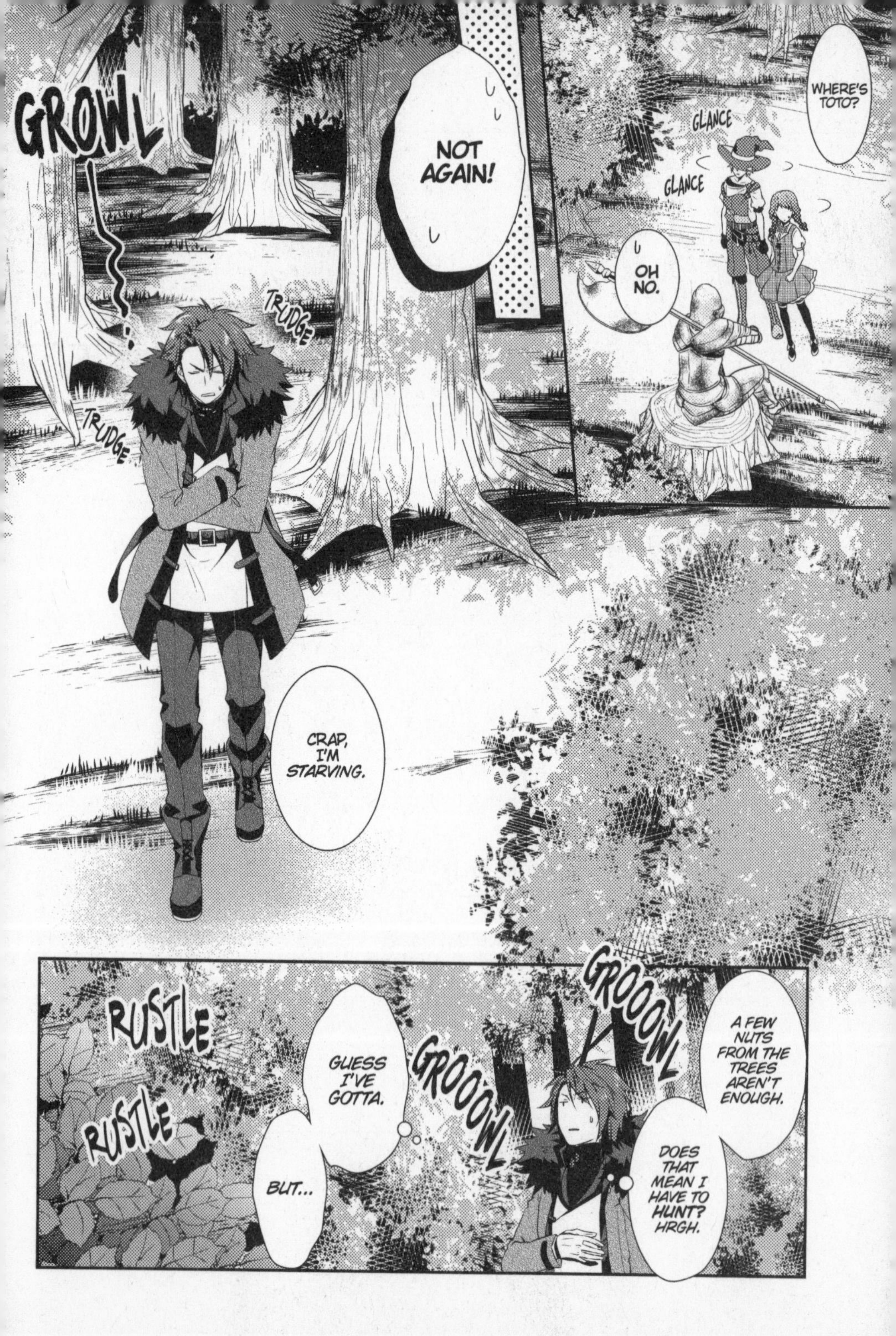
WHERE'S TOTO?
GLANCE
GLANCE
OH NO.
NOT AGAIN!
GROWL
TRUDGE
TRUDGE
CRAP, I'M STARVING.
GROOOWL
A FEW NUTS FROM THE TREES AREN'T ENOUGH.
DOES THAT MEAN I HAVE TO HUNT? HRGH.
GROOOWL
GUESS I'VE GOTTA.
BUT...
RUSTLE
RUSTLE

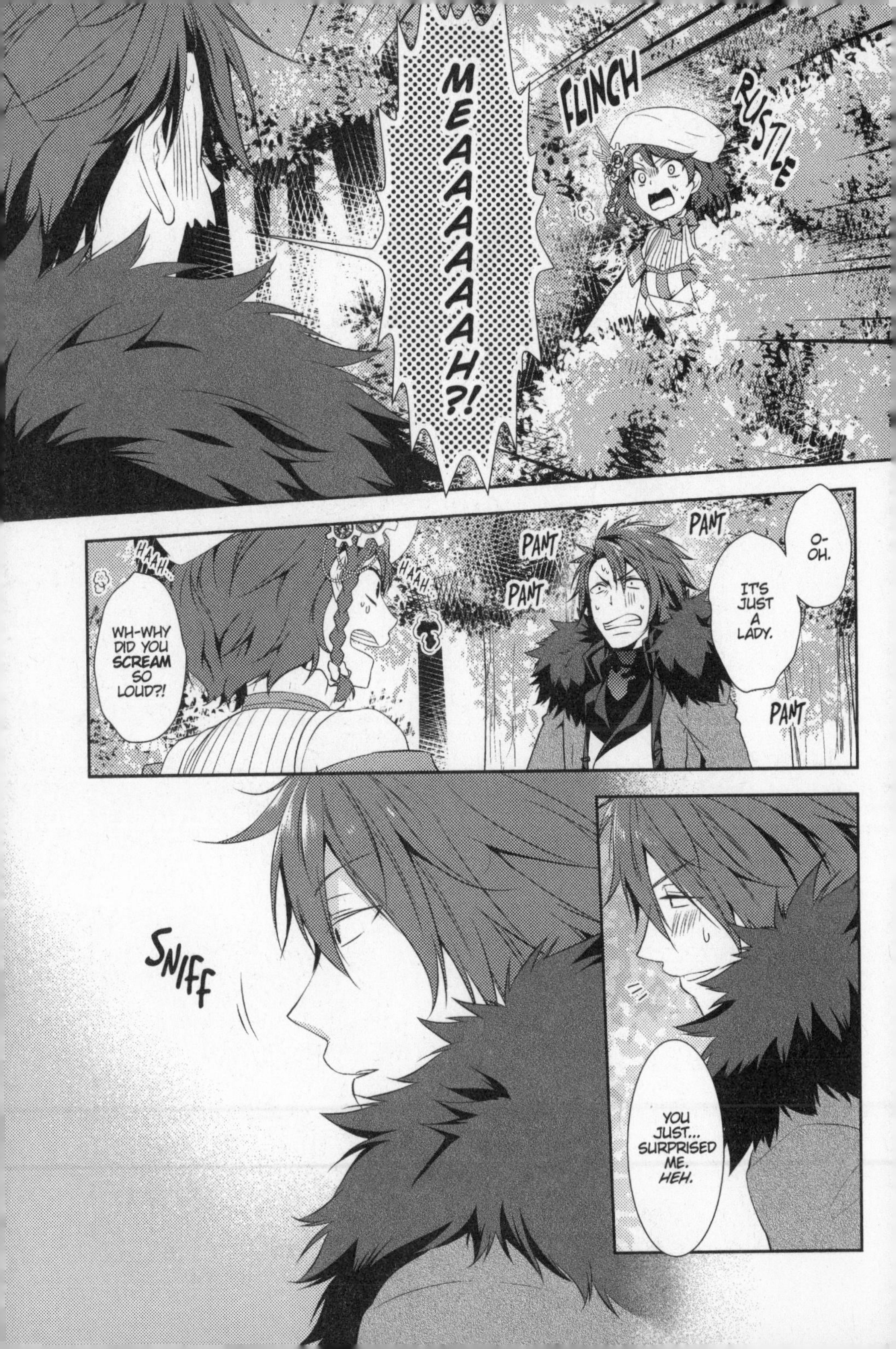
RUSTLE
FLINCH
MEAAAAAAH?!
PANT
O-OH.
IT'S JUST A LADY.
PANT
PANT
PANT
HAAH
WH-WHY DID YOU SCREAM SO LOUD?!
HAAH...
YOU JUST... SURPRISED ME. *HEH.*
SNIFF

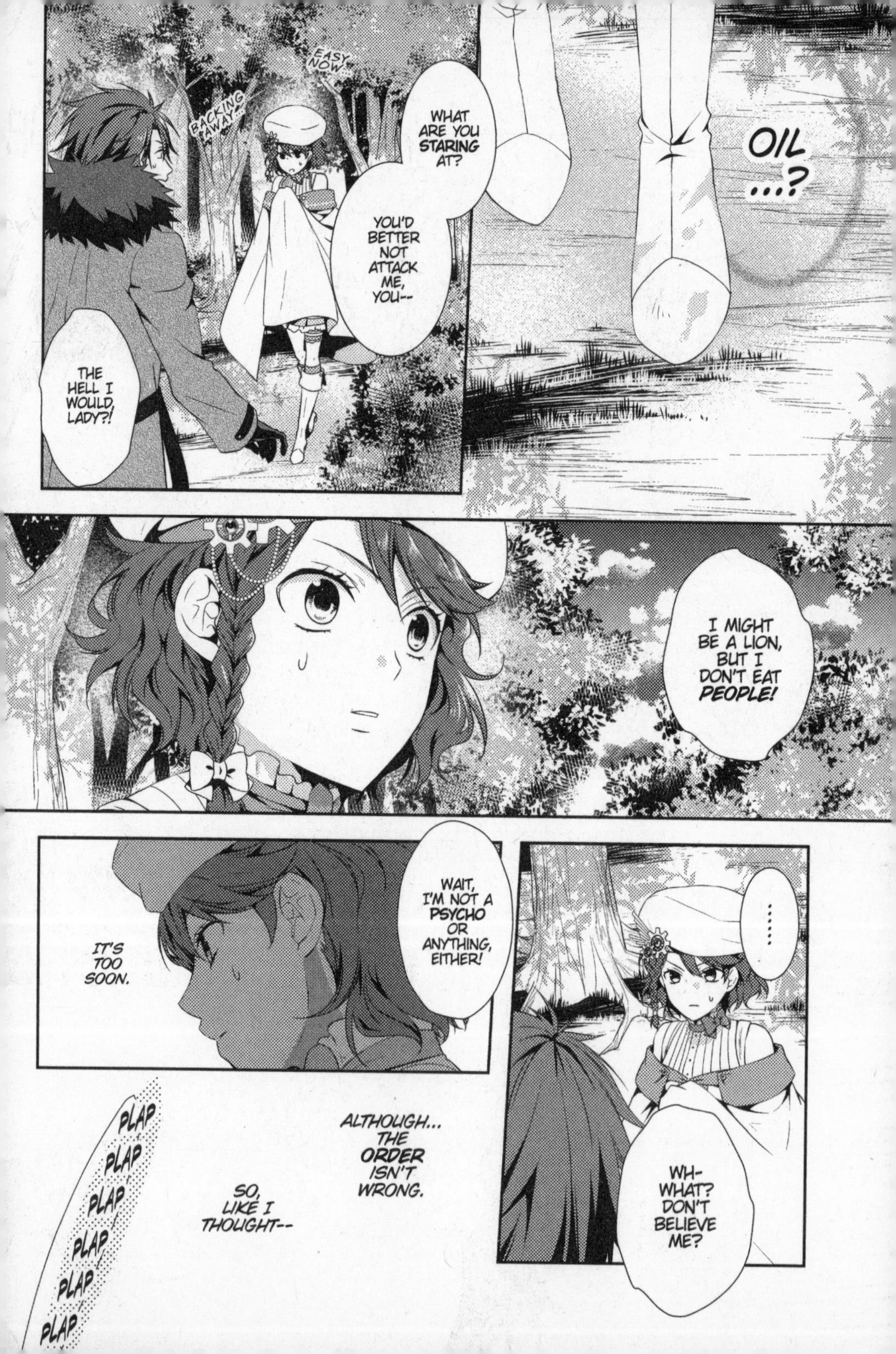
OIL ...?
EASY NOW
WHAT ARE YOU STARING AT?
BACKING AWAY...
YOU'D BETTER NOT ATTACK ME, YOU--
THE HELL I WOULD, LADY?!
I MIGHT BE A LION, BUT I DON'T EAT PEOPLE!
......
WH- WHAT? DON'T BELIEVE ME?
WAIT, I'M NOT A PSYCHO OR ANYTHING, EITHER!
IT'S TOO SOON.
ALTHOUGH... THE ORDER ISN'T WRONG.
SO, LIKE I THOUGHT--
PLAP PLAP PLAP PLAP PLAP PLAP

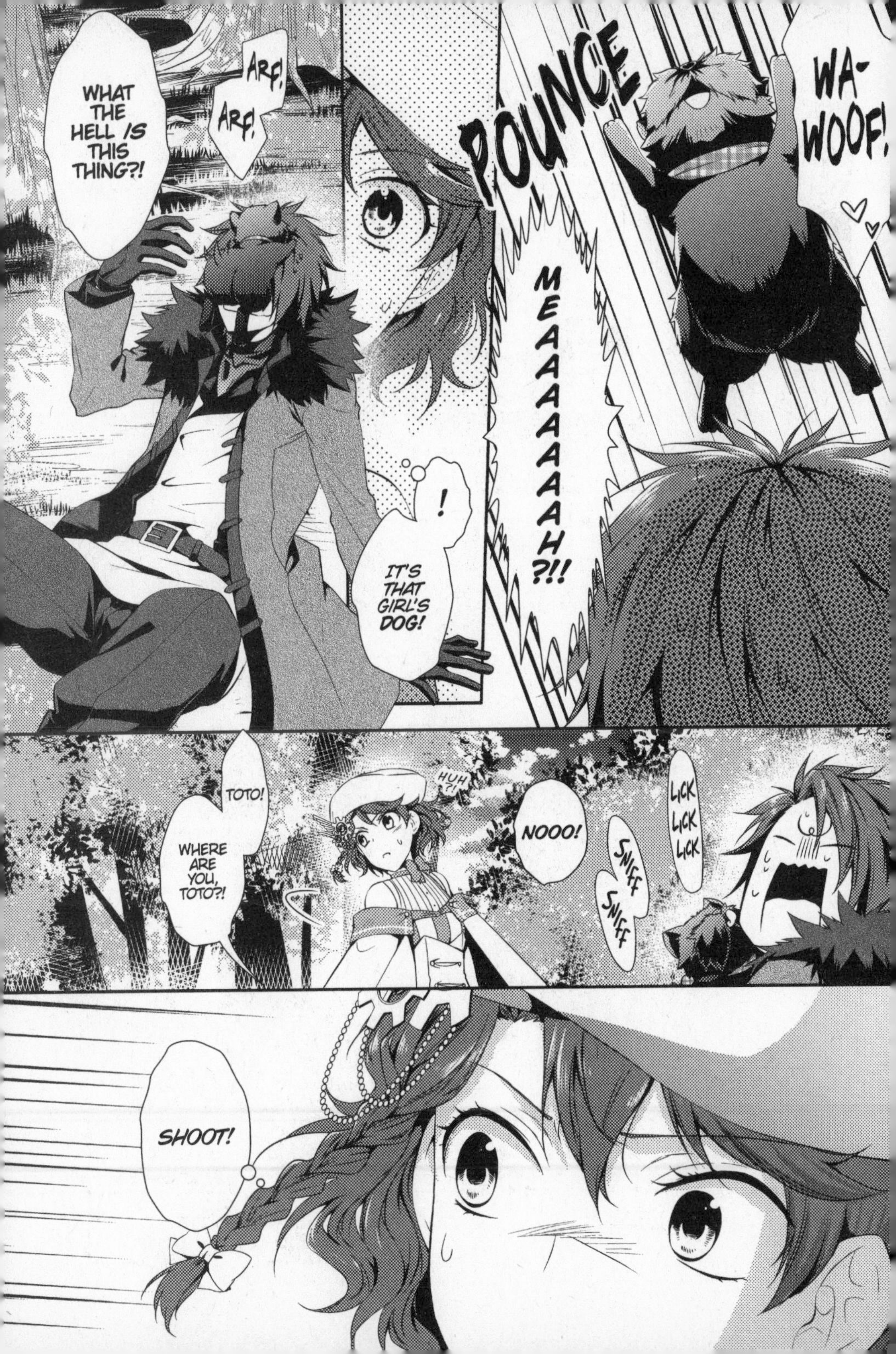
WA-WOOF!
POUNCE
MEAAAAAAAH?!!
ARF!
ARF!
WHAT THE HELL IS THIS THING?!
!
IT'S THAT GIRL'S DOG!
LICK LICK LICK
SNIFF SNIFF
NOOO!
HUH?!
TOTO!
WHERE ARE YOU, TOTO?!
SHOOT!

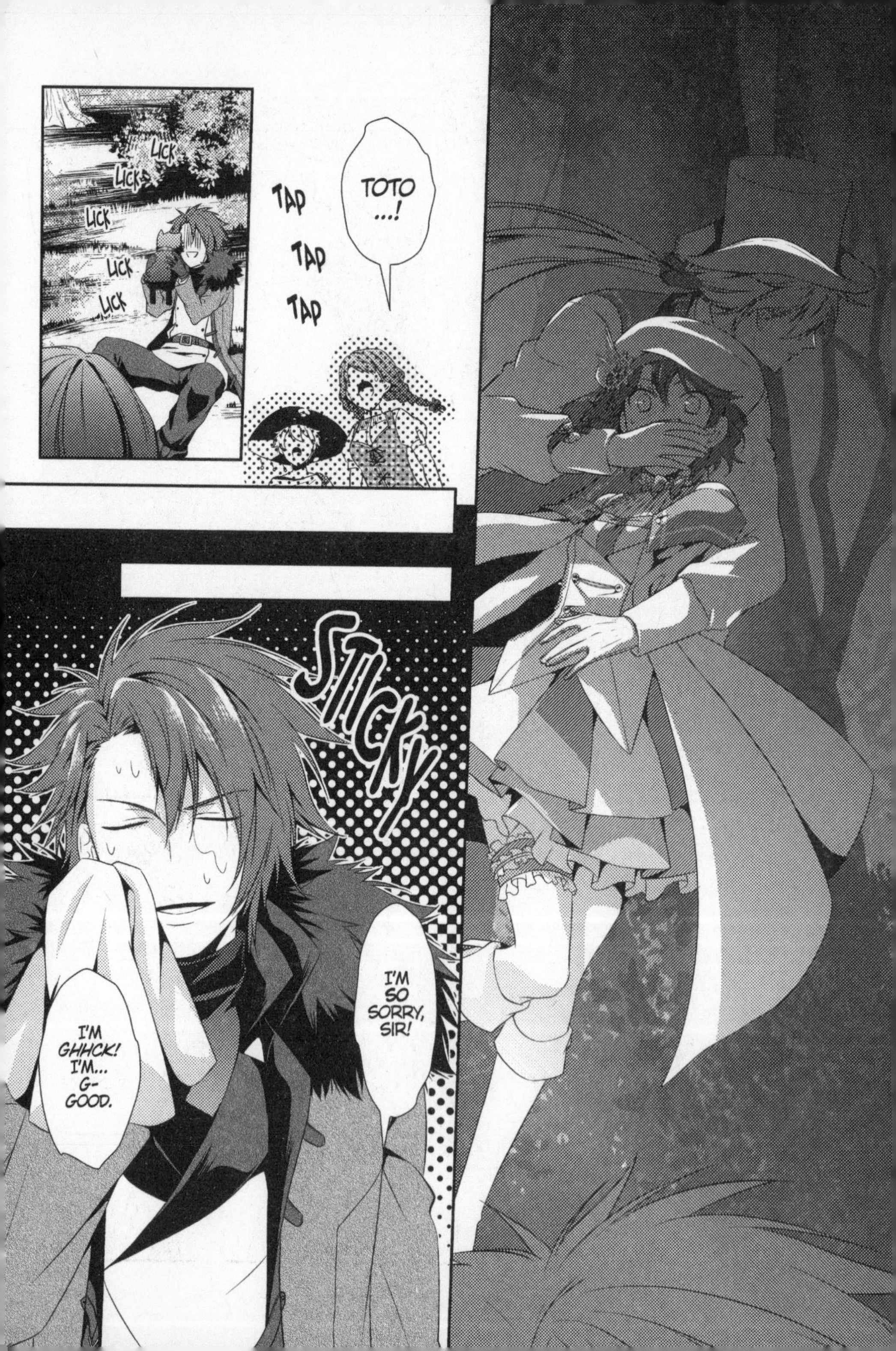
TOTO ...!
TAP
TAP
TAP
LICK
LICK
LICK
LICK
LICK
STICKY
I'M SO SORRY, SIR!
I'M GHHCK! I'M... G-GOOD.

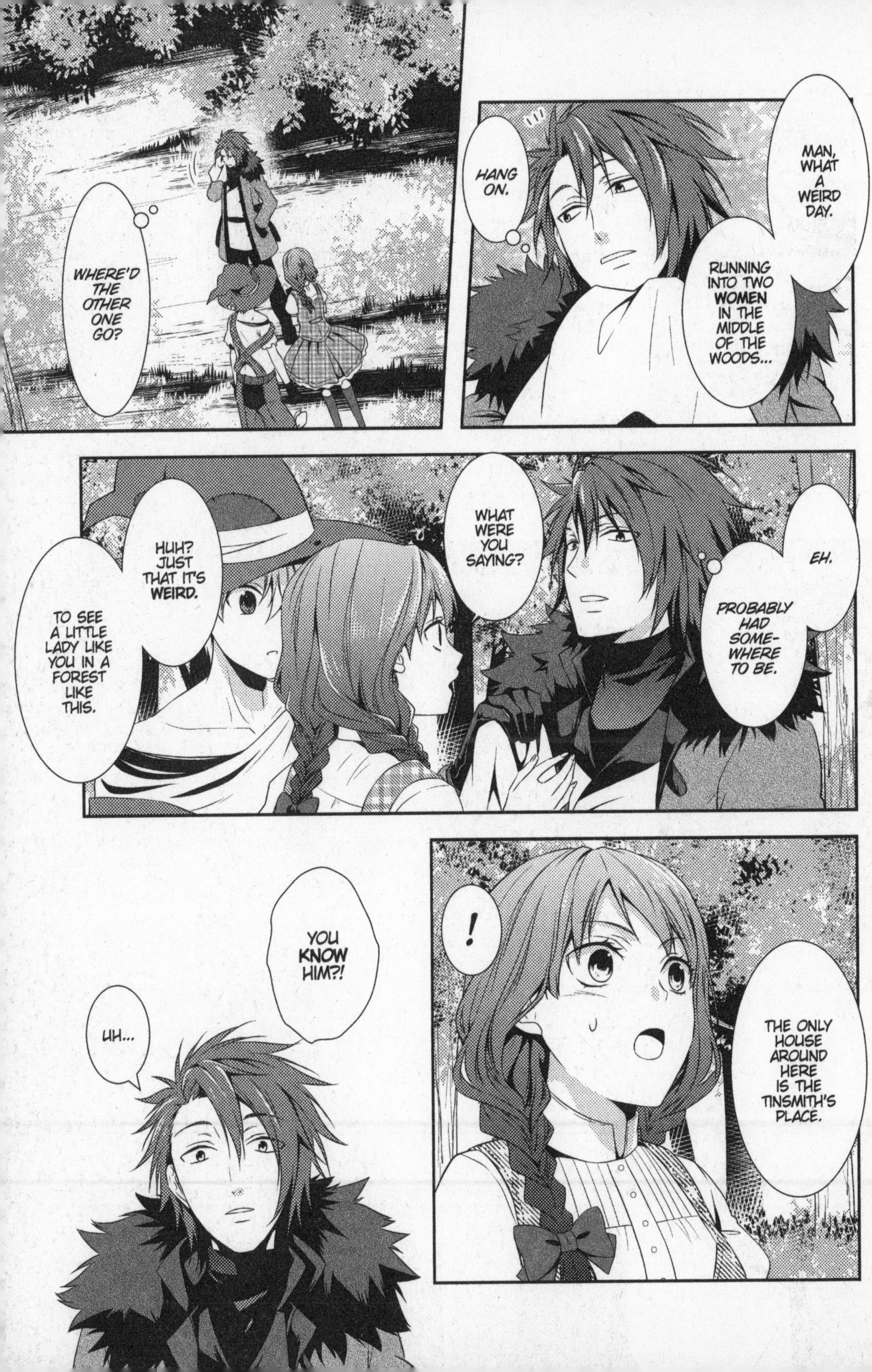
MAN, WHAT A WEIRD DAY.
RUNNING INTO TWO WOMEN IN THE MIDDLE OF THE WOODS...
HANG ON.
WHERE'D THE OTHER ONE GO?
EH.
PROBABLY HAD SOMEWHERE TO BE.
WHAT WERE YOU SAYING?
HUH? JUST THAT IT'S WEIRD.
TO SEE A LITTLE LADY LIKE YOU IN A FOREST LIKE THIS.
THE ONLY HOUSE AROUND HERE IS THE TINSMITH'S PLACE.
!
YOU KNOW HIM?!
UH...

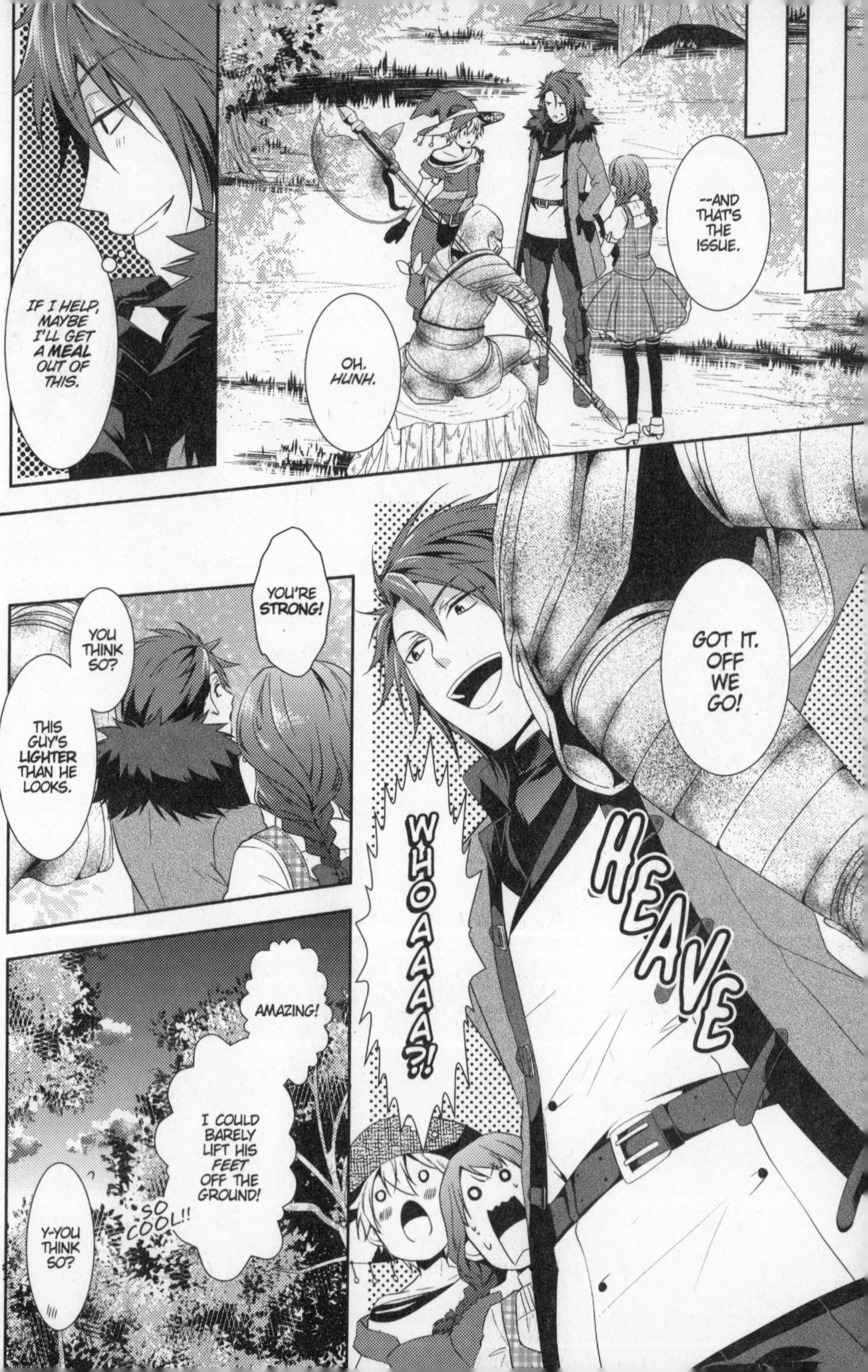
--AND THAT'S THE ISSUE.
OH. HUNH.
IF I HELP, MAYBE I'LL GET A MEAL OUT OF THIS.
GOT IT. OFF WE GO!
HEAVE
WHOAAAAA?!
YOU'RE STRONG!
YOU THINK SO?
THIS GUY'S LIGHTER THAN HE LOOKS.
AMAZING!
I COULD BARELY LIFT HIS FEET OFF THE GROUND!
SO COOL!!
Y-YOU THINK SO?

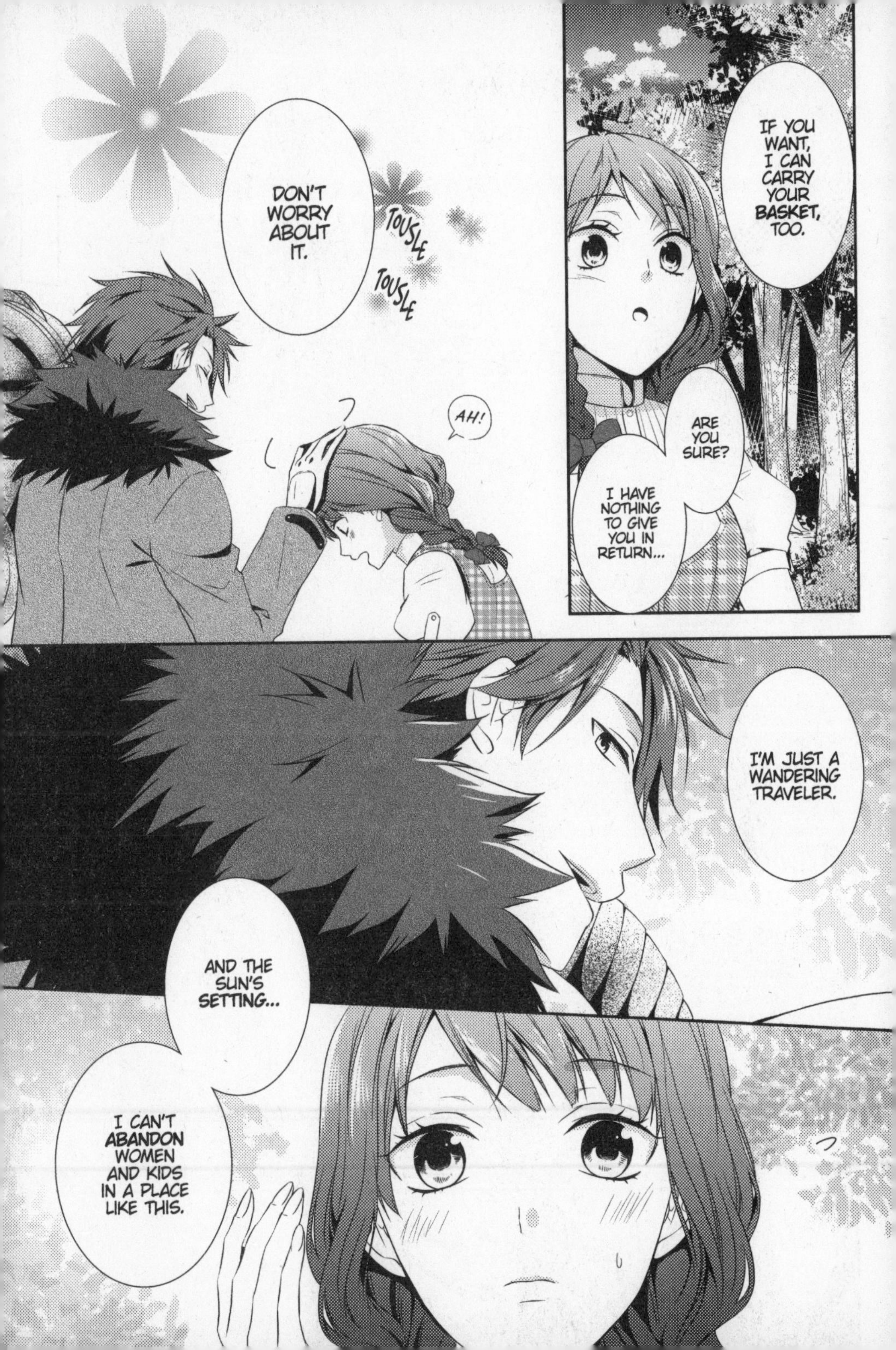
IF YOU WANT, I CAN CARRY YOUR BASKET, TOO.
ARE YOU SURE?
I HAVE NOTHING TO GIVE YOU IN RETURN...
DON'T WORRY ABOUT IT.
TOUSLE
TOUSLE
AH!
I'M JUST A WANDERING TRAVELER.
AND THE SUN'S SETTING...
I CAN'T ABANDON WOMEN AND KIDS IN A PLACE LIKE THIS.

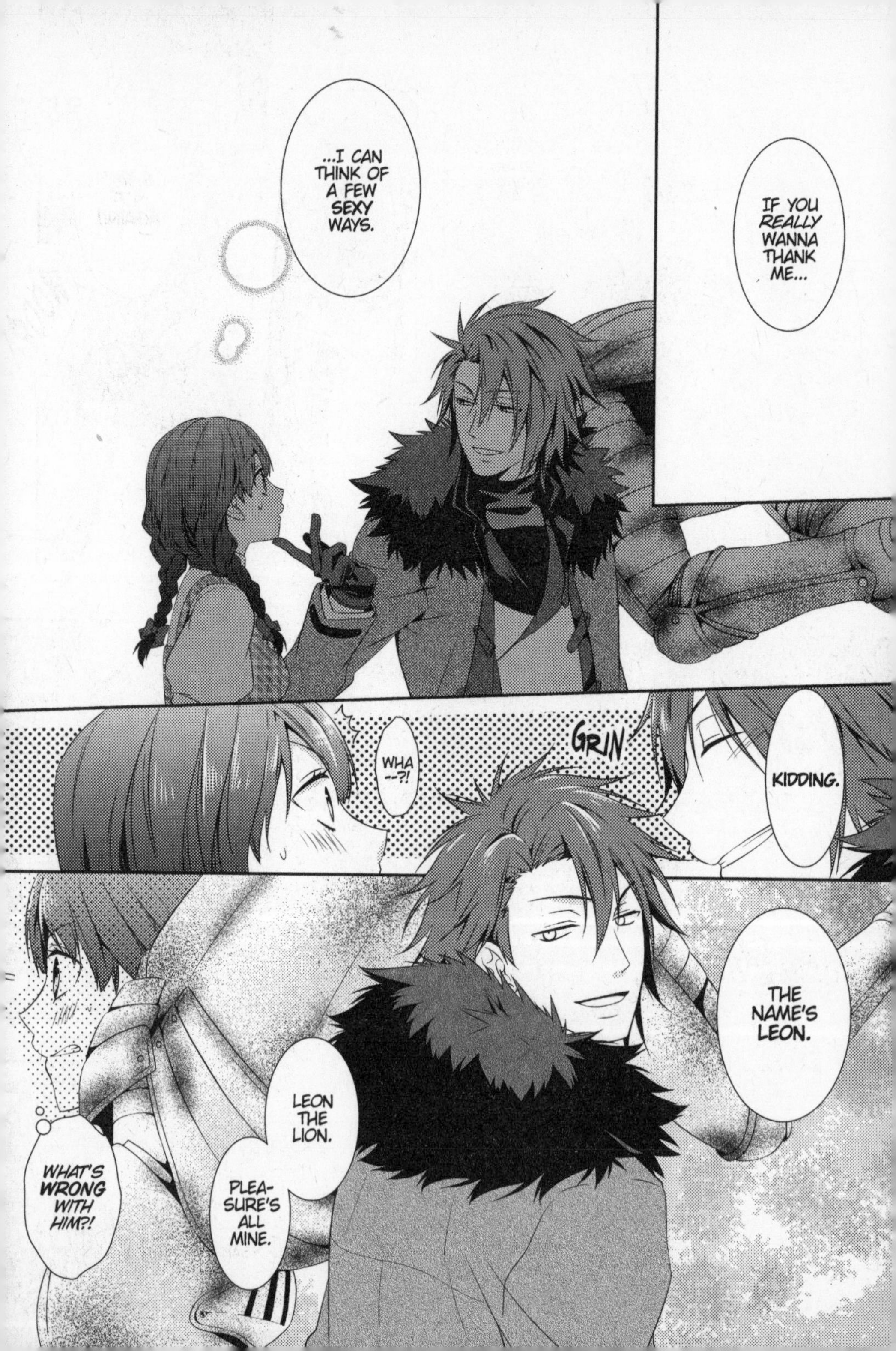
IF YOU REALLY WANNA THANK ME...
...I CAN THINK OF A FEW SEXY WAYS.
KIDDING.
GRIN
WHA--?!
THE NAME'S LEON.
LEON THE LION.
PLEA-SURE'S ALL MINE.
WHAT'S WRONG WITH HIM?!

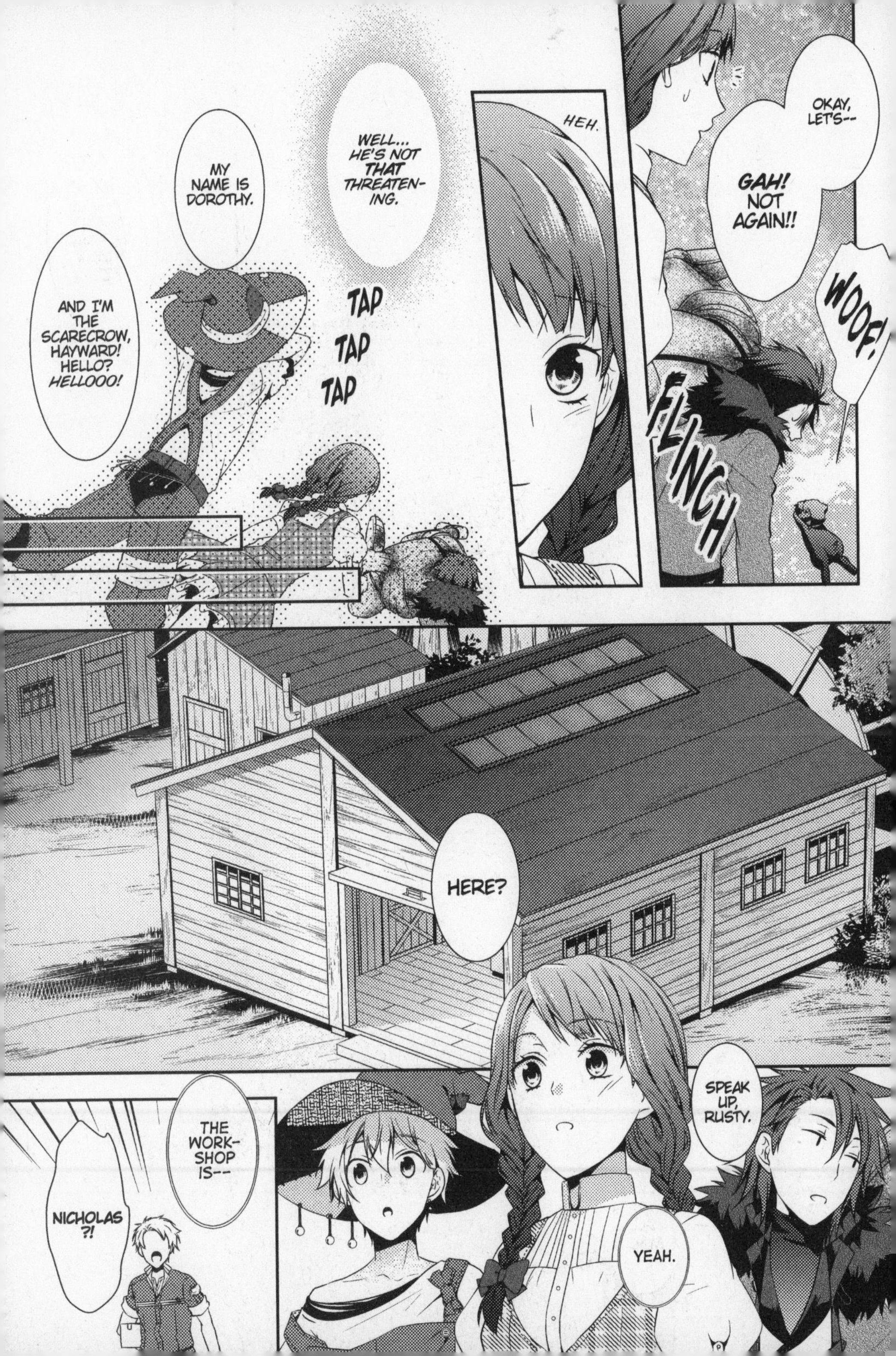
OKAY, LET'S--
GAH! NOT AGAIN!!
WOOF!
FLINCH
HEH.
WELL... HE'S NOT THAT THREATEN-ING.
MY NAME IS DOROTHY.
TAP TAP TAP
AND I'M THE SCARECROW, HAYWARD! HELLO? HELLOOO!
HERE?
SPEAK UP, RUSTY.
YEAH.
THE WORK-SHOP IS--
NICHOLAS ?!

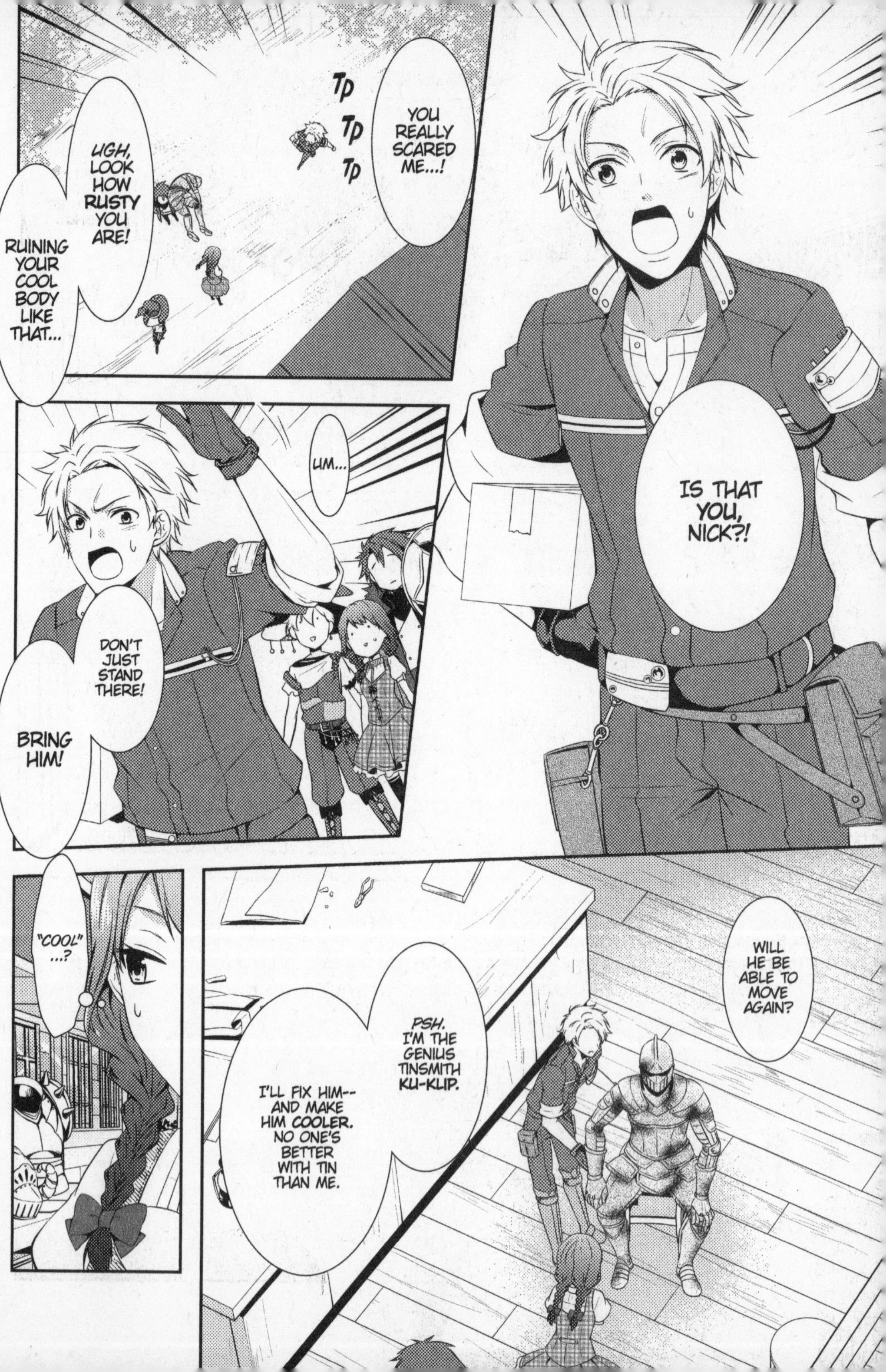
IS THAT YOU, NICK?!
YOU REALLY SCARED ME...!
Tp Tp Tp
UGH, LOOK HOW RUSTY YOU ARE!
RUINING YOUR COOL BODY LIKE THAT...
UM...
DON'T JUST STAND THERE!
BRING HIM!
WILL HE BE ABLE TO MOVE AGAIN?
PSH. I'M THE GENIUS TINSMITH KU-KLIP.
I'LL FIX HIM-- AND MAKE HIM COOLER. NO ONE'S BETTER WITH TIN THAN ME.
"COOL" ...?

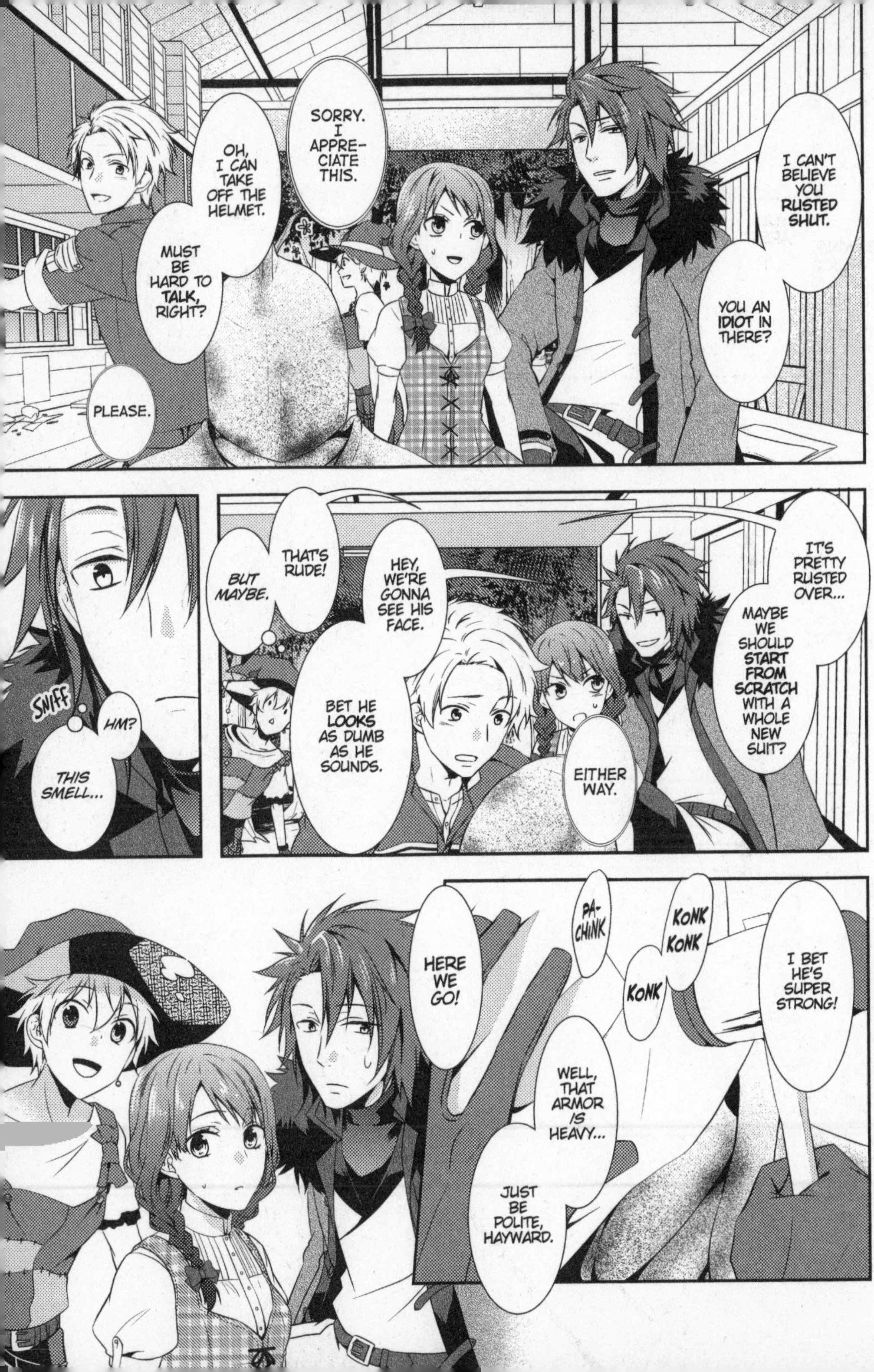
I CAN'T BELIEVE YOU RUSTED SHUT.
YOU AN IDIOT IN THERE?
SORRY. I APPRECIATE THIS.
OH, I CAN TAKE OFF THE HELMET.
MUST BE HARD TO TALK, RIGHT?
PLEASE.
IT'S PRETTY RUSTED OVER...
MAYBE WE SHOULD START FROM SCRATCH WITH A WHOLE NEW SUIT?
EITHER WAY.
HEY, WE'RE GONNA SEE HIS FACE.
THAT'S RUDE!
BUT MAYBE.
BET HE LOOKS AS DUMB AS HE SOUNDS.
SNIFF
HM?
THIS SMELL...
I BET HE'S SUPER STRONG!
KONK KONK
PA-CHINK
KONK
HERE WE GO!
WELL, THAT ARMOR IS HEAVY...
JUST BE POLITE, HAYWARD.

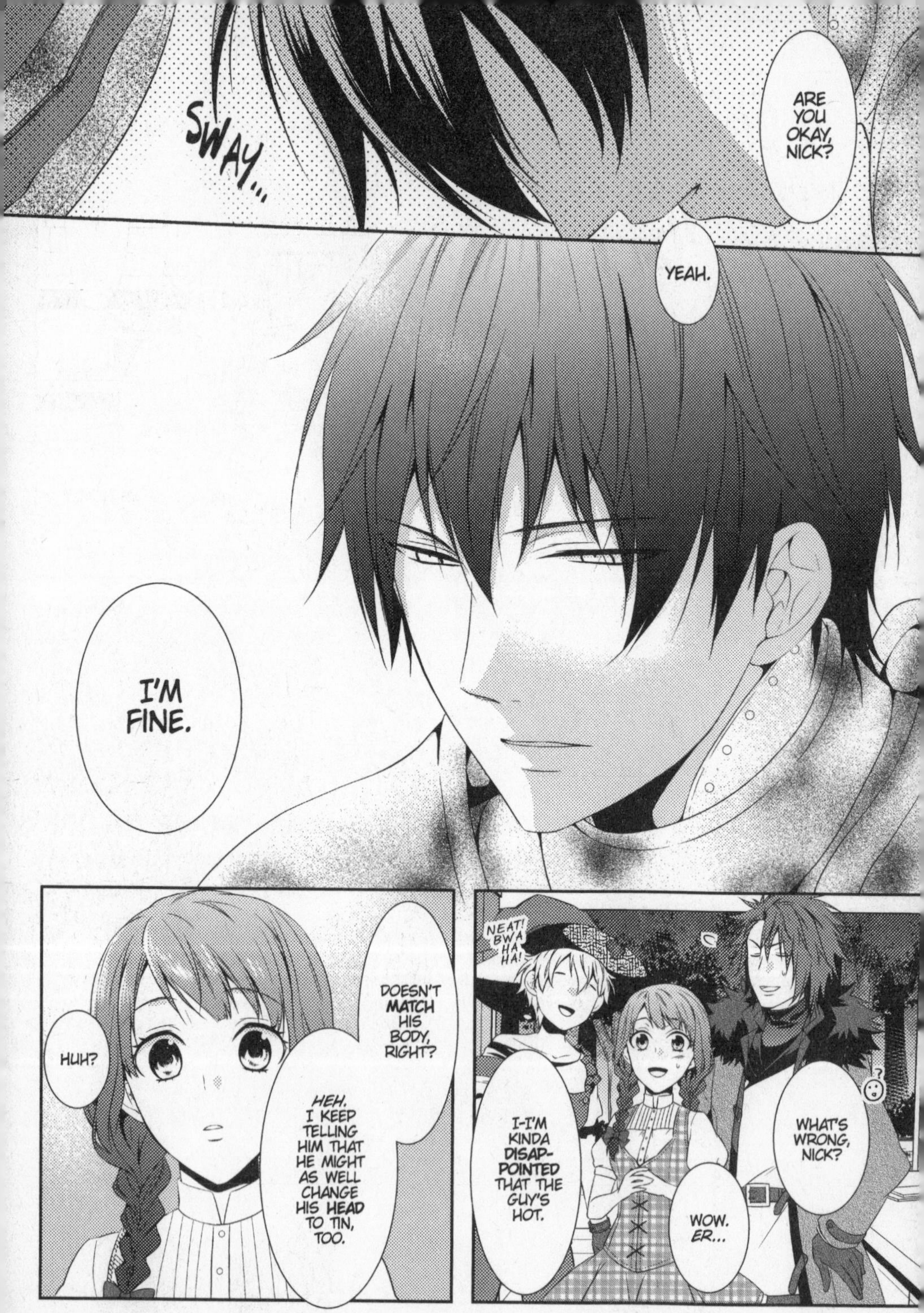
SWAY...
ARE YOU OKAY, NICK?
YEAH.
I'M FINE.
NEAT! BWA HA HA!
WHAT'S WRONG, NICK?
I-I'M KINDA DISAPPOINTED THAT THE GUY'S HOT.
WOW. ER...
DOESN'T MATCH HIS BODY, RIGHT?
HEH. I KEEP TELLING HIM THAT HE MIGHT AS WELL CHANGE HIS HEAD TO TIN, TOO.
HUH?

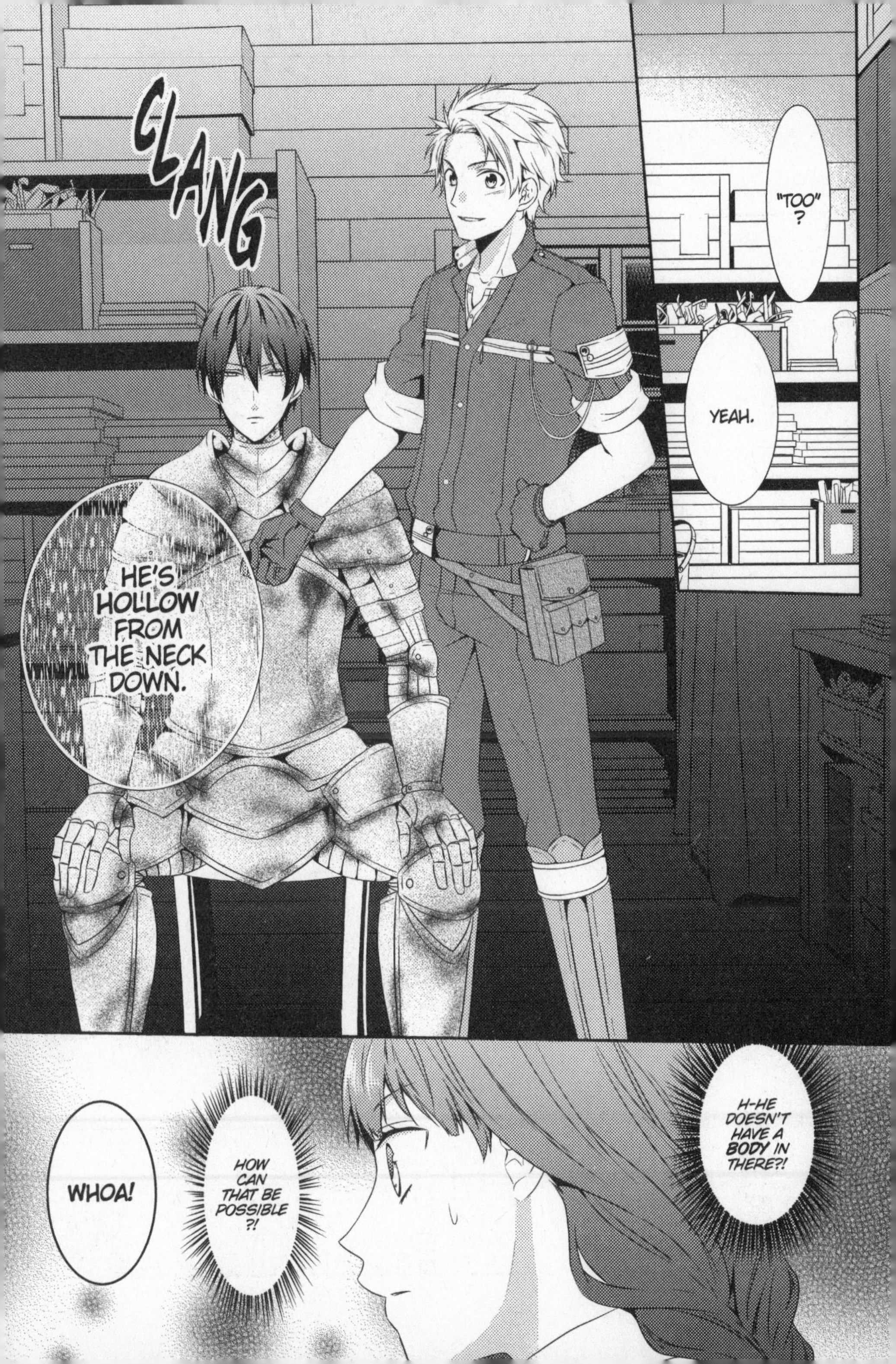
"TOO" ?
YEAH.
CLANG
HE'S HOLLOW FROM THE NECK DOWN.
H-HE DOESN'T HAVE A BODY IN THERE?!
HOW CAN THAT BE POSSIBLE ?!
WHOA!

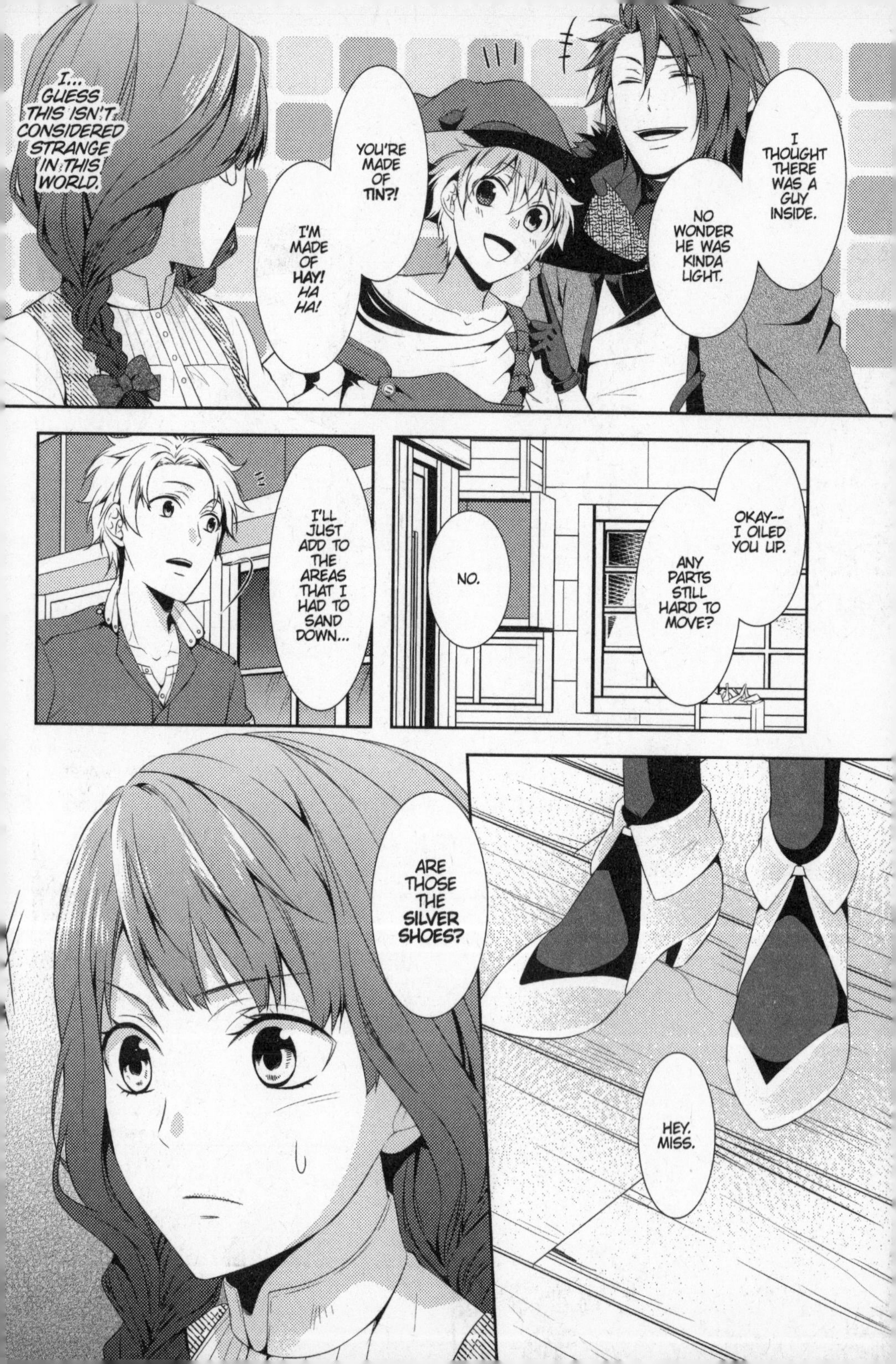
I THOUGHT THERE WAS A GUY INSIDE.
NO WONDER HE WAS KINDA LIGHT.
YOU'RE MADE OF TIN?!
I'M MADE OF HAY! HA HA!
I... GUESS THIS ISN'T CONSIDERED STRANGE IN THIS WORLD.
OKAY-- I OILED YOU UP.
ANY PARTS STILL HARD TO MOVE?
NO.
I'LL JUST ADD TO THE AREAS THAT I HAD TO SAND DOWN...
HEY. MISS.
ARE THOSE THE SILVER SHOES?

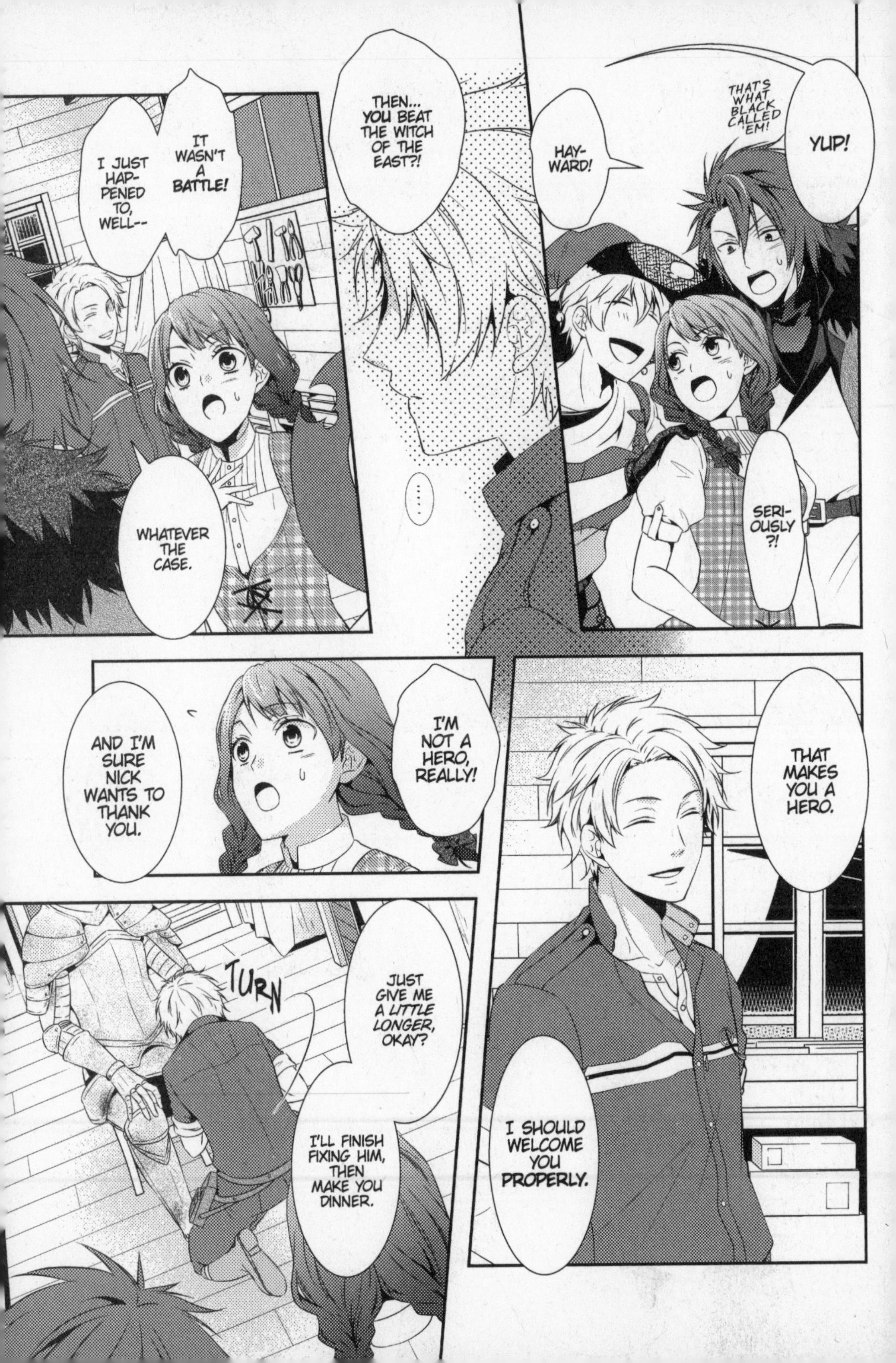
YUP!
THAT'S WHAT BLACK CALLED 'EM!
HAY-WARD!
SERIOUSLY?!
THEN... YOU BEAT THE WITCH OF THE EAST?!
......
IT WASN'T A BATTLE!
I JUST HAP-PENED TO, WELL--
WHATEVER THE CASE.
THAT MAKES YOU A HERO.
I SHOULD WELCOME YOU PROPERLY.
I'M NOT A HERO, REALLY!
AND I'M SURE NICK WANTS TO THANK YOU.
JUST GIVE ME A *LITTLE LONGER*, OKAY?
TURN
I'LL FINISH FIXING HIM, THEN MAKE YOU DINNER.

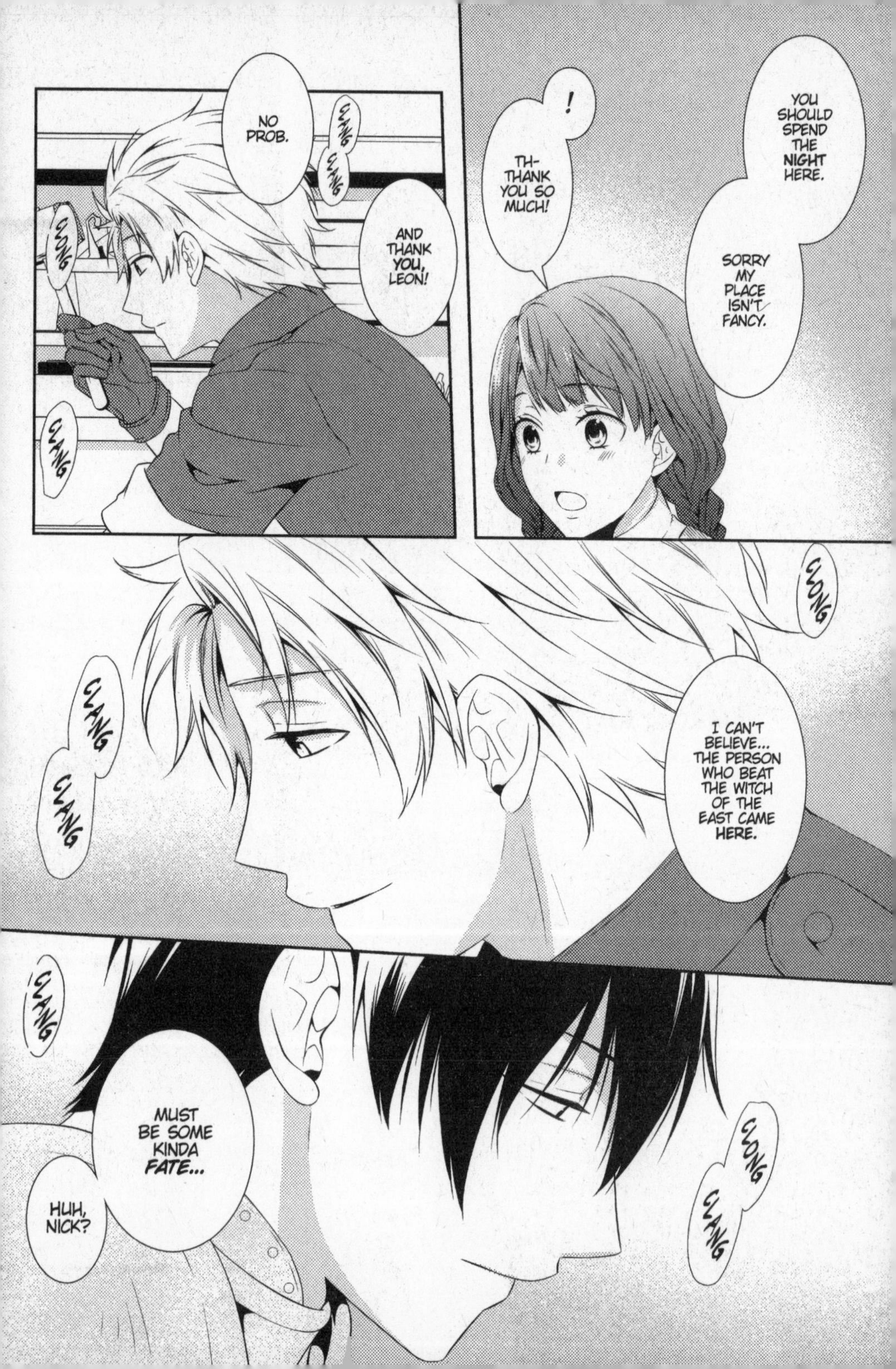
YOU SHOULD SPEND THE NIGHT HERE.
SORRY MY PLACE ISN'T FANCY.
!
TH-THANK YOU SO MUCH!
AND THANK YOU, LEON!
NO PROB.
CLANG CLANG
CLONG
CLANG
CLONG
I CAN'T BELIEVE... THE PERSON WHO BEAT THE WITCH OF THE EAST CAME HERE.
CLANG
CLANG
CLONG
CLANG
MUST BE SOME KINDA FATE...
HUH, NICK?
CLANG

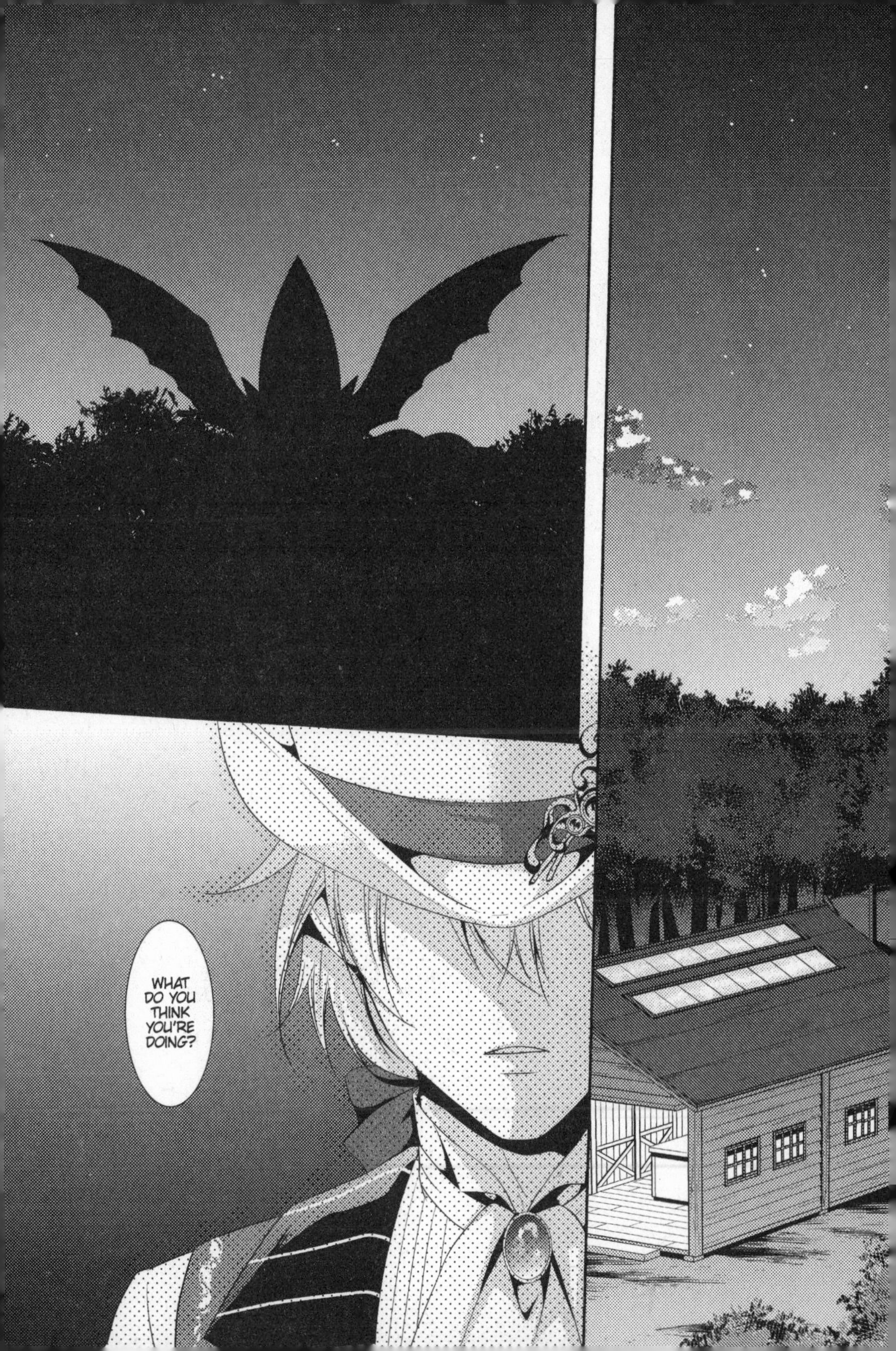
WHAT DO YOU THINK YOU'RE DOING?

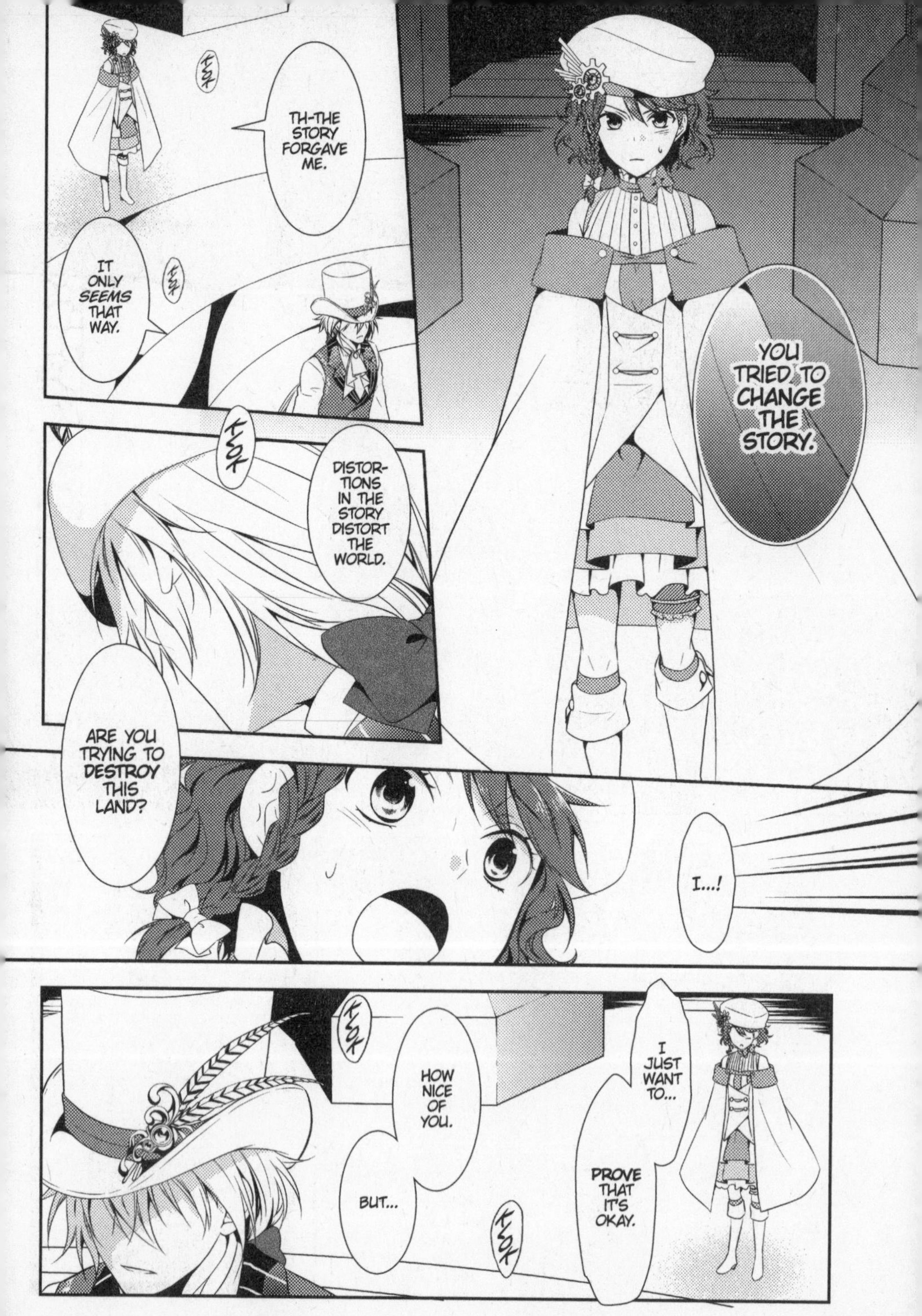
YOU TRIED TO CHANGE THE STORY.
KLOK
TH-THE STORY FORGAVE ME.
KLOK
IT ONLY SEEMS THAT WAY.
KLOK
DISTORTIONS IN THE STORY DISTORT THE WORLD.
ARE YOU TRYING TO DESTROY THIS LAND?
I...!
I JUST WANT TO...
PROVE THAT IT'S OKAY.
KLOK
HOW NICE OF YOU.
BUT...
KLOK

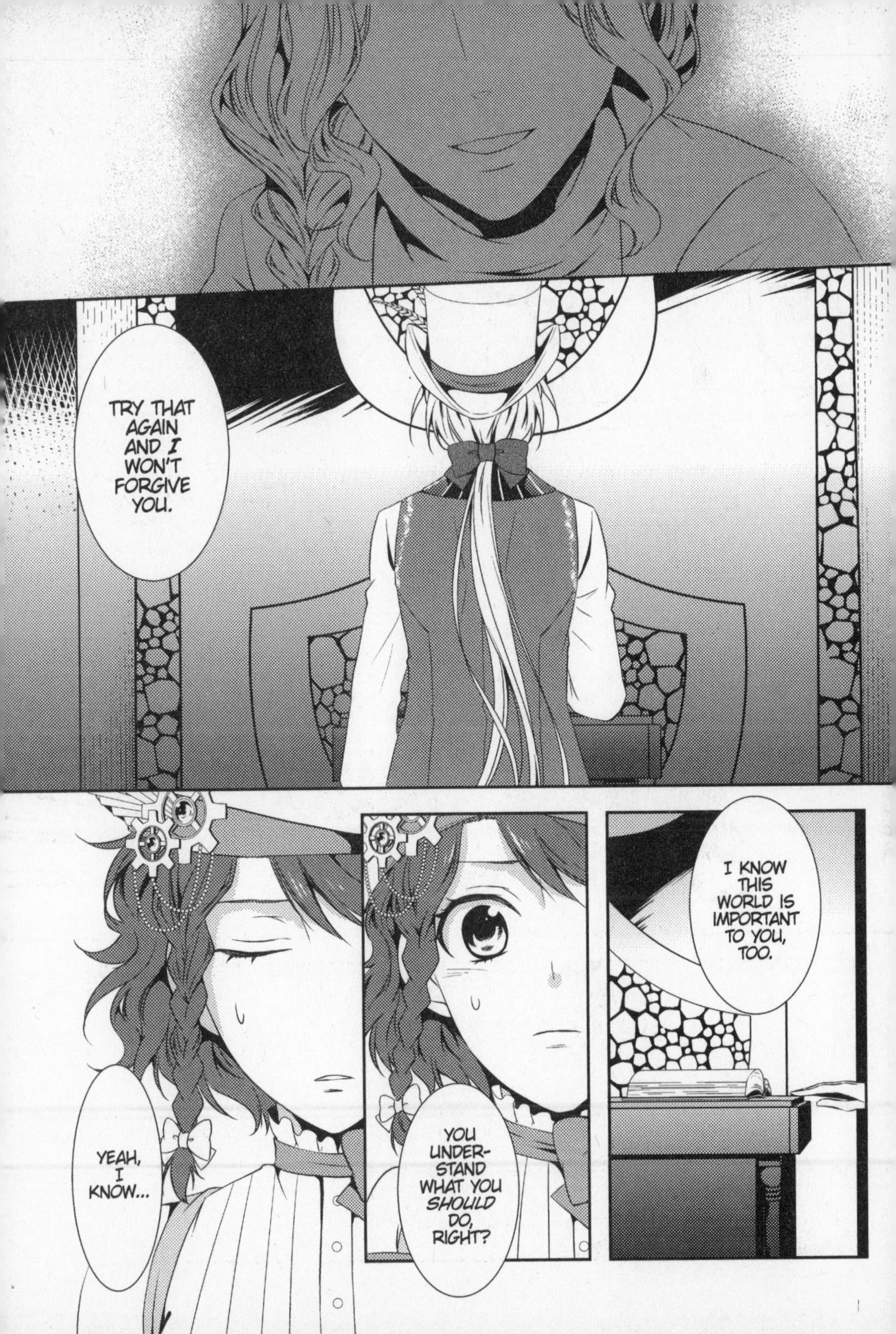
TRY THAT AGAIN AND *I* WON'T FORGIVE YOU.
I KNOW THIS WORLD IS IMPORTANT TO YOU, TOO.
YOU UNDER-STAND WHAT YOU *SHOULD* DO, RIGHT?
YEAH, I KNOW...

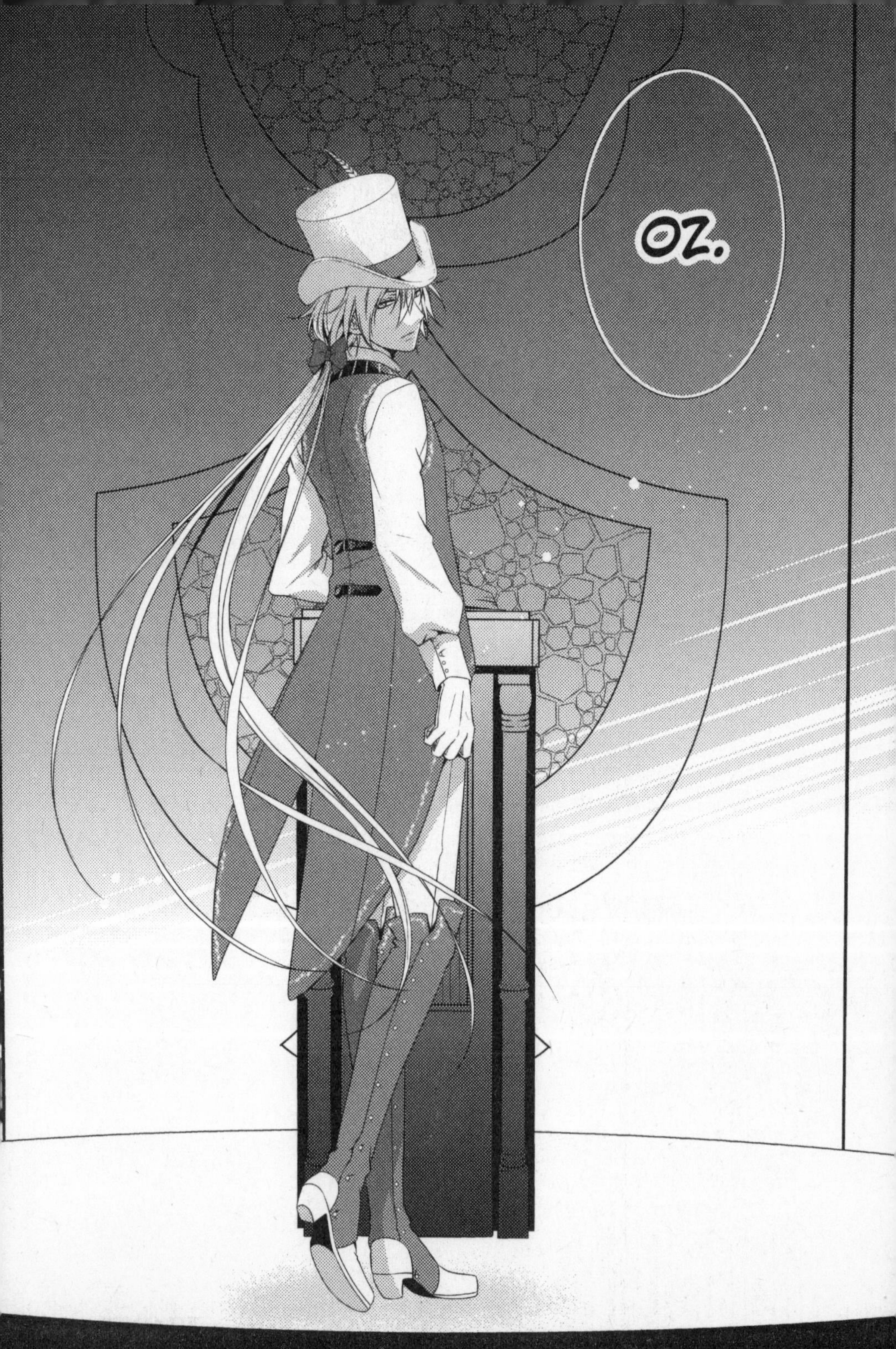
OZ.

Captive Hearts of Oz

Captive Hearts of Oz

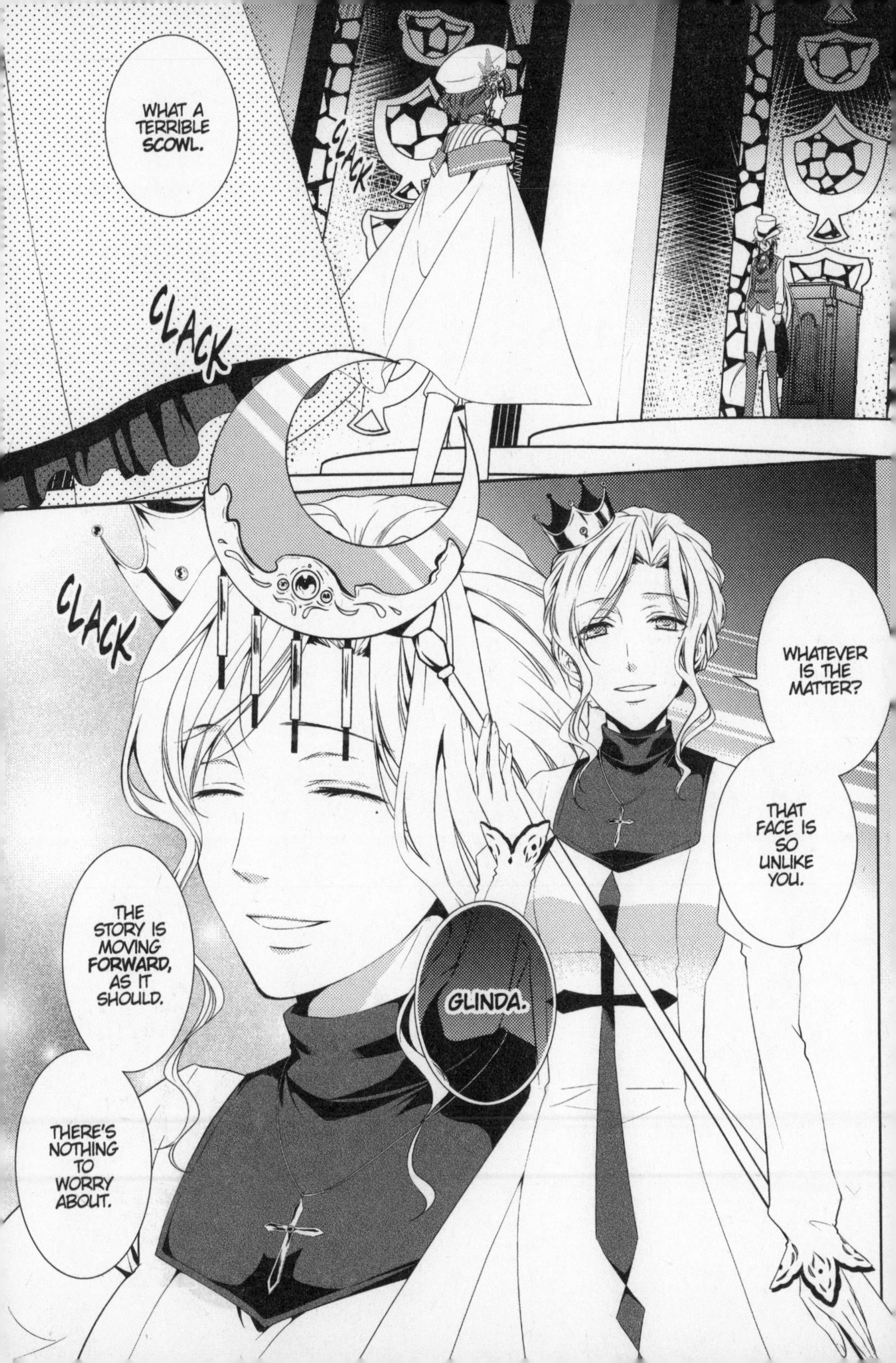
CLACK
WHAT A TERRIBLE SCOWL.
CLACK
CLACK
WHATEVER IS THE MATTER?
THAT FACE IS SO UNLIKE YOU.
GLINDA.
THE STORY IS MOVING FORWARD, AS IT SHOULD.
THERE'S NOTHING TO WORRY ABOUT.

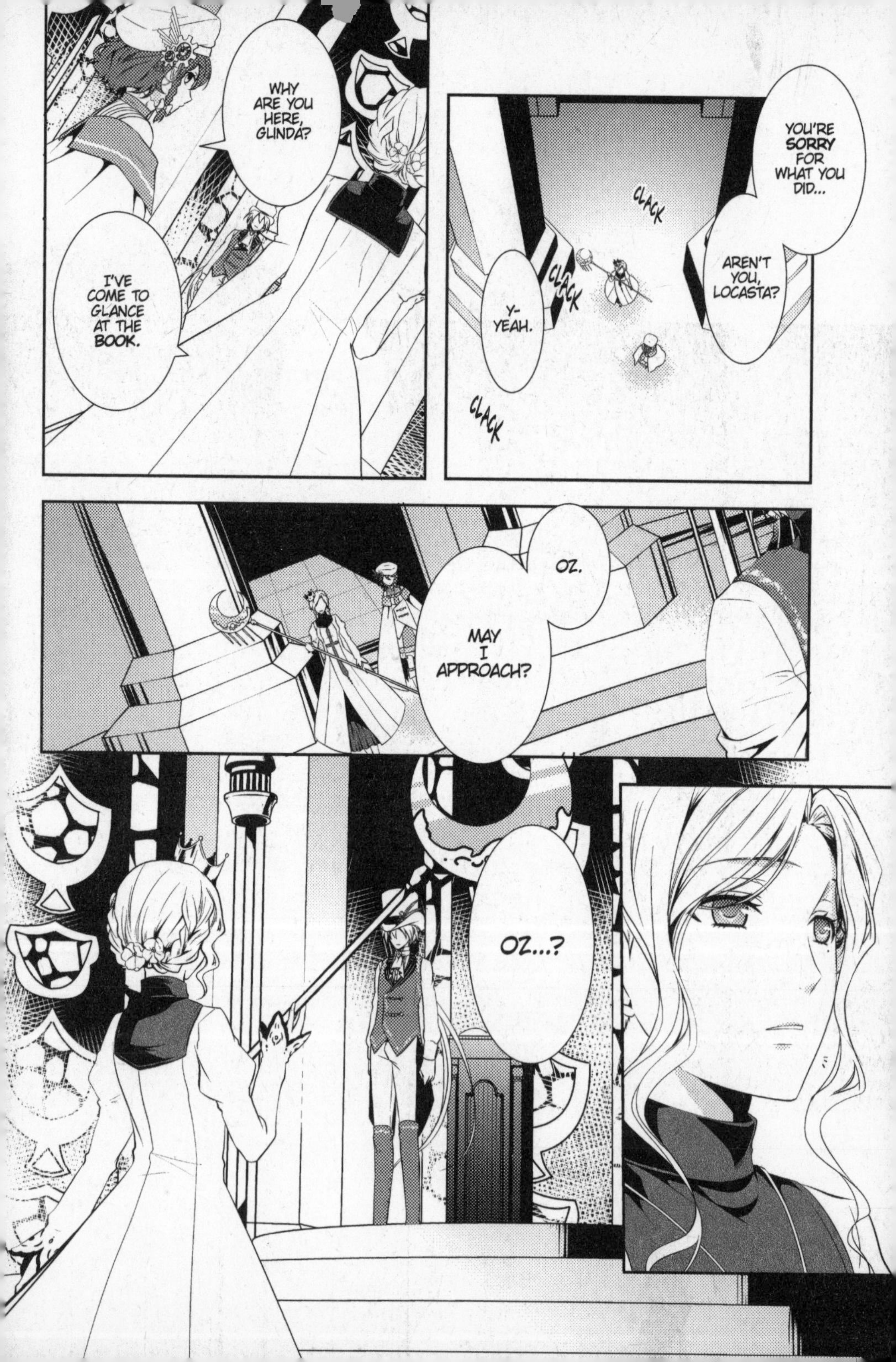
YOU'RE SORRY FOR WHAT YOU DID...
CLACK
AREN'T YOU, LOCASTA?
CLACK
Y-YEAH.
CLACK
WHY ARE YOU HERE, GLINDA?
I'VE COME TO GLANCE AT THE BOOK.
OZ.
MAY I APPROACH?
OZ...?

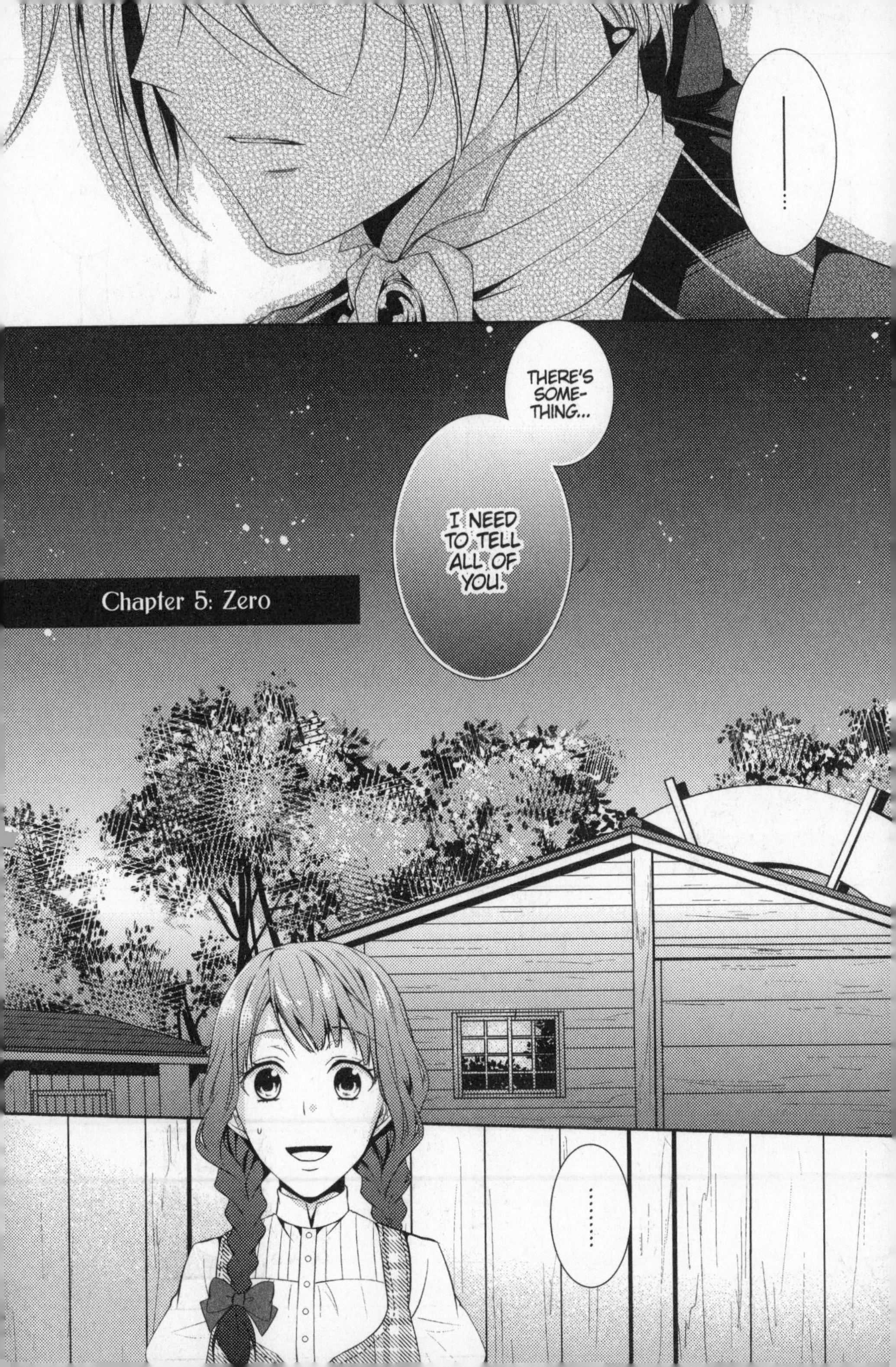
—……
THERE'S SOME-THING...
I NEED TO TELL ALL OF YOU.
Chapter 5: Zero
……

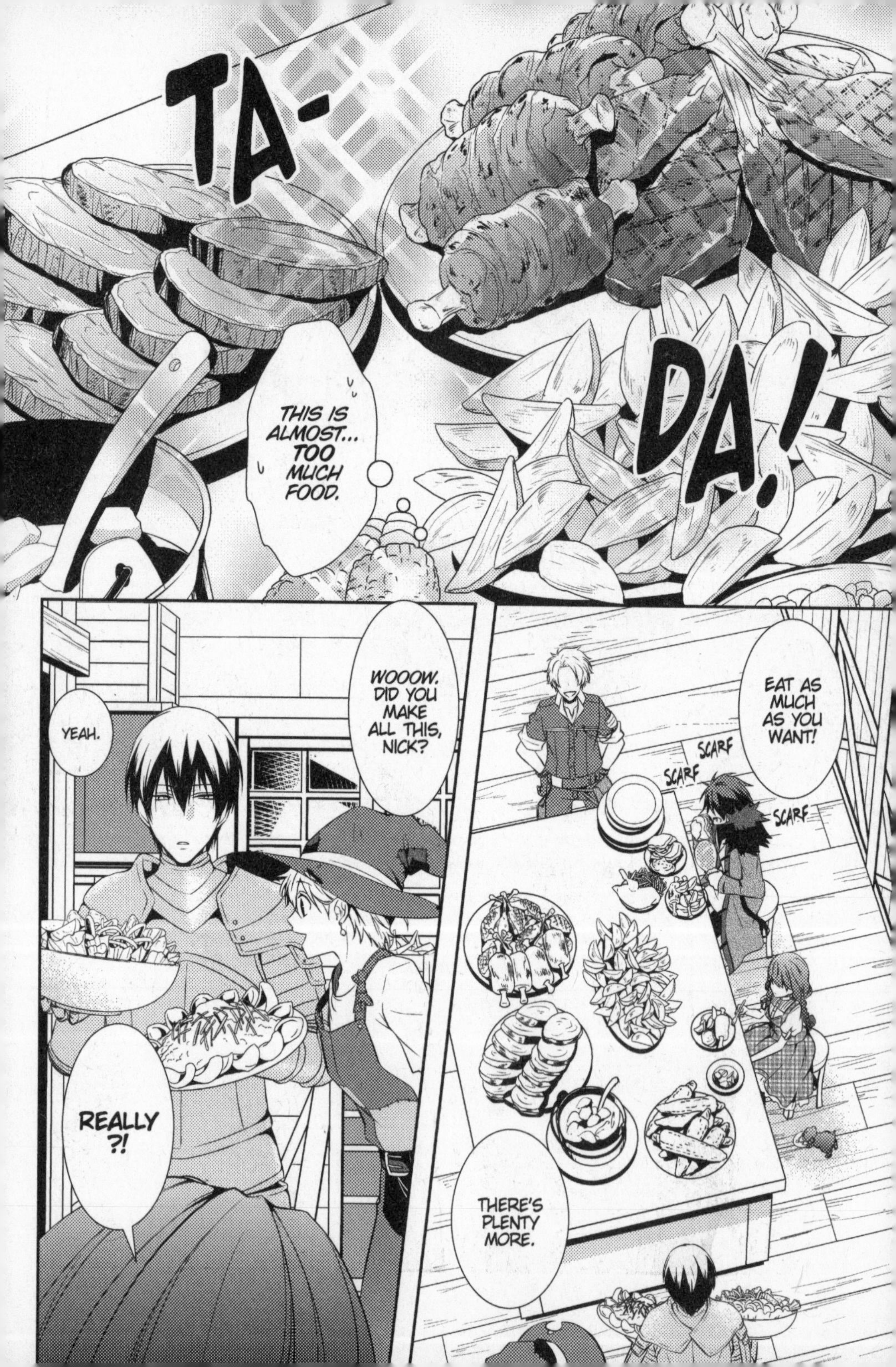
TA- DA!
THIS IS ALMOST... TOO MUCH FOOD.
EAT AS MUCH AS YOU WANT!
SCARF
SCARF
SCARF
THERE'S PLENTY MORE.
WOOOW. DID YOU MAKE ALL THIS, NICK?
YEAH.
REALLY?!

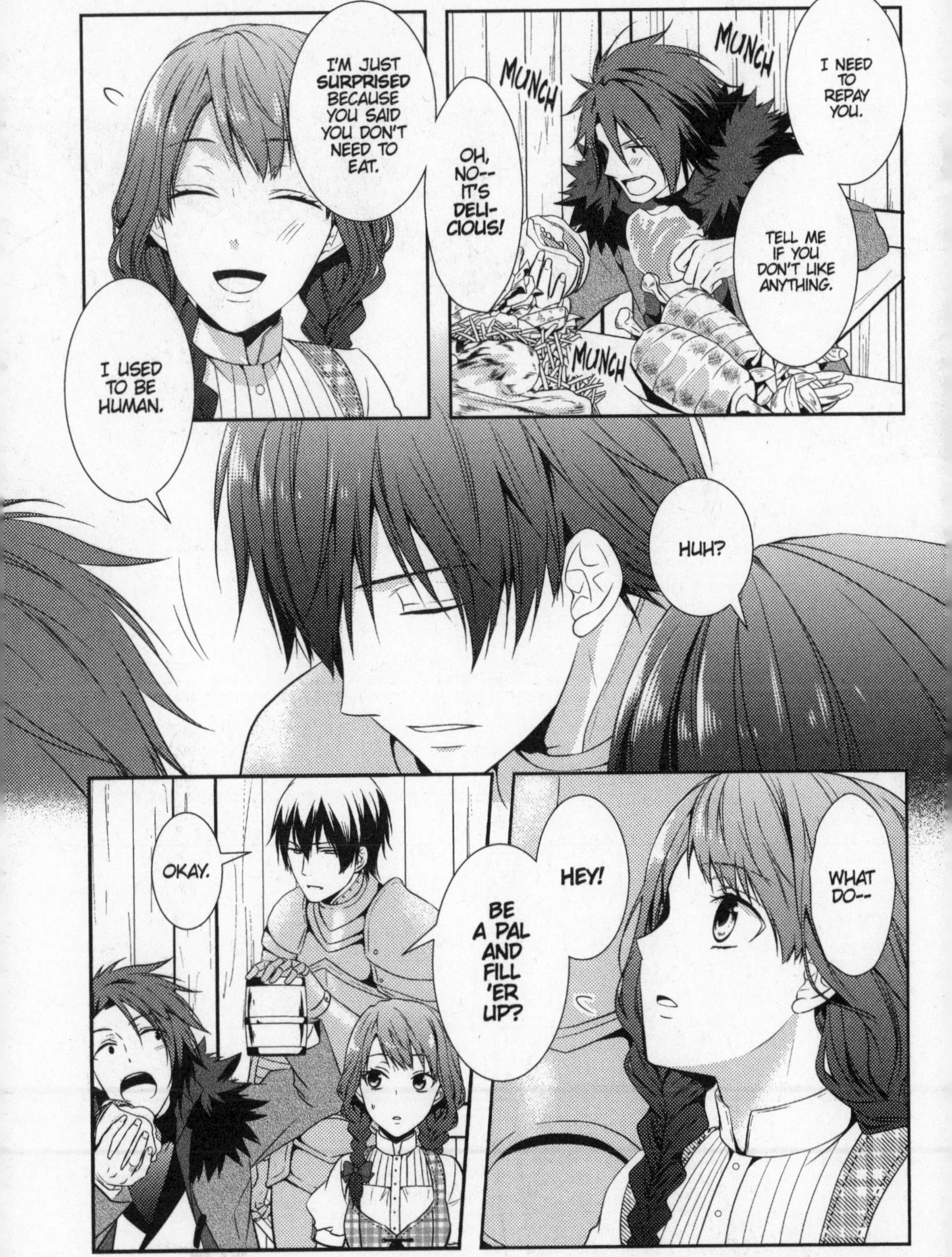
MUNCH
I NEED TO REPAY YOU.
MUNCH
TELL ME IF YOU DON'T LIKE ANYTHING.
MUNCH
OH, NO-- IT'S DELICIOUS!
I'M JUST SURPRISED BECAUSE YOU SAID YOU DON'T NEED TO EAT.
I USED TO BE HUMAN.
HUH?
WHAT DO--
HEY!
BE A PAL AND FILL 'ER UP?
OKAY.

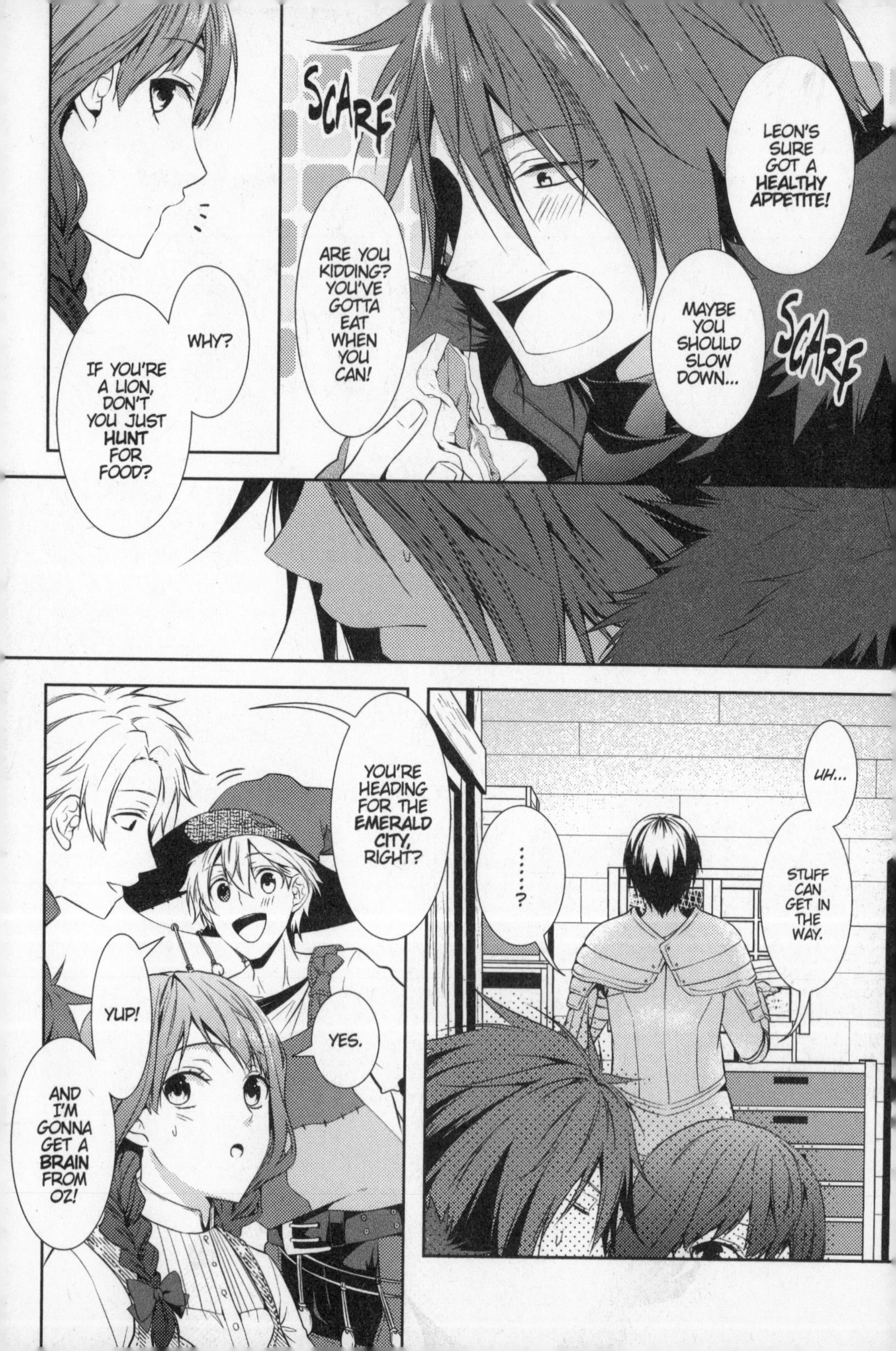
LEON'S SURE GOT A HEALTHY APPETITE!
MAYBE YOU SHOULD SLOW DOWN...
SCARF
SCARF
ARE YOU KIDDING? YOU'VE GOTTA EAT WHEN YOU CAN!
WHY?
IF YOU'RE A LION, DON'T YOU JUST HUNT FOR FOOD?
UH...
STUFF CAN GET IN THE WAY.
......?
YOU'RE HEADING FOR THE EMERALD CITY, RIGHT?
YES.
YUP!
AND I'M GONNA GET A BRAIN FROM OZ!

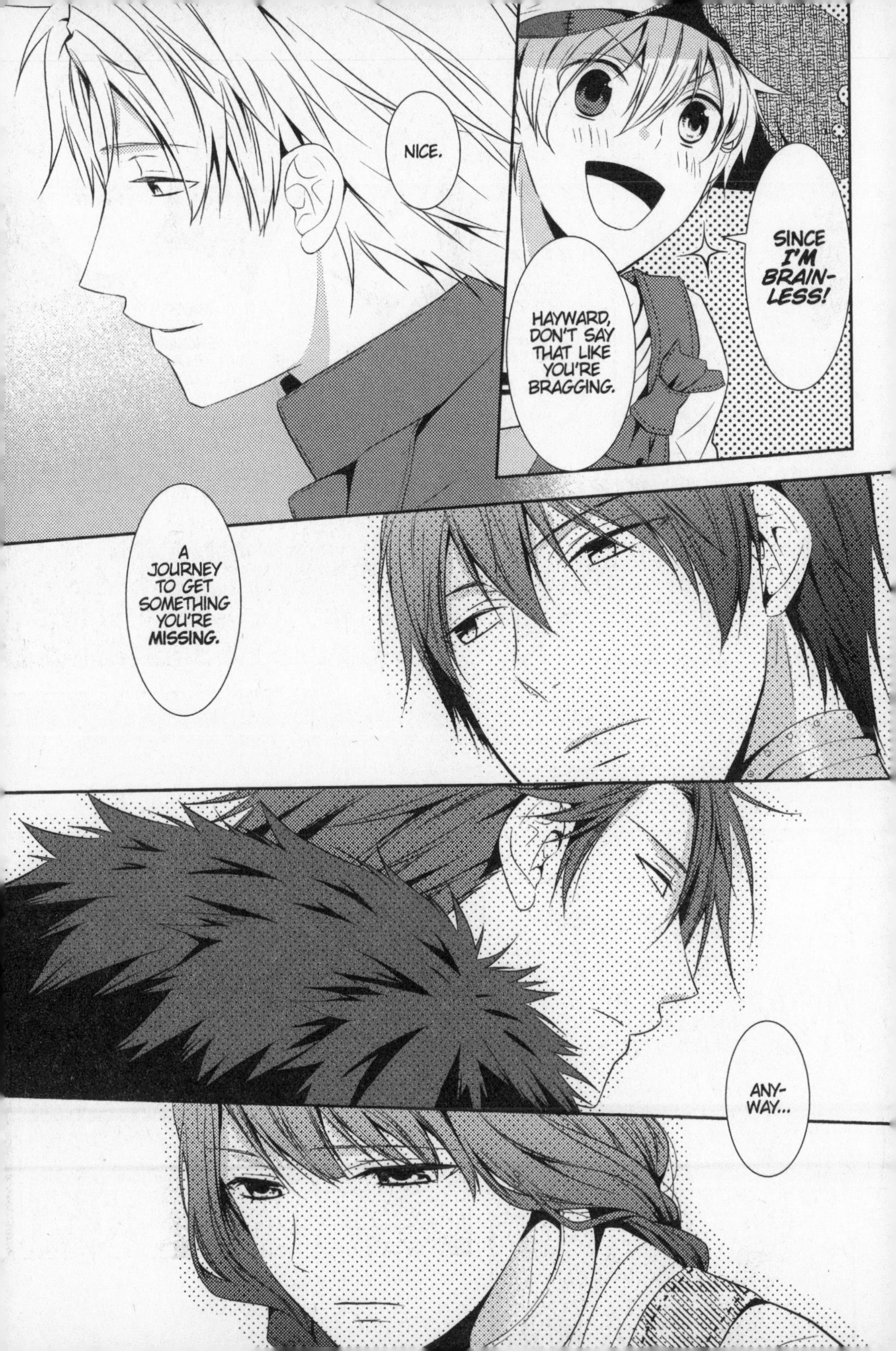
SINCE I'M BRAIN-LESS!
HAYWARD, DON'T SAY THAT LIKE YOU'RE BRAGGING.
NICE.
A JOURNEY TO GET SOMETHING YOU'RE MISSING.
ANY-WAY...

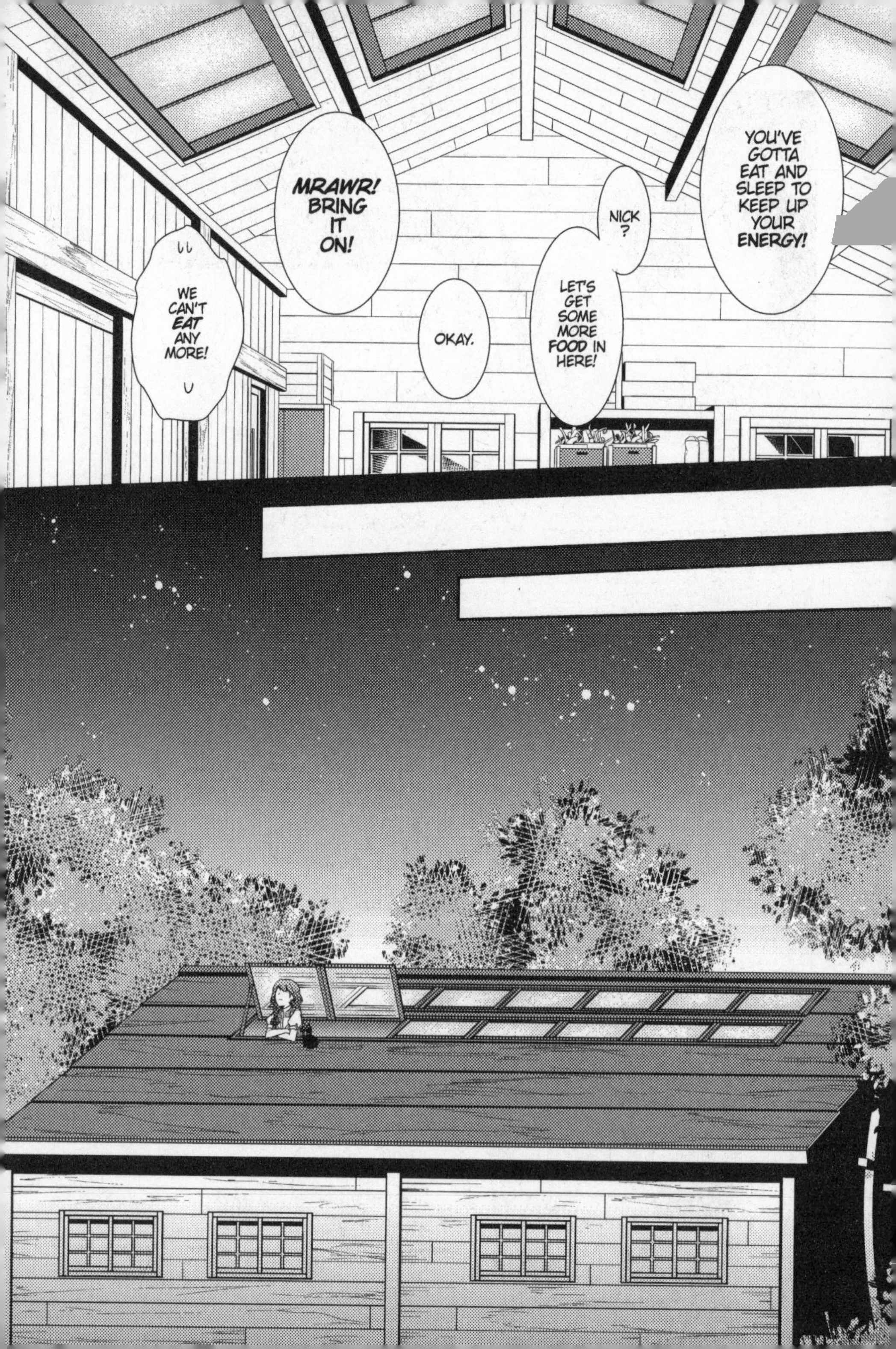
YOU'VE GOTTA EAT AND SLEEP TO KEEP UP YOUR ENERGY!
NICK?
LET'S GET SOME MORE FOOD IN HERE!
OKAY.
MRAWR! BRING IT ON!
WE CAN'T EAT ANY MORE!

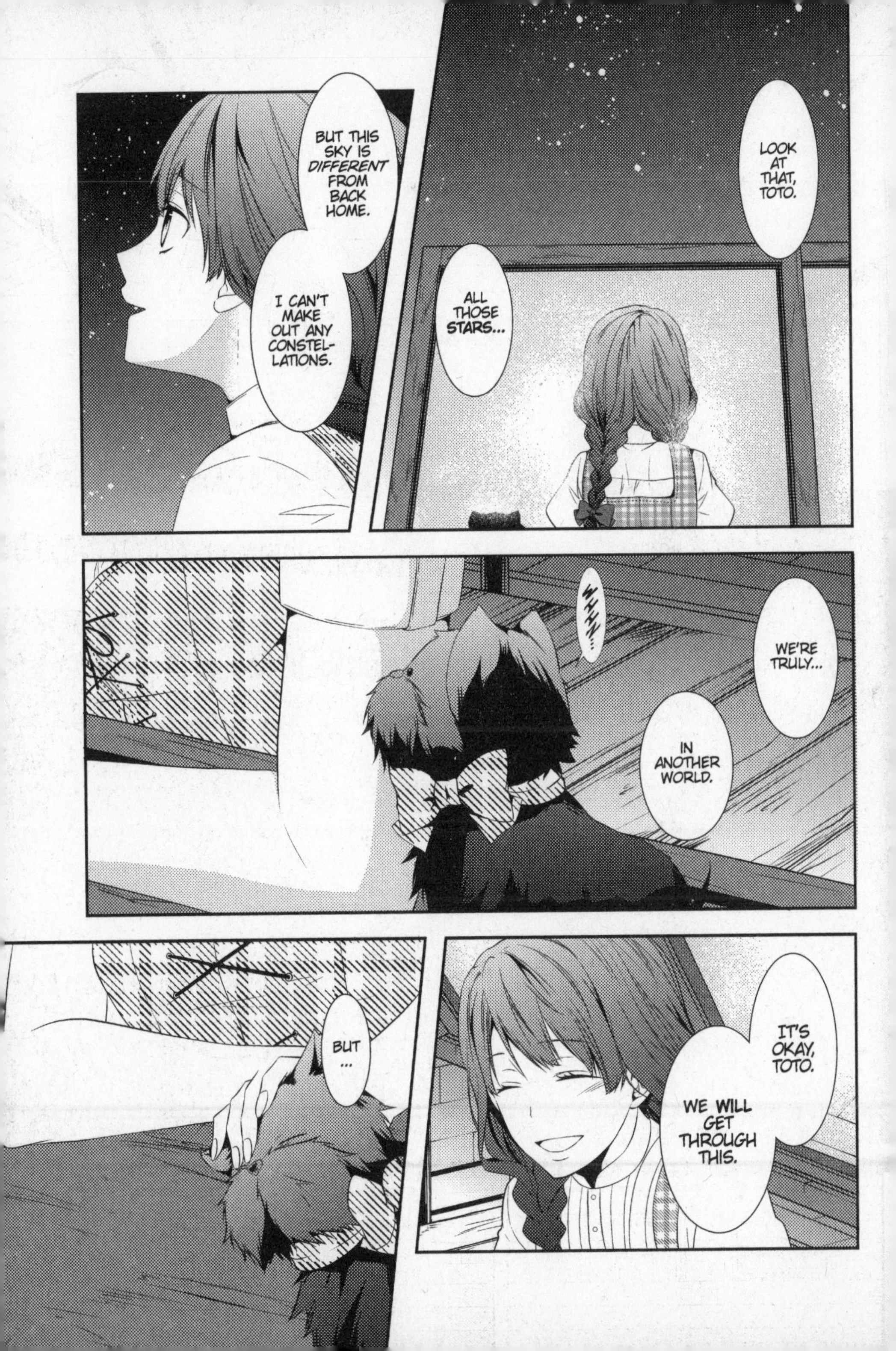
LOOK AT THAT, TOTO.
ALL THOSE STARS...
BUT THIS SKY IS *DIFFERENT* FROM BACK HOME.
I CAN'T MAKE OUT ANY CONSTEL-LATIONS.
WE'RE TRULY...
IN ANOTHER WORLD.
WHHN...
IT'S OKAY, TOTO.
WE WILL GET THROUGH THIS.
BUT ...

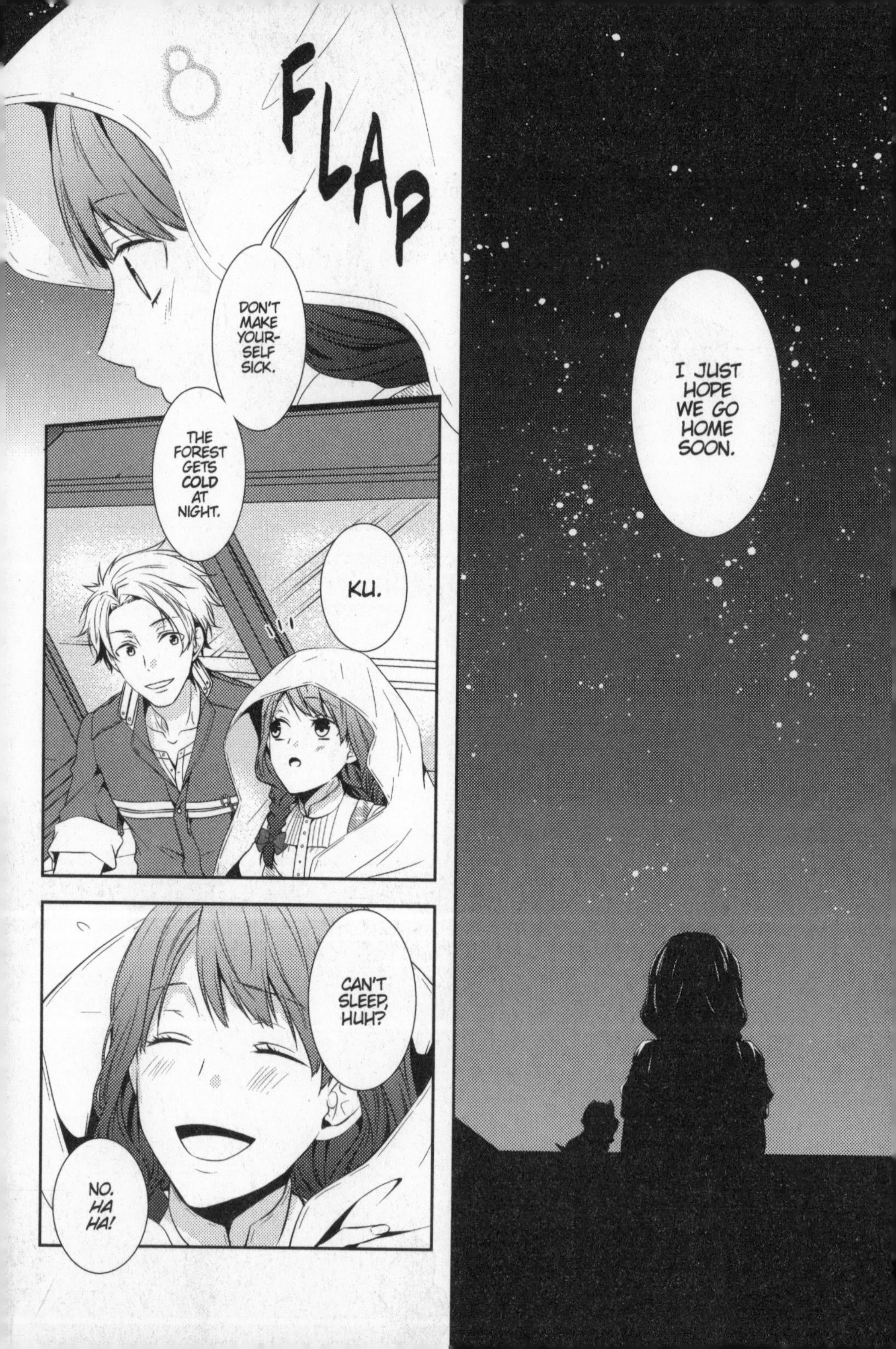
I JUST HOPE WE GO HOME SOON.
FLAP
DON'T MAKE YOUR-SELF SICK.
THE FOREST GETS COLD AT NIGHT.
KU.
CAN'T SLEEP, HUH?
NO. HA HA!

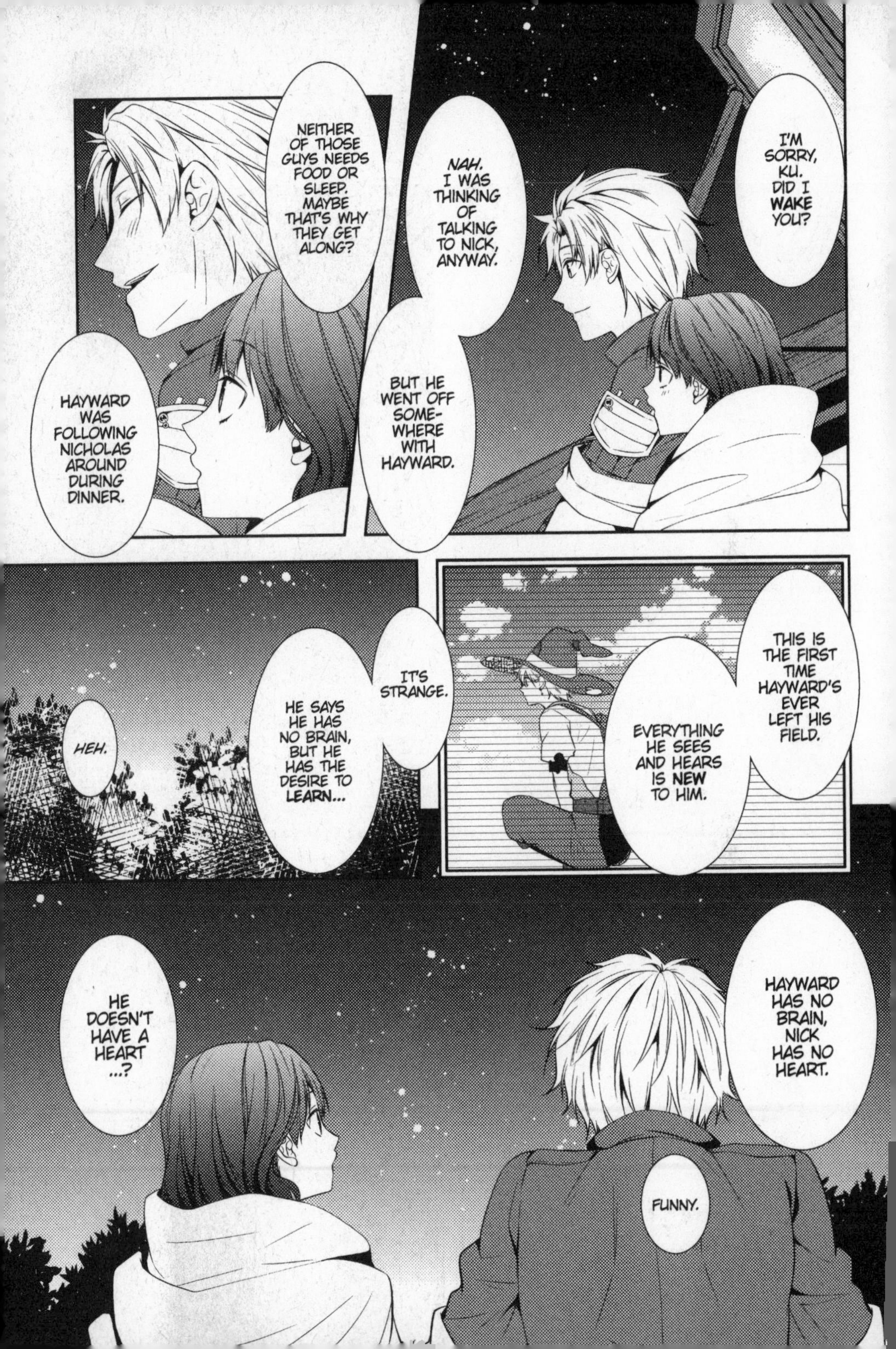
I'M SORRY, KU. DID I WAKE YOU?
NAH. I WAS THINKING OF TALKING TO NICK, ANYWAY.
BUT HE WENT OFF SOMEWHERE WITH HAYWARD.
NEITHER OF THOSE GUYS NEEDS FOOD OR SLEEP. MAYBE THAT'S WHY THEY GET ALONG?
HAYWARD WAS FOLLOWING NICHOLAS AROUND DURING DINNER.
THIS IS THE FIRST TIME HAYWARD'S EVER LEFT HIS FIELD.
EVERYTHING HE SEES AND HEARS IS NEW TO HIM.
IT'S STRANGE.
HE SAYS HE HAS NO BRAIN, BUT HE HAS THE DESIRE TO LEARN...
HEH.
HAYWARD HAS NO BRAIN, NICK HAS NO HEART.
FUNNY.
HE DOESN'T HAVE A HEART ...?

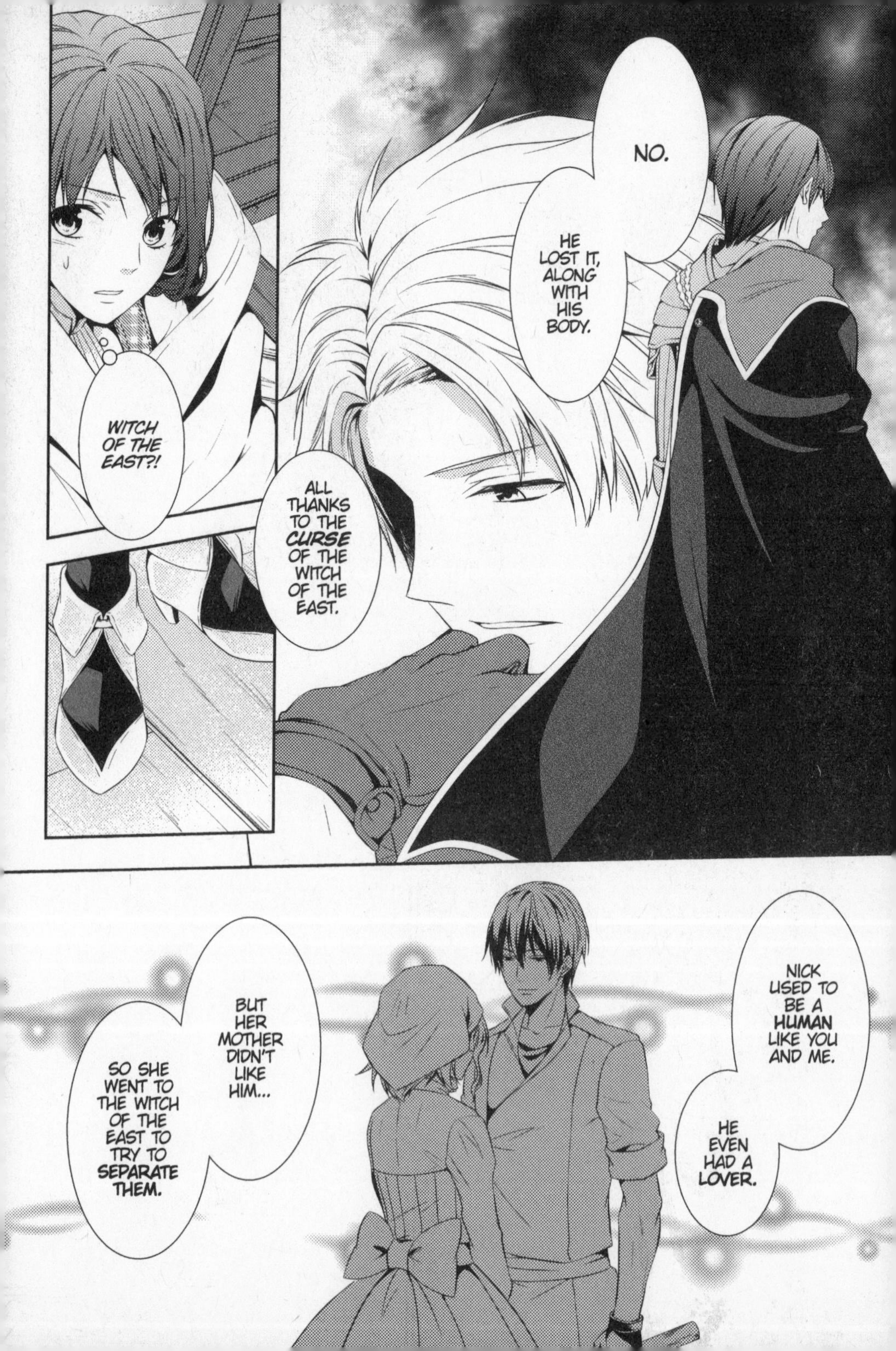
NO.
HE LOST IT, ALONG WITH HIS BODY.
ALL THANKS TO THE *CURSE* OF THE WITCH OF THE EAST.
WITCH OF THE EAST?!
NICK USED TO BE A HUMAN LIKE YOU AND ME.
HE EVEN HAD A LOVER.
BUT HER MOTHER DIDN'T LIKE HIM...
SO SHE WENT TO THE WITCH OF THE EAST TO TRY TO SEPARATE THEM.

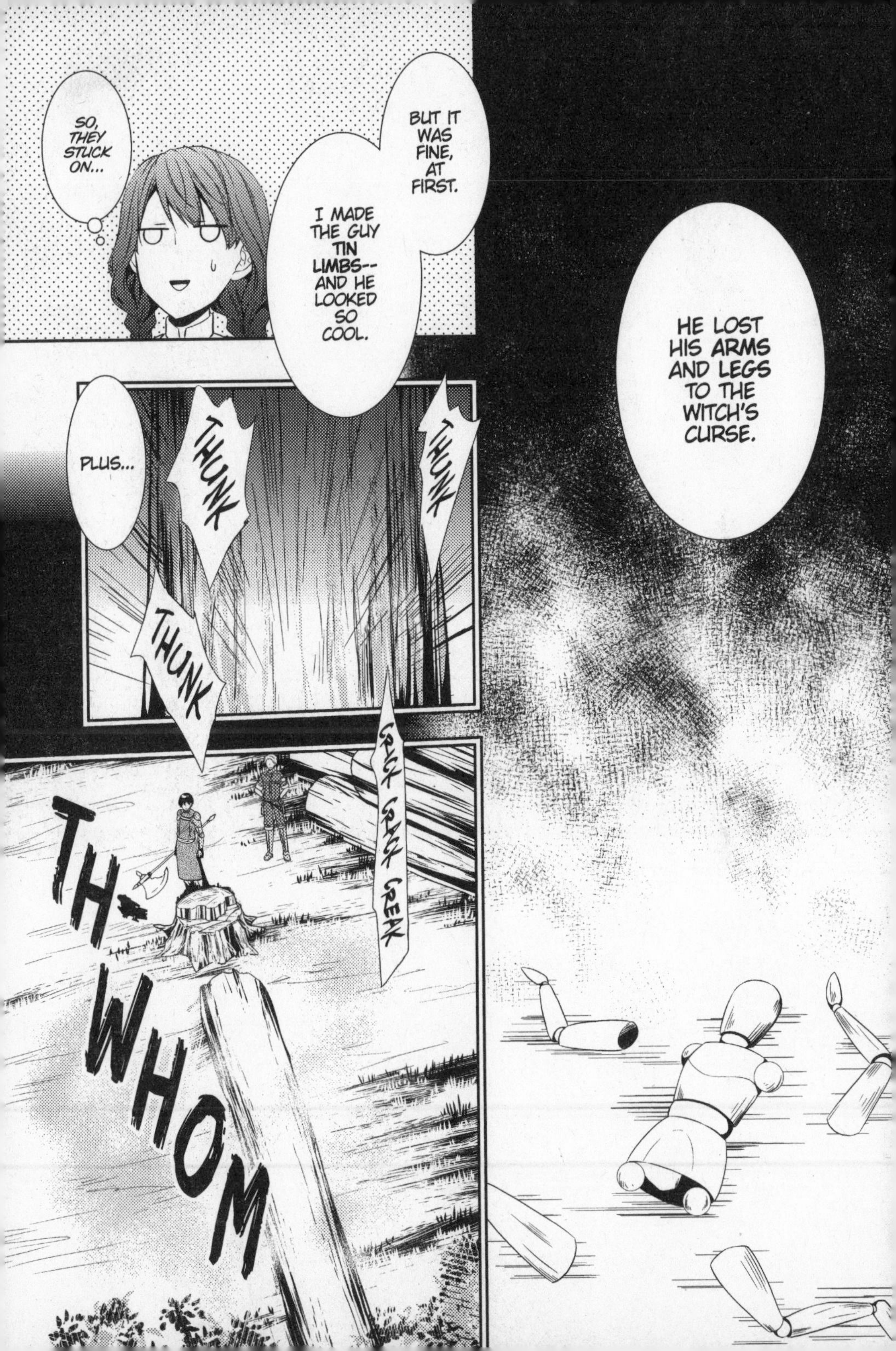
HE LOST HIS ARMS AND LEGS TO THE WITCH'S CURSE.
BUT IT WAS FINE, AT FIRST.
I MADE THE GUY TIN LIMBS-- AND HE LOOKED SO COOL.
SO, THEY STUCK ON...
THUNK
PLUS...
THUNK
THUNK
CRACK CRACK CREAK
THWHOM

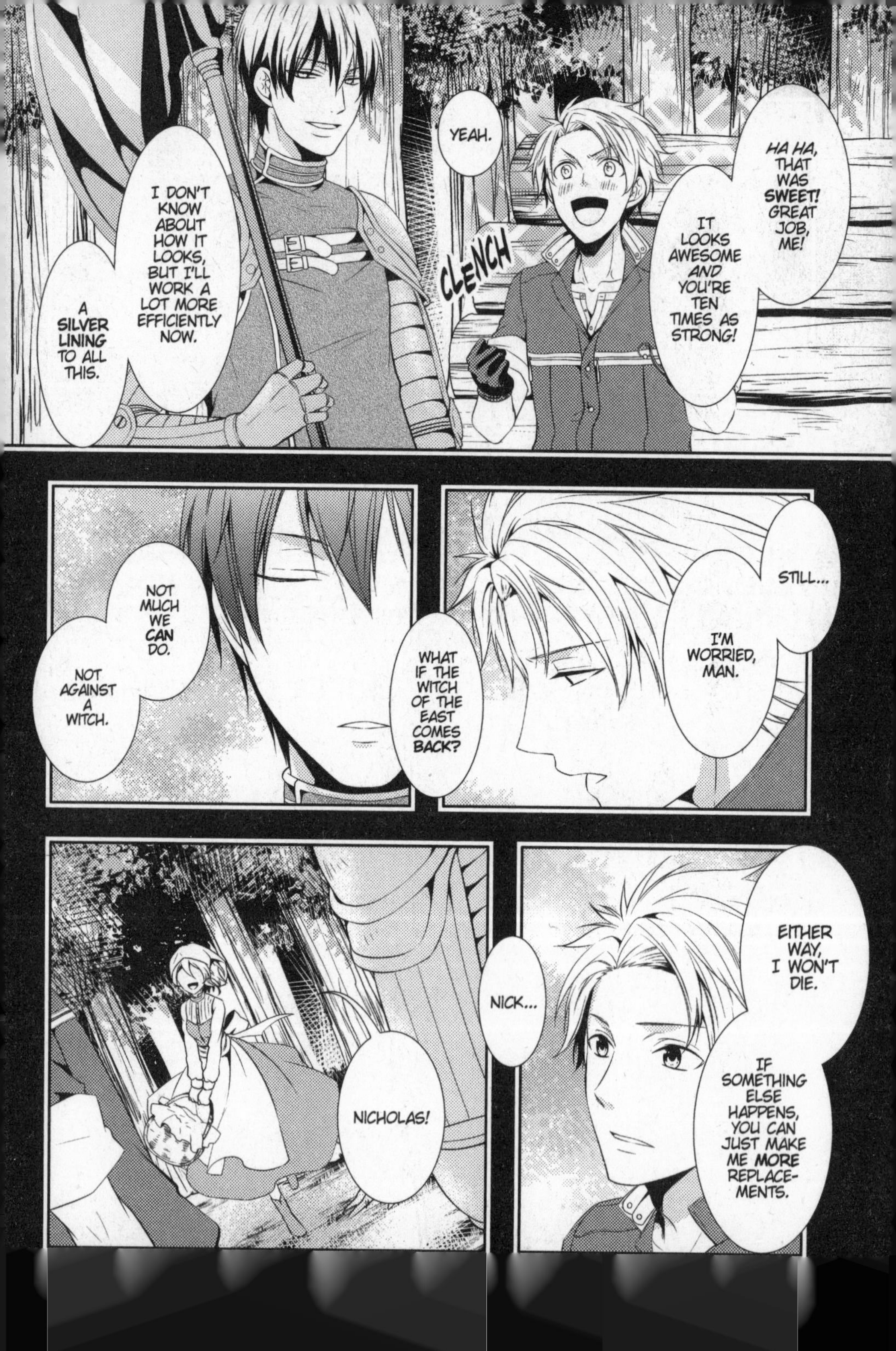
HA HA, THAT WAS SWEET! GREAT JOB, ME!
IT LOOKS AWESOME AND YOU'RE TEN TIMES AS STRONG!
CLENCH
YEAH.
I DON'T KNOW ABOUT HOW IT LOOKS, BUT I'LL WORK A LOT MORE EFFICIENTLY NOW.
A SILVER LINING TO ALL THIS.
STILL...
I'M WORRIED, MAN.
WHAT IF THE WITCH OF THE EAST COMES BACK?
NOT MUCH WE CAN DO.
NOT AGAINST A WITCH.
EITHER WAY, I WON'T DIE.
IF SOMETHING ELSE HAPPENS, YOU CAN JUST MAKE ME MORE REPLACEMENTS.
NICK...
NICHOLAS!

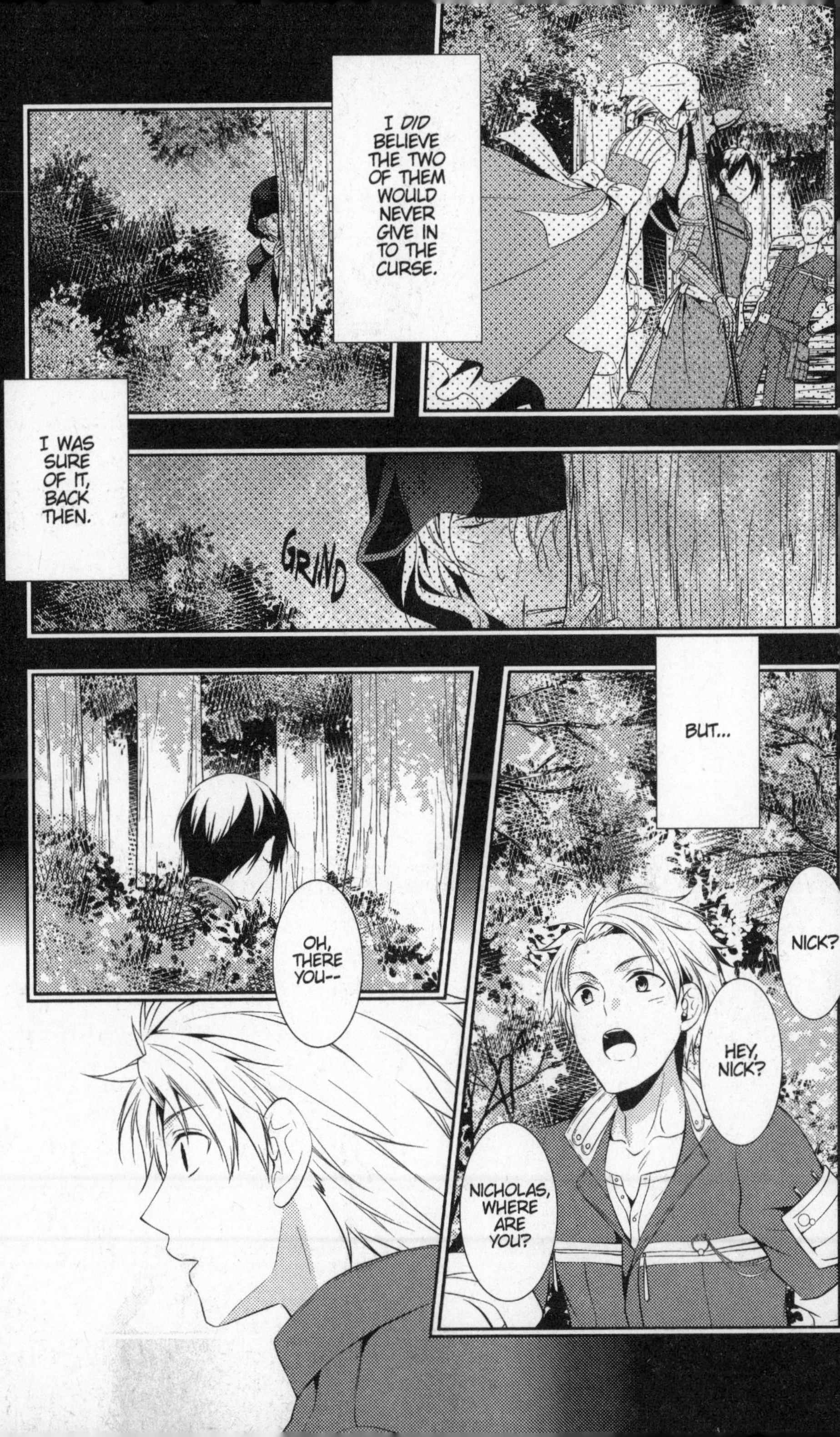
I *DID* BELIEVE THE TWO OF THEM WOULD NEVER GIVE IN TO THE CURSE.
I WAS SURE OF IT, BACK THEN.
GRIND
BUT...
NICK?
HEY, NICK?
NICHOLAS, WHERE ARE YOU?
OH, THERE YOU--

ROLL..

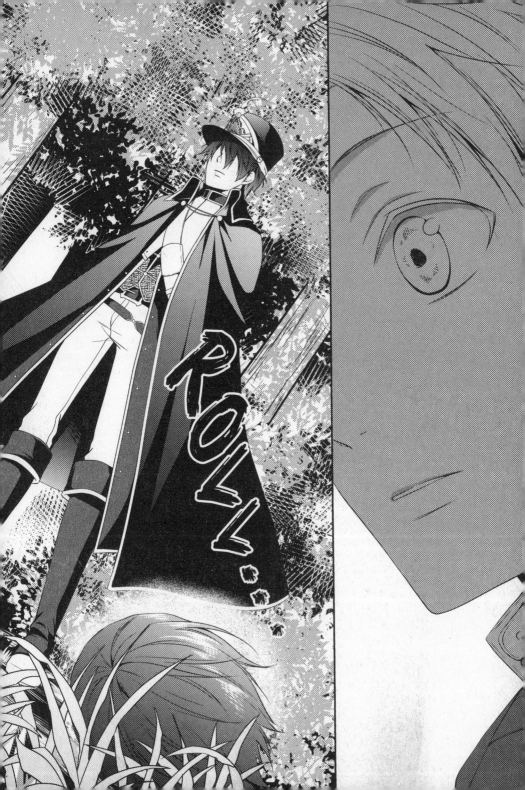

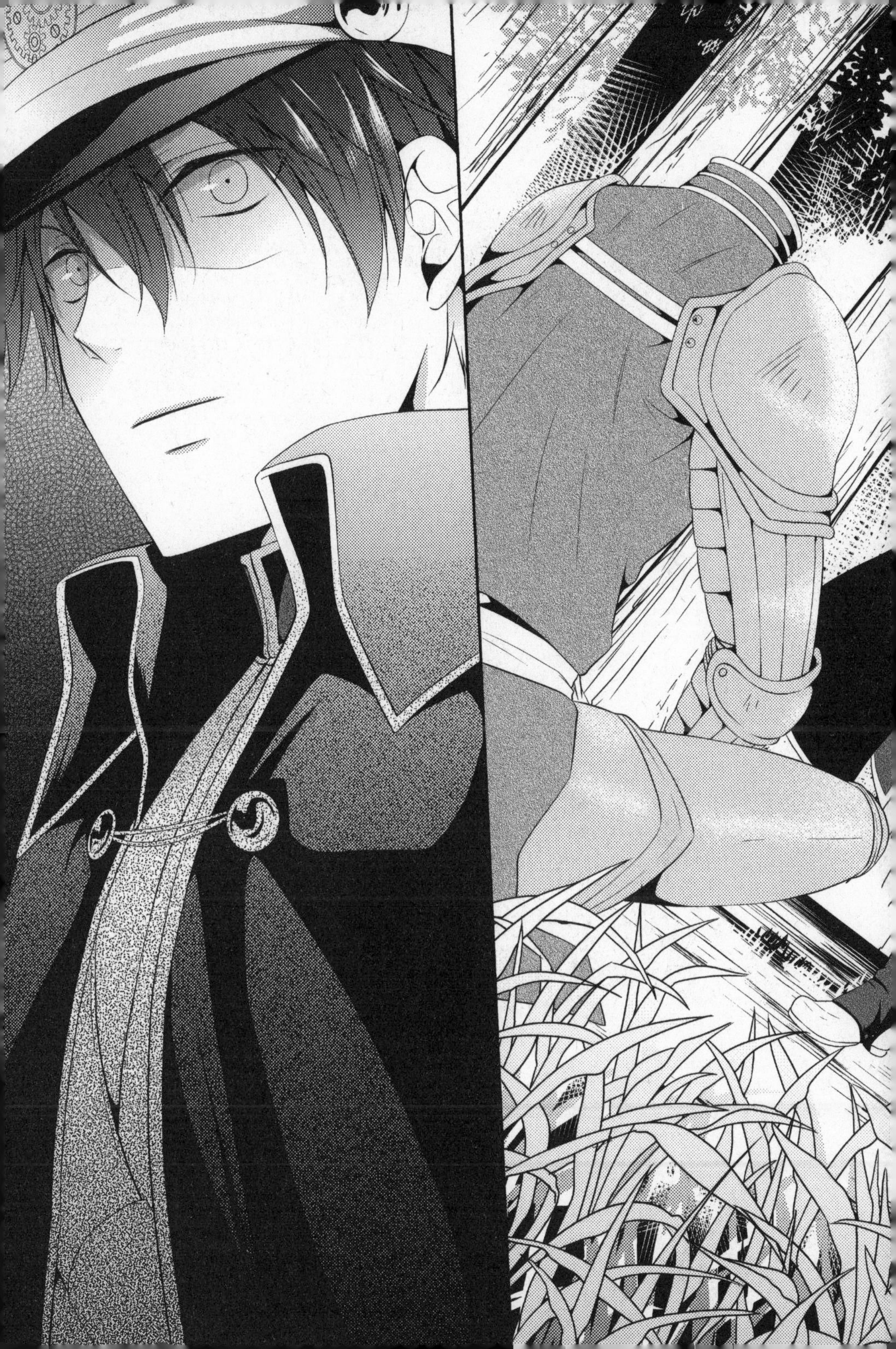

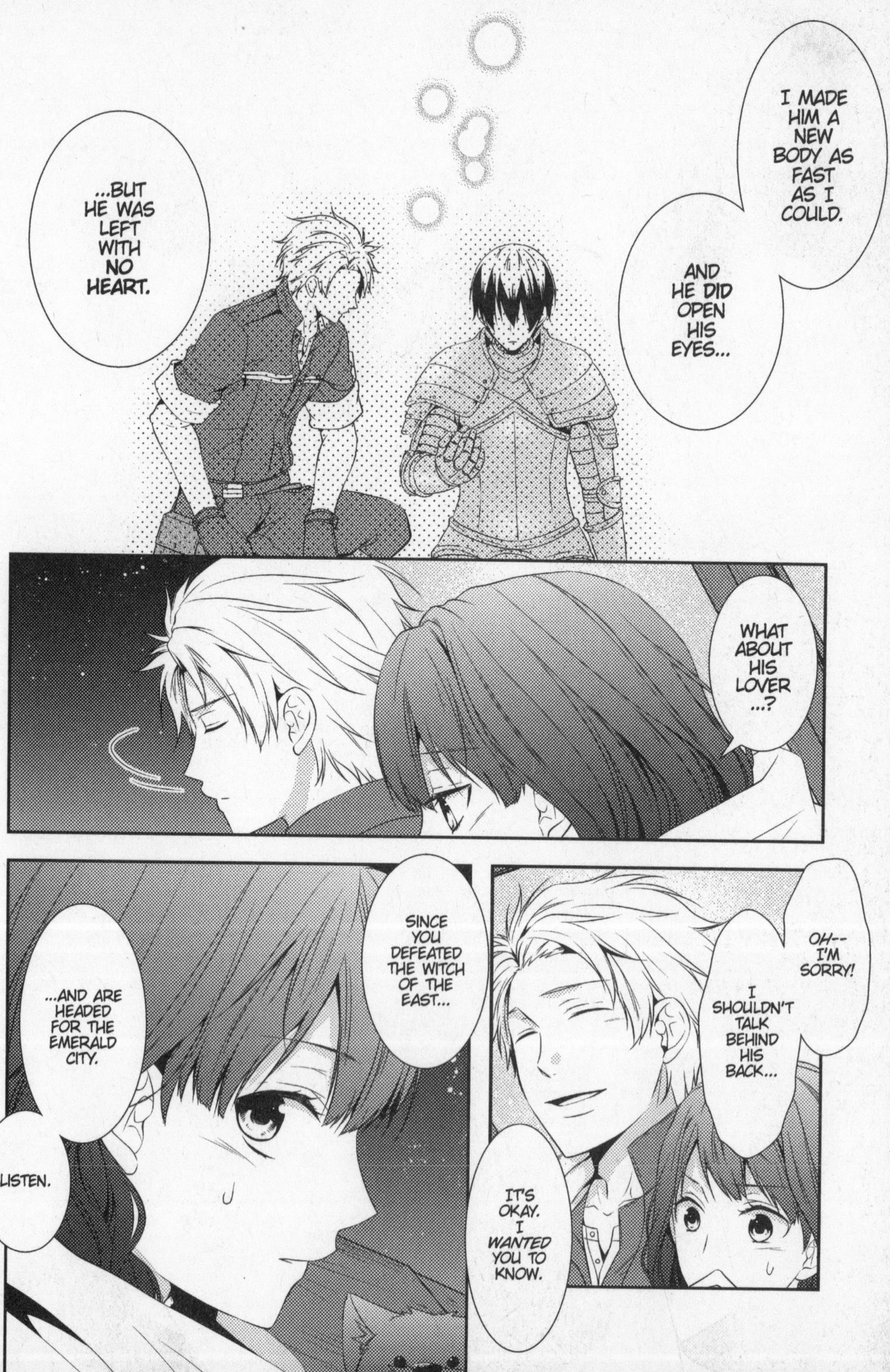
I MADE HIM A NEW BODY AS FAST AS I COULD.
AND HE DID OPEN HIS EYES...
...BUT HE WAS LEFT WITH NO HEART.
WHAT ABOUT HIS LOVER ...?
OH-- I'M SORRY!
I SHOULDN'T TALK BEHIND HIS BACK...
IT'S OKAY. I *WANTED* YOU TO KNOW.
SINCE YOU DEFEATED THE WITCH OF THE EAST...
...AND ARE HEADED FOR THE EMERALD CITY.
LISTEN.

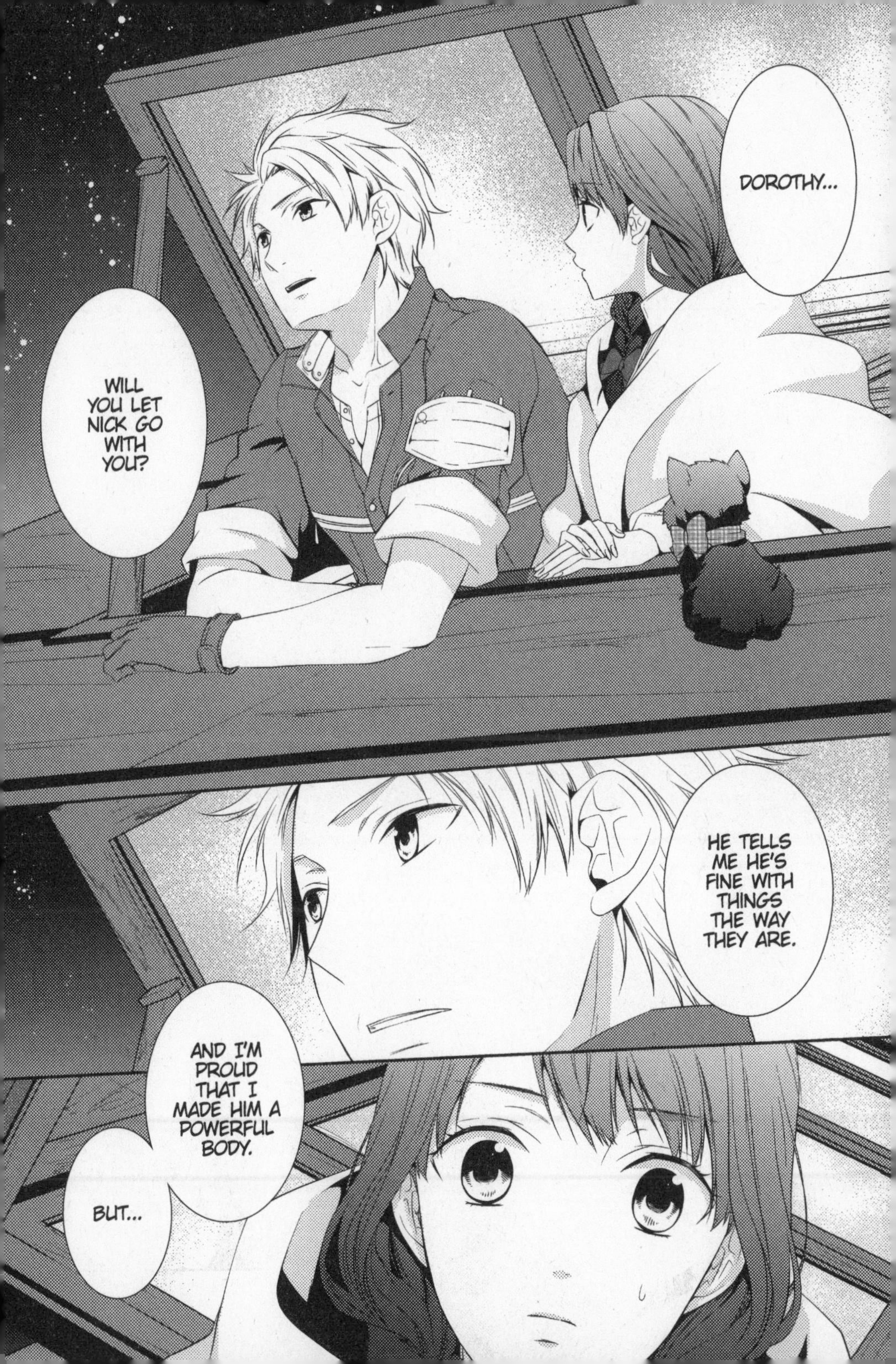
DOROTHY...
WILL YOU LET NICK GO WITH YOU?
HE TELLS ME HE'S FINE WITH THINGS THE WAY THEY ARE.
AND I'M PROUD THAT I MADE HIM A POWERFUL BODY.
BUT...

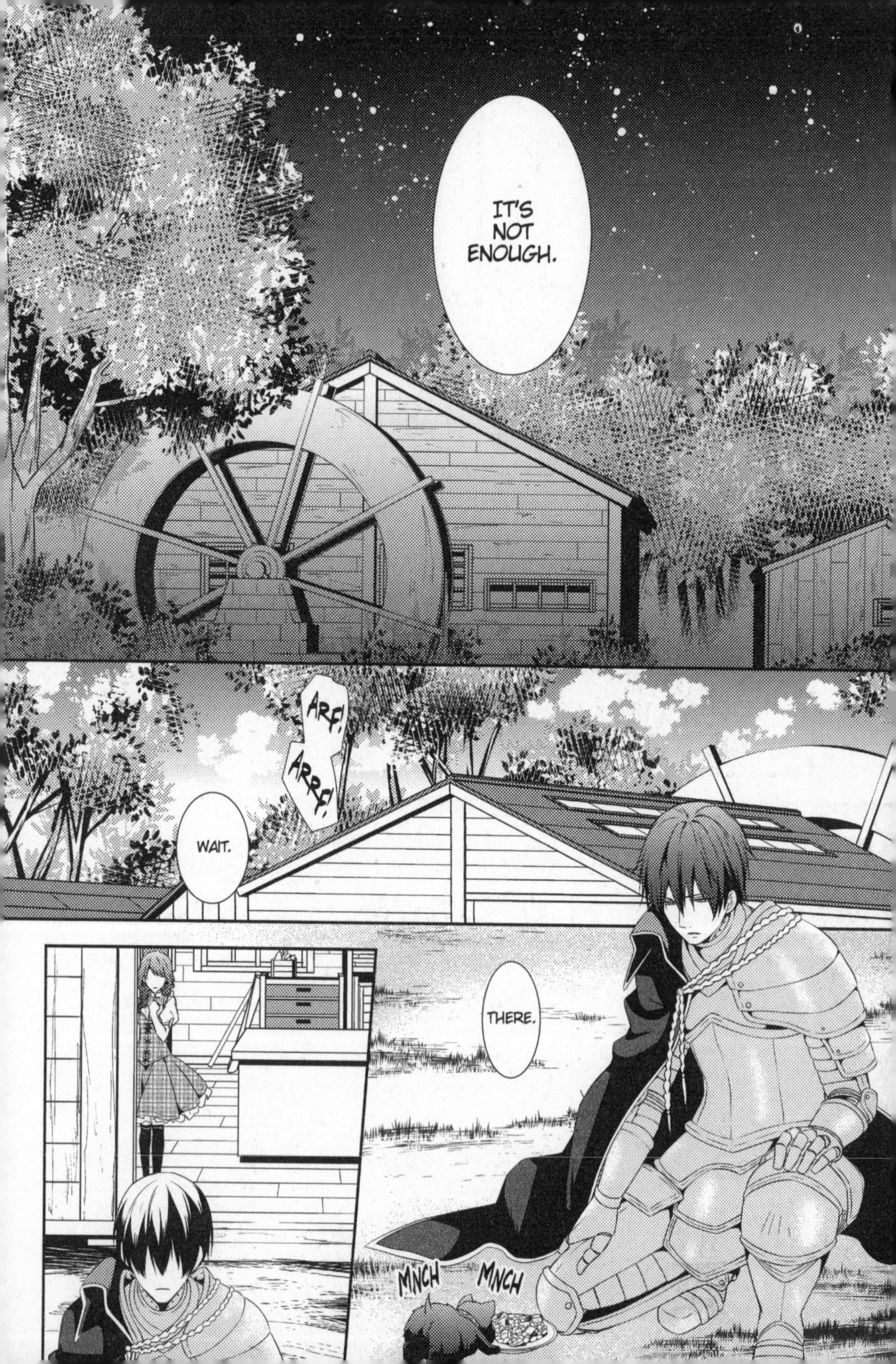
IT'S NOT ENOUGH.
ARF!
ARRF!
WAIT.
THERE.
MNCH
MNCH

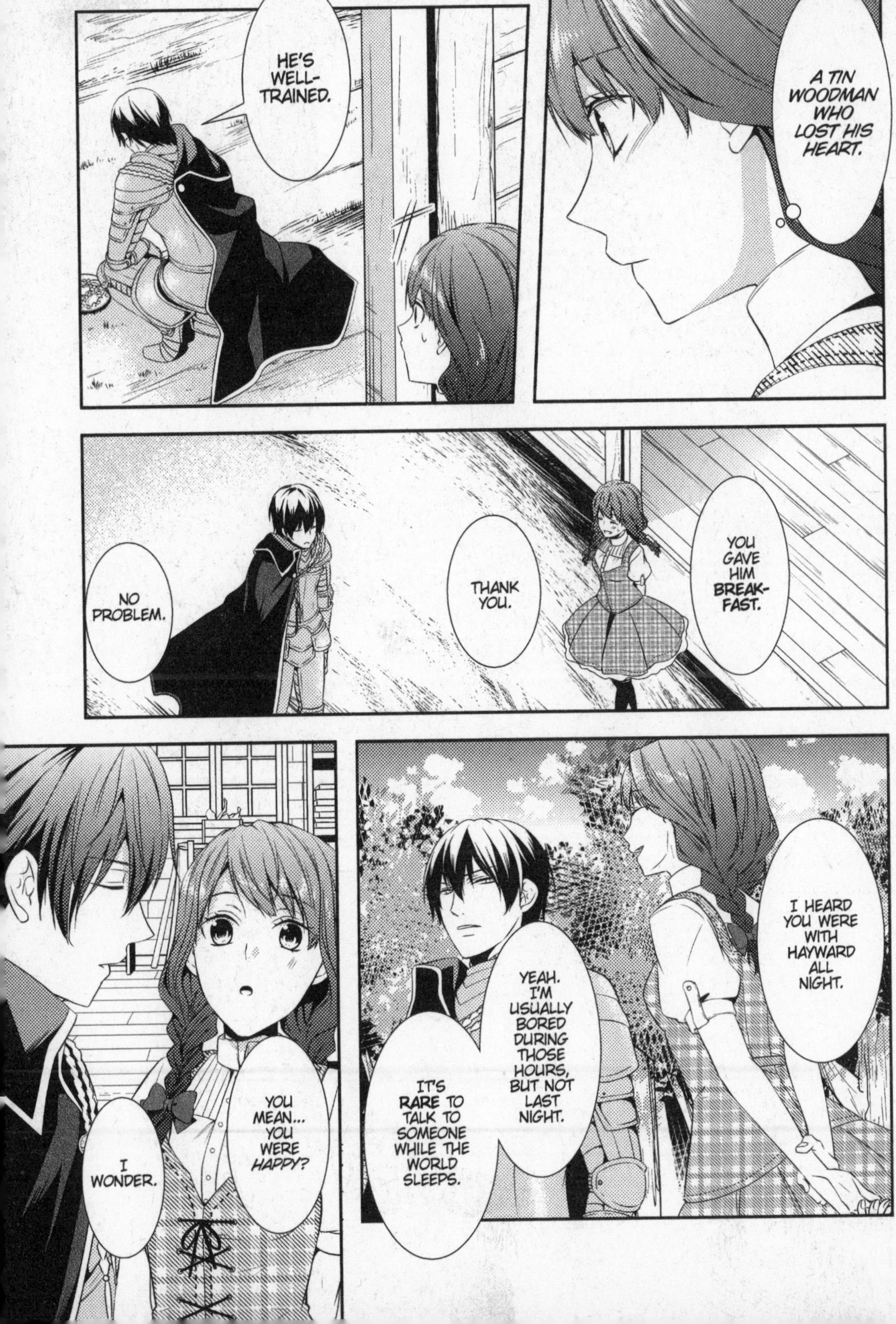
A TIN WOODMAN WHO LOST HIS HEART.
HE'S WELL-TRAINED.
YOU GAVE HIM **BREAKFAST.**
THANK YOU.
NO PROBLEM.
I HEARD YOU WERE WITH HAYWARD ALL NIGHT.
YEAH. I'M USUALLY BORED DURING THOSE HOURS, BUT NOT LAST NIGHT.
IT'S **RARE** TO TALK TO SOMEONE WHILE THE WORLD SLEEPS.
YOU MEAN... YOU WERE *HAPPY*?
I WONDER.

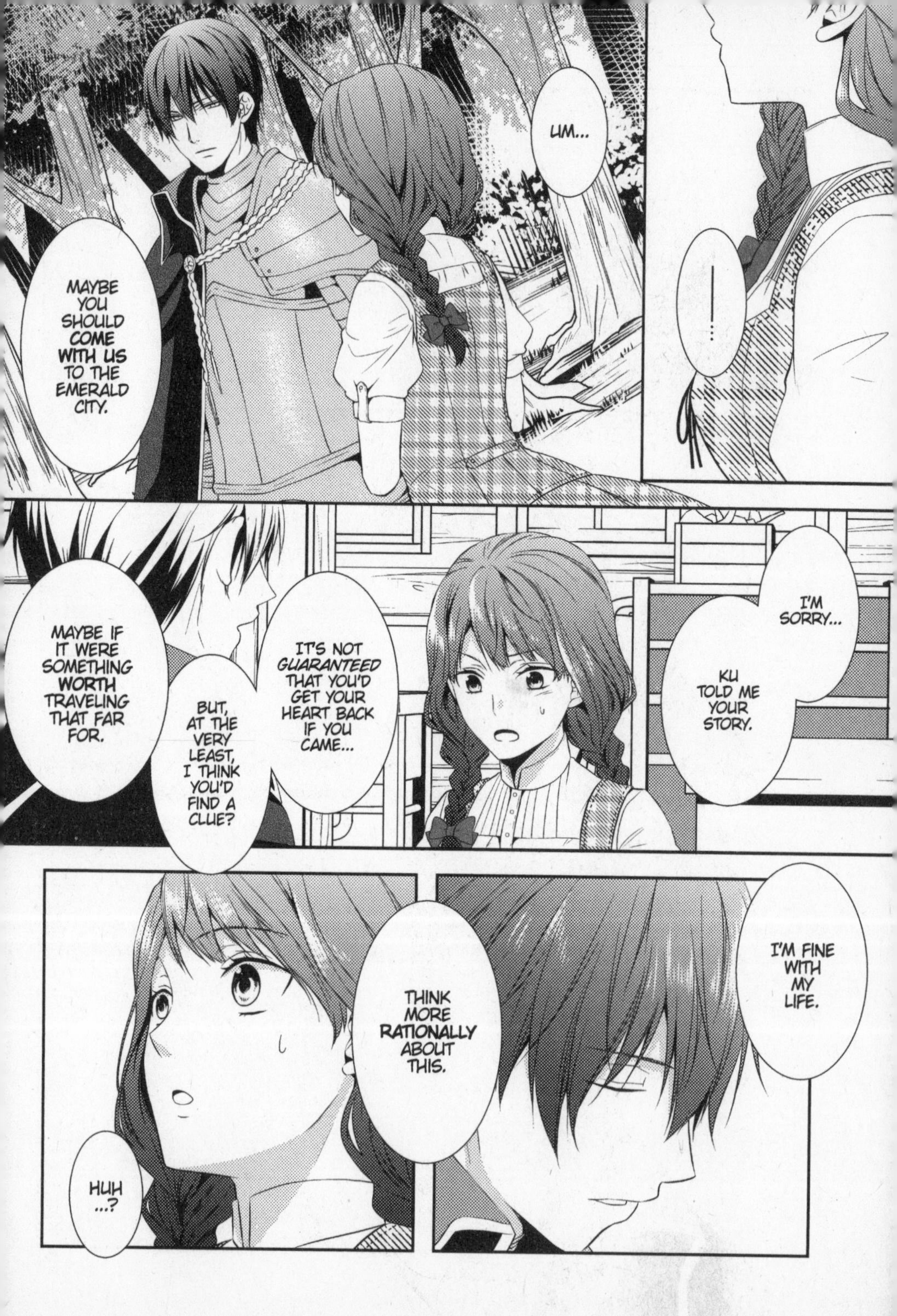
!......
UM...
MAYBE YOU SHOULD COME WITH US TO THE EMERALD CITY.
I'M SORRY...
KU TOLD ME YOUR STORY.
IT'S NOT GUARANTEED THAT YOU'D GET YOUR HEART BACK IF YOU CAME...
BUT, AT THE VERY LEAST, I THINK YOU'D FIND A CLUE?
MAYBE IF IT WERE SOMETHING WORTH TRAVELING THAT FAR FOR.
I'M FINE WITH MY LIFE.
THINK MORE RATIONALLY ABOUT THIS.
HUH ...?

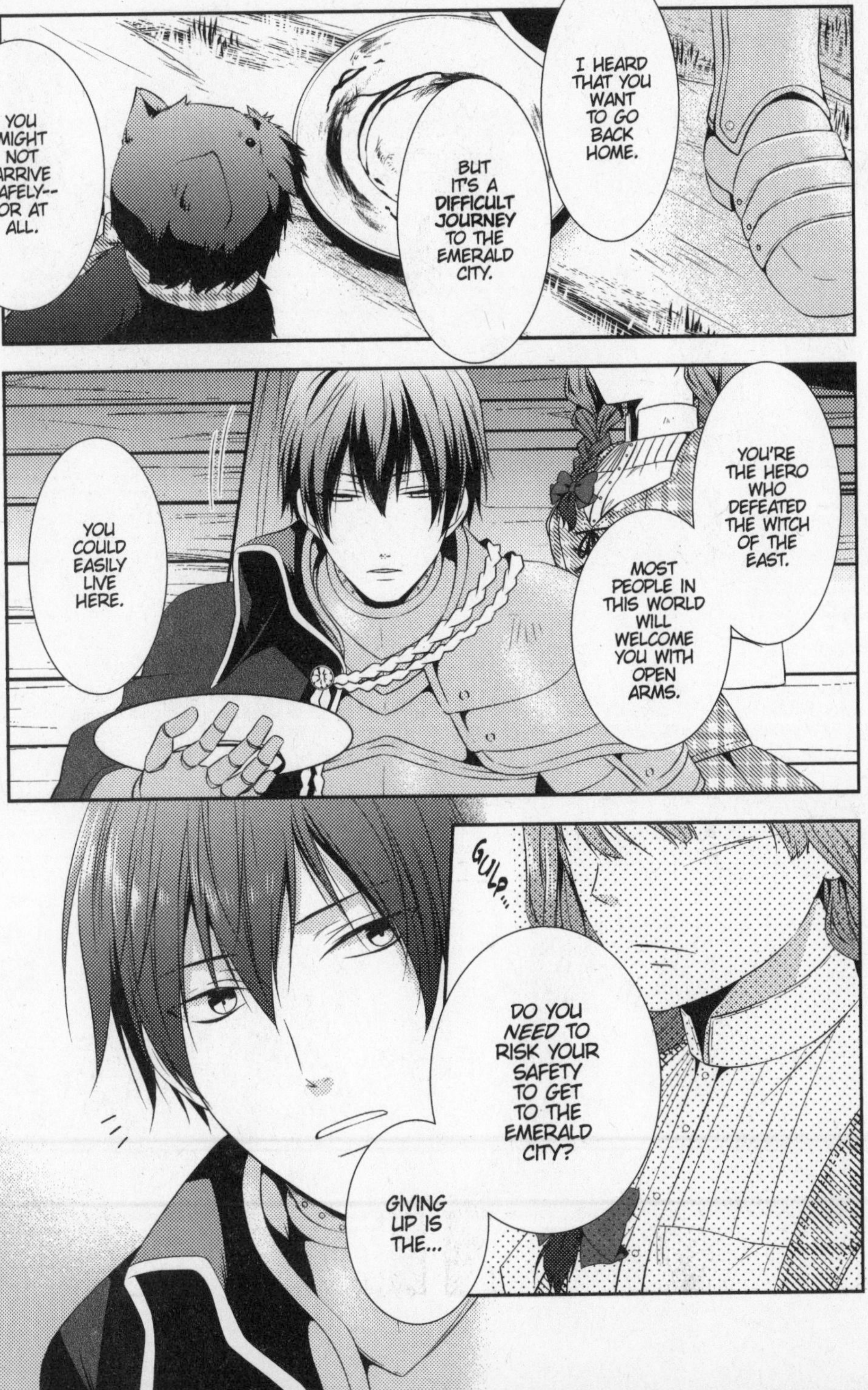
I HEARD THAT YOU WANT TO GO BACK HOME.
BUT IT'S A DIFFICULT JOURNEY TO THE EMERALD CITY.
YOU MIGHT NOT ARRIVE SAFELY-- OR AT ALL.
YOU'RE THE HERO WHO DEFEATED THE WITCH OF THE EAST.
MOST PEOPLE IN THIS WORLD WILL WELCOME YOU WITH OPEN ARMS.
YOU COULD EASILY LIVE HERE.
GULP...
DO YOU NEED TO RISK YOUR SAFETY TO GET TO THE EMERALD CITY?
GIVING UP IS THE...

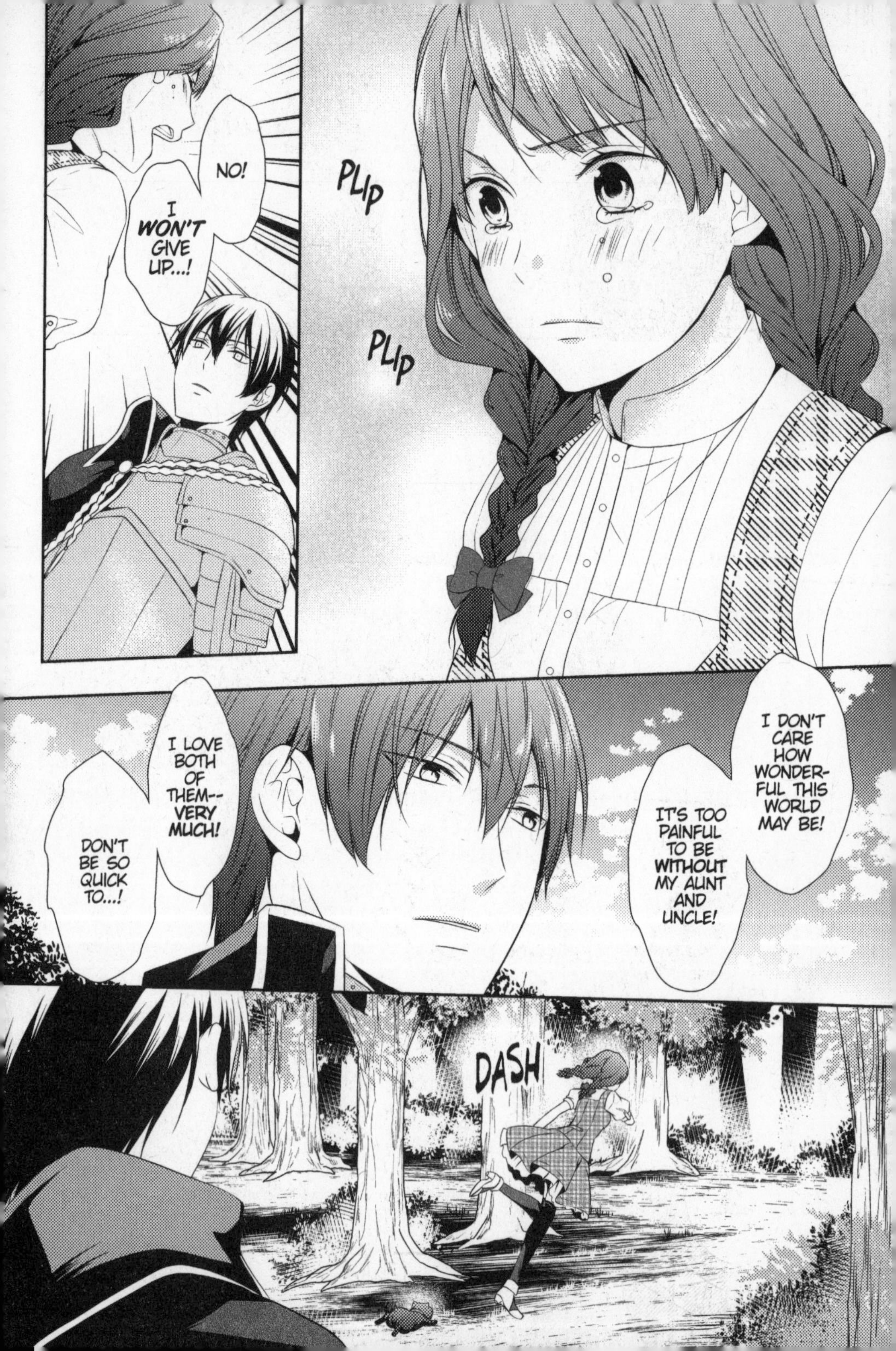
PLIP
PLIP
NO!
I WON'T GIVE UP...!
I DON'T CARE HOW WONDERFUL THIS WORLD MAY BE!
IT'S TOO PAINFUL TO BE WITHOUT MY AUNT AND UNCLE!
I LOVE BOTH OF THEM--VERY MUCH!
DON'T BE SO QUICK TO...!
DASH

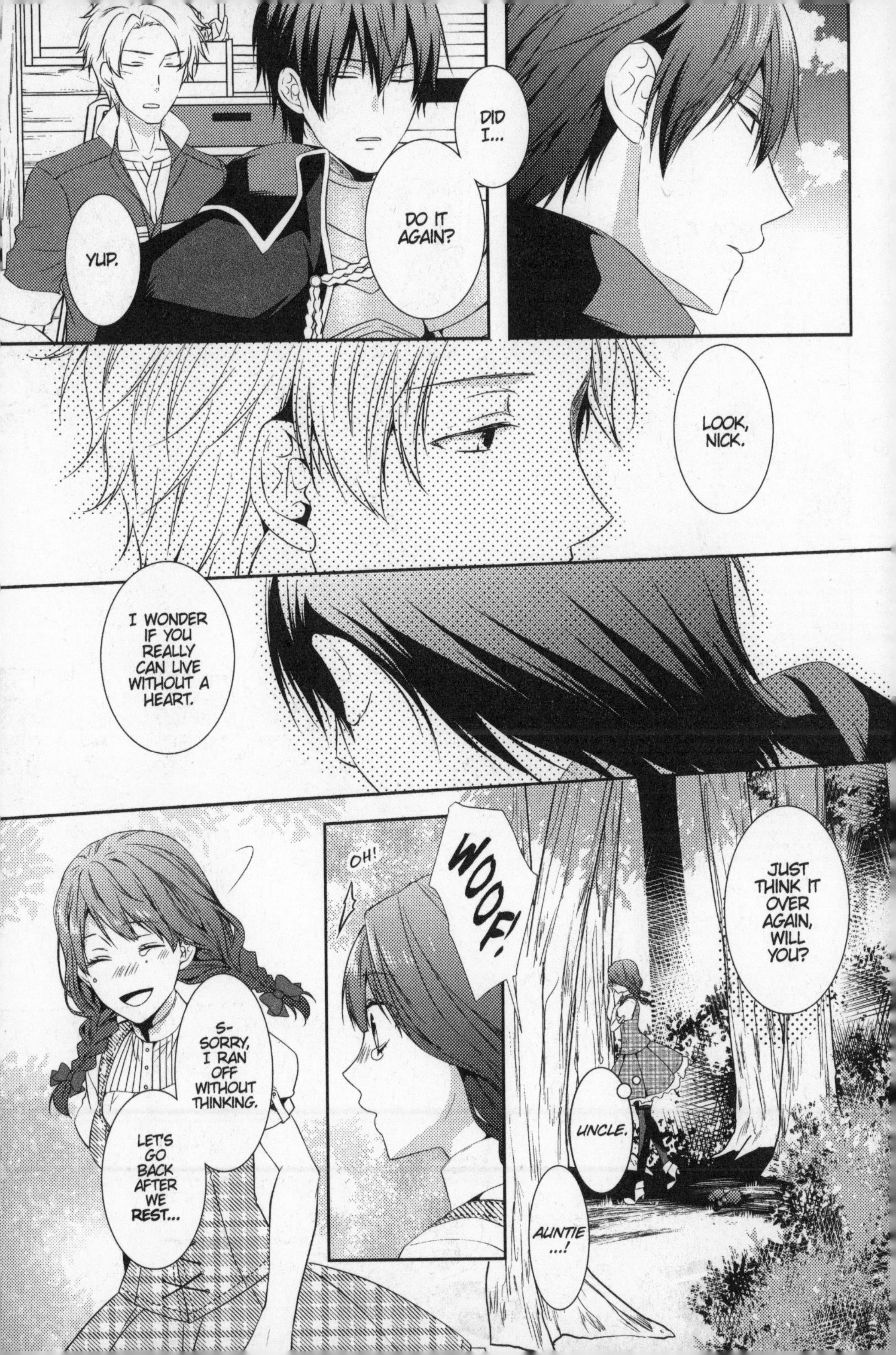
DID I...
DO IT AGAIN?
YUP.
LOOK, NICK.
I WONDER IF YOU REALLY CAN LIVE WITHOUT A HEART.
JUST THINK IT OVER AGAIN, WILL YOU?
UNCLE.
AUNTIE ...!
WOOF!
OH!
S-SORRY, I RAN OFF WITHOUT THINKING.
LET'S GO BACK AFTER WE REST...

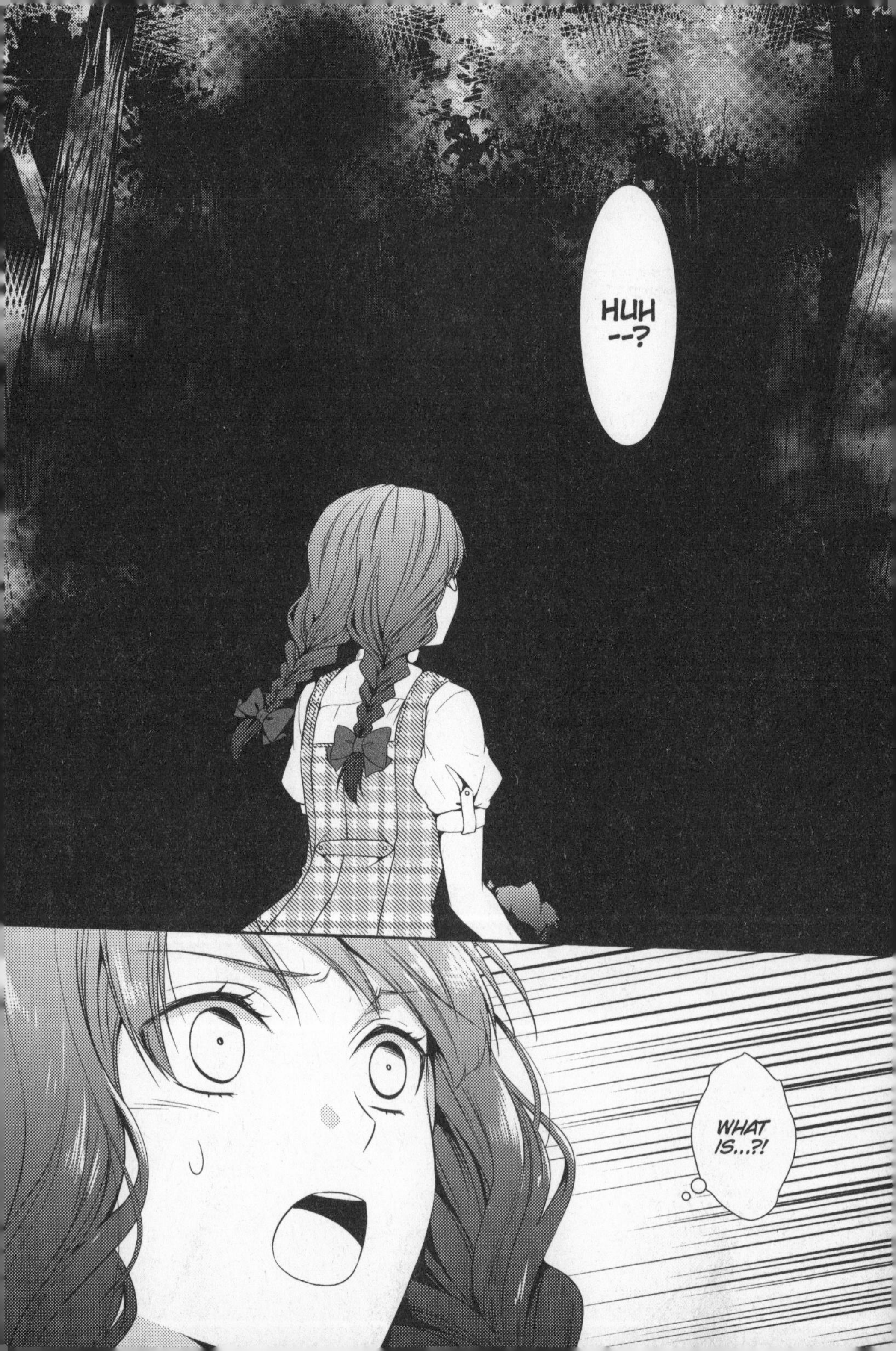
HUH --?
WHAT IS...?!

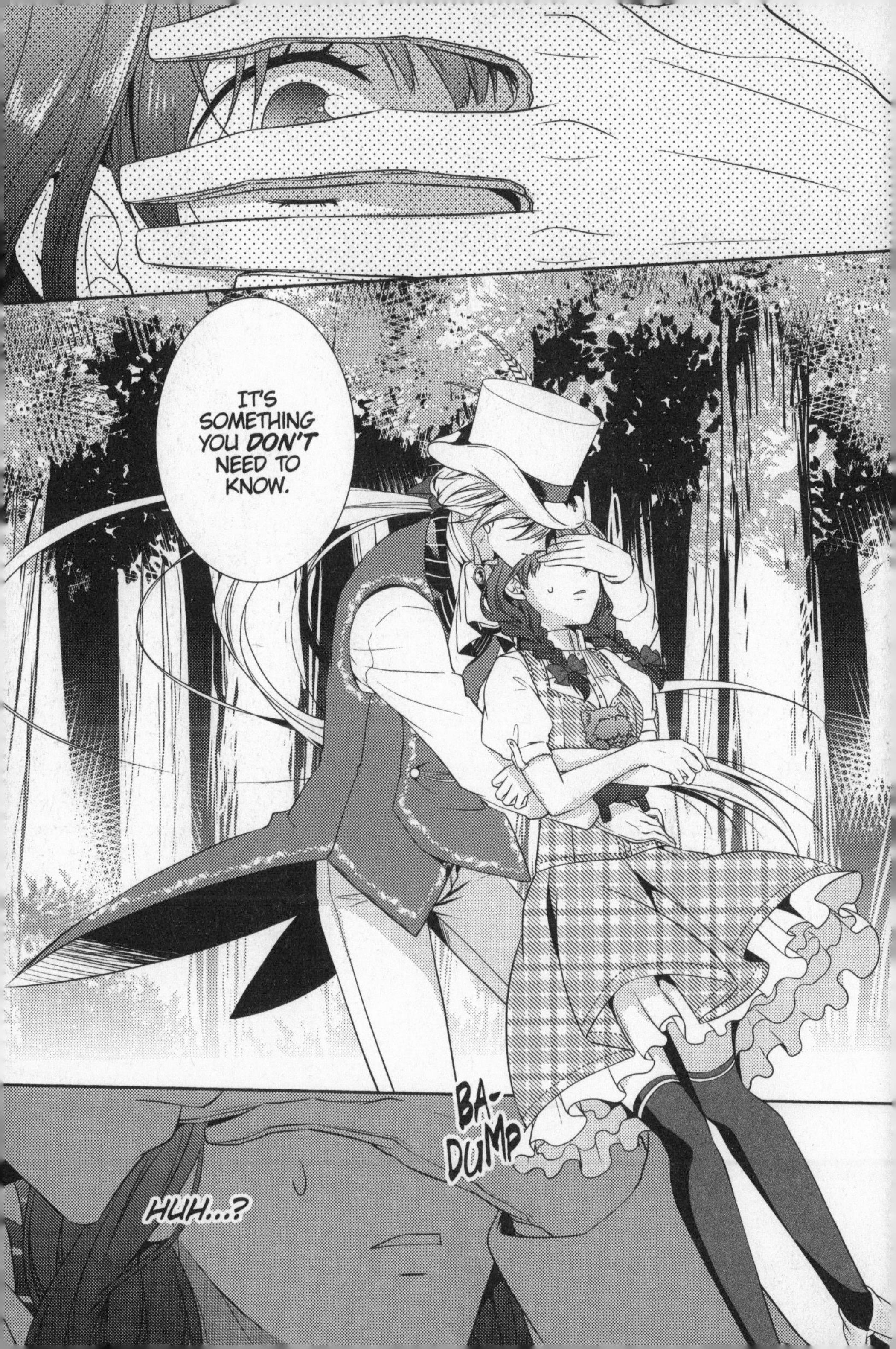
IT'S SOMETHING YOU **DON'T** NEED TO KNOW.
BA-DUMP
HUH...?

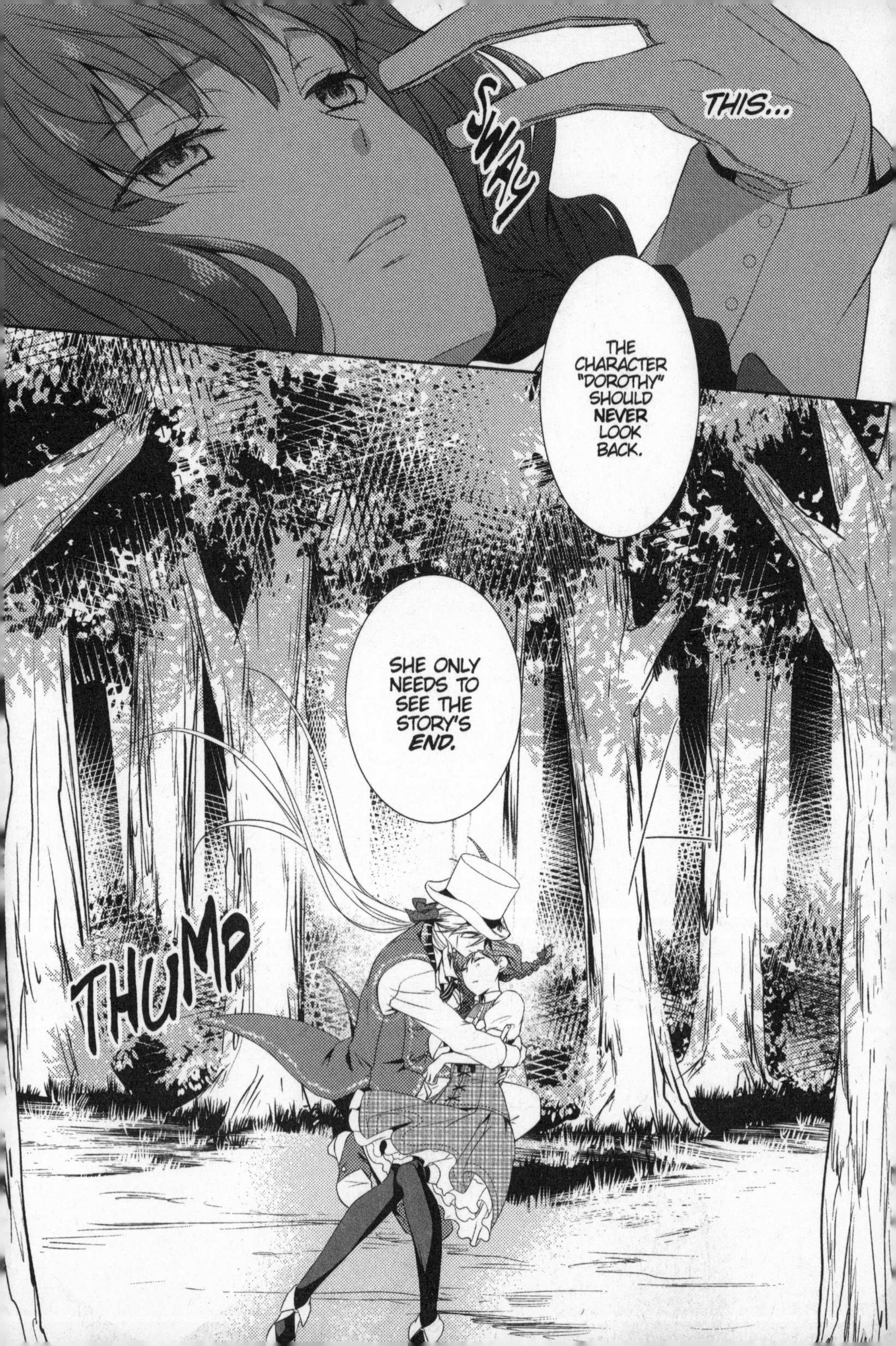
THIS...
SWAY
THE CHARACTER "DOROTHY" SHOULD NEVER LOOK BACK.
SHE ONLY NEEDS TO SEE THE STORY'S END.
THUMP

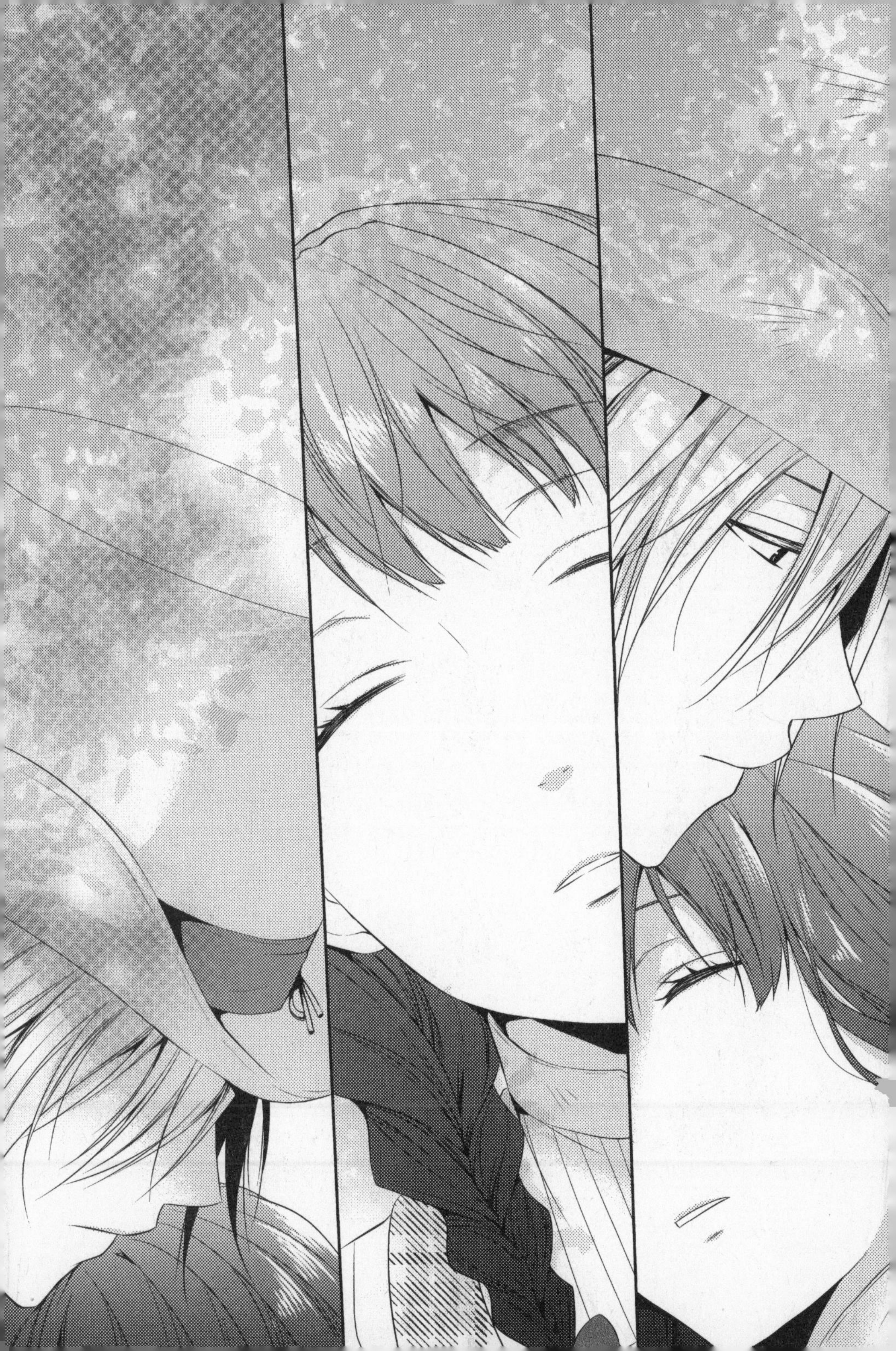

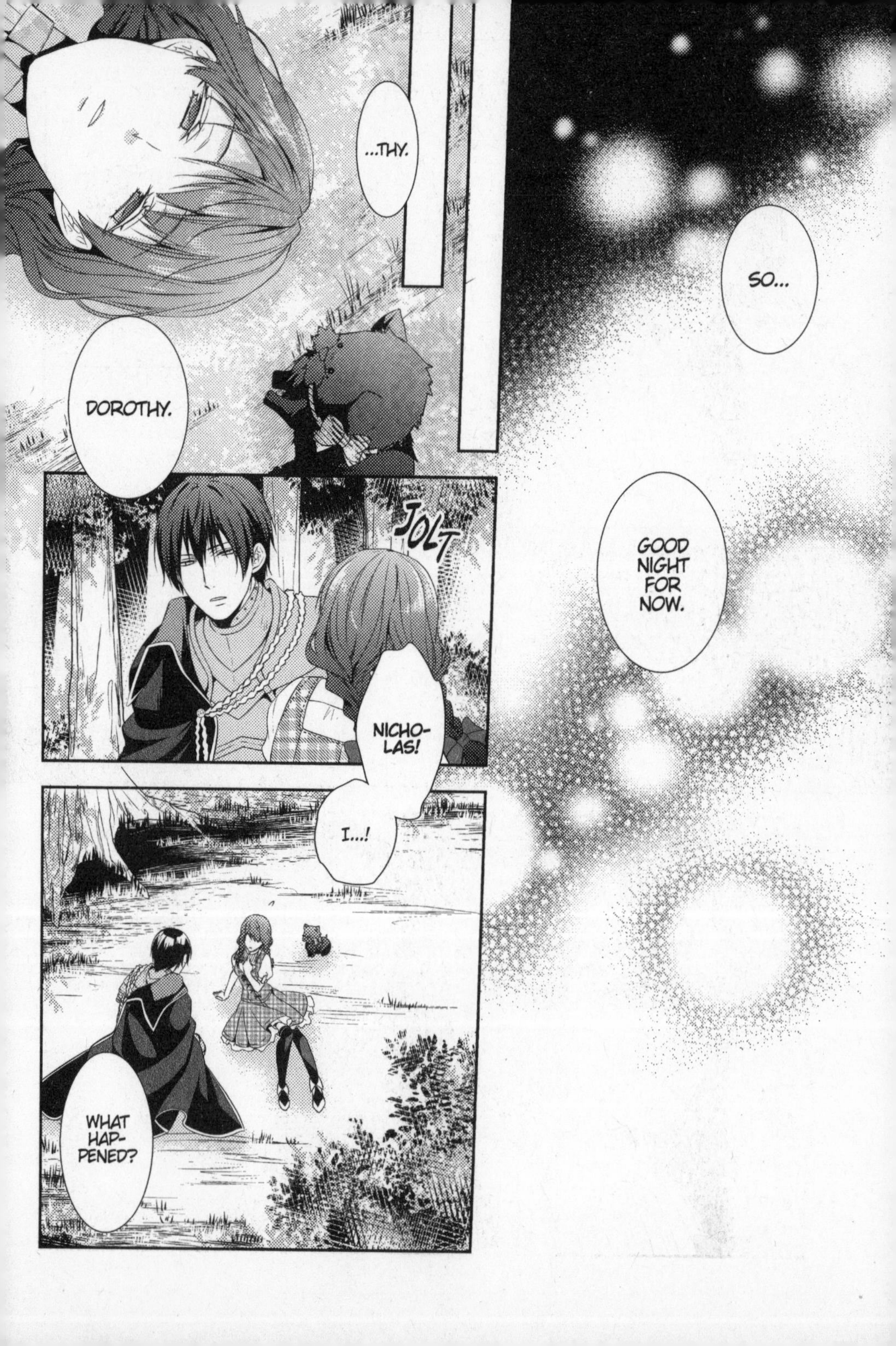
SO...
GOOD NIGHT FOR NOW.
...THY.
DOROTHY.
JOLT
NICHO-LAS!
I...!
WHAT HAP-PENED?

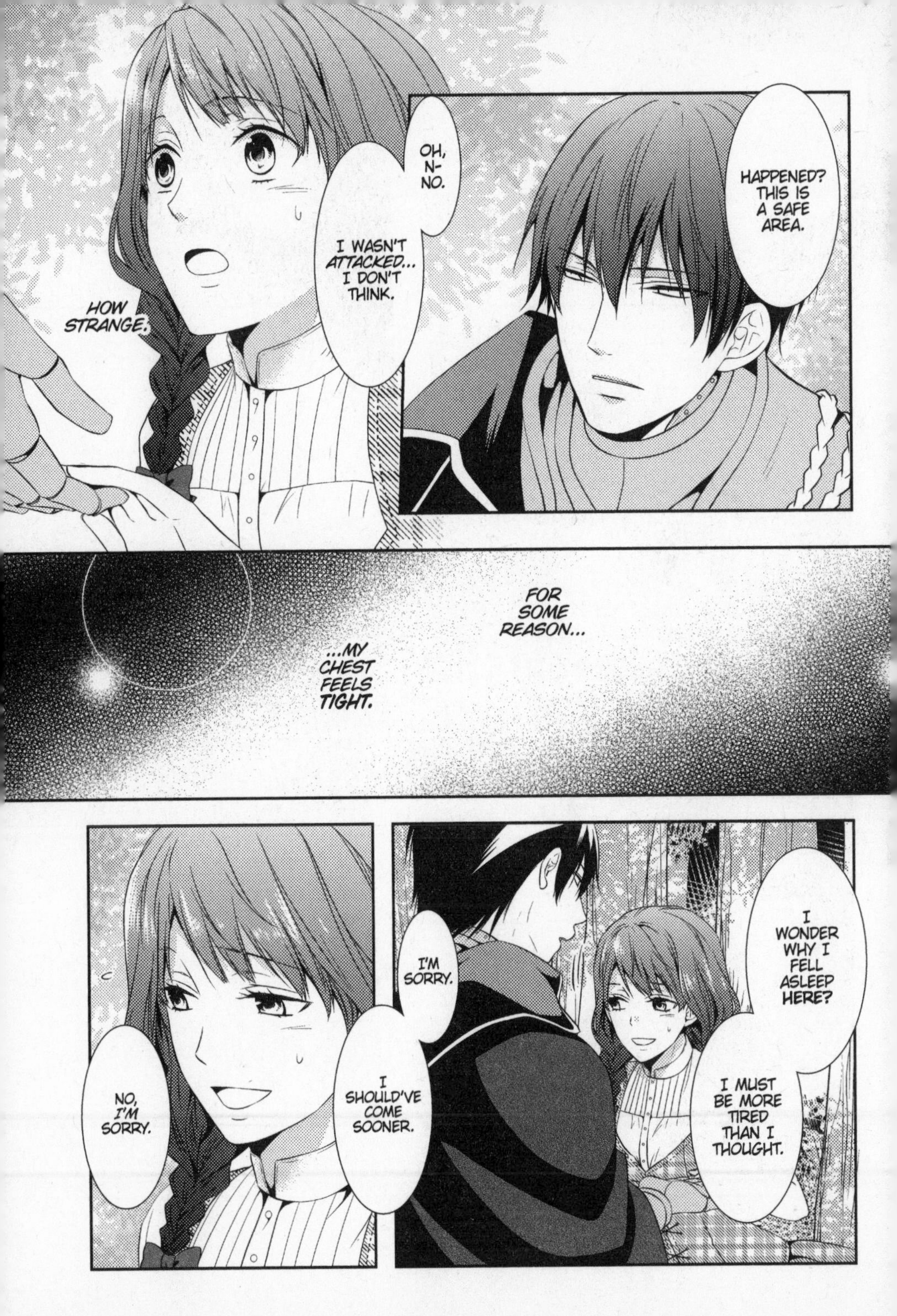
HAPPENED? THIS IS A SAFE AREA.
OH, N-NO.
I WASN'T ATTACKED... I DON'T THINK.
HOW STRANGE.
FOR SOME REASON...
...MY CHEST FEELS TIGHT.
I WONDER WHY I FELL ASLEEP HERE?
I MUST BE MORE TIRED THAN I THOUGHT.
I'M SORRY.
I SHOULD'VE COME SOONER.
NO, I'M SORRY.

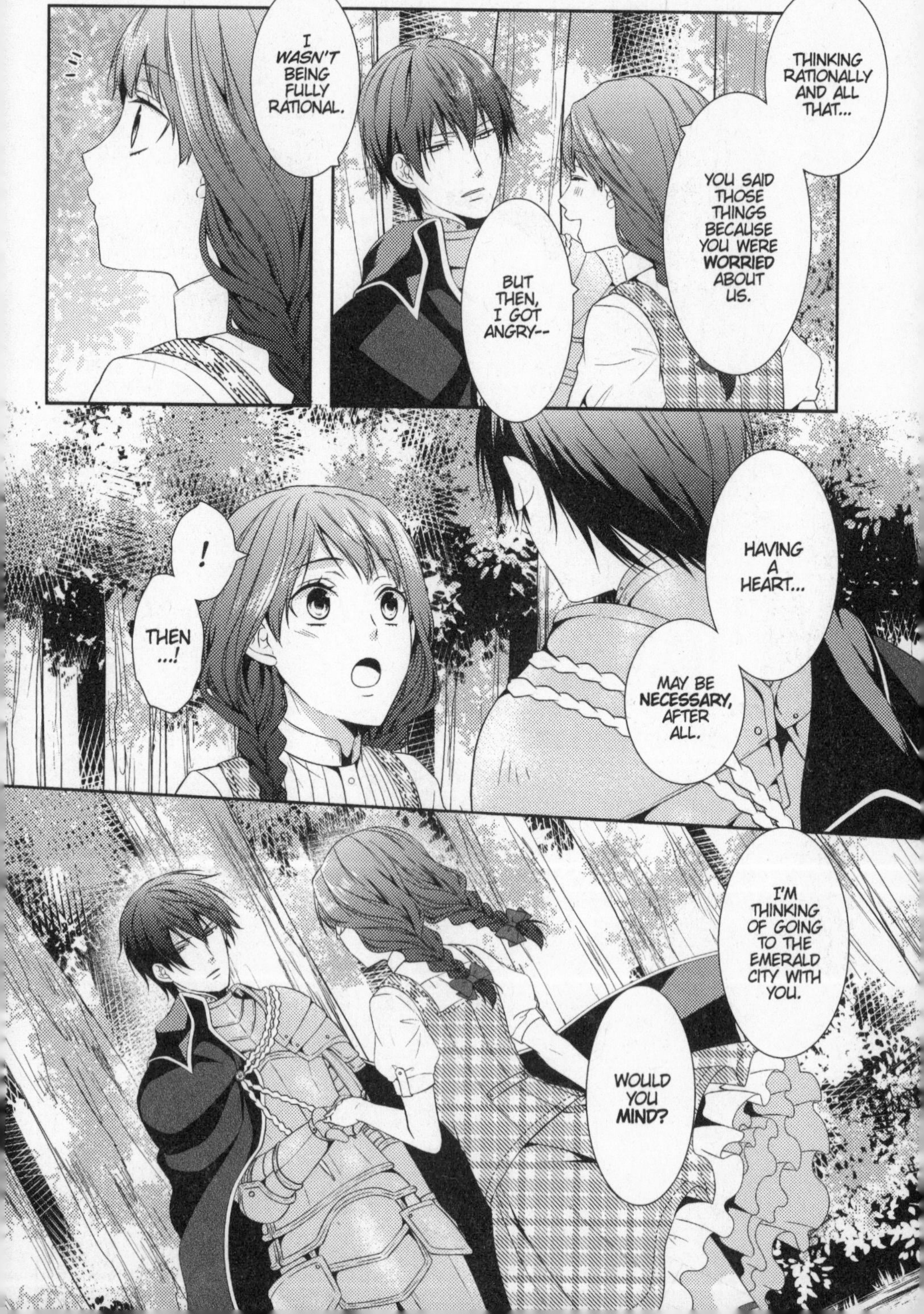
THINKING RATIONALLY AND ALL THAT...
YOU SAID THOSE THINGS BECAUSE YOU WERE WORRIED ABOUT US.
BUT THEN, I GOT ANGRY--
I WASN'T BEING FULLY RATIONAL.
HAVING A HEART...
MAY BE NECESSARY, AFTER ALL.
!
THEN ...!
I'M THINKING OF GOING TO THE EMERALD CITY WITH YOU.
WOULD YOU MIND?

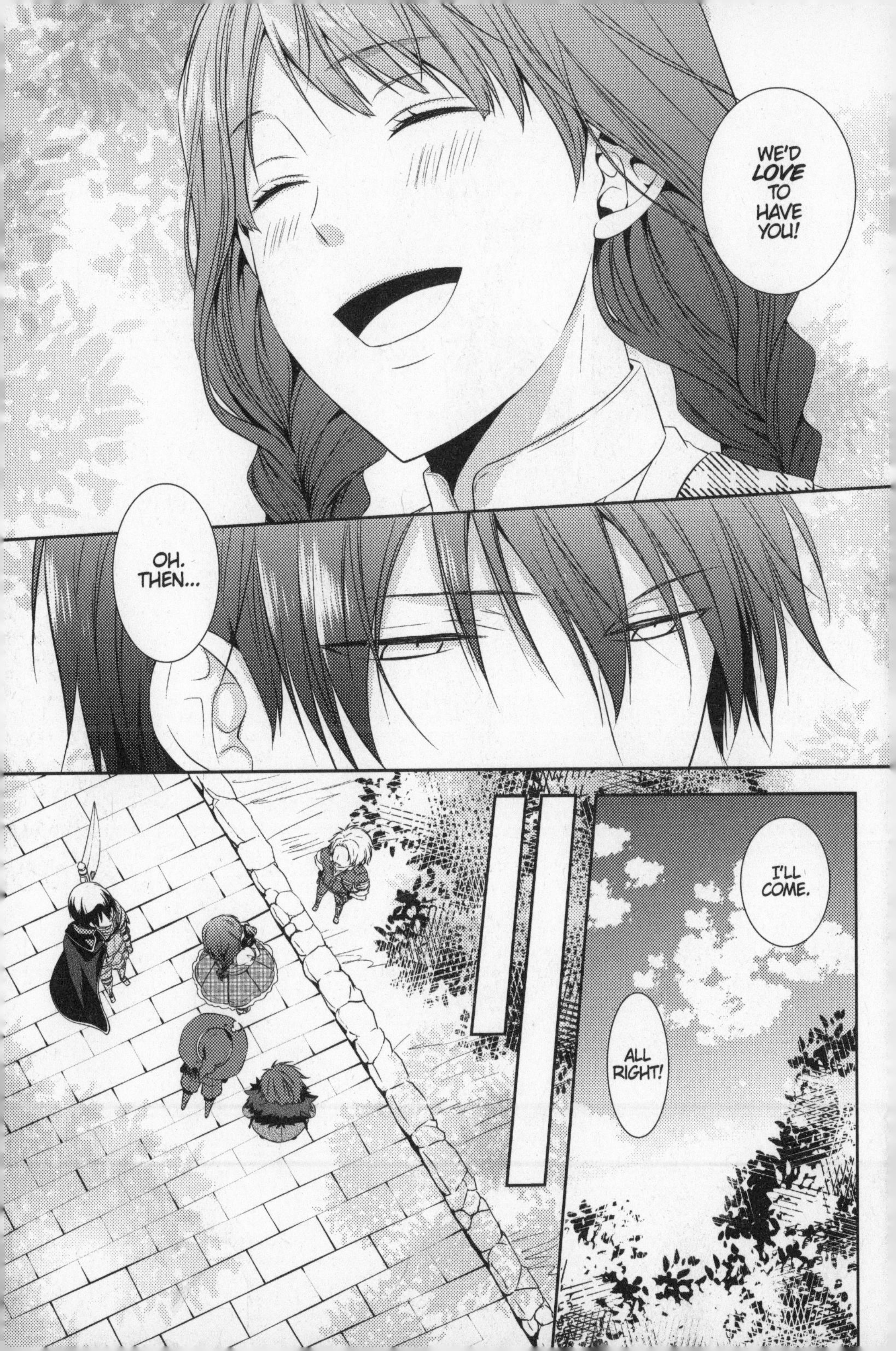

WE'D LOVE TO HAVE YOU!
OH. THEN...
I'LL COME.
ALL RIGHT!

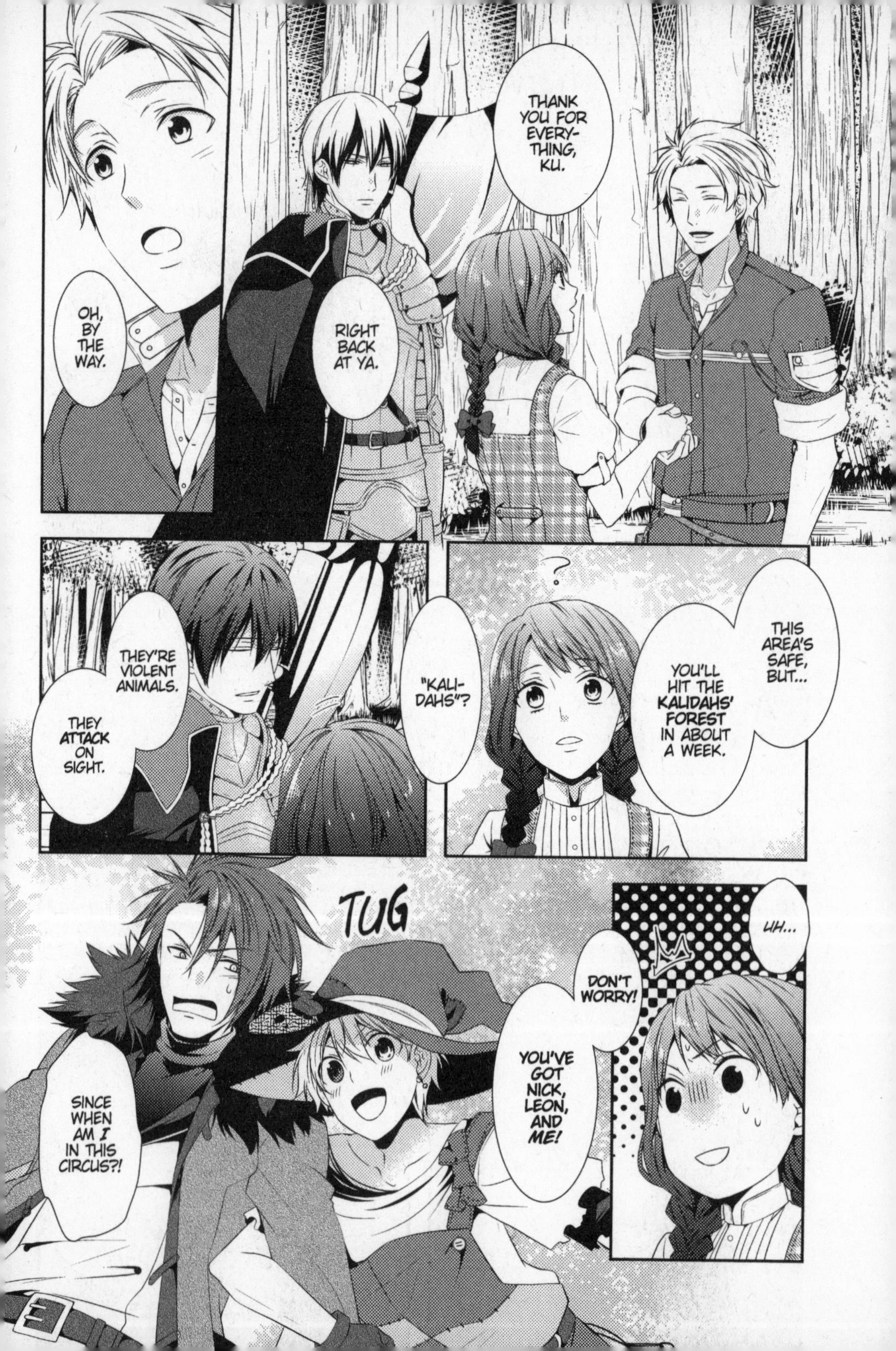
THANK YOU FOR EVERYTHING, KU.
RIGHT BACK AT YA.
OH, BY THE WAY.
THIS AREA'S SAFE, BUT...
YOU'LL HIT THE KALIDAHS' FOREST IN ABOUT A WEEK.
"KALIDAHS"?
THEY'RE VIOLENT ANIMALS.
THEY ATTACK ON SIGHT.
UH...
DON'T WORRY!
YOU'VE GOT NICK, LEON, AND ME!
TUG
SINCE WHEN AM I IN THIS CIRCUS?!

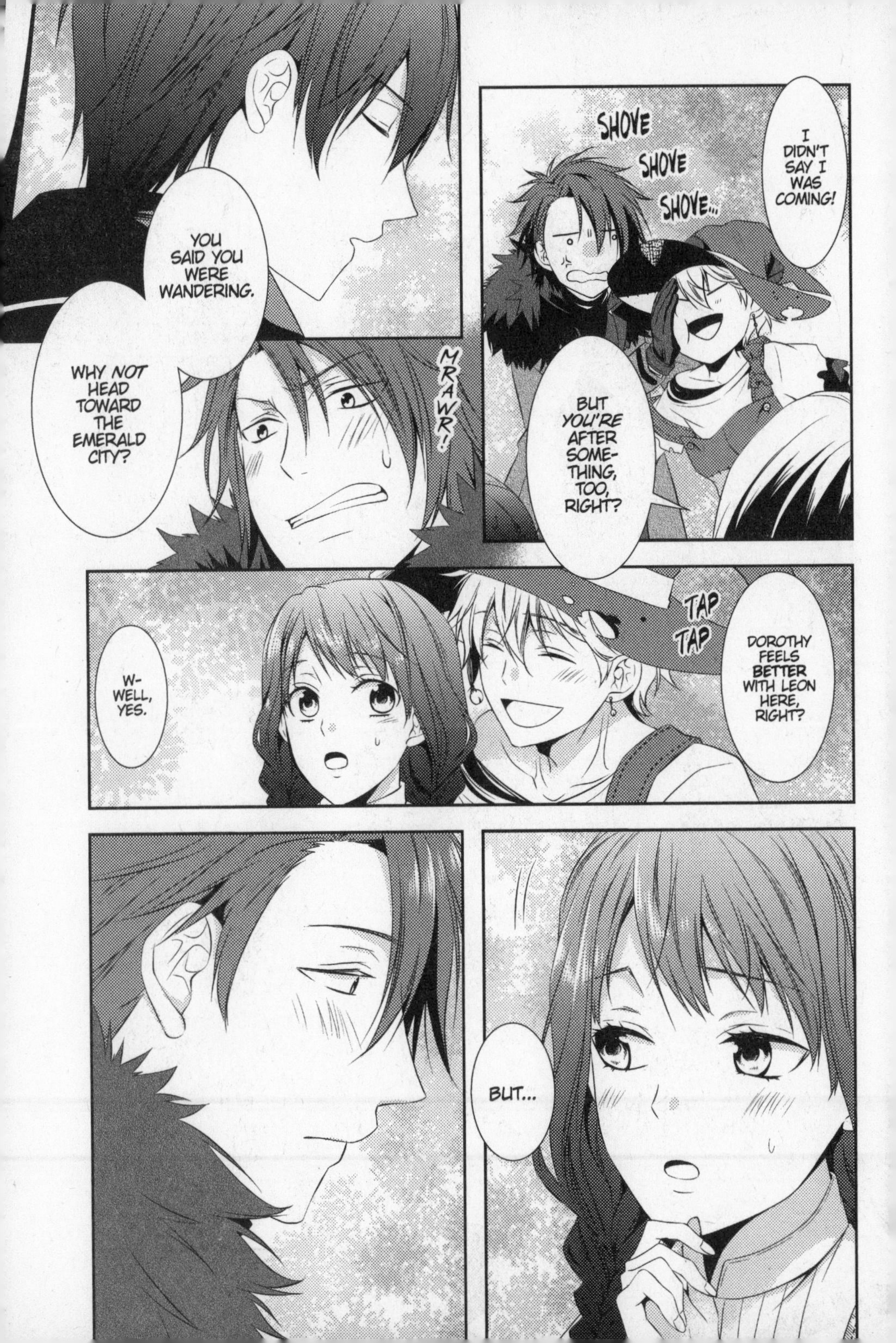
I DIDN'T SAY I WAS COMING!
SHOVE
SHOVE
SHOVE...
BUT YOU'RE AFTER SOME-THING, TOO, RIGHT?
YOU SAID YOU WERE WANDERING.
WHY NOT HEAD TOWARD THE EMERALD CITY?
MRAWR!
TAP TAP
DOROTHY FEELS BETTER WITH LEON HERE, RIGHT?
W-WELL, YES.
BUT...

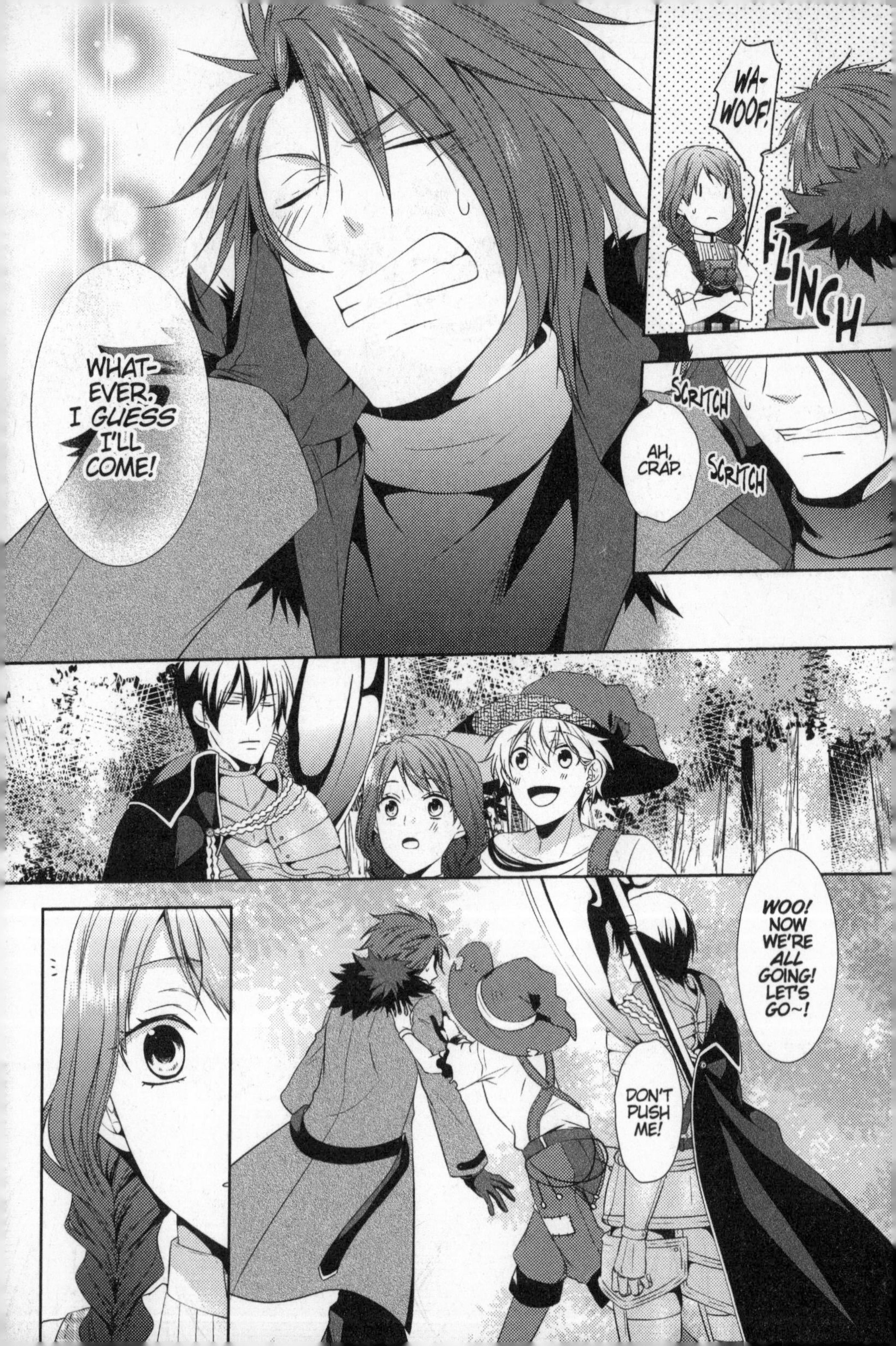
WA-WOOF!
FLINCH
SCRITCH
AH, CRAP.
SCRITCH
WHAT-EVER, I GUESS I'LL COME!
WOO! NOW WE'RE ALL GOING! LET'S GO~!
DON'T PUSH ME!

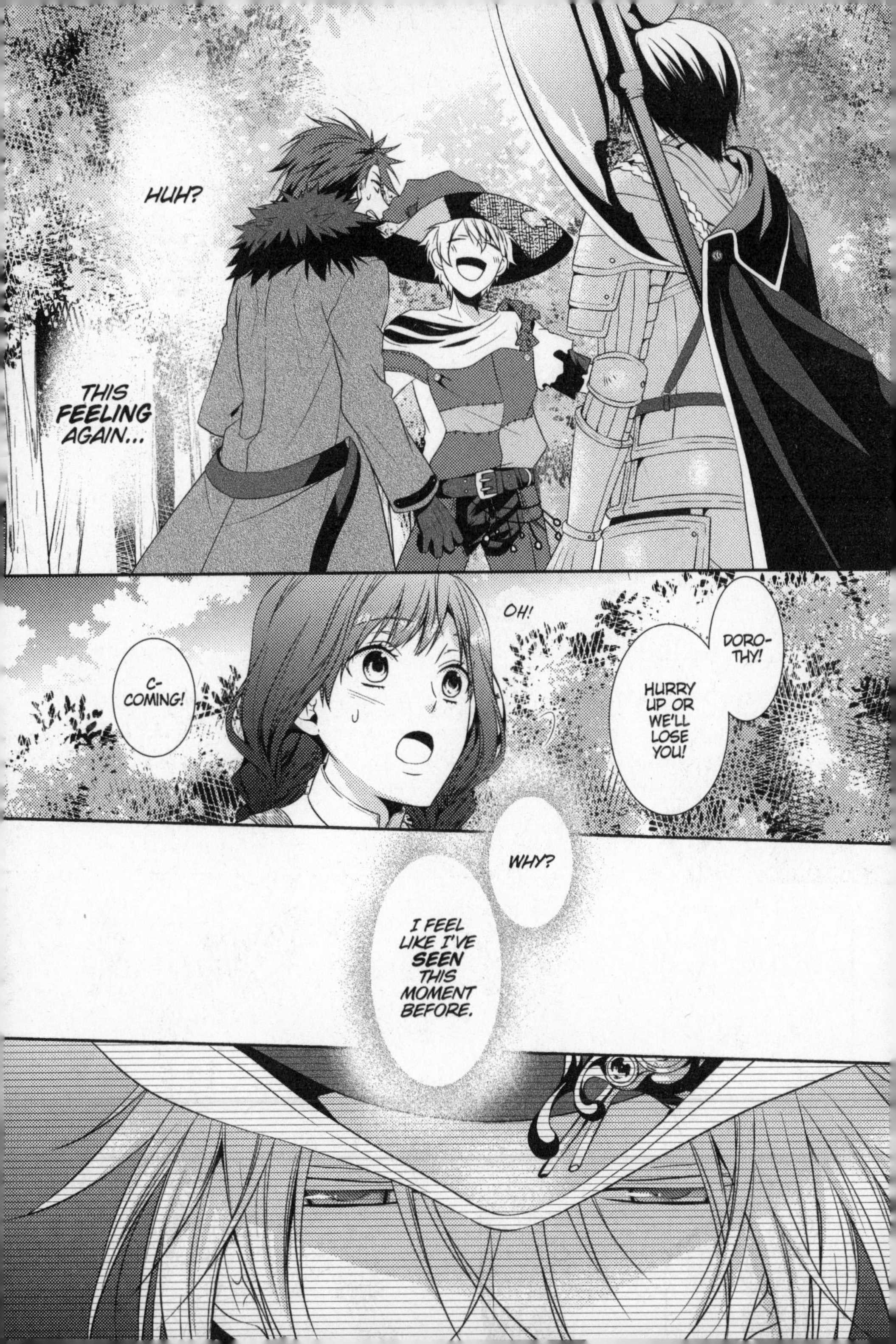
HUH?
THIS FEELING AGAIN...
DORO-THY!
HURRY UP OR WE'LL LOSE YOU!
OH!
C-COMING!
WHY?
I FEEL LIKE I'VE SEEN THIS MOMENT BEFORE.

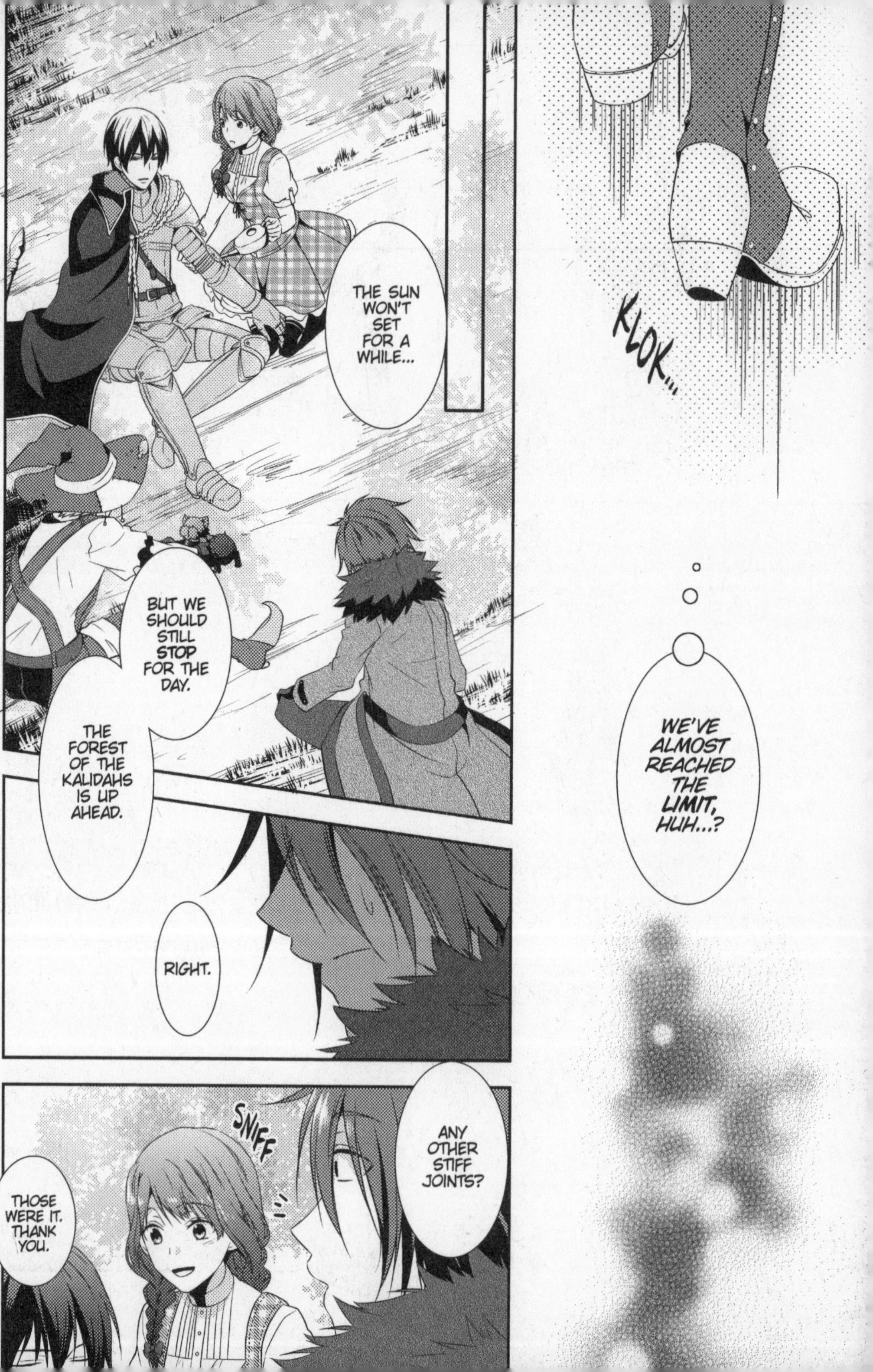
KLOK...
WE'VE ALMOST REACHED THE LIMIT, HUH...?
THE SUN WON'T SET FOR A WHILE...
BUT WE SHOULD STILL STOP FOR THE DAY.
THE FOREST OF THE KALIDAHS IS UP AHEAD.
RIGHT.
SNIFF
ANY OTHER STIFF JOINTS?
THOSE WERE IT. THANK YOU.

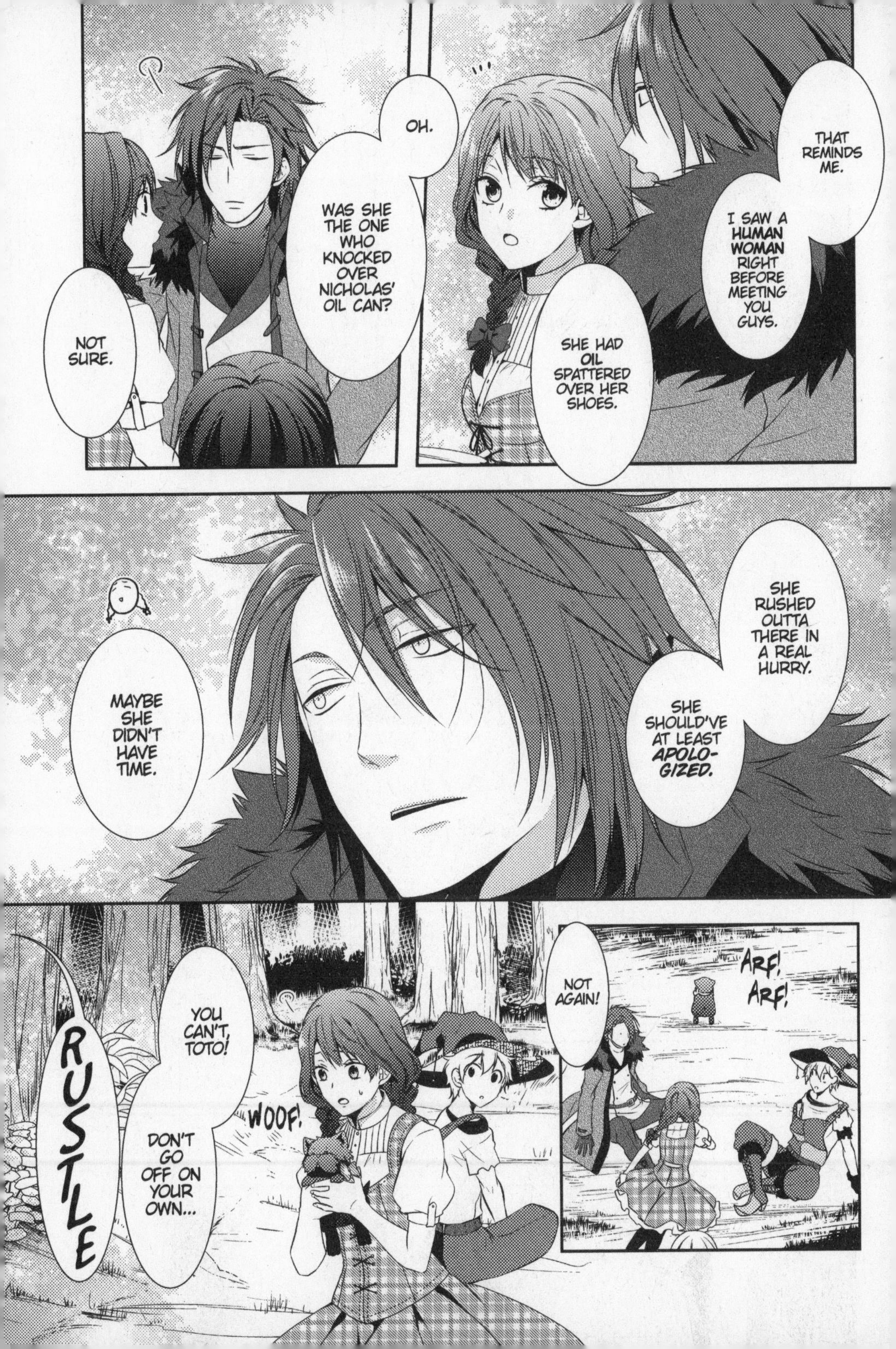
...
THAT REMINDS ME.
I SAW A HUMAN WOMAN RIGHT BEFORE MEETING YOU GUYS.
SHE HAD OIL SPATTERED OVER HER SHOES.
OH.
WAS SHE THE ONE WHO KNOCKED OVER NICHOLAS' OIL CAN?
NOT SURE.
SHE RUSHED OUTTA THERE IN A REAL HURRY.
SHE SHOULD'VE AT LEAST APOLOGIZED.
MAYBE SHE DIDN'T HAVE TIME.
ARF! ARF!
NOT AGAIN!
WOOF!
YOU CAN'T, TOTO!
DON'T GO OFF ON YOUR OWN...
RUSTLE

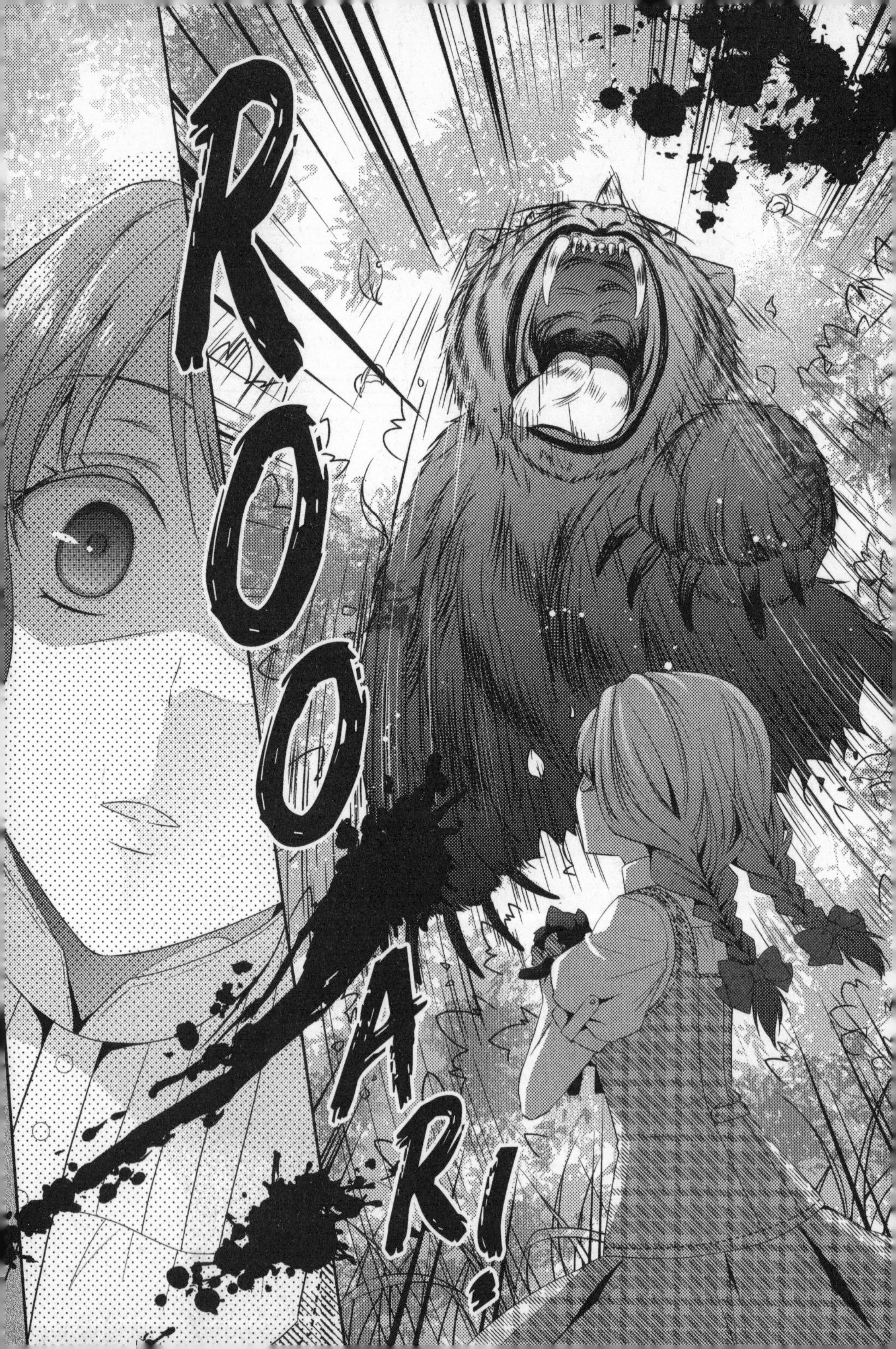
ROOAR!

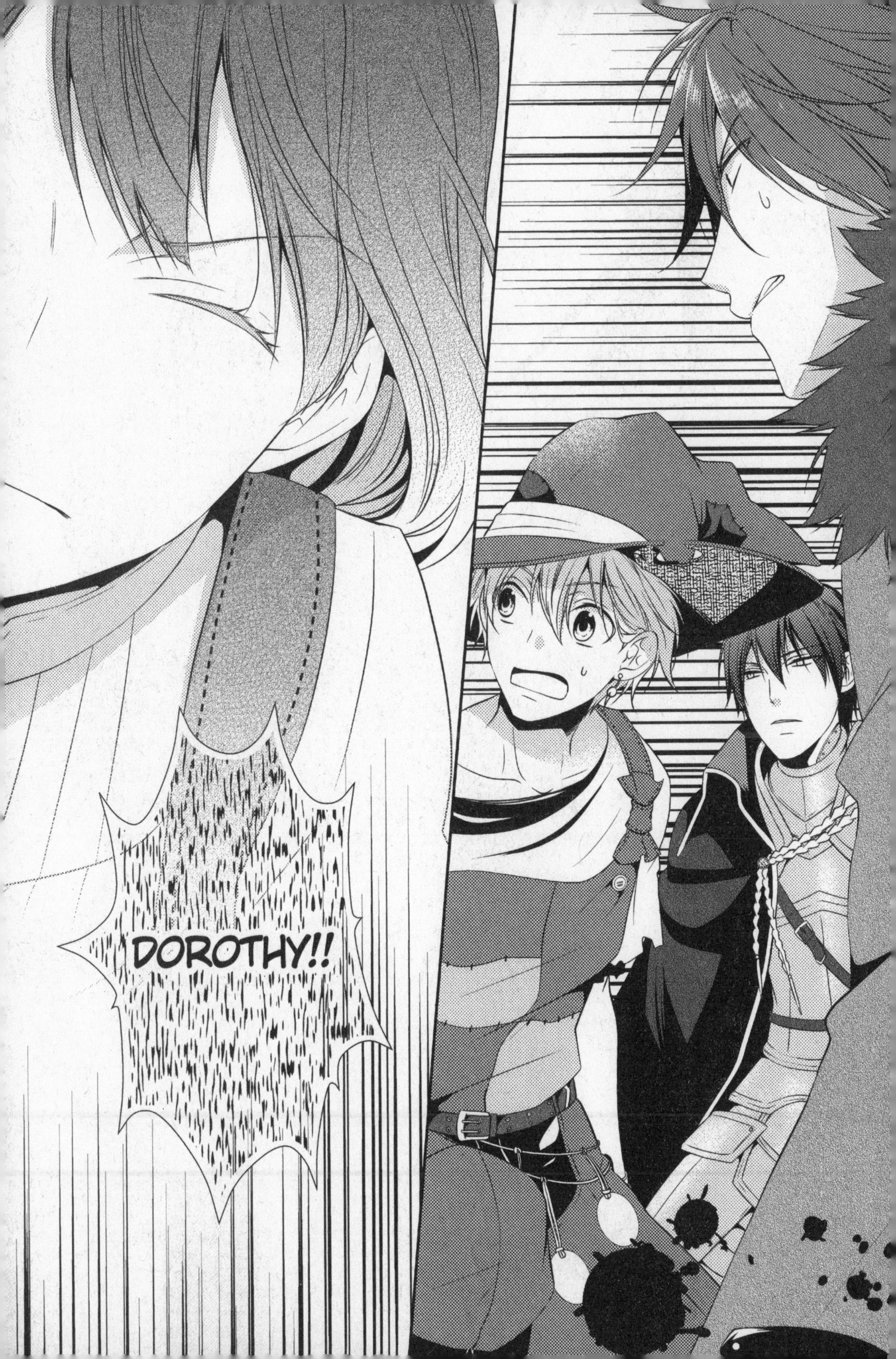
DOROTHY!!

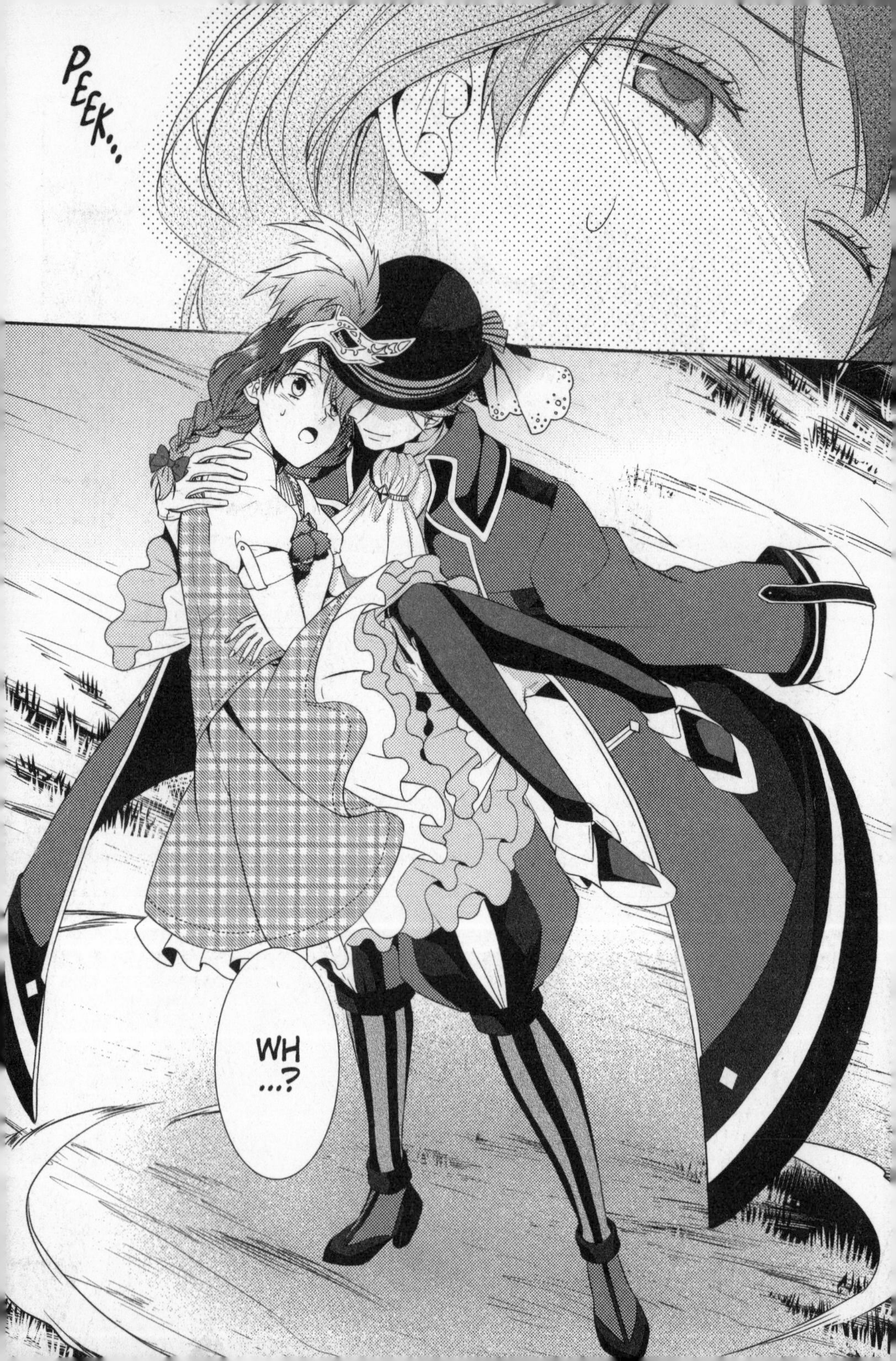
PEEK...
WH...?

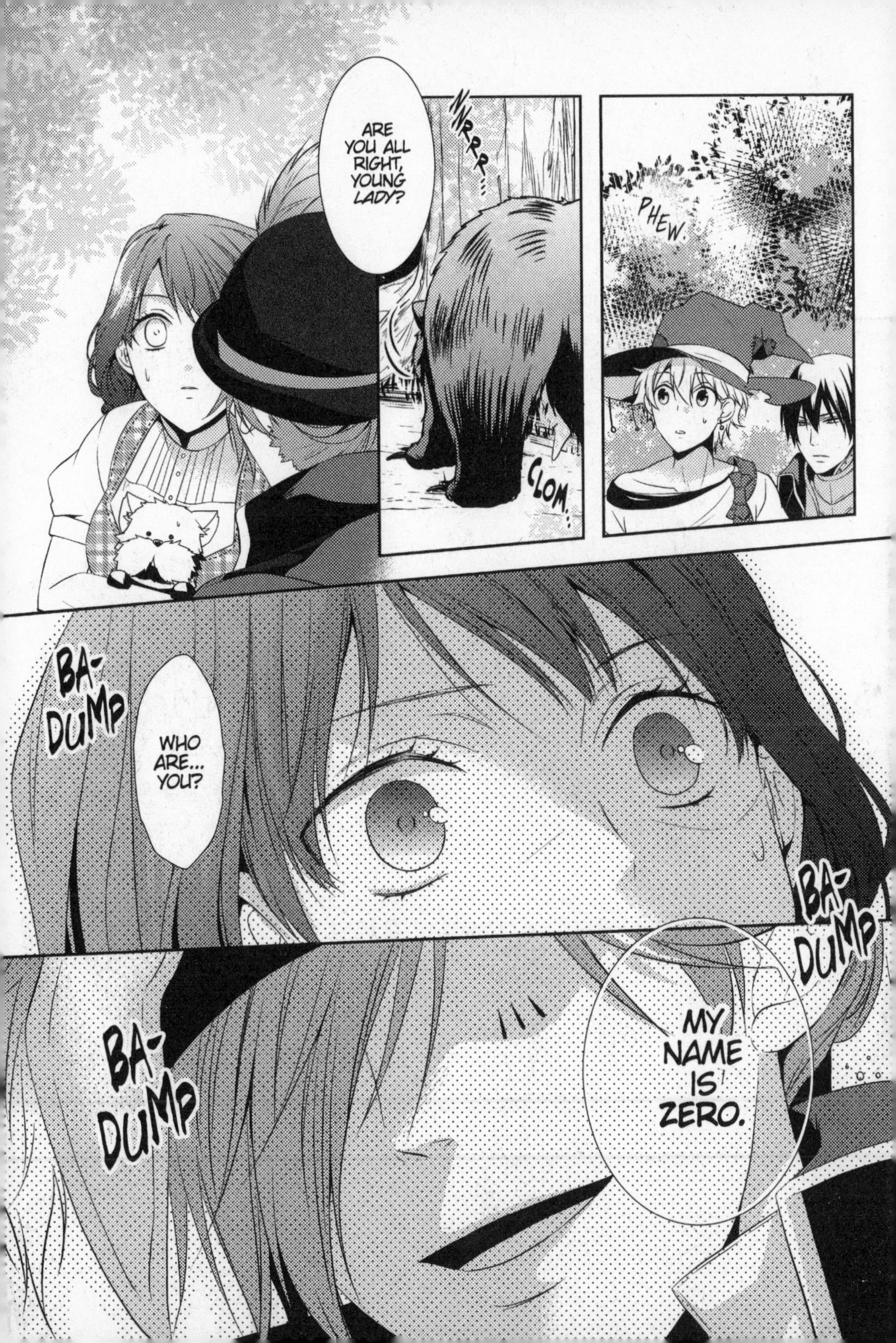
PHEW.
NNRRR...
CLOM...
ARE YOU ALL RIGHT, YOUNG LADY?
BA-DUMP
WHO ARE... YOU?
BA-DUMP
MY NAME IS ZERO.
BA-DUMP

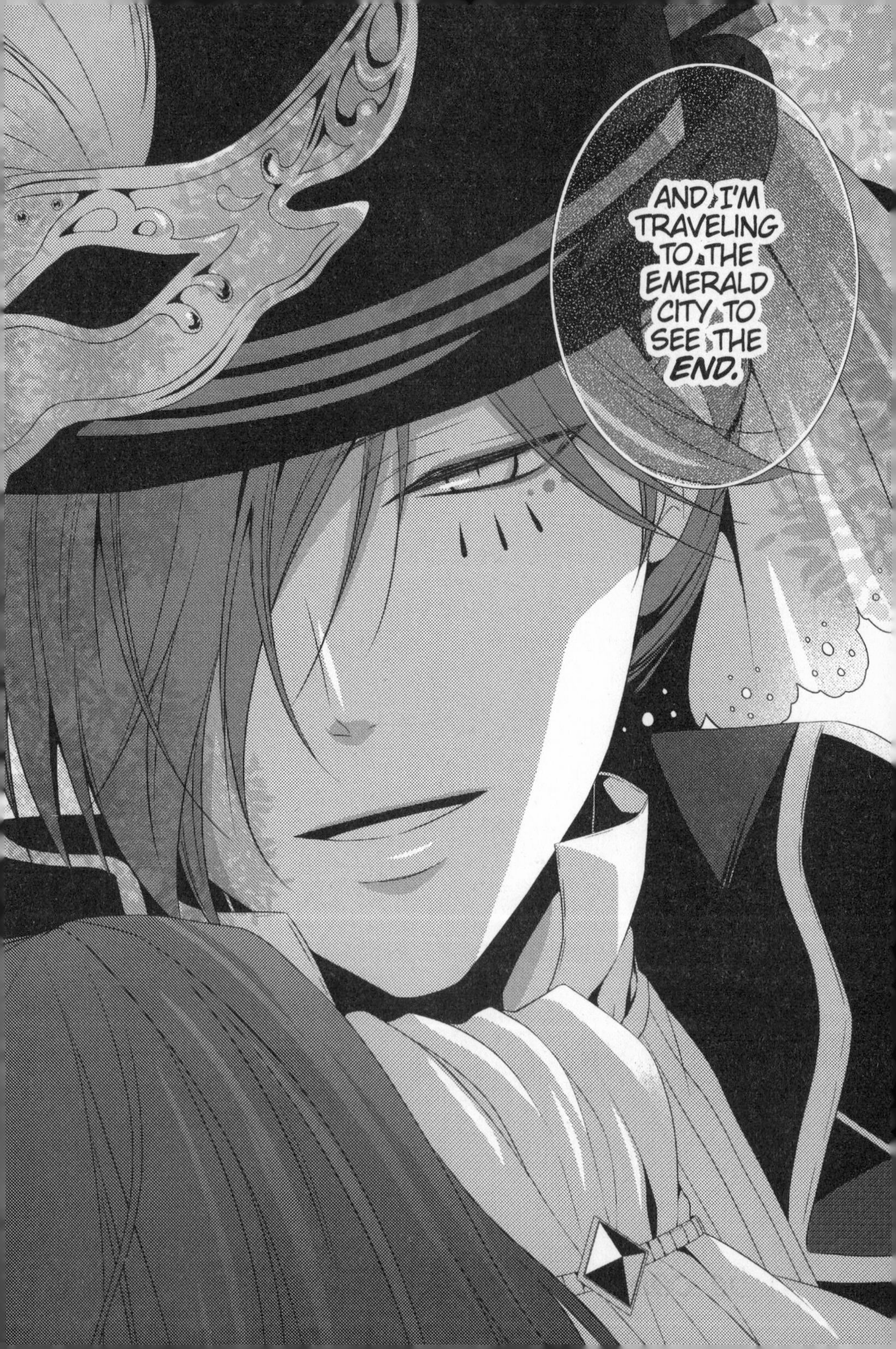
AND I'M TRAVELING TO THE EMERALD CITY TO SEE THE *END.*

To be continued...

SEVEN SEAS ENTERTAINMENT PRESENTS

9348

Captive Hearts of Oz

story by RYO MARUYA   art by MAMENOSUKE FUJIMARU   VOLUME 1

TRANSLATION
Angela Liu

ADAPTATION
Lianne Sentar

LETTERING AND RETOUCH
Roland Amago
Bambi Eloriaga-Amago

LOGO DESIGN
Karis Page

COVER DESIGN
Nicky Lim

PROOFREADER
Shanti Whitesides
Jenn Grunigen

PRODUCTION MANAGER
Lissa Pattillo

EDITOR-IN-CHIEF
Adam Arnold

PUBLISHER
Jason DeAngelis

CAPTIVE HEARTS OF OZ VOLUME 1
© 2017 Ryo Maruya / Mamenosuke Fujimaru / Seven Seas Entertainment, LLC.

Seven Seas books may be purchased in bulk for promotional, educational, or business use. Please contact your local bookseller or the Macmillan Corporate and Premium Sales Department at 1-800-221-7945, extension 5442, or by e-mail at MacmillanSpecialMarkets@macmillan.com.

Seven Seas and the Seven Seas logo are trademarks of Seven Seas Entertainment, LLC. All rights reserved.

ISBN: 978-1-626924-20-8

Printed in Canada

First Printing: January 2017

10 9 8 7 6 5 4 3 2 1

FOLLOW US ONLINE: *www.gomanga.com*

READING DIRECTIONS

This book reads from *right to left*, Japanese style. If this is your first time reading manga, you start reading from the top right panel on each page and take it from there. If you get lost, just follow the numbered diagram here. It may seem backwards at first, but you□ll get the hang of it! Have fun!!

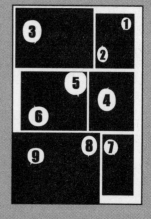